Social Security and Solidarity
in the European Union

Contributions to Economics

Giuseppe Gaburro (Ed.)
Ethics and Economics
1997. ISBN 3-7908-0986-1

Frank Hoster/Heinz Welsch/
Christoph Böhringer
**CO_2 Abatement and Economic
Structural Change in the European
Internal Market**
1997. ISBN 3-7908-1020-7

Christian M. Hafner
**Nonlinear Time Series Analysis
with Applications to Foreign Exchange
Rate Volatility**
1997. ISBN 3-7908-1041-X

Sardar M.N. Islam
**Mathematical Economics of
Multi-Level Optimisation**
1998. ISBN 3-7908-1050-9

Sven-Morten Mentzel
Real Exchange Rate Movements
1998. ISBN 3-7908-1081-9

Lei Delsen/Eelke de Jong (Eds.)
The German and Dutch Economies
1998. ISBN 3-7908-1064-9

Mark Weder
Business Cycle Models with Indeterminacy
1998. ISBN 3-7908-1078-9

Tor Rødseth (Ed.)
**Models for Multispecies
Management**
1998. ISBN 3-7908-1001-0

Michael Carlberg
Intertemporal Macroeconomics
1998. ISBN 3-7908-1096-7

Sabine Spangenberg
**The Institutionalised Transformation
of the East German Economy**
1998. ISBN 3-7908-1103-3

Hagen Bobzin
Indivisibilities
1998. ISBN 3-7908-1123-8

Helmut Wagner (Ed.)
Current Issues in Monetary Economics
1998. ISBN 3-7908-1127-0

Peter Michaelis/Frank Stähler (Eds.)
**Recent Policy Issues in Environmental
and Resource Economics**
1998. ISBN 3-7908-1137-8

Jessica de Wolff
**The Political Economy
of Fiscal Decisions**
1998. ISBN 3-7908-1130-0

Georg Bol/Gholamreza Nakhaeizadeh/
Karl-Heinz Vollmer (Eds.)
**Risk Measurements, Econometrics
and Neural Networks**
1998. ISBN 3-7908-1152-1

Joachim Winter
**Investment and Exit Decisions
at the Plant Level**
1998. ISBN 3-7908-1154-8

Bernd Meyer
Intertemporal Asset Pricing
1999. ISBN 3-7908-1159-9

Uwe Walz
Dynamics of Regional Integration
1999. ISBN 3-7908-1185-8

Michael Carlberg
European Monetary Union
1999. ISBN 3-7908-1191-2

Giovanni Galizzi/Luciano Venturini (Eds.)
**Vertical Relationships
and Coordination in the Food System**
1999. ISBN 3-7908-1192-0

Gustav A. Horn/Wolfgang Scheremet/
Rudolf Zwiener
Wages and the Euro
1999. ISBN 3-7908-1199-8

Dirk Willer
**The Development of Equity Capital
Markets in Transition Economies**
1999. ISBN 3-7908-1198-X

Karl Matthias Weber
**Innovation Diffusion and Political
Control of Energy Technologies**
1999. ISBN 3-7908-1205-6

Heike Link et al.
**The Costs of Road Infrastructure
and Congestion in Europe**
1999. ISBN 3-7908-1201-3

Simon Duindam
Military Conscription
1999. ISBN 3-7908-1203-X

continued on page 289

Joos P. A. van Vugt · Jan M. Peet (Editors)

Co-editors: Irene Asscher-Vonk, Lout Bots,
Lei Delsen, Nicolette van Gestel, Frans Pennings,
Cees Sparrius, Kees Tinga, and Egon Verbraak

Social Security and Solidarity in the European Union

Facts, Evaluations, and Perspectives

With 5 Figures
and 26 Tables

Physica-Verlag

A Springer-Verlag Company

Series Editors
Werner A. Müller
Martina Bihn

Authors
Dr. Joos P.A. van Vugt
Catholic University of Nijmegen
Catholic Study Centre
Erasmusplein 1, P.O. Box 9103
6500 HD Nijmegen
The Netherlands

Dr. Jan M. Peet
Wezenlaan 197
6521 MP Nijmegen
The Netherlands

"This publication is part of the series 'Publications of the Catholic Study Centre'"

ISSN 1431-1933
ISBN 3-7908-1334-6 Physica-Verlag Heidelberg New York

Cataloging-in-Publication Data applied for
Die Deutsche Bibliothek – CIP-Einheitsaufnahme
Social security and solidarity in the European Union: facts, evaluation and perspectives; with 27 tables
/ Joos P.A. van Vugt; Jan M. Peet (ed.). – Heidelberg; New York: Physica-Verl., 2000
  (Contributions to economics)
  ISBN 3-7908-1334-6

Physica-Verlag Heidelberg, New York
a member of BertelsmannSpringer Science+Business Media GmbH

© Physica-Verlag Heidelberg 2000
Printed in Germany

The use of general descriptive names, registered names, trademarks, etc. in this publication does not imply, even in the absence of a specific statement, that such names are exempt from the relevant protective laws and regulations and therefore free for general use.

Softcover Design: Erich Kirchner, Heidelberg

SPIN 10779952   88/2202-5 4 3 2 1 0 – Printed on acid-free paper

Preface

In 1996 the *Katholiek Studiecentrum* (Catholic Study Centre) of the Catholic University of Nijmegen, the Netherlands, initiated a discussion of recent developments in social security in the member states of the European Union. One reason for this initiative lay on a national level: in a trend towards privatisation and in other changes in the system of social security in the Netherlands, since the early 1990s. In addition, however, the Catholic Study Centre was aware that, on a European level, the process of European integration and the demands of integration on economic and social developments had a substantial impact on the evolution of national social security systems – in the Netherlands and in other European member states. As a result of European integration, especially economic and monetary integration, the Catholic Study Centre presumed a trend towards convergence of systems of social security in the European member states. As a possible result of this convergence, a trend towards structural change and a deterioration of the quality of social security in the Netherlands – but also, perhaps, in other European member states – were assumed.

Within the academic community of Nijmegen University, the Catholic Study Centre presents itself as a platform for discussing issues of religious, ethical or social importance. To this end it founds and coordinates a range of special working committees in which interested persons of different academic backgrounds meet for discussion. For the discussion of developments in European social security, a Committee on Social Security was created. This committee consisted of members of the academic staffs of Nijmegen and Tilburg universities: experts on social law, on social security, on economics, on political sciences and on social and economic history. External experts on theology and on social well-being also participated. The members were: Prof. Irene Asscher-Vonk (chair), Dr. Lout Bots, Dr. Lei Delsen, Dr. Nicolette van Gestel, Prof. Dr. R. Muffels, Dr. Jan Peet, Dr. Frans Pennings, Cees Sparrius, Kees Tinga, Dr. Egon Verbraak. Dr. J. van Vugt and Dr. Jan Peet acted as secretaries to the Committee and editors of its publication.

In order to create a European dimension, the Catholic Study Centre contacted experts on social law and social security in nine European Union member states: in Belgium, Denmark, France, Germany, Greece, Ireland, Italy, Spain and the United Kingdom.[1] The participants, including a team from the Catholic Study Centre's Committee on Social Security itself, were invited to submit for discus-

---

[1] Readers will find the names of participants in the list of contributors, elsewhere in this book. As for the cooperation of Catholic universities, the Catholic Study Centre and its Committee on Social Security wish to thank the *Fédération des Universités Catholiques Européennes* (FUCE) for its assistance in establishing our network of contributors.

sion a report on trends and developments in social security in their countries –
especially as a consequence of European integration. In this book, on the basis of
these reports, we present ten national perspectives on changes in social security, in
a European Union on the road to a closer integration. We also offer an evaluation
of these perspectives.

Two basic considerations have been especially influential as to the form and the
contents of this book. First, in order to maintain some unity and coherence in the
national reports on social security, the Committee decided to choose as a point of
departure two Recommendations of the Council of the European Communities to
the Member States. The recommendations are:

• 'Council Recommendation of 24 June 1992 on common criteria concerning sufficient resources and social assistance in social protection systems' (92/441/EEC,
published in: *Official Journal of the European Communities*, L 245, 26.8.92, p.
46-48);

• 'Council Recommendation of 27 July 1992 on the convergence of social protection objectives and policies' (92/442/EEC, published in: *Official Journal of the
European Communities*, L 245, 26.8.92, p. 49-52).

On the basis of the recommendations a proposal and a series of questions for the
participants were formulated.

Secondly, the committee decided that each national report, and this book as a
whole, should be more than a mere description of developments in social security.
Therefore, the participants were invited expressly to reflect on the quality, and on
the merits and shortcomings of the systems of social security in their countries –
'quality' being defined as the ability of a system of social security to shape solidarity of the well-to-do and the employed with those who, through no fault of their
own, cannot sufficiently support themselves. The participants were also asked
explicitly, to express their views on possible trends and developments regarding
the quality of social security in their countries, as a consequence of the process of
European integration. The committee, on its part, proposed to make a final
evaluation of these trends and developments.

To sum up, this book discusses social security and solidarity in the European Union – now and in the near future. It does so from the basic conviction that a social
security system of sufficient quality should be able to shape solidarity of the well-
to-do and the employed with those who, through no fault of their own, cannot
sufficiently support themselves. In the first chapter members of the committee
present a short sketch of the development of social security in Europe. After the
contributions on the various European countries, two more chapters are added.
The first of these describes the current trends and problems in European social
security, and presents some possible scenarios for the future. The second is of a
more philosophical nature. Social security is not only a matter of structures, interests and calculations but also an ethical issue. Social security systems, in spite of

their formal and detached character, are a mechanism for society to care for those of its members who are in some kind of need. Of course, in the rise of social security systems some degree of enlightened self-interest has always played a part. The well-to-do have always realised that social peace, even at a cost, is in their own interest and also that they themselves may, at one time or another, fall on hard times and need the support of their fellow-citizens. But on the other hand, social security systems reflect a sense of ethical obligation of the young, the healthy, the employed, the well-to-do *vis-à-vis* the old, the sick, the unemployed, and the poor. The latter aspect is explored in this final chapter.

The Committee wishes to thank all authors for their excellent contributions, and the *Stichting Sormanifonds* and *Stichting Mr. H.P.L.C. de Kruijff-fonds*, two Dutch charitable funds, for their generous financial support in the preparation of this publication. Finally, the committee wishes to commemorate mrs. Sue Houston, who meticulously edited its texts. She died in April 2000.

Nijmegen, May 2000 Prof. Irene Asscher-Vonk, *chair*
Dr. Joos van Vugt, *secretary*

Contents

I Introduction: Changes in European social security

Lei Delsen, Nicolette van Gestel, and Frans Pennings

1 Introduction

In this chapter we will present a classification of models of social security to help us develop a framework for the analysis of recent changes in European social security systems. To that end we will first, in section 2, give a brief survey of some historical roots of social security systems in the countries of Europe. We will also present a classification of social security models, as developed in the early 1990s. In section 3, subsequently, we will attempt to define some of the main dimensions of change in social security since then. In both section 2 and section 3 we will also touch on European integration, and its consequences for the development of social security in the European Union countries.

2 Historical developments in European social security

2.1 Social security before the Second World War: the development of the 'Bismarck model'

In 1981 social security in Europe was one hundred years old. This centennial was commemorated by several books and conferences.[1] Since then, social security has developed further. It is useful to look again at the roots of our present social security systems.

Of course, there were already systems of 'social security' before 1881, and it is more precise to say that the hundredth birthday of social security, concerned *statutory* social security. We will not discuss here the 'social security' systems of the Middle Ages and Early Modern Times, but it is useful to mention some of the social provisions as developed in the nineteenth century, by trade unions and by

---

[1] See for instance: P.A. Köhler and H.F. Zacher (Eds.), *The evolution of social insurance, 1881-1981. Studies of Germany, France, Great Britain, Austria and Switzerland*, London, New York 1982.

other workers' organisations. These workers' funds were based on an insurance principle: members of the funds had to pay contributions, and only contributors were eligible for benefits after materialisation of the insured risks. The early insurances were, however, not strictly actuarially based and showed several elements based on a solidarity principle. Contributions were not strictly related, on a basis of equivalence, to the dimensions of the insured risk, and benefits were not strictly related to the contributions paid. These elements of 'organised solidarity' were meant to mitigate the equivalence aspects of the insurances. They also had, to some extent and perhaps not fully intentionally, a redistributive effect. The first insurance schemes concerned the contingencies of occupational accidents, occupational diseases, invalidity and old age. Unfortunately, the early 'social security' schemes were often incapable of meeting all demands.

The first country to adopt statutory social security was Imperial Germany. In 1881 Chancellor Otto von Bismarck was the initiator of an accident insurance bill. Bismarck accepted statutory social security not in the first place for social reasons, but mainly in order to curb socialist political agitation. Indeed, his social policies – including the accident insurance bill (adopted in 1884) and an old age and disability insurance scheme – did help calm down social unrest in Germany for some time. From a point of view of organisation, Bismarck's social security schemes were, at least to some extent, not unlike the earlier non-statutory security schemes. They were industrial schemes, though more employer than employee-based. They were based on the insurance idea, and again Bismarck's insurance schemes were *social* insurances.[2] Elements of organised solidarity mitigated equivalence aspects. The old age and disability scheme even included a modest State subsidy. Still, the insurance principle was predominant: the schemes were financed by contributions, and only members, *i.e.* employees, were eligible for benefits. Benefits could be paid only for specified risks, as mentioned in the laws. The insurances' objective was to guarantee the economic and social status of the insured in the event of materialisation of these risks. Insurance benefits were, therefore, income-related.[3]

In Great Britain, from 1911 on, statutory social insurance schemes were also developed. Here, the idea of insurance identified strongly with a resistance to the alternative idea of free State social benefits. Moreover, insurances fitted into the prevailing ideology that an individual had to help himself by his own efforts. To this ideology the ideas of property rights and of contractual duties were closely connected: the right to benefit, based on previous contributions of the individual,

[2] *Cf.* J.M. Roebroek, *The imprisoned state. The paradoxical relationship between state and society* (Tilburg 1993), p. 33-40.
[3] See, for the view of an influential economist in the beginning of the 20th century on the development of social insurances: F. Pennings, 'Is Schmoller's view on the principles of social security still relevant in present debates on the future of social security?', in: J.G. Backhaus (Ed.), *Essays on social security and taxation. Gustav von Schmoller and Adolph Wagner reconsidered* (Marburg 1997), p. 595-616.

could be regarded as a contractual right.[4] Employees' contributions made a Government contribution to the insurance funds acceptable as well. As a British variation on the insurance theme, flat-rate contributions for flat-rate benefits also constituted a principle none could impugn.[5] Moreover, contributions for social security were seen as an instrument to select the genuine unemployed from amongst the broader destitute segments of the population. Thus benefits would only be payable to a person who had been regularly employed, as only he or she would be able to satisfy the contribution conditions: '[...] whilst it was extremely unlikely that a genuine worker would be unemployed long enough or often enough for the rule to operate, the malingerer would soon exhaust his right to benefit'.[6]

Today, some countries still have social security systems with a predominant workers' insurance character. Persons not covered by their personal scope have to buy their own provisions – such as private insurances.

2.2 Social security during and immediately after the Second World War: the development of the 'Beveridge model'

During and after the Second World War there were new developments. In Great Britain William Beveridge was greatly opposed to the prevailing system of public social assistance, which had developed to supplement the system of statutory workers' insurances in the pre-war years. In fact, hostility towards social assistance and towards the practice of means-testing that it implied – the 'household test' – was widespread. A report which reflected Beveridge's views, the *Beveridge Report,* was written during the Second World War. It was, as the reactions it invoked, very much influenced by a feeling of 'one society' which arose during the war. The report was very popular in Great Britain, and it would also be influential internationally. The main ideas in the report were to restrict the number of means-tested social assistance benefits in favour of contributory social insurance benefits, and to create a comprehensive scheme of social insurances, providing cover against the loss or interruption of earnings due to unemployment, sickness and old age. In addition, the social insurance benefits were (though not income-related) to be sufficient for subsistence on an accepted social minimum level, and of unlimited duration. Finally, in Beveridge's view, the social insurance system should be universal: it should provide not only the workers, but all British residents with a guarantee of freedom from want. This, the Beveridge Report intended, would ensure that after the Second World War, means-tested assistance was to play a minor role only in social protection in Great Britain.

---

[4] A.I. Ogus, 'Great Britain', in: Köhler and Zacher, *The evolution of social insurance, 1881-1981,* p. 183.

[5] M. Bruce, *The coming of the welfare state* (London 1961), p. 200.

[6] A. Deacon, *In search of the scrounger* (London 1976), p. 10.

The importance of the Beveridge Report lay in the comprehensiveness of the social security system it proposed, and in the elaboration of the principles underlying this system. In themselves, however, Beveridge's proposals were not really revolutionary in character. In September 1944, the British Government published a white paper on social insurance, in which many proposals of the Beveridge Report were incorporated. The proposals were subsequently enacted in the National Insurance Act (1946). In accordance with the report, this act created a public universal social insurance system, providing cover against the loss or interruption of earnings due to unemployment, sickness or old age. However, though still in accordance with the proposals of the Report, the right to unemployment benefits was restricted, and a main departure from Beveridge's proposals was that benefits were not set at subsistence level. The Government contended that the costs of subsistence varied widely from one claimant to another depending on the amount of housing rent claimants had to pay. This meant that for claimants who had to pay high rents, the benefits could reach the subsistence level only if excessive additions were paid. Such a varying benefit rate, the Government felt, would infringe upon the contributory principle. Beveridge's proposals regarding the duration of benefits were also not accepted. The Government argued that an unlimited duration of benefit entitlement would give rise to abuse. A proposal for compulsory training after six months of unemployment, to help limit the duration of benefit, was found impracticable.[7]

As a result, two main models of social security were created, which can be represented as in Table 1:[8] There were, of course, many national variations on these two models. For instance, the British system, though universal in its objectives, did not insure all residents against all social risks. As stated above, coverage in the event of unemployment was not extended to all residents. Neither did the system of means-tested social assistance benefits vanish completely in Great Britain. On the contrary: as social insurance benefits were flat-rate, they had to be set at a low level in order not to exceed the lowest wage levels. In fact insurance benefits were often too low, in any case, to support a family. As a result, though the idea of national insurances was very attractive, the elaboration of the idea led to critical publications such as *Social security: Another British failure?*.[9]

---

[7] W.H. Beveridge, *Social insurance and allied services,* London 1942. See also: W.H. Beveridge, *The pillars of security and other war-time essays and addresses,* London 1943. See also: F.J.L. Pennings, *Benefits of Doubt. A comparative study of the legal aspects of employment and unemployment schemes in Great Britain, Germany, France and The Netherlands,* Deventer 1990.

[8] The model is derived from M. Einerhand *et al., Sociale zekerheid: stelsels en regelingen in enkele Europese landen* [Social security: systems and regulations in some European countries] (The Hague 1995), p. 28. The scheme was originally published in Dutch as *Model Bismarck en Beveridge* (Model Bismarck and Beveridge). Some adjustments have been made.

[9] J. Walley, *Social security: another British failure?,* London 1972.

Table 1: Models of social security.

	Bismarck model	Beveridge model
Objective	guaranteed social and economic status	guaranteed minimum income
Scope	selective (workers only)	universal (all residents)
Benefits	income-related	not income-related
Funding	contributions	taxes
Administration	private law organisations	public authority

2.3 Developments in social security since the late 1940s

From about the end of the 1940s, social security lived a rather quiet life. Almost all over Europe the coverage of social security systems was extended – preferably to all residents – and benefit levels were raised. In the late 1940s and the 1950s, with the depression of the 1930s still in living memory, the main objective of this expansionist social security policy was to ban poverty, and to provide workers and other residents with, if possible, an all-embracing protection against the financial consequences of social and economic adversity. In the 1960s and the early 1970s policy objectives became more ambitious still. Unprecedented economic growth and a generally optimistic view of social development made equal opportunities for all, a substantial redistribution of wealth, and public care for almost every social or cultural need seem realistic goals. In this context, social security became a mainstay of the Western European welfare states. In the process, some countries borrowed their social security ideas from both the Bismarck model and the Beveridge model. With both employees' insurances and national (universal) insurances, the 'hybrid' social security systems in these countries offer a more general coverage of social risks than either the Bismarck or the Beveridge model.

However, the heyday of social security did not last. Since the 1970s – partly as a result of the oil crises of 1973 and 1979 – European economies have been suffering from serious structural problems. The costs of social security, and of welfare state provisions in general, were seen as a part of the problems. There have been frequent reductions in social security expenditure in all Western European countries since then. Benefit rates were reduced continually and the duration of benefit entitlement shortened. Moreover, since the 1980s and the early 1990s, in a changing ideological and cultural climate, more fundamental questions concerning social security and society in general have been asked. What is the proper task of Government, and what are the responsibilities of individual citizens and their organisations? Was social security really to achieve a redistribution of wealth and income, or rather just to give a reasonable measure of financial protection? Did social security contribute to the goal of equal opportunities for all, or did it rather have an adverse effect – by discouraging many beneficiaries from re-entering working life? Discussions on these, and on other questions, were more conspicuous in some countries than in others but they had an impact all over Europe, wherever extensive social security systems had developed.

In a European context, the development of an internal market (completed at the end of 1992) and the creation of the European Union (completed by the Treaty of Maastricht, in December 1991) also had an impact on social security systems in the European member states. The completion of the European internal market within the European Union (EU) emphasised an increased competition between companies and between countries, that had already been present as a result of a process of internationalisation of the European national economies.[10] It was thought that a reduction in labour costs, including the costs of social security, would be necessary for business and for the member states in order to survive in the competition. Moreover, the creation of the *Economic and Monetary Union* (EMU) was envisaged to take place before the end of the century. According to article 2 of the Maastricht Treaty, the aim of the EMU is to promote 'sustainable and non-inflationary growth respecting the environment, a high degree of convergence of economic performance, a high level of employment and of social protection, the raising of the standard of living and quality of life, and economic and social cohesion and solidarity among Member States'. The implementation of the first phase of building the EMU, in 1990, coincided with the European Directive on the liberalisation of capital markets.

At the Maastricht summit, agreement was reached on the second stage (to be started on January 1, 1994) and the third and final stage of the EMU (as of January 1, 1999). In addition, convergence-criteria for joining the EMU in 1999 were defined. To be eligible for the EMU, a country's inflation rate should not exceed the lowest three European Union member states' inflation rates by more than 1.5%-points. Its interest rate on long-term Government bonds should not exceed by more than 2%-points those of the three EU member states with the best performance. Its total Government deficit must not exceed 3% of gross domestic product (GDP), and its outstanding Government debt is not to exceed 60% of GDP. For at least two years, the country's exchange rates *vis-à-vis* other curren-

---

[10] The large European market generates cooperation and mergers of enterprises and also a greater mobility of companies or their component parts. There is evidence that cross border flows of capital and the exchange of technology have increased markedly over the past decades and that total inward and outward foreign direct investments in the European Union have risen. The international trade in goods and services has also shown an increasing trend. However, in Europe import- and export-to-GDP ratios are more or less constant. The increasing shares of intra-EU trade imply trade diversion/substitution from extra-EU trade. The internationalisation of the economies is not global, in fact internationalisation is mainly regionalisation: the data show an increasing interdependence of European economies. *Cf.* B. van Aarle, *Essays on monetary and fiscal policy interaction. Applications to EMU and Eastern Europe* (Tilburg 1996), p. 129; L. Delsen and E. de Jong, 'Germany and The Netherlands: Who follows whom?', in: L. Delsen and E. de Jong (Eds.), *The German and Dutch economies: Who follows whom?* (Heidelberg 1998), p. 8-10.

cies in the *European Monetary System* (EMS) must have remained within its EMS band without a devaluation of its central parities.[11] Finally, the statutes of its national central bank must be compatible with the European Central Bank (ECB) statute as established by the Maastricht Accord. All in all, the perspective of the EMU became a further argument for European member states to brace themselves for competition, reduce public expenditure, and thus reduce social security benefits and benefit conditions.

As said before, the discussions on social security in the EU member states, in this context, were to a large extent similar. However, the policy measures that were taken to encourage labour market participation and to reduce expenditure on social security varied considerably. The United Kingdom and the Netherlands went a long way in a privatisation of social security but in other countries too, benefit schemes were revised and benefit rates were reduced. To be sure, European Community law also became relevant in this area but, apart from a number of directives and regulations on the social security rights of migrant workers, European law on social security mainly concerned the equal treatment of men and women. This did not lead to a general improvement of benefit conditions; on the contrary, some national Governments even deteriorated their national schemes in order to comply with European legislation. In addition, European treaties and other agreements – from the 1957 Treaty of Rome to the Maastricht 'social chapter' of 1991 – have dealt with social security policies, but only in very general terms. Finally, Council Recommendations nos. 92/441 and 92/442 on minimum benefits and convergence of benefits were made – which have been presented, in the preface, as a point of departure for this study. It can be said here, though, that they are of a weak legal nature. All in all, few European Union requirements concern the social security policies of the member States.

3 Social security in the early 1990s

3.1 Models of social security

In the 1990s, the systems of social security in Europe are not based on uniform objectives, and they are often the result of different and – in terms of the two models we presented above – 'mixed' historical developments. In their study of

---

[11] The EMS was initiated in 1979 to create monetary stability within Europe after the collapse of the postwar global monetary system in 1971. The system is based on fixed exchange rates of the participating currencies. However, a currency is allowed to deviate from its exchange rate within narrow margins (its EMS band). The EMS virtually collapsed in August 1993 as a result of massive speculation against key currencies.

social security systems and arrangements in some European countries, M. Einerhand *et al.* have aggregated eleven aspects of social policies in Europe. Across these aspects of social policies, since the 1970s (and especially in the early 1990s), four models of social policy and welfare state development have been suggested.[12] These models can also serve as a classification of social security systems:

Table 2: Models of social security.

		Scandinavian model	Anglo-Saxon model	Continental model	Southern European model
1	*Type*	aimed at full employment; welfare state in the first place 'employer', in the last place payer of benefits	aimed at economic growth; welfare state in the last place payer of benefits, and strict focus on work on labour market	aimed at economic growth; welfare state in the first place payer of benefits, in the last place employer	economically aimed at catching up with northern states; welfare state is only a semi-institutionalised promise
2	*Right to*	work	transfer of income	social security	work and social security (only partly implemented)
3	*Primary responsibility*	the State	the State	labour market	family and church
4	*Solidarity based on*	society	individual (no solidarity)	economic sector	family
5	*Redistributive effect*	large	average	restricted	restricted
6	*Support (reintegration etc.)*	extensive	restricted	average	restricted
7	*Level of benefits*	average/high	average/high	differentiated	low
8	*Scope*	all residents	all residents	employees	aimed at the poor
9	*Aim*	guarantee social protection	guarantee social protection	maintaining income	combat poverty
10	*Funding*	taxes	taxes	contributions	contributions and other sources (church etc.)

[12] Einerhand *et al., Sociale zekerheid: stelsels en regelingen in enkele Europe landen*, p. 30. The scheme was originally published in Dutch as *Aspecten van modellen van sociale politiek* [Aspects of models of social policy]. Numbers 1-11 and element no. 12 were added.

11	*Financial independence of labour market*	high	low	average	high
12	*Administration*	trade unions/ central	central/State	private	private

As can be seen from a comparison with Table 1 – especially for aspects nos. 8, 9, 10 and 12 – in the early 1990s social security in 'Continental' countries still largely reflected the Bismarck model, while social security in Anglo-Saxon countries in many ways reflected the Beveridge model. There were however, again, national variations. In Great Britain, for instance, social insurance was still paid from contributions instead of taxes – though contributions may have been supplemented by public funds. Again in Great Britain, social insurance knew some form of solidarity: from the 1960s, social insurance contributions were earnings-related, whereas benefits remained flat-rate. This implied an income redistributive effect. As for the other models, the 'Scandinavian' model combined elements of both the Bismarck and the Beveridge model, and added a stress on reintegration in the labour market. Social security in the 'Southern European' countries appears to have followed a course of its own.

From a systematic point of view, two dimensions of change in social security in the 1990s can be discerned: a policy dimension and an organisational dimension. In each of these dimensions (in the context of this project, as set forth in the preface to this volume) some questions can be asked.

• Referring to Table 2, six aspects belong to the policy dimension: the right to work and/or income (2); the redistribution effects of social security (5); the capacity of social security to support the claimants in their efforts at reintegration (6); the level of benefits and of income support (7); the scope of social security (8); and the capacity to give social protection, maintaining income levels and fighting poverty (9). Questions can be asked as to the performance of social security systems and as to changes in this dimension.

• Also referring to Table 2, three aspects belong to the organisational dimension: the organisation of responsibilities for social security (3); the structure of organised solidarity in the context of social security (4); and the basis of social security funding (10).[13] Questions can be asked as to changes in the roles and the responsibilities of public actors (especially the State) and private actors (employers and employees, their organisations, households, private citizens on an individual basis etc.).

---

[13] The organisational dimension of social security also covers the administration of social security regulations (12). However, our study will not deal with this aspect of social security.

3.3 European perspectives

From a European policy perspective, too, the four models of social security show
different characteristics, and different levels of performance. The European Council Recommendations no. 92/441 and no. 92/442 on minimum benefits and convergence of benefits mainly recommended:
• that employed persons be provided with a level of social security, sufficient to
maintain their standard of living in the event of the materialisation of social risks;
and
• that all residents be provided with a minimum level of social assistance and protection, sufficient to cover their essential needs.

Generally, according to these recommendations, social policy (and social security)
should combat poverty and social exclusion, and should aim at integrating, economically and socially, those people who rely on social security provisions.[14] In
fact – as can be seen from Table 2 (aspect no. 9: *Aim*) – in the early 1990s, social
security in 'continental' countries still mainly aimed at maintaining employees'
incomes, while 'Scandinavian' and 'Anglo-Saxon' social security aimed to provide a more general social protection. Only 'Southern European' social security
systems expressly aimed to combat poverty. However, as aspects nos. 5 (*Redistributive effect*) and 7 (*Level of benefits*) indicate, these systems probably performed rather poorly in this respect. Conditions for combating poverty in countries with other models of social security (especially with a 'Scandinavian' model)
have probably been better. As aspects nos. 2 (*Right to...*) and 6 (*Support: reintegration etc.*) indicate, economic integration was a social security objective only in
the 'Scandinavian' and 'Southern European' countries – the 'Scandinavian' countries making the bigger effort. From an organisational point of view, moreover,
aspects nos. 3 (*Primary responsibility*), 4 (*Solidarity based on...*), 10 (*Funding*)
and 12 (*Administration*) indicate that the respective roles and responsibilities of
the State, of voluntary social organisations, and of households and individuals
were still very different in the four social security models.

The prospects of social security – of all models – looked rather bleak in the early
1990s European context. As we have seen above, European Union law had so far
had little influence on the development of social security in the member states,
and the influence it did have, had not always been for the better. The process of
economic integration and the prospect of Economic and Monetary Union also

---

[14] 'Council Recommendation of 24 June 1992 on common criteria concerning sufficient resources,
social assistance in social protection systems (92/441/EEC)', in: *Official Journal of the European
Communities*, L245 (August 26th, 1992), p. 46 (5) and 47-48 (I, A; I, B2; I, C1 sub a and sub c);
'Council Recommendation of 27 July 1992 on the convergence of social protection objectives and
policies (92/442/ EEC)', in: *Official Journal of the European Communities*, L245 (August 26th, 1992),
p. 50 (I, A, sub 1 (d)).

gave rise to a strong suspicion that social security in Europe might have to pay a heavy price for both. And with good reason. As we have seen here above, there were in the early 1990s, in the field of social security – and, more generally, in labour law – still considerable differences between the European Union member states. In the internal market these differences had already resulted in an increase in distortions of competition, which was emphasised by the development towards the EMU. Because not all member states had the same level of social development at the time of completion of the internal market, the increased competition put pressure on the social policies in the member states and created competition between national systems of social policy. This competition mainly concerned taxes, social security and working conditions. In the context of the development towards the EMU, in the years ahead, a more restrictive system of employment protection and more sober social security arrangements were expected to become national selling points, to attract investments and hence jobs from abroad. Social dumping (unfair competition between national systems caused by differential wages, social costs and working conditions) was expected to have a major impact on national social security systems. Simultaneously, social tourism (increased flows of labour to the richer regions of the European Union, with more generous social policies) was expected to occur.

As for social dumping, on the integrated European market of the early 1990s, countries with low levels of social protection, and hence lower labour costs, had a comparative advantage. There was also pressure on certain countries to maintain or gain comparative advantages by keeping their labour costs low. In the single market of the early 1990s, European currencies were not yet irrevocably fixed in value in relation to one another. The effects of social dumping – based on lower levels of social costs – could still be compensated for by adjustments in the exchange rates of the participating countries and by differing rates of inflation. As of 1999, however, under the EMU, the option of monetary adjustments would no longer be available. Comparative advantages would gain more weight in a common market with fixed exchange rates or with a single currency. An increase in social dumping was expected. Specifically, three forms of dumping were distinguished:[15] replacement of products, movement of capital and low wage policy, and policies to create a secondary labour market to obtain a competitive advantage. All three were expected to result in a downward spiral of underbidding national states within the European Union.[16] In general, A. Lejour concluded in 1995 that increasing integration exerts a downward pressure on the social insurance

---

[15] H.G. Mosley, 'The social dimension of European integration', in: *International Labour Review,* 129 (1990), no. 2, p. 147.

[16] J. Muysken and C. de Neubourg, 'Hoe sociaal is de EG? Het sociaal beleid' [How social is the EC? Its social policy]', in: J. Muysken and L.L.G. Soete, *Maastricht 1991 kritisch beschouwd. Preadviezen van de Koninklijke Vereniging voor de Staathuishoudkunde 1993* [Maastricht 1991: a critical review. Preliminary reports of the Royal Society for Economy 1993], Utrecht 1993.

budget.[17] Social dumping may result in social convergence towards an ever lower level. Only countries that can keep wages and social costs permanently low will have an advantage. They will be tempted to adjust continuously to shocks by wage cuts and cuts in social contributions and taxes. However, other countries with higher wage costs and social costs will be put under pressure by such competition to make corresponding cuts. If this analysis is correct, a race to the bottom will result. None of the countries will actually bear the fruits of their restrictive social policy measures. There will be only losers.

As for social tourism, as a result of the internal market, the mobility of labour was also expected to increase. On the one hand, citizens from member countries with low levels of social security benefits would decide to make use of their rights under European Community law to settle in other member countries with more generous welfare payments. Adverse selection would be the result: countries with relatively high protection – especially benefit – levels would attract high risk individuals, resulting in increasing costs to the social security system. On the other hand, high benefit levels imply high tax and premium rates, and the latter would induce people with low risks to leave their area or country. As a result, the basis to finance social security would become narrower. Hence, free movement of people was expected to make it increasingly difficult to maintain relatively high protection standards. Finally, from a general point of view of social policy, adaptability of economies became a central issue in the early 1990s. The internationalisation of the economies and the establishment of the European internal market was expected to imply a reduction in the relevancy and effectiveness of national economic policy of national Governments. In Europe, the room for a national macroeconomic policy would also be limited, because more and more decisions were taken and would be taken in Brussels or in Frankfurt. Not only was the number of policy instruments reduced, the aims of socio-economic policy were actually set more and more at the European level. The capacity to counteract, on a national level, adverse developments in the social field, was expected to diminish.

Developments towards European integration, in the 1990s, in many ways unrolled as had been expected at the beginning of the decade. On January 1, 1994 the second stage of the EMU started, providing a period of transition and preparation of at most five years, to successfully launch a stable EMU in 1999. A European Monetary Institute (EMI) was created to coordinate the national monetary preparations for the final stage of the EMU and the establishment of the European Central Bank. National Central Banks will have to be made independent of the Government. To achieve convergence of the national economies, member states had to satisfy the criteria defined by the Maastricht summit of 1991 for entering the EMU. The pursuit of these criteria has often be considered an implementation of

---

[17] A.M. Lejour, *Integration of disintegrating welfare states? A qualitative study to the consequences of economic integration on social insurance*, Tilburg 1995.

sound economic policies, which are desirable in their own right, and which would need to be introduced even in the absence of the EMU. In this view, what the Maastricht Treaty did was advancing those policies in time.[18] Indeed, for most member states, the predominant task in the 1990s was to meet the convergence criteria. Moreover, in the December 1996 Dublin Stability Pact, member states have agreed not only to comply with the Maastricht criteria concerning budget deficits for joining the EMU in 1999, but also for supporting the single European currency. In 1999, EMU became a fact of life for eleven European governments, companies and citizens, and the majority of national currencies were permanently pegged in *Euro*. The die was cast.

---

[18] J. Vinals and J.F. Jimeno, *Monetary union and European unemployment,* London 1996. Discussion paper series, no. 1485.

II Belgium

Maureen Verhue

1 Introduction

1.1 The system of social security in Belgium

In many ways, the Belgian system of social security is one of the most developed in the world. Firmly rooted in the industrial organisation and class struggles of the nineteenth century, it has come a long way since the formation in 1850 of pension funds which employees could voluntarily join. Nowadays, nearly every Belgian citizen is protected by some form of social security legislation. Different arrangements were established, providing social security for employees, Government officials, the self-employed, and other 'minor' categories such as seamen and miners. The scheme covering employees is by far the largest.

Social security for employees in Belgium received its legal basis through the Social Security Act of December 28, 1944. It was replaced by the Act of June 27, 1969, which extended the range of application. Basically, the system comprises four schemes, each of which were installed in order to meet the need for insurance against the contingencies which confront large numbers of employees:
• old age and survivors' pensions
• health care insurance and sickness and disability payments (including maternity benefits)
• unemployment insurance; and
• family allowances.

Work accidents and professional diseases are not formally covered by social security legislation. Their coverage is (to a large part) not financed through the regular federal institution which covers the financial flows related to the other social security schemes. Their insurance is organised by private insurance companies. However, these contingencies are considered to be a part of social security *sensu lato*.

The social security act of 1967, which gave social security for the self-employed its legal organisation, was the natural consequence of an evolution aimed at providing coverage to the broadest possible range of people. Social protection of the self-employed is less extended than the employees' scheme and comprises child benefits, old age and survivors' pensions, sickness and disability insurance and insurance against 'large' health care risks (small health care costs being mainly doctors' costs and medicinal expenditures when not hospitalised).

Typically, allowances to the self-employed are lower in amount than benefits to employees or civil servants. For purposes of poverty alleviation, 'residual', income-tested schemes were set up to guarantee minimum levels of protection to the disabled, pensioners, families with children and people with simply insufficient resources on which to live.

Belgium is commonly perceived to be a prototype of federalism. The whole concept of Belgian federalism has evolved through numerous stages and is still not fully developed. Belgium now consists of three geographical regions which comprise its linguistic communities (Flemish, French, German), each with its own regional authorities. Social security is, however, still organised at a national level. We will not tackle this topic extensively, but content ourselves with the summary remark that federalisation of social security, in particular of health care and family allowances, has recently obtained serious legitimacy as a subject of debate.

Table 1: Social protection expenditure as a percentage of GDP and the allocation of social benefits according to social risks (1980-1994).[1]

	1980	1984	1988	1990	1991	1993	1994
Social protection expenditure (% of GDP)	28.0	29.9	27.8	26.9	27.4	27.0	27.0
Allocation of social benefits:							
• health care	21.8	20.8	22.1	22.9	23.4	24.1	25.0
• invalidity, disability	9.6	9.8	9.4	9.1	8.7	8.9	8.9
• occupational accidents and diseases	3.2	2.6	2.2	2.2	2.1	2.0	2.0
• old age	28.6	30.2	32.2	33.4	34.1	33.9	33.9
• survivors	13.0	12.5	11.9	11.8	11.5	11.0	10.9
• maternity	0.6	0.6	0.5	0.9	0.9	0.8	0.8
• family	10.7	9.0	8.6	8.2	8.0	7.7	7.4
• unemployment	9.2	11.1	9.9	8.7	8.7	9.9	9.5
• other	3.4	3.7	3.1	2.8	2.7	1.7	1.6

As in most other western countries, budgetary constraints have acted as a break on the growth of social security. In particular, the large national debt haunting the Belgian Government (a magnificent 133.5% of GDP in 1995) seriously limits the freedom of policymakers to implement whatever measures social policy might require. Social protection expenditures in 1994 represented 27% of GDP, against a European Union average of 28.7%. Old-age pensions are by far the largest category of social protection expenditures, followed by health care insurance, the percentage of which shows a steadily increasing trend.

---

[1] Eurostat, *Social Protection Expenditure and Receipts 1980-1994,* Luxembourg 1996.

Table 2 shows that there is little disparity between Belgium and other European countries, both regarding the level of social protection expenditure and the allocation of social benefits according to social risks. Health care and old age insurance typically are the largest programmes in all countries considered.

Typical of the Belgian situation is the high degree of centralisation, both with respect to the revenue side as to expenditure. Unlike several other European countries (like the United Kingdom or, to a decreasing extent, the Netherlands), social security benefits in Belgium are granted by national organisations, with only a few intermediary institutions: the unions with respect to unemployment benefits, health services with respect to health care costs and funds for child allowances with respect to child benefits.

1.2 The financing of social security

Social security is financed primarily through contributions which are related to earnings in a uniform, linear manner. Contributions are paid partly by employees and partly by the employer, and they differ according to the scheme under consideration. Since 1982 all earnings are taken into account, without limitation. Contributions are also levied at various levels on some benefits, including pensions, invalidity benefits, occupational injury benefits and survivors' benefits. Benefits which are the sole source of income in the family are, however, exempt from premium imposition. Government subsidies serve to finance the whole of the expenses related to the residual schemes and any deficits that social security schemes may incur. In 1997, the total of Government subsidies was set at 188.2 billion Belgian Francs (BFr). This amount serves as a basis for indexation in the years after.

To these traditional financial sources are added the revenues from certain taxes (*e.g.* on premiums paid for car insurance or supplementary hospital insurance), which are directed towards the schemes for which they were installed; and revenues from specific withholdings, such as a special social security contribution which was set up in 1994 on the family income of employees or social security beneficiaries, the revenues of which are used to help finance employee social security benefits. Until 1995, revenues raised with respect to the compulsory social security contributions were allotted to the scheme for which they were imposed. Any surpluses or losses were compensated for by the Government subsidies and by transferring resources between the several schemes. Since 1995, however, all revenues (except for the affected taxes) are generalised and divided over the several schemes according to need (the so-called *Globaal Beheer*, or global financing system). Several other countries have applied the same kind of centralisation to the revenue side of social security – Spain, Portugal, the UK and Ireland being a few examples. However, since this system is bound to reduce transparency with respect to the financial flows that the social security scheme entails, its introduction is not an entirely positive development. Furthermore, there is an ongoing trend towards less 'direct' Government subsidisation and more of what is called 'alternative financing', which means that sources other than labour income (such as VAT) become part of the basis for the financing of social security.

Table 2: Social protection expenditure as a percentage of GDP, and the allocation of social benefits according to social risks, in Belgium and other Western European countries (1993; 1994).[2]

	Netherlands (1994)	Germany (1994)	France (1994)	United Kingdom (1993)	Belgium (1994)
Social protection expenditure (% of GDP)	32.3	30.8	30.5	28.1	27.0
Division:					
• health care	22.4	27.7	26.7	19.7	25.0
• invalidity and disability	22.5	9.2	6.0	11.1	8.9
• occupational accidents and diseases	--[3]	2.9	1.9	0.4	2.0
• old age	32.2	31.7	37.8	41.1	33.9
• survivors	5.6	10.5	6.6	1.3	10.9
• maternity	0.6	0.7	1.4	1.3	0.8
• family	5.0	7.1	8.3	10.4	7.4
• unemployment	10.7	7.0	6.2	6.3	9.5
• other	1.1	3.1	5.2	8.4[4]	1.6

Social benefits for Government officials largely come directly from the State. Contributions are paid only with respect to health care and pensions. Unemployment insurance for Government officials is non-existent since State employment has a permanent character. The self-employed, who are mandated to join a social security fund, pay contributions on their professional earnings. Unlike the wages earned by employees, which are taken into account in their entirety with respect to the premium imposition, a ceiling is imposed on self-employed earnings above which no social security contributions are paid.

1.3 Social security benefits

Table 3 provides an overview of the sources of social security financing in Belgium.

---

[2] *Ibid.*

[3] Included in 'invalidity and disability'.

[4] Housing subsidies constitute the main part of the category 'other'.

Table 3: Sources of social protection receipts (1980-1994).[5]

	1980	1984	1988	1990	1991	1993	1994
Employers	44.5	39.7	41.8	44.8	45.3	42.0	43.1
Protected persons	17.8	21.9	25.6	26.5	26.7	26.5	26.6
Government	34.0	34.6	28.5	25.6	24.8	22.2	20.6
Other	3.8	3.8	4.2	3.1	3.2	9.4	9.8

The Belgian social security scheme is of the Bismarckian type, hence most bene-fits are earnings-related. Eligibility is related to the applicant's employment his-tory. Minimum and maximum amounts add significantly to the redistributive character of social security benefits in Belgium. No means-test is required in order to be eligible for social security benefits except, of course, regarding the residual schemes. However, most benefits differ according to some broad categories that correspond to some measure of 'supposed' need. Table 4 provides information on the main social security benefits in Belgium.

Table 4: The level of main social security benefits for private sector employees (1996).

	Earnings-related	*Flat-rate*
Old-age pensions	family benefit: 75% of gross wages	
	• minimum: 34,709 BFr per month	
	• maximum: 65,315 BFr per month for women, 61,200 BFr per month for men[6]	
	individual benefit: 60% of gross wages	
	• minimum: 27,775 BFr per month	
	• maximum: 48,960 BFr per month for women, 52,252 BFr per month for men	
Survivors' pensions	80% of old-age family pension	
	• minimum: 27,308 BFr per month	
	• maximum (when combined with old-age pension): 30,039 BFr per month	
Health care insurance		reimbursement of medical payments (minus personal

---

[5] Eurostat, *Social Protection Expenditure and Receipts 1980-1994.*

[6] Regarding what one might call an unjustified differential treatment of men and women with respect to old age pensions, we should mention that this phenomenon is on its way back due to recent legislative reforms. For further remarks on differential treatment we refer to section 5 of this chapter.

		contributions, varying according to the item and the personal situation of the insured)
Sickness benefit (first year of disability)	60% of gross wages (max: 2,175 BFr per day)	
Invalidity benefit (after the first year of disability)	head of household: 65% (max: 2,175 BFr per day)[7] cohabiting: 40% (max: 1,450 BFr per day) single: 45% (max: 1,450 BFr per day)	
Maternity benefit	first period of 30 days: 82% of gross wages after 30 days: 75% of limited wages	
Unemployment insurance	head of household: 60% of gross wages[8] • minimum: 30,030 BFr per month • maximum: 34,190 BFr per month cohabiting: 55% of gross wages • minimum: 17,134 BFr per month • maximum: 31,356 BFr per month single: 60% of gross wages • minimum: 21,502 BFr per month • maximum: 34,190 BFr per month	flat-rate 'waiting benefit' for all new graduates (after waiting for a period of 9 months)[9] flat-rate benefit after 15 months of unemployment flat-rate interruption benefit • minimum: 11,830 BFr per month • maximum: 14,082 BFr per month
Child benefits		1st child: 2,653 BFr per month[10] 2d child: 4,909 BFr per month 3d child (and following): 7,329 BFr per month

---

[7] Minimum amounts depend on whether the employee enjoyed regular employment or not.
[8] Gross wages used for calculation of benefits are limited to 56,994 BFr a month.
[9] The amount differs according to the family composition of the recipient and to their age.
[10] The exact amount depends on the age of the child as well as on its 'rank' in the family with respect to the other children.

2 Maintaining living standards

We shall restrict our analysis to the social security scheme which has the broadest field of application, *i.e.* the scheme for employees who work in the private sector. Eligibility for social security benefits in Belgium typically depends on the applicants' work history. The actual conditions vary depending on the benefit in question.

2.1 Old age and survivors' pensions

If there is one sector in which the actuarial relationship between benefits and former earnings is more or less preserved (see the table above), it is that of old-age and survivors' pensions, typically the arrangements for which private sector alternatives are blooming. In Belgium, the pensionable age is flexible and benefits can be drawn for the first time between the ages of 60 and 65. The average replacement rate of old-age pension payable to a single person who was on the average industrial wage when in work and who is entitled to a full pension on the basis of his or her contribution record, was 73% in 1993, close to the European Union average of 75% (1993).[11] Survivors' pensions are 80% of the family old age pension benefit, which is a theoretical amount if the spouse has deceased before the age of retirement, and the actual amount if otherwise. One can be eligible for both a retirement and a survivor's pension, although cumulation is restricted.

Financial constraints and an ageing population are forcing the Belgian Government towards a tightening of eligibility requirements. The replacement ratio in effect can hardly be altered since the average of all earnings over the working period is already used to calculate the benefits. The Government has taken steps to encourage occupational pension schemes (firm-related pension funds or mutual insurance) and individual saving by instituting a legal framework and by introducing fiscal deductions. However, the use of occupational pensions in order to achieve a decent old-age income level is not as widespread in Belgium as is *e.g.* the case in the Netherlands or Denmark. Some 10% of all pensioners in the private sector are entitled to an occupational pension and 35% of all currently active employees are involved in some pension plan – these are rather unimpressive figures. Nonetheless, it seems that the rise of occupational pension schemes and private savings plans will continue, since public pensions can no longer guarantee an adequate standard of living, particularly to higher income earners. This trend is likely to increase income inequality among pensioners. It may also affect the attractiveness of the public pension scheme for high income earners. In the long run, this may well jeopardise the scheme's very existence.

---

[11] European Commission, *Social protection in Europe 1993* (Luxembourg: Office of Official Publications of the European Union, 1994), p. 54.

Specific to the Belgian situation is the widespread occurrence of 'early retirement' (*brugpensioen*: bridging pension). The scheme in question, which was introduced in 1975, guarantees applicants who have contributed for at least 25 years and who lose their job before the legal retirement age (generally from the age of 58 onwards), a supplementary transfer on top of their unemployment benefit, amounting to half the difference between the former net wages and the unemployment benefit. This scheme, which is in fact a part of unemployment insurance, was installed and is still operating because of its positive labour market effects: employers who make use of the scheme to dismiss an elderly employee are obliged to take one or two unemployed persons in his or her place. Large numbers of employees have taken up this opportunity to retire early without too large an income loss. Consequently, Belgium has one of the lowest percentages of people still working above the age of 55: 47% of the male labour force between the age of 55 and 59 were still participating in 1993, as compared to 62.2 % in the Netherlands and 68% in France.[12] The huge financial burden that this scheme puts on social security funds has, however, resulted in a tendency to make conditions more strict, and even to doubts about the scheme's advisability altogether.

Pensions for public service employees are calculated as a percentage of the average wages over the five years prior to the age of retirement, instead of the average over the whole career in the case of private sector employees. Furthermore, pension amounts are adapted whenever the wages of the still active public sector employees are raised, and with the same percentage. This system, called *perequatie,* was guided by the notions that public sector pensions are a sort of 'deferred wages' and that the living standard of pensioners should keep pace with that of current employees. However, its automatism is now under heavy criticism due to the huge costs it incurs. The Government thus faces a dilemma since public sector wages are still considerably below private sector earnings and pensions are considered to be a compensation for this fact.

2.2 Health, sickness and disability

Health insurance in Belgium consists of two rather distinct branches. On the one hand, nearly all Belgian residents are entitled to medical insurance which provides reimbursement of medical expenses. On the other hand, all employees (be it in the private or in the public sector) have a right to a sickness or invalidity benefit in the event that they should fall ill. Although in most European countries medical insurance is not considered to be a part of social security we emphasise that there is

---

[12] Figures taken from the *Organisation for Economic Cooperation and Development* (OECD) and the *Nationaal Instituut voor Statistiek* (National Institute for Statistics, NIS), *Arbeidskrachtentelling* (Labour force count) figures.

still consensus in Belgium concerning the legitimate place of medical insurance in the whole of social security.

Medical insurance in Belgium is characterised by its broad range: hardly anyone is exempted from health care insurance, which is quite remarkable. Anyone who resides in Belgium and cannot make a claim to medical insurance on behalf of some social security scheme, can voluntarily join the residual medical insurance scheme for the 'persons not yet protected'. A co-insurance premium is installed, which is reduced for particular categories such as widows, orphans, the disabled and pensioners. Moreover, in order to encourage long-term unemployed and people on social assistance to make use of available medical facilities a 'social deductible' was introduced in 1994: above a certain amount all medical expenses are reimbursed. Finally, a fiscal deductible is in place for all beneficiaries: all but medicinal costs are reimbursed above a certain amount, dependent on income.

As in many other countries, health costs in Belgium are steadily increasing. The causes are to be found in the health care system itself with its surplus of doctors and its lack of incentives towards economy. The steadily increasing health care expenditures coincide with the need to control Government expenditures. For this reason the Government is under a lot of pressure to restrict the scope of health insurance. It intends to limit the increase in health care costs to no more than 1.5% annually in real terms, although this budgetary constraint is not enforceable. Furthermore, the co-insurance premiums installed with respect to several categories of health expenditures have been increased on several occasions in the recent past. In spite of these measures, total health costs in 1996 amounted to 442 billion BFr, some 10.3% higher than in 1995. Both in 1997 and 1998 the health care budget has risen by far more than the cap of 1.5%. Due to the effect of ageing, which will lead to large health costs in the future, there is a call for some kind of 'dependency insurance', as already exists in France. So far, private insurance companies have not been very keen to provide this kind of insurance for elderly people.

Sickness and invalidity benefits are the least extended branch of social security benefits in Belgium, apart from family and maternity allowances.[13] They represent about the same percentage of GDP as unemployment benefits, *i.e.* 9%. Amazingly, sickness and invalidity benefits have never encountered the same hostile reaction as unemployment benefits. The right to sickness and invalidity allowances is tightly linked to the labour relationship. It is probably the best embedded of all social insurance rights, both in the minds of the public as in the mind of public decision-makers. A clear distinction should be made between sickness benefits (duration of illness is less than one year) and invalidity benefits (duration of illness extends beyond one year), since the latter are related to the household composition of the employee. Although social security law states that sickness

[13] See Table 1. This presupposes, of course, that the coverage of occupational accidents and diseases is not a part of social security.

benefits are due after the first day of illness, most employees receive full pay during the first month of sickness, due to collective agreements with employers.

2.3 Family allowances

Since the early 1980s the Government has made effective use of family allowances in its fight against poverty. Although several austerity measures were taken that led to lower benefits,[14] improvements were made regarding benefits for children who live in deserving families (children of the long-term unemployed, pensioners and the disabled). Benefit levels of the basic family allowance were also significantly raised on different occasions. Figures prove child allowances have been, and still are, a significant help in strengthening the financial security of families at the bottom of the income distribution.

2.4 Unemployment benefits

Unemployment benefits in Belgium are granted, in theory, for unlimited duration but are widely considered to be insufficient to maintain living standards, or even to prevent people from falling into dire poverty. When compared to neighbouring countries (in particular France and the Netherlands), Belgian unemployment insurance grants lower benefits, both as regards the maximum amount (due to the low earnings ceiling for benefit calculation) and as regards the minimum income guarantee. Unemployment benefits have proven to be insufficient especially for one-income-families. One of the main reasons why actual replacement rates are lower in Belgium than in neighbouring countries, is that the Belgian scheme does not provide housing subsidies. In 1981, the current modulation of benefits was introduced based on categories of 'supposed need'. Hence, replacement rates, minimum and maximum benefits are higher when the applicant is a single person than when he or she is living with other family members earning an income (cohabiting). They are highest in the case of heads of household (breadwinners in one-earner-families, single parents). Long-term unemployed who are not the sole breadwinner in the family eventually fall back on rather low flat-rate benefits.

The requirement concerning the work history of the applicant does not apply to newly graduated persons who are eligible for a 'waiting allowance'. New graduates who are not head of a household are entitled to a (low) flat-rate waiting benefit, which is granted without any eligibility requirements other than having finished school and having waited a period of 9 months. New graduates who are head of a household are entitled to an unemployment benefit based on the minimum

---

[14] Automatic price indexation was suspended on several occasions between 1982 and 1987 and a temporary deduction of 375 BFr a month was made between 1983 and 1992. See below.

wage.[15] Nearly 40% of all the unemployed are entitled to low flat-rate benefits, and minimum and maximum benefits show very little disparity, thus limiting the insurance character of the benefits. Furthermore, minimum unemployment benefits are only slightly higher than the so-called Minimex (*i.e.* the basic income granted as a flat-rate residual allowance). All benefits are lower than the 'social minimum' proposed by B. Cantillon *e.a.* in 1996.[16]

Employees who decide to interrupt their work for a minimum of six months and a maximum of one year, or to move from full-time to part-time work for a maximum of five years, are entitled to an 'interruption benefit'. This is also payable for up to five years to unemployed persons who choose to leave the labour market for social or family reasons, in which case it replaces the unemployment benefit. Approximately 90% of people claiming this benefit are women. Many of them use this benefit to carry them through a period of childcare.

In view of financial constraints, the work test to which unemployment benefit applicants are submitted, has recently been tightened. Suspension of benefits to unemployed people cohabiting with an earning partner, is now more readily applied. In 1995, no less than 200,046 decisions were made concerning non-admissibility, suspension or limitation of the right to benefits, as compared to 196,287 in 1994 and 154,523 in 1993. Married women most frequently qualify for a suspension of benefits due to a longer than average duration of unemployment.

2.5 Some concluding remarks

Since the late 1970s the Government's austerity policy has implied that benefits are no longer adapted to the overall level of prosperity. Moreover, since the early 1980s full price indexation of social insurance benefits has been discontinued. In 1984, 1985 and 1987 benefits, like overall wages, were not indexed at all. The burden of this policy has fallen mainly on supra-minimum benefits because there were compensating mechanisms installed to protect minimum benefits, chiefly those of single people and heads of household.

Since 1994, benefits have been indexed according to the 'health index' (*i.e.* the consumer price index without the effects of tobacco, alcohol and petrol prices) and adjusted with a two-month delay (for benefits with monthly payments).

Social benefit applicants in Belgium are protected by law from discretionary and unjust decisions by the Government. Disputes arising from social security benefits fall within the competence of the Labour Court, in which labour unions, employ-

---

[15] The parents' right to child benefit is not affected by this waiting allowance.

[16] B. Cantillon, I. Marx, and K. Van den Bosch, 'Is the welfare state really in need of a radical overhaul?', paper presented at the international colloquium *Repenser (radicalement?) la solidarité* [Rethinking Solidarity (Radically?)], Louvain-la-Neuve, December 19-20th, 1996.

ers and the Government are represented. Specific well-defined rules govern the relationship between the applicant and the administration if the former is unhappy about a decision by the latter. For example, in the case of unemployment insurance the applicant whose benefit has been suspended due to an abnormally long duration of unemployment has two ways to appeal against this decision, provided the appeal is lodged within the month following the decision by the unemployment administration. He or she can appeal on objective grounds to the official who ordered the suspension. Subjective reasons may be called in before a special National Administrative Commission. Many people make use of these possibilities.

On the whole, social security benefits have been successful in alleviating the financial consequences of social risks. Between 80% and 85% of all individuals who are dependent on social insurance for continuous income benefit from the security provided by income replacement benefits. The system owes this success to the existence of minimum benefits related to pensions, disability and unemployment allowances, social assistance benefits, the (in principle) unlimited duration of unemployment benefits, universal and high child benefits, the automatic indexation with respect to the general price level, and the decentralisation of specific services (such as social assistance). Recent changes to the several schemes, in particular unemployment insurance, have detracted from the principle of insurance that initially inspired Belgian social security. As in other western countries, there is a trend towards flat-rate and universal benefits, which are less dependent on the applicants' employment history and increasingly selective in determining their supposed or actual need.

3 The level of social assistance arrangements

In Belgium, social assistance is generally regarded as a residual and relatively minor part of social security. More than in other European countries social insurance is the rule, social assistance the exception. No wonder, since most social insurance benefits have minimum levels and unemployment benefits are granted, at least in theory, for unlimited duration. Nevertheless, the number of people receiving a social assistance allowance has grown substantially over the last ten years.

Social assistance consists principally of four benefits: disability allowance, guaranteed income for older people, guaranteed family allowance, and Minimex. Disability allowance and guaranteed income for older people represent by far the largest of the minimum income schemes, both as regards numbers of recipients and as regards expenditure figures.

All basic social assistance benefits have a national statutory framework, but policy and administration are split between different departments. One particular feature regarding the organisation of Minimex is the fact that, although policy responsibility is exercised by the Ministry of Social Integration, Health and the Environment, it is actually administered by the *Openbaar Centrum voor Maatschappelijk Welzijn* (Public Centres for Social Welfare, OCMW) at the local municipality level. These centres have quite some discretionary power in allocating benefits. Hence benefits for the same categories of people may differ from one municipality to another. Half the budget on Minimex benefits stems from the Government and half is financed by the local municipalities.

3.1 Entitlement to social assistance

Entitlement to all social assistance benefits is dependent on the applicant's resources being below prescribed limits. The exact level of these limits depends on the sort of benefit under consideration. With respect to Minimex and disability allowance, the rule is that the benefit is reduced by the positive difference between the benefit and income from other sources, in so far as the latter exceeds the annual amount of 12,500, 10,000 or 6,250 BFr, depending on whether the applicant is married (Minimex) or has dependants (disability allowance), is single, or cohabiting. The means-test is slightly different with respect to guaranteed income for older people since here the determining factor for reducing the benefit is whether the applicant is head of family (12,500 BFr) or not (10,000 BFr). With respect to guaranteed family allowance, the means-test is applied in yet another way since now the level of the allowance is independent of income, but the eligibility is not.

Other specific entitlement conditions apply, depending on which benefit is considered. The disability allowance can be granted only to applicants whose earning capabilities have been reduced to less than one third of the earning capacity of a 'representative employee on the labour market'. This is similar to the conditions prevalent for the more common invalidity scheme. The right to disability allowance does not, however, require any previous work records and benefits are flat-rate. Older people can be granted a guaranteed income provided the applicant has reached the required pension age. If the applicant is entitled to some sort of pension, the amount of the minimum benefit is reduced by 90%, irrespective of the means-test (which also takes account of all income sources, including pensions). Parents who have no other means of entitlement to a family allowance on behalf of their children, may apply for a guaranteed allowance, the amount of which is equal to that applied in the employee scheme. The right to family allowance is, however, not (yet) a 'right of the child *in se*' and some children may be exempted from that right. For example, children who are not tied by a family bond to the person who claims the benefit only have right to benefits after five years of residence in Belgium.

Availability for work is also an entitlement condition regarding Minimex. The minimum age for entitlement is 18, unless a claimant is pregnant or has children.

Since 1992, recipients under 25 years of age have to make an 'integration agreement' with the OCMW. For the Guaranteed Income for Older People, claimants have to be 65 (men) or 60 (women) years old. Applicants for the Disability Allowance must be over 20 and under 65. To be eligible they must demonstrate that their earnings on the open labour market have been reduced to less than one-third of that of a healthy person. All social assistance benefits are available for unlimited duration as long as conditions are met and personal resources remain insufficient.

3.2 Benefit levels

Social assistance rates in Belgium have never been based on an objective measure of adequacy. They are based on political decisions, and there is no official poverty line, in spite of proposals made to the Government by, among others, the *Commissie voor de bestaanszekerheid van de armsten* (Commission on Social Security for the Poorest) in 1987. Minimex amounts, for instance, are still considerably lower than the proposed poverty line. Hence, H. Deleeck and others state that an increase in all social assistance benefits is absolutely necessary if the Government aims to push poverty back further.[17] Furthermore, there is a growing concern about the economic position of young people. Since the lowering of the age of majority in 1990, people under the age of 21 have become entitled to Minimex. In 1993 they made up just over 10% of all recipients. In January 1995, no less than one quarter of all Minimex recipients were young people. Social assistance benefit levels are given in Table 5.

As a result of the selective nature of Government cuts official policies have been more or less adequate in protecting the less fortunate against poverty. Between 1980 and 1995 social assistance benefits were extended in actual fact to people aged between 18 and 21 years (due to the lowering of the age of majority) and eligibility conditions for people who do not hold Belgian nationality were relaxed. The means-test (in particular regarding Minimex) has become less strict and benefits were raised in real terms, in particular those regarding one-parent families.

The gap between social assistance benefits and minimum benefit levels in the social insurance schemes has decreased over the years since Government policy to combat poverty in recent years has focused on increasing social assistance benefits. Hence, the gap between Minimex and the minimum unemployment benefit for single people has almost completely disappeared. If poverty alleviation is to be the main rationale of Government policy in years to come, care should be taken that the increase in basic and minimum social insurance benefits does not further

---

[17] H. Deleeck, 'Sociale zekerheid en armoede [Social security and poverty]', in: *Belgisch Tijdschrift voor Sociale Zekerheid* [Belgian Social Security Review], (1996), no. 3, p. 451-497.

affect the insurance character of social insurance benefits and hence stays within the boundaries of political feasibility.

Table 5: Social assistance benefit amounts (1996).

Social insurance benefit	Monthly benefit (in BFr)
Minimex	
• spouses living together	27,341
• people living with at least one minor	27,341
• singles	20,505
• people cohabiting	13,670
Guaranteed income for older people	
• family allowance	27,342
• singles	20,506
Guaranteed family allowance	
• first child	4,004
• second child	5,746
• third child and so on	7,476
Disability allowance (income replacement allowance)	
• with dependent(s)	27,341
• singles	20,506
• people cohabiting	13,672
Socio-professional reintegration premium	
• first year	6,757
• second year	5,631
• third year	3,379

As a result of the severity of the Minimex means-test people on social assistance find it difficult to overcome their precarious financial situation. They can easily find themselves in a vicious circle of poverty (the so-called poverty trap). To prevent this measures have been taken to promote their reintegration, such as the introduction of the 'socio-professional reintegration premium' and the exemption of revenues from Local Employment Agencies (*Plaatselijke Werkgelegenheidsagentschappen*) in calculating benefit entitlements. The reintegration premium grants exemption of a certain amount of earnings from the Minimex means-test to applicants who take up training or who are employed with the help of a Public Centre. Their extra earnings are not deducted from their Minimex income. Some other sources of income have also been exempted from means-test such as scholarships and maintenance money for children. Applicants under the age of 25 are induced to sign an integration contract with the Public Centre as contracting partner. These contracts contain mutual obligations with respect to training and employment. However, in spite of the legal pressure to sign such contracts, their application is still not very widespread.

4 Household and individual

In general, social insurance benefits in Belgium are granted on an individual basis, based on the work experience that the recipient can demonstrate. In some cases, however, an individual related to the 'insured employee' is entitled to benefits, in which case a 'derived right' is established: the benefits are derived from the relationship that the eligible person has or had *vis-à-vis* the employee. They are calculated on the basis of the income and, occasionally, the career of the insured employee. Derived rights exist only in a few, though significant cases. For instance, the right to medical insurance does not only apply to the insured employee but also to his or her dependants or surviving spouse. Survivors' pensions and (in the event of divorce) old-age pensions also fall into this category. Finally, derived rights are granted with respect to work injuries and professional disease if the insured dies due to one of these misfortunes.

The existence of derived rights is heavily criticised since they may reinforce the dependence of a married woman on her husband. Another issue of criticism lies in the fact that the level of the survivor's pension depends only on the income and the career of the deceased, with no relationship whatsoever to the needs of the spouse or his or her efforts towards society. Hence, it is possible that a woman who has worked all through her life may be entitled to a lower pension than another woman who never worked but whose husband has died, only because the husband of the latter woman earned a higher income. This is all the more inequitable since female employees still earn lower wages than their male colleagues. Nonetheless, the bulk of social insurance benefits are granted as an individual right. They do, however, take account of the family composition of the recipient. This is done in three different ways:

• *Old-age pensions.* When the recipient has a spouse under his or her charge, the old-age pension percentage used to calculate benefits is 75%, as compared to 60% in all other cases. Hence, the only distinction made here is between pensioners who have a spouse to look after and the other pensioners, regardless of the actual family burden. This kind of modulation is subject to criticism since it strengthens the dependent position of women in the family.

• *Unemployment benefits and sickness and disability benefits.* In both these cases a distinction is made between three categories as far as benefit calculation is concerned: heads of household, single people and people living with someone who earns an income which exceeds some specific amount (cohabiting). Sickness benefits are the same regardless of the category (60% of gross wages) during the first year of disability and are modulated according to family composition only afterwards. Unemployment benefits are lower when recipients have been cohabiting from the first year onwards. After 15 months of unemployment, recipients who are in the category 'cohabiting' are entitled only to a flat-rate amount; this category is furthermore the only category of unemployed whose benefit can be suspended when unemployment duration exceeds 1.5 times the average unemployment duration of their region. Hence, a distinction is made here according to some broad measure of family burden, but also between people who only have their own income to provide their income security and people who can rely on another income to be income secure.

• *Social assistance benefits*. Although the same flat-rate benefits apply to Minimex, guaranteed income for older people and disability allowance, descriptions of the household categories are not fully the same in each case, which is the cause of some criticism. Again, three categories can be distinguished: recipients with dependants, single people, and cohabiting recipients.[18] The ensuing benefit amounts can be found in Table 5.

The flat-rate family allowance can be considered to be a case on its own: it is neither a derived right, nor an increase in some replacement income in order to take account of the family burden. Child allowances are dependent on the specific scheme of which one is part (public or private employee, self-employed or guaranteed child allowance), the child's rank within the family, the number of children, and supposed needs of the child (due to age, disability or orphanage).

We may conclude that Belgian social security schemes are more or less, though with some major exceptions, in line with European recommendations concerning individual rights and modulation of benefits according to different types and sizes of household.

5 Differential treatment of men and women in Belgian social security

With respect to social security in Belgium it is safe to say that most 'formal' differences in the treatment of men and women have been abolished. However, the complex mixture of labour market evolutions and social security legislation (which always entails some fragmentation of the public into distinct, artificial categories) may still leave some unwanted effects with respect to this problem. We shall demonstrate this statement by referring to the examples of old age pensions and of unemployment benefits.

Until 1991, the retirement age was set at 65 for men and at 60 for women. Although this differential treatment was done away with after 1991, the required number of contribution years still remained 45 for men and 40 for women. Hence, after having worked for 40 years, male pensions – presuming a man and a woman

---

[18] The guaranteed income for older people only distinguishes between two categories: single people and families (as is the case for the earnings-related old-age pension).

have experienced the same wage evolution, which is nowhere near the reality – were still 11% below female pensions. This, of course, was an outright discrimination against men. The recent reforms with respect to the legal pension scheme (equalisation in stages of the calculation method with respect to the benefit amount) will also entail effects that may not be entirely in line with the principle of equal treatment.

Before these reforms women benefited from this so-called preferential treatment. This was always justified by referring to differences in labour market experience between men and women, especially the persistent differences in wages. However, some authors believe that the preferential treatment did not so much benefit women as men above the age of 60 who experienced a period of illness, invalidity or early retirement. This category represented 75% of those aged between 60 and 65. The reason for this adverse effect lies in the combination of pension, sickness and invalidity and early retirement legislation. Hence, the intended improvements to the pension situation of men may in effect impair the pension rights of most men, and the intended reductions to the pension situation of women may lead to some women improving their position.

Current unemployment insurance regulation poses a problem not so much with respect to formal differential treatment, as to the effects of some formal legal arrangements on actual benefit amounts and eligibility. Since most women find themselves in the category of the 'cohabitants' – living with someone who earns an income exceeding some specific amount – they are entitled to the smallest benefit amounts. They also face a much higher chance of suspension of benefits due to abnormally long unemployment duration. This statistical fact does not, however, justify the notion of 'discrimination'. Belgian legislation, with its inherent 'modulation' of benefits according to (some reformulation of) 'marital status', has been acknowledged as non-discriminatory with respect to equal treatment of men and women by the European Court of Justice. Taking account of hypothesised need through modulation of benefits according to family composition, however commendable, can nonetheless still be discriminatory in its application. The whole concept of 'head of family' involves criteria that cannot be justified by referring to hypothesised need. Unquestionably, these criteria penalise any professional activity by the partner or keep this partner from making an appeal to his or her own rights to benefits. Since it is very rare for men to perform no labour activity whatsoever or to be entitled to no social security benefit, this aspect of regulation will, on the whole, affect women more than men. Whether this amounts to discrimination and contravenes European Union regulations is, however, debatable and not the subject of this contribution.

6 European unity and its consequences

When confronting Belgian social security schemes with the recommendations formulated by the Council of Ministers dating from 27 July 1992 (92.442/EEC) on the convergence of social protection objectives and policies between member states of the (then so-called) European Community, it seems that most social security schemes in Belgium require little or no adaptation. However, in order to be in line with the European Community recommendation 79/7/EEC on equal treatment of men and women with respect to social security, the Belgian Government had to adapt the pension scheme and equalise the pension age of men and women. Now, women are entitled to pension benefits from the age of 61 onwards; this pension age will be raised by one year every three years. Eventually, in 2009, pension ages for men and women will be equalised at 65. Analogously, the required number of working years necessary for women to be entitled to a full pension will gradually increase to 45 years in 2009.

In anticipation of the monetary union, member states of the European Union need to fine-tune their economic and budgetary policies in favour of price stability, reduction of budgetary deficits and control of Government debt. Evidently, the repercussions of these goal-induced policies with respect to social security cannot go unnoticed. It is in this context that the Belgian Government's *Globaal Plan* (Global Plan) was agreed upon at the end of 1993. This plan included measures related to employment as well as two new concepts concerning the organisation of social security: alternative financing and the *globaal financieel beheer* (global financial administration), as mentioned above. Between 1992 and 1995, budgetary measures of a one-off nature were taken in order to ensure that the accounts would balance at the end of the budgetary year. Furthermore, the share of all contributing parties in the overall social security budget has been subject to some alterations. Between 1990 and 1994 employee and State contributions were raised by 1% and 0.6% respectively; employer contributions were decreased by the sum of these percentages while other sources maintained the status-quo. Hence, the European unification process has already had severe effects on social security rules and generosity.

In its recommendation of 27 May 1997 the European Council of Ministers insisted that, with respect to cuts in large Government deficits, the Belgian Government pay attention to tax revenues and social expenditures and take measures to counteract any increases in social security expenditures. If Belgium was to be one of the countries to become members of the European Monetary Union from its beginning in 1999, it should reduce its deficit firmly and the proposed way to do this was to cut social security benefits.

Whether European unity will turn out to be a good development for social security in Belgium is a matter of debate. The outcome will first and foremost depend on the willingness of the other European partners to commit themselves to the objectives as they are laid down in the recommendation (92.442/EEC) on the convergence of social protection objectives and policies. Belgian social security, with its high levels of employer contributions, stands to lose a lot should the installation of the European Monetary Union not be accompanied by a certain amount of convergence towards some commonly defined goals. We believe that the fears of social tourism, and especially of social competition, are well-founded. Therefore, it is our understanding that besides economic codes there is a great need for social codes in order to provide each country with equal opportunities to compete and every European citizen with equal levels of social protection.

7 Conclusion

Belgian social security is, first and foremost, characterised by its very broad range of application. Nearly everyone receives legal protection against such contingencies as job loss, illness, old age and family extension. In particular, health cost insurance and family allowances are attainable by all, irrespective of work history. Social protection in Belgium plays a major role in preventing people from falling into poverty. Some 6% of the Belgian population can be considered 'poor' and 1.5% 'chronically poor', *i.e.* remaining poor over several years (in terms of the European Union poverty line[19]). These figures prove that, from the viewpoint of poverty alleviation, Belgian social security is amongst the best performing in the world.

However, there remain some flaws as far as protection against poverty is concerned. Despite the overall adequacy in keeping people above the poverty line, social security is inadequate in guaranteeing income security to some groups of single people and sole-wage-earners. Living in a family with more than one income seems to be the best guarantee of income security. The work-related character of social security in Belgium is also responsible for some people not having any entitlements to social security benefits (such as some categories of female part-time employees). In a few, though significant, cases no individual entitlements exist, thus enforcing dependence of women on their husbands. Furthermore, the increasingly exacerbated situation of poorly educated employees with a high risk of unemployment, calls for adaptations to several social security schemes which might limit their universal insurance character. For instance, unemployment insurance is no longer able to meet the requirement of guaranteeing a decent standard of living to the non-poor part of the insured. For large groups of high income earners, old age pensions are also insufficient to maintain their former standard of living, which explains the growing adherence to private insurance plans and the

---

[19] Eurostat, *Social Protection Expenditure and Receipts 1980-1994.*

need for decent regulation of these private sector alternatives. In the context of an ageing population and the efforts that the Maastricht criteria require with respect to Government debt and expenditures, there is an on-going debate on how social security expenditures would best be spent. It raises the question of selectivity versus universality of social security benefits. This, of course, leads to discussions over the pros and cons of selectivity *vis-à-vis* universality, on issues such as political sustainability, dependence traps, administrative feasibility and income distribution. The main issue in ongoing debates on social security reform in Belgium, however, is entirely politically determined and focuses on the extremely delicate question of social security federalisation.

It seems that social security in Belgium, as in several other western countries, is at the crossroads of major evolutions. Probable reforms relate not only to technicalities or changes on the margin but, first and foremost, to the issue as to how the burden of these changes will be distributed between several groups in society, between labour and capital, between those on the winning side and the losers. The future of Belgian social security will be shaped entirely by the future of social solidarity.

Bibliography

In addition to the references given in the footnotes, we refer to:

M. Andries, 'Het bestaansminimum als laatste wapen van de sociale zekerheid in de strijd tegen de armoede [Subsistence levels as the last weapon of social security in the war on poverty]', in: *Tijdschrift voor Sociale Zekerheid* [Belgian Journal on Social Security], (1996), no. 3, p. 655-673.

Belgisch Tijdschrift voor Sociale Zekerheid [Belgian Social Security Review], (1997), no. 2 (Special issue on social security in Belgium).

P. Brouwers, 'Financiële toegankelijkheid tot de geneeskundige verzorging [Financial accessibility to medical care]', in: *Belgisch Tijdschrift voor Sociale Zekerheid,* (1996), no. 3, p. 531-577.

D. Coeurnelle, 'De 'omgekeerde' herverdelingen op het vlak van de uitkeringen voor bejaarden [The 'reversed' redistributions in the field of benefits for the elderly]', in: *Belgisch Tijdschrift voor Sociale Zekerheid,* (1996), no. 3, p. 579-597.

P. Palsterman, 'Werkloosheidsverzekering en armoede [Unemployment insurance and poverty]', in: *Belgisch Tijdschrift voor Sociale Zekerheid,*(1996), no. 3, p. 623-653.

P. Pestieau and F. Spinnewijn, 'Sociale zekerheid en armoede: debat tussen twee economisten [Social security and poverty: a debate between two economists]', in: *Belgisch Tijdschrift voor Sociale Zekerheid,* (1996), no. 3, p. 431-449.

H. Verlinden, 'De gezinsbijslag: een huis op maat van de kansarme? [Family benefits: a suitable home for the underprivileged?]', in: *Belgisch Tijdschrift voor Sociale Zekerheid,* (1996), no. 3, p. 599-622.

III Denmark

Bent Greve

1 Introduction

The European Union does not have a direct right to intervene in matters in relation to the welfare state, including the main fields of social security. So far, these have been seen as belonging to the national prerogative. The European Union does, however, have an impact on social security, mainly by setting the agenda, and through the impact of the internal market on the economic situation in the member states.[1] In addition, the European Union has an impact on the welfare state through its directives on equal treatment, equal pay and safety at work. The European Union also has the authority to make certain binding rules regarding migrant workers. These include the coordination and regulation of people moving and working across the European Union.[2] On the whole, though, its ability to determine welfare state matters in the member states is limited. These limitations are the main reason why the European Union mainly acts by issuing recommendations. This type of intervention may have an impact in the sense that these recommendations can promote ideas and inspire developments within national systems. On the other hand, as these recommendations are often vague and unspecific they are a weak instrument. Recent changes in the Amsterdam treaty and the new employment policy can be seen as a new trend moving the European Union more in a direction that will enable it to intervene.

In this chapter I will, mainly from the Danish perspective, examine how social security in Denmark is organised and structured, and how it can be expected to develop in the future. Furthermore, I will briefly discuss if and how the European Union will have an impact on Danish social security and, if so, in what way. First, in section 2, I will provide a short introduction to the main characteristics of the Danish system. This will be followed, in section 3, by a more precise survey of how living standards are maintained, given specific contingencies: unemployment, sickness, early retirement and old age. I will also present a short empirical excursion on living standards by referring to recent comparative analyses of poverty in Denmark. In section 4, I will reflect on the tendencies and future developments. In

---

[1] B. Greve, 'Indications of Social Policy Convergence in Europe', in: *Social Policy and Administration*, 30 (1996), no. 4, p. 348-367.

[2] *Cf.* E. Eichenhofer, *European social security law. A case book*, Osnabrück 1995.

section 5, I will discuss how the development of the European Union might affect the social security system in Denmark. Finally, in section 6, I will present some observations on welfare state development.

It is often assumed that there will be a tendency towards convergence of the welfare systems in Europe,[3] but even with no convergence hypothesis in mind there is ample reason for a debate on the impact of the European Union on various national social security systems. There seems to be a creeping convergence towards a mixture of Beveridgean universal flat-rate low coverage and a Bismarckian supplementary system, mainly based on labour market participation.

2 The Danish system

The Danish welfare state is, in principle, a universal type of welfare state – sometimes labelled the Scandinavian Welfare State. This type of welfare state uses general financing, *i.e.* revenue through the tax- and duty-system, for the bulk of its expenditure and system expenses.[4] In principle, social rights apply to all citizens, and individuals have access to services which in many areas are free of user charges, provided that the individual meets certain legal criteria. Day-care is an

---

[3] Greve, 'Indications of Social Policy Convergence in Europe'.

[4] The main laws in relation to social security are the following, which besides the overview from *Forsikringsoplysningen* 1999 (Insurance information, 1999) have been used as a basis for this chapter. The main law and latest legal instructions, which includes recent minor changes in the laws, are shown.

• *Lov om offentlig sygesikring* (Law on National Health Security) (Act no. 311, June 9th, 1971, published in: *Lovbekendtgørelse* (Legal instruction) no. 509, July 1st, 1998).

• *Lov om sygehusvæsenet* (Law on Hospitals) (Act no. 324 of June 19th, 1974, *Lovbekendtgørelse* no. 687, August 16th, 1995).

• *Lov om dagpenge ved sygdom eller fødsel* (Daily Sickness Benefits Act) (Act no. 852, December 20th, 1989, *Lovbekendtgørelse* no. 632, June 22nd, 1997).

• *Lov om social pension* (Social Pension Act) (Act no. 217, May 16th, 1984, *Lovbekendtgørelse* no. 22, January 14th, 1998).

• *Arbejdsmarkedets Tillægspension* (Labour market supplementary pension, ATP) (Main law from 1964, *Lovbekendtgørelse* no. 752, October 20th, 1998).

• *Lov om en børnefamilieydelse* (Law on the General Allowances for Families with children) (Act no. 147, March 19th, 1986, *Lovbekendtgørelse* no. 609, June 30th, 1994).

• *Lov om arbejdsformidling og arbejdsløshedsforsikring m.v.* (Law on the Public Employment Service and Unemployment Insurance) (Act no. 114, March 24th, 1970, *Lovbekendtgørelse* no. 897, December 16th, 1998).

• *Lov om Aktiv Socialpolitik* (Law on active Social Policy) (Act no. 455 of June 10th, 1997)

• *Lov om Social Service* (Law on Social Services) (Act no. 454 of June 10th, 1997)

• *Lov om Retssikkerhed og Administration på det sociale område* (Law on administration and justice in relation to social security) (Act no. 453 of June 10th, 1997).

example of a system where parents, low income families excepted, pay up to 30% of the cost of having a child in day-care. In general, basic social security rights are not restricted to certain groups or linked to, for example, work experience. Rights are based on laws which imply that all citizens can receive public support for themselves and their dependants, if they are in need and other avenues have been exhausted. The health care system is a national system which covers all residents, yet many benefits (both in kind and in cash) are only available under certain conditions. In some cases these conditions include previous employment. As stated above, the system is mainly financed from general taxation and, to a lesser extent, from contributions by employers and employees. These contributions are especially related to the risk of unemployment because unemployment is covered by a system of the social insurance type in which previous contributions to and membership of the unemployment insurance system are a pre-requisite for receiving benefits.

Although the Danish social security system mainly depends on direct State financing, part of its funding takes place *indirectly* through the tax-system (tax-expenditures).[5] For example, individuals have a right to deduct interest payments on mortgages from their income. In this way the State indirectly supports housing by a reduced tax-payment. In this way, the right to deduct payment to unemployment insurance is also a support, besides the direct payment of unemployment insurance, to the financing of unemployment benefit. In 1996 tax-expenditures were calculated as being 2.4% of the Gross National Product[6] (the figures do not include the preferential fiscal treatment of savings for pension purposes). The total direct public sector outlay on social security was 278.8 billion Danish Kroner (Dkr) or € 37.4 billion in 1998[7] – nearly 43% of total public sector outlay. Of this sum, 198 billion DKr (€ 26.6 billion) were spent on income transfers, 71.1 billion (€ 9.6 billion) on services and 9.7 billion (€ 1.3 billion) on administration. The total spending equalled 23.9% of GNP. These figures do not include expenditures on housing benefits and sickness. If these are included the total spending on social security was 30.8% of GNP (1997 figures). *Per capita* the amount was 62,465 DKr in 1997 prices (€ 8,395). Pensions and care for the elderly constituted the single largest sector, consuming 129.7 billion DKr (€ 17.4 billion). Expenditures on sickness (in kind and in cash) made up the second largest area with 59.8 billion

---

[5] B. Greve, 'The Hidden Welfare State', in: *Scandinavian Journal of Social Welfare*, (1994), no. 4, p. 203-211; *Skatteudgifter i Danmark* [Tax-Expenditures in Denmark], København: Skatteministeriet (Ministry of Taxation) *et al.*, October 1996.

[6] *Skatteudgifter i Danmark* (1996).

[7] The figures in this paper are mainly taken from *Statistisk 10 års oversigt*, 1999 [Statistical Ten-Year Overview 1999] from *Danmark Statistik* (The Danish Statistical Office). The information concerning the social security system and the legal position will mainly be taken from: *Sociale Ydelser. Håndbog i den sociale lovgivning og ydelser pr. 1. januar 1999* [Social Benefits. Handbook of Social Law and Benefits on January 1st, 1999], Viborg: Forsikringsoplysningen (Insurance Information), 1996.

DKr (€ 8.0 billion) and labour market benefits, including unemployment benefits, the third largest sector with 41.6 billion DKr (€ 5.6 billion).

Two areas which need to be examined more closely are pensions and unemployment benefits. The reason for not analyzing expenditures on sickness in greater depth is that a high proportion of expenditure in this area are services, rather than income transfers. Therefore, expenditure depends more upon the individual being sick than on testing whether or not certain criteria are fulfilled.

Pensions in Denmark are a mixed system within a mainly universal system. The basic pension is flat-rate and not directly means-tested. It is only reduced if the pensioner receives income from paid labour above a ceiling. The equally flat-rate pension supplement, on the other hand, is means-tested, based on all the income the pensioner receives, including income from private pensions exceeding 45,000 DKr (for a single person in 1999). In addition to the public pension system all those on the labour market have what is labelled 'labour market supplementary pension' (ATP).[8] It is not a very large amount, but for low income earners it implies that the fall in disposable income after retirement is small. Furthermore, pension funds have been established as a part of many collective labour agreements. It is estimated that approximately 80% of the labour force is by now covered by such a pension.[9]

Unemployment benefits are, in principle, earnings-related. The maximum benefit available amounts to 90% of one's previous income – with a maximum amount. However, this figure solely applies to low income earners: the average replacement rate is 63.5% for men and 70.9% for women.[10] This implies that, although it is an earnings-related benefit, for most people it is more in line with a flat-rate benefit, due to the ceiling.

Social assistance is in principle based on a flat rate, depending on age and on whether or not the applicant is a breadwinner. The amount is lower than the unemployment benefit. On top of the normal social assistance benefit it is possible to

---

[8] *Arbejdsmarkedets Tillægspension* (Labour market Supplementary Pension). The name derives from the fact that payment is conditional on having been employed on the labour market and on the amount of working hours. In 1999 the yearly pension for an individual who has paid contributions since 1964 is 18,600 Dkr.

[9] *Pensionssystemet og fremtidens forsørgerbyrde* [The pension system and the future dependency level], København: Finansministeriet (Ministry of Finance), 1995. It must, however, be borne in mind that of those 1.5 million citizens covered in these mainly occupational based supplementary systems 650,000 persons have entered the system in 1989, 1991 and 1993. It will thus take thirty to thirty-five years before their pension, as part of a collective agreement, will have a real impact.

[10] A. Møller Jensen and M. Verner, 'Dagpengenes betydning for omfanget af arbejdsløshed i Danmark [Unemployment benefits impact on the level of unemployment in Denmark]', in: *Nationaløkonomisk Tidsskrift* [Journal of National Economics], 134 (1996), no. 3, p. 238-256.

apply for extra support on account of high housing costs or other specific high costs associated with being a breadwinner or single parent.

In the last ten to fifteen years the Danish system has been moving towards benefits based on rights more than on discretion. On the positive side, the individual now has access to well-known rights in case of need. On the negative side, street-level bureaucrats now enjoy less leeway in assessing an individual's needs from a broader viewpoint. Discretion has always permitted local administrators to take more specific needs into consideration, and to cover certain expenses (like, for instance, children's participation in school camps) which cannot be covered in a more legalistic system.

3 Maintaining living standards outside of the labour market

3.1 Introduction

The European Communities Council's recommendation of July 27th, 1992, concerning convergence of national welfare systems contains, among other elements, the provision that member states 'provide employed workers who cease work at the end of their working lives or are forced to interrupt their careers owing to sickness, accident, maternity, invalidity or unemployment, with a replacement income [...] which will maintain their standard of living in a reasonable manner in accordance with their participation in appropriate social security schemes'.[11] This recommendation is vague in the sense that it does not specify 'a reasonable manner'. Nor does it explain how 'participation in appropriate social security schemes' has a role in determining a reasonable living standard. If the text is taken on its own unspecified terms, implying that no person should live in poverty or below the poverty line as defined by the European Community (*i.e.,* 50% of the average income), it would seem that this recommendation is met by most countries.

The Danish system, with its largely universal approach, does not give rise to specific problems in relation to the criteria of having been a member of a social security scheme, as the analysis on specific contingencies will show. In the following, I will touch upon four main areas: old age, sickness, unemployment and early

---

[11] 'Council Recommendation of 27 July 1992 on the convergence of social protection objectives and policies' (92/442/EEC), in: *Official Journal of the European Communities,* L245, August 26th, 1992, p. 49-52, I, A, sub 1 (d).

retirement. These four contingencies cover both permanent and short-term periods in which income replacement is needed.

3.2 Pensions

In Denmark, the right to pensions depends mainly on reaching a specific age (67 years for both men and women) and on being a Danish citizen. However, some special categories – refugees, citizens of countries with which Denmark has an agreement, and citizens from EEA-countries[12] – do not have to meet the citizenship requirement. Furthermore, in order to qualify for full State pension one must have lived in Denmark for at least forty years after reaching the age of 15. Consequently, a person who has lived in Denmark for, say, twenty years will receive half this pension. Similarly, and in accordance with the European Union regulations, a citizen of the European Union who has worked in Denmark for twenty years receives half a State pension.

On average, State social pensions account for approximately 62% of pensioners' income.[13] The category with the lowest income[14] receive a gross income of 95,600 DKr for single persons and 139,000 DKr for couples (1999). Nearly half of the pensioners have a higher gross income, primarily due to labour market pensions. The replacement rate varies depending on one's income during the years preceding retirement.

The ATP administration has calculated that with the latest increase in ATP, a labour market pension of 9% established in 1993 (6% paid by employers and 3% by employees), and a yearly income of 200,000 DKr, the replacement rate in disposable income will gradually rise from nearly 60% in 1995 to over 75% in 2035.[15] Similarly, it has been calculated that with a disposable income of 105,800 DKr the replacement rate will be 71% in 2005, and increase to 86% in the year 2040 when the ATP system has matured.[16] It thus seems possible to achieve decent living standards for pensioners by combining a universal pension with the agreed labour market supplementary and collective pensions.

The question remains how individuals will be covered who are not employed on the labour market or who, owing to spells of unemployment, do not form part of the core labour force. Since 1993, individuals receiving social benefits because of unemployment, sickness, maternity or participation in a labour market programme

---

[12] European Economic Area.

[13] *Pensionssystemet og fremtidens forsørgerbyrde* (1995).

[14] I leave aside the approximately 6% of the pensioners who live in a home for the elderly and who do not receive a pension but a small allowance, instead.

[15] *Supplementary pensions in Denmark – a description of the future pension system,* Hillerød: ATP, 1995.

[16] *Pensionssystemet og fremtidens forsørgerbyrde* (1995).

are covered by ATP. This amendment will naturally increase their ATP pension. As low income earners run a higher risk of long-term unemployment, ATP is especially important for them since their replacement rate will be boosted by this extra pension income (even despite the fact that the supplementary ATP pension is low in absolute terms). However, those individuals who have remained permanently outside of the labour market, will receive the social pension and nothing else. Because their income has always been small, their replacement rate will be relatively high but in absolute terms their income will be much lower than that of people who have at any time been employed on the labour market. Whether this outcome constitutes the maintainance of a reasonable standard of living is largely a matter of personal moral perception. However, it seems in accordance with the second part of the European recommendation, as people who were never employed on the labour market will not have contributed to specific social security schemes.

3.3 Unemployment benefits

Old age pensions represent a permanent income transfer and, consequentially, the income replacement they produce is also permanent. The income transfers needed by people who leave the labour market for a limited period are of a different nature. Normally, unemployment benefits are transitory in character. They replace a person's income for a short time, during unemployment spells or during a transition period towards permanent retirement from the labour market.

Although membership of unemployment insurance funds is optional, their coverage is quite high. In 1998, they had a membership of nearly 2.2 million out of a total labour force of around 2.87 million persons. Non-members generally belong to three groups: people with a very low risk of ever becoming unemployed (often highly salaried employees), people who work too few hours to be covered, and finally people from professions without a membership tradition (many self-employed and civil servants). In order to qualify for membership one has to be employed within the field of the specific unemployment fund, to have taken vocational training for at least eighteen months, or to have been an army conscript. Unemployment insurance in Denmark is mainly organised by the trade unions – there is no specific insurance market for unemployment benefits. Traditionally, members of unemployment insurance funds are also members of the corresponding trade union, although this is not obligatory.

In order to be eligible for an unemployment benefit one must have been a member for at least one year, or one must have finished a vocational training of at least eighteen months less than a fortnight after entering the unemployment insurance fund. Furthermore, the right to unemployment benefit is dependent on having worked at least 52 weeks within the last three years. One cannot receive unemployment benefit when one is receiving a study grant,[17] during sickness, or during unemployment through one's own fault (five weeks waiting period first time).

Unemployment insurance is financed partly by fixed contributions from employers and employees. These contributions are related to the level of unemployment benefits. The State pays most, since it guarantees the actual payment of unemployment benefits. The State's contribution varies with the level of unemployment because its economic responsibility is restricted to the marginal cost of having unemployment insurance funds. In recent years unemployment in Denmark has dropped to a low level and the State's role in unemployment insurance has declined accordingly.

The maximum level of unemployment benefit is, as already mentioned, 90% of one's previous income with a ceiling of 143,520 DKr a year in 1999 (though never more than 552 DKr a day). The level is lower for persons who have just taken vocational training or who have been conscripts, and have not been able to find a job. They receive 117,782 Danish Kroner (82% of the maximum unemployment benefit). It is possible to receive unemployment benefit for up to four years. This four year period is split between one year on benefits, and a three year period of 'activation': people who receive unemployment benefits are obliged to search actively for a job, and must be prepared to accept any reasonable job offer by the employment exchange. For individuals over twenty-five years of age, continuance of the benefit after the first year of unemployment depends on their willingness to accept a so-called pool job. Pool jobs are considered a kind of training. Payment is equal to the unemployment benefit. The time spent in a pool job cannot be used in order to qualify for a new period of unemployment benefit. This implies that if a person is unable to get at job after this period he or she will have to live on social assistance.

For low income earners the consequences of the transition from employment to unemployment may be small in terms of loss of income. However, the impact of the loss of contact with other people and other psycho-sociological problems cannot be assessed in terms of money. Low income earners without a job represent between 15 and 20% of the total number of unemployed.[18] This implies that for 80 to 85% of jobless people the economic consequences of unemployment can be quite dramatic with a high decline in income. There has been debate on the possibility of introducing additional voluntary insurance systems in order to raise the replacement rate. Presumably, such systems would have to survive without the substantial financial support of the State. They would be organised along the lines of the existing unemployment insurance fund system, either as an element in the existing system, *i.e.* mainly through the trade unions, or as a service of private

---

[17] Except when education is part of a plan for the unemployed to return to the labour market. There are further specific rules for youngsters under 25 years of age which I will leave aside here.

[18] Møller Jensen and Verner, 'Dagpengenes betydning for omfanget af arbejdsløshed i Danmark'.

insurance companies. The discussion has focused on the question whether such a scheme would really promote equity and equality. In an unmitigated market situation, people with the highest risk of unemployment would have to pay the highest insurance premium – if they could be covered at all. This effect would clash with the intentions of the present system in which coverage and payment are solidaristic, at least as regards the State contribution which is mainly based on the universal tax-system. So far there has been no tendency towards privatisation in this area.

The unemployed who are not members of an unemployment insurance fund have to rely on social assistance which is means-tested, as mentioned earlier. Their right to receive social assistance does not depend on whether or not they have lost their jobs through their own fault.

3.4 Sickness and early retirement benefits

The last two benefits to be included in this presentation are sickness benefits and early retirement benefits. Both kinds of benefits are relevant for those who are employed or have been employed on the labour market, but sickness benefits can also be obtained by other persons – a point I shall return to later.

Early retirement benefit can be given to all persons between the ages of 60 and 67 who are members of an unemployment insurance fund. They must have been members for at least twenty-five of the last thirty years, and they must continue their membership of the fund after retirement. They must not have applied for or received a social pension of any kind. Employees must be eligible for unemployment benefit in order to start receiving early retirement benefit. Self-employed persons must be able to prove that their activities as self-employed persons have ceased, for example by showing that their firm has been closed down. The level of benefits is dependent on the age of retirement. One level is applicable to those who enter at the age of between 60 and 62. For them the level of benefit is 91% of unemployment benefit. Those who enter at the age of between 63 and 65 receive a retirement benefit which equals the benefit level for unemployed persons – provided the resulting income remains below the ceiling of 90% of their previous income. In 1998 it was decided that from 1 July 1999 onwards those who continue working up to the age of 65 (and who have been a member and paid membership fees) are entitled to a tax-premium of 8,600 Danish Kroner for each quarter they work after becoming 62, up to a maximum of 103,200 Danish Kroner. The overall intention was to create incentives for people to stay longer on the labour market. One may argue that this decision indicates a shift away from the fully universal model, as only those who have paid the specific premium are eligible for the early retirement benefit or, in the event that they apply for early retirement, the extra State premium. More than before, the whole system of early retirement benefits now resembles an insurance scheme.

A high proportion of those receiving early retirement benefits are unskilled. In recent years other groups have increasingly used the opportunity to retire before the official pension age of 65. Nowadays, withdrawal from the labour market often takes place around the age of 61 or 62. Given the fact that retirement is voluntary,[19] the level of support seems reasonable, especially for low income earners. In most cases pensioners enjoy a decent living standard compared to their situation prior to retirement. It has also to be borne in mind that the usual 8% tax-contribution for employees need not be paid over the early retirement benefit. Instead normal income tax applies.

Sickness benefits can be obtained after having worked for 13 weeks and for a total of at least 120 hours. The benefit is paid from the first day of sickness and for a maximum of 52 weeks within a period of 18 months. Self-employed persons and their spouses (if the latter work as their assistant) need to take out a voluntary insurance (within the public sector) in order to be covered in the first two weeks of sickness. In this case the benefit also relates to previous income, which is calculated differently for different categories (employed, self-employed persons and assistant spouses). The overall maximum level of benefit is 143,416 Danish Kroner (approx. € 19,275). The system carries an obligation for municipalities to take action if a person is sick for more than three months, in order to prevent prolonged sickness.[20] Intervention can take different forms, from an interview on individual possibilities to training programmes, additional education *etc.* Invariably, it aims to promote a way back to the labour market or to clarify the individual's future prospects. Employers are held responsible for healthy and safe working environments and for paying premiums for work accident insurance. In many collective agreements there are rules concerning the payment of wages in the event of sickness. These rules often imply that employees receive full salary during a period of sickness. For this, their employer is partially reimbursed by the State. They also guarantee that a person cannot be sacked during sickness (unless his sickness lasts for a very long period). Employers in general have an interest in reducing sickness among their employees as this will increase productivity.

The level of sickness benefits *per se* seems reasonable. It is more questionable whether enough efforts are being made to reintegrate recuperated employees and whether preventive measures currently taken to reduce the risk of sickness are sufficient.

---

[19] I am aware that for some people on the Danish labour market it is mainly a choice between different types of income support, but for others it is a choice reflecting preferences concerning their personal arrangement of free time and working time and the income to go with these preferences.

[20] For persons who are unable to return to the labour market a specific anticipatory pension exists, which can be given on medical and, for persons above 50, also on social grounds.

3.5 Some general remarks and an evaluation of the system

All the benefits mentioned in this section are adjusted on an annual basis in relation to the average income on the labour market. As a consequence, income transfers will follow the changing standard of living in Danish society unless specific
political intervention takes place. Such an intervention took place between 1983
and 1985, when unemployment benefits were reduced in real terms as a result of a
political decision not to index these benefits.

In principle, benefits are awarded to individuals. However, there is no rule without
an exception. Social assistance and housing benefits are based on household income.[21] Some specific allowances to pensioners also depend on whether the applicant is single or a member of a household.

Overall, the generosity of the Danish system ensures that fewer people live in
relative poverty than without this tax- and transfers-system. M. Förster[22] has calculated that 20.2% of the Danish population belong to the low income category,
i.e. persons living in a household with an income below 50% of the median income before taxes and transfers. When the effect of taxes and transfers is included
this percentage drops to 5.7%. It can therefore be concluded that the system does
indeed redistribute income within Danish society, both within and between generations. Denmark has one of Europe's highest degrees of equality as measured by
the GINI-coefficient.[23] This does not necessarily imply, however, that all citizens
are actively involved in society and in production. There is a great deal of debate
in Denmark as to the extent of social marginalisation and how this phenomenon
should be defined. For example, how long must an individual remain outside of
the labour market before he or she is considered to be marginalised? A recent
report by O. Ingerslev and L. Pedersen[24] supplies some information on the number
of marginalised persons in Denmark. Ingerslev and Pedersen base their figures on
register data files. Their definition of marginalisation implies that anyone who has
been unemployed for more than 15% of the time within the last three years, is to
be considered excluded from what is labelled the core of the labour market and
thereby socially marginalised. Their figures indicate that in 1994, out of a total of
just over 3.4 million citizens between 18 and 66 years of age 429,000 were loosely
connected to the labour market, 255,000 belonged to the marginal group, 370,000
were living permanently on public benefit, and 150,000 were living on alternative

---

[21] In general, household income implies the income of people cohabiting, regardless of their marital
status.

[22] M. Förster, *Measurement of low incomes and poverty in a perspective of international comparisons*,
Paris: Organisation for Economic Cooperation and Development (OECD), 1994. Labour market and
Occasional Papers no. 14.

[23] See Bent Greve (Ed.), *What Constitutes a Good Society*, Houndsmills: Macmillan, 1999.

[24] O. Ingerslev and L. Pedersen, *Marginalisering: 1990-1994* [Marginalisation: 1990-1994], København: Socialforskningsinstituttet (Institute for Social Research), 1996.

income types (living at the expense of relatives or friends, or making money in the hidden economy). This means that more than 1 million people do not receive the main part of their income from the labour market. In this respect a very high proportion of the 18-66 age groups rely to some degree on the public system and the benefits and services connected with it. The social benefit system succeeds in maintaining a decent standard of living for those who are temporarily or permanently excluded from the labour market. However, for many thousands, achieving a higher standard of living by rejoining the labour market for a longer timespan seems no real option. In this respect the welfare state has not been able to achieve equality.

4 Some reflections on the future

The trend in Denmark seems to be towards means-tested benefits, and towards a system in which the continuation of various short-term benefits is made conditional on accepting offers of work,[25] training or further education. Permanent benefits such as pensions and early retirement benefits are not affected by this trend which reflects, to some degree, public opinion on 'deserving' and 'undeserving' receivers of benefits, and public notions on the merits and faults of the social security system. Sometimes there is, so it seems, a fear that some people can too easily cheat the system, *i.e.* receive benefits and still be working clandestinely or receiving other types of income. Various control actions from the social security system and the tax and duty system, however, do not confirm this general impression.

Two proposals sent out for debate by the Ministry of Social Affairs in the early autumn of 1996[26] confirmed that the strategies and the perception of responsibilities, ideas and visions for the welfare state are gradually undergoing change. The system will become more individualistic, implying a bigger role for the subsidiarity principle in the process of social policy in Denmark. More than ever before the welfare state will be the last lender of resort. In the future many people who receive social assistance – and not just the young among them – will also find themselves under pressure to search for work or to join educational programmes.

---

[25] For this purpose various work schemes exist in the public sector, as well as work projects and the special jobs mentioned above, intended for those unemployed for more than two years.

[26] *Rapport fra udvalget om bistandslovens serviceydelser* [Report of the committee on service in the social area], København: Socialministeriet (Ministry of Social Affairs), 1996; *Rapport fra udvalget om kontanthjælp, aktivering og revalidering m.v.* [Report of the committee concerning social assistance, activation and rehabilitation *etc.*]), København: Socialministeriet, 1996.

It is not obvious why these changes have taken place or why they seem to continue. Tentatively, several reasons may be suggested. First and foremost the fact that a growing number of people depend on social benefits. It is feared that the rising dependency ratio (which will rise even further as a result of demographic developments) will make it difficult to finance the welfare state in the future. This fear of demographic transition is also seen in international studies from the OECD and the European Union, but its consequences are often overestimated – provided the countries in question stick to a sound fiscal policy, and the overall economic possibilities continue to grow as they have done in the past. Secondly, there is a fear that public support for the welfare state will crumble if voters feel that there are too many scroungers. Thirdly, the globalisation of the economy makes it increasingly difficult to maintain current Danish policies on income and taxes.

Between 1993 and 1999 a change in labour market and social policies has revealed a clear push towards activating people into resuming their place on the labour market. Perhaps these policies have had some effect, but presumably the decrease of unemployment in Denmark is chiefly due to better overall economic conditions combined with the implemented leave schemes.[27] Nevertheless, the policy changes indicate a process of rethinking and a move towards higher demands on those who wish to receive a benefit for a longer period (unless they are elderly or severely disabled). They will notice that the requirements for eligibility have been sharpened considerably.

In spite of all this, the welfare state in Denmark will, in the foreseeable future, remain universal and driven mainly by the public sector. The debate on privatisation of the welfare state has petered out. Nevertheless, a thorough discussion about the financing and the goals of the welfare state should take place, preferably in a public debate, because changes in the provision of social services within the welfare state may well be under way. The boundaries between state and market may no longer be the centre of interest but the quality of social services is. While financing still seems to be the more common approach, it may well be the historical distinction between public and private delivery that is in the process of changing.[28]

Solidarity with the weakest still seems to prevail. This impression is supported by surveys of voters' attitudes.[29] It is, however, difficult to determine exactly what is meant by the 'weakest persons in society'. Furthermore, support for the welfare state seems to focus increasingly on areas where all citizens need support from the State at some time during their lifes: childcare, care for the elderly, and health care

---

[27] Schemes which enable workers to leave the labour market for shorter or longer intervals for educational or parenting purposes.

[28] *Cf.* Bent Greve and Danny Pieters (Ed.), *Social security in an interdisciplinary approach,* Brussels: Maklu, 1999.

[29] *Velfærd – for hvem. Social forskning* [Welfare – for whom. Social research], København: Socialforskningsinstituttets, 1998.

(including hospitals). The growing wealth accrued in pension funds may also, although more indirectly, push in this direction. In the years to come, an increasing number of senior citizens will have a very high level of income. As a result, less and less elderly will need support from the welfare state. The debate on universal or more targeted support to the elderly is already taking place. This may result in a decline of support for the welfare state among the elderly too. If these trends continue, it is to be feared that over time the financial support for the genuinely poor in Danish society will become less well developed, less positive and less thorough.

5 The impact of the European Union

The European Union's direct impact seems to be quite limited within the sphere of social policy. Under the prevailing good economic conditions in Denmark the introduction of the third stage of the Economic and Monetary Union (EMU), in which Denmark will not participate for the time being, does not seem to be an issue which will influence Danish economic decision-making or Danish expenditure on social security. Nevertheless, there may be an indirect effect from the Maastricht criteria which countries need to fulfil in order to enter the third stage of the EMU.

In comments and official publications the Danish Government and the Ministry of Economic Affairs are continuously pointing out that the Danish economy – especially with regard to the level of public debt and deficit – must be able to fulfil the Maastricht criteria in order to prevent any negative impact on the Danish economy of an increase in interest rate. This means that if the economic climate deteriorates and problems occur with the public sector deficit, the level of benefits and services may be affected. It is only in this broader context and more indirect way that the European Union may have an impact on the development of the welfare state in Denmark. Apart from this, it seems that changes in the Danish welfare state will only take place when preferences in Danish society change.

6 Concluding comments

It is notoriously difficult to predict future developments on the basis of present and past. Likewise, it is difficult to predict how the Danish welfare state will develop in the years to come. At times its prospects look bright, then again bleakness prevails.

In the late 1960s and the early 1970s, many people believed in a golden age of economic growth and prosperity. Shortly afterwards, rising oil prices and the transfer of money from the western world to the Arab world radically changed the economic climate. The economy of most European countries flagged. Not before the middle of the 1980s and again in the 1990s, did western economies combine growth with a decline in unemployment. It was in the intermediate years of economic crisis and uncertainty that the welfare state came under fire. The crisis of the welfare state seemed apparent. In retrospect, one wonders[30] if there really ever was a crisis of the welfare state. It is a fact that in many countries, in spite of the economic crisis, the welfare state continued to grow. Only in a few countries did its development come to standstill (if one takes the proportion of GNP spent on social security as a benchmark). Soon, rhetoric about the crisis of the welfare state was replaced by concerns about more pressing ecological matters.

Seen in this light, the globalisation of economies and external economic disturbances may well affect the welfare state but, if this is not the case, one may well expect the future welfare state in Denmark to be both solidaristic and universal.

---

[30] Greve, 'Indications of Social Policy Convergence in Europe'.

IV France

Dominique Greiner

1 Introduction

Over the past ten years, the social security system in France has been the subject of rapid change and all sectors have been influenced. In 1988, the law of Minimum Income for Adults was established. Also, a reform of the old Age Insurance came into effect in August 1994 and in November 1995, the Government took an ambitious step towards reorganising the health care system and its insurance. By the end of 1996, the social partners had come to an agreement regarding unemployment insurance. In January 1997, an allowance for elderly dependent individuals was created. In February 1997, Parliament adopted a law on pension plan introducing capitalisation in the retirement scheme. As a consequence of employment problems encountered at the end of 1997 and the beginning of 1998, levels of minimum assistance benefits have been exhausted. In 1999-2000, a universal coverage of health expenses should be implemented.

2 The French system

2.1 General overview

In 1945, the objective of the French social security system was defined as: 'To protect the workers and their families against all susceptible risks that can impede or halt one's work, to cover maternity leave and the expenses of their family.'[1] The initial goal was to establish a unified system. However, certain social groups benefiting from specific professional systems refused to be included in the new one. Thus the unification of the system was jeopardised from the beginning and has never been achieved. Today, the French social security system is composed of 145 basic *régimes* or 'schemes', of which 122 benefit salaried workers and 19 non-salaried non-agricultural workers. Of these schemes the social security scheme for the salaried (the so-called general system) is by far the most important.

---

[1] Fundamental Law of Social Security, October 4th, 1945.

It covers a large population and it is practically the only scheme to cover a wide range of risks and charges. It is subdivided into four divisions: illness (illness, health-care and invalidity), workplace accidents, family (maternity and family), and old age (old age and widowhood). The unemployment compensation scheme is not administered by the social security system; it has been jointly regulated and managed by the social partners since 1959.

The basic social security system (consisting of the general system and numerous specific schemes) has been subject to the addition of complementary schemes (health, old-age pension). Some of these are compulsory, especially those which relate to retirement.

Table 1: Social benefits in percentages of GNP.[2]

	1981	1985	1990	1995	1996
Old age benefits					
• Retirement	9.4	10.2	10.5	11.7	11.9
• basic benefits	7.3	7.8	7.8	8.5	8.6
• complementary benefits	2.1	2.4	2.7	3.2	3.3
• Means-tested benefits	0.5	0.5	0.3	0.2	0.2
• Other	0.6	0.6	0.5	0.5	0.4
Total	10.5	11.3	11.3	12.4	12.5
Health					
• Illness	6.5	6.9	7.0	7.7	7.7
• Invalidity	1.5	1.7	1.6	1.7	1.8
• Work accidents	0.8	0.7	0.6	0.5	0.5
Total	8.8	9.3	9.2	9.9	10.5
Workforce					
• Unemployment	1.4	1.4	1.5	1.6	1.7
• Reintegration in the labour market	0.2	0.2	0.3	0.5	0.5
• Early retirement	0.5	1.2	0.5	0.3	0.2
Total	2.2	2.8	2.2	2.4	2.4
Family					
• Maternity	0.5	0.5	0.4	0.5	0.4
• Family	3.7	4.1	3.8	4.1	4.2
Total	4.2	4.6	4.2	4.6	4.6
Other					
• RMI and private charities)	0.2	0.2	0.3	0.5	0.5
Total	25.9	28.2	27.2	29.8	30.0

[2] Source: SESI. *Comptes de la protection sociale;* INSEE, *Comptes Nationaux.*

In addition to these systems, *social assistance* offers benefits to those who cannot apply for contributory benefits. It provides medical assistance, minimum benefits for old-age or disabled people, housing assistance and programmes for reintegration in the labour market.

2.1 Social security expenses

The social security expenses consist of the expenses of basic and complementary schemes, family allowances and unemployment benefits. In 1981, total expenses represented 25.9% of the GNP; in 1996, they rose to 2,300 billion French Francs (FFr) or € 350.6 billion, that is 30% of the GNP (see Table 1 above). This significant increase is to be attributed to the ageing of the population, the rise in unemployment rate, the growth of medical expenditures and growing needs of poor people.

The structure of the expenses has remained unchanged since the 1980s (see Table 2 below). In 1996, care for the elderly (early retirement benefits excepted) represents 41.9% of total expenditures; health (illness, handicap, work accident) totals 33%; family related benefits (family, housing, maternity) amounts to 15.2% and work related benefits (unemployment, professional inadaptation and early retirement) to 8%.

Table 2: Structure of expenses per risk.[3]

	1981	1985	1990	1995	1996
Old Age	40.5	40.1	41.3	41.5	41.9
Health	34.1	32.9	33.9	33.3	33.3
Family	16.2	16.2	15.4	15.3	15.2
Employment	8.4	10.0	8.2	8.2	8.0
Other	0.8	0.8	1.2	1.7	1.6
Total	100.0	100.0	100.0	100.0	100.0

2.2 The financial aspect of the social security system

75% of the social security system is financed by social contributions by employers and salaried workers. To face the increase in expenses, contribution rates have been raised and the contribution basis has been extended (suppression of maximum ceiling for contribution). In addition, a new tax was introduced in 1991 to finance the social security deficit. This so-called *contribution sociale généralisée* (CSG, generalised social contribution) is applied to nearly all types of income.

---

[3] Source: SESI. *Comptes de la protection sociale.*

This wide fiscal basis ensures a high fiscal return: one point of CSG yields FFr 38.2 billion against 13.5 billion for one point of income tax. Only a few portions of income remain outside of the CSG: some special forms of compensation such as the returns of profit-sharing, and half the income of social benefits or property. In 1996, the CSG and other specific taxation (on tobacco, alcohol) cover 7.9% of the social security budget (Table 3).

Table 3: The financing of social protection, Structure in % (1981-1996).[4]

	1981	1985	1990	1991	1992	1993	1994	1995	1996
Contributions	76.8	75.0	78.3	77.4	76.8	75.4	74.2	74.5	75.1
• by employers	53.8	50.9	50.3	49.8	48.4	47.6	47.7	47.9	47.9
• by employees	17.9	18.8	22.2	21.8	21.8	21.7	21.4	21.7	21.7
• other (self-employed, retired people)	5.1	5.3	5.8	5.8	5.6	5.3	5.2	5.1	5.5
State contributions and specific taxation	17.6	19.0	16.2	17.2	17.8	19.2	20.9	20.4	20.0
• State contribution	15.3	15.9	12.8	12.9	13.2	13.6	13.4	12.8	12.1
• specific taxation (CSG etc.)	2.3	3.1	3.4	4.3	4.6	5.6	7.5	7.6	7.9
Other	5.6	6.0	5.5	5.4	5.4	5.4	4.9	5.1	4.9
Total	100.0	100.0	100.0	100.0	100.0	100.0	100.0	100.0	100.0

The financing of social security is based upon occupational earnings. However, this principle does not extend to the method of access to allowances. Some benefits, like family allowances, are financed by contribution of wage-earners but since 1978 they have been available to all residents in charge of families. Currently, the tendency is towards a change in the financing of family allowances: the lowest wages have already been exonerated from family contribution payments.

3 Maintaining living standards

The French social security system is based on paid professions and occupations. Access to the main allowances depends on former employment or previously paid contributions. This applies to every type of social risk.

---

[4] Source: SESI. *Comptes de la protection sociale.*

3.1 Illness

Social protection against the consequences of illness is primarily covered by health insurance. The various insurance schemes relate to different categories of professions. All wage-earners are covered in the event of illness. Non-wage-earners can take out a private insurance. For those who can ill afford such an insurance, premiums may be covered by social assistance. Yet, in 1996, 98% were covered in case of illness, leaving an estimated 500,000 people that encounter difficulties in obtaining health care. The main reason for this deficiency is the lack of coordination between medical aid and social security administrations. However, the introduction of a universal health insurance plan is currently in progress and should be completed in the next few months.

Table 4: The French health care coverage.

Category	Percentage
Enjoying a basic coverage (social security plus medical aid)	99.8
Linked to the general system	69.7
Linked to a particular scheme	20.4
Linked to a special group	10.3
In receipt of medical aid	2.7
Exempt from the *ticket modérateur* for health care[5]	8.7
Enjoying a supplementary coverage	83.0

3.1.1 Reimbursement of medical expenses

The reimbursement of medical expenses is open to all insured people. The rate of reimbursement depends on the nature of the care. The supplementary health insurance raises the reimbursement rate, sometimes up to 100%. The average rate of reimbursement (basic and complementary) decreased from 84.4% of expenses in 1978 to 81.5% in 1993. This can be explained by the reduction that the social security system carried through in its reimbursement rates.

3.1.2 Illness, maternity, and accident benefits

All wage-earners are eligible for a partial income compensation in case of illness, maternity or accident. This benefit is paid by the social security system and, in many cases, the employer provides complementary compensation. He continues to

---

[5] The *ticket modérateur* is the portion of health care expenses paid directly by people themselves (30% for medical fees, about 40% for medication, 20% for hospital care).

pay the entire salary while being partially reimbursed by the daily compensation of the social security system.

Insured employees who fall ill, are paid a benefit by the health insurance after three days. This benefit is paid for a maximum duration of 120 days per year on average, and three years if the illness is one of a list of so-called 'long illnesses'. The amount of the benefit is equal to 50% of the usual salary during the first 30 days, two thirds after the 31st day if the patient has at least three children. The gap between these benefits and the normal salary is filled by supplementary occupational or private insurance plans.

In the event of an accident at work, the benefit is equal to 60% of the salary in the first month and 80% thereafter. It is paid for the entire duration of the employee's inability to work. In case of permanent disability, the victim has a right to an annuity. Its amount depends on the previous income and on the degree of disability. Each of these allowances has a floor and a ceiling. Table 5 gives the amounts as of January 1st, 1997.

Table 5: Floor and ceiling of daily compensation in the event of illness, invalidity and work accident (January 1997).

	Minimum		Maximum	
	FFr	€	FFr	€
Illness	47.00	7	228.70	35
Maternity	46.40	7	362.20	55
Work accident				
• for the first 28 days:			823.85	126
• thereafter:			1,098.50	167

Maternity benefits are paid for a minimum period of 16 weeks. The amount varies with the number of previous children and is adjusted in the event of multiple birth (see Table 6). More favourable arrangements can be made if previewed in a conventional manner.

Table 6: Length of leave allowed before and after birth (or adoption).

	Maternity			Adoption
	before delivery	after delivery	total	after arrival at home
Birth or adoption:				
• 1 or 2	6 weeks	10 weeks	16 weeks	10 weeks
• 3 or more	8 weeks	18 weeks	26 weeks	18 weeks
Multiple births or adoptions:				
• twins	12 weeks	22 weeks	34 weeks	22 weeks
• triplets or more	24 weeks	22 weeks	46 weeks	

3.2 Unemployment

Two kinds of unemployment benefits must be distinguished: benefits paid by the conventional insurance scheme and benefits paid by the assistance scheme. Over the past few years, restrictions have been imposed on eligibility for benefits.

3.2.1 Unemployment insurance

Table 7: Duration and rate of unemployment insurance (January 1997).[6]

Duration of previous contributions	Total duration of compensation	Of which at full rate
4 months over last 8 months	4 months	4 months
6 months over last 12 months	7 months	4 months
8 months over last 12 months		
• less than 50 years	15 months	4 months
• 50 years and over	17 months	7 months
14 months over last 24 months		
• less than 50 years	30 months	9 months
• 50 years and over	45 months	15 months
27 months over last 36 months		
• 50 to 54 years	45 months	20 months
• 55 years and more	60 months	27 months

A new law on unemployment insurance was implemented since on January 1st, 1997 (Table 7). Eligibility conditions have been slightly modified. The duration of coverage depends on the duration of one's subscription. Benefits are paid for a minimum of 4 months to employees who have worked 4 months or less in the course of the last 8 months, and up to 60 months for employees aged 55 and over, who have contributed for at least 27 months in the course of the last 36 months.

Table 8: Unemployment insurance: full-rate compensation.[7]

Basic salary	Monthly compensation
Lower than or equal to FFr 5,690 (€ 867)	75% of salary
Between FFr 5,690 (€ 867) and 6,230 (€ 950)	FFr 4,267.20 (€ 651) (flat amount)
Between FFr 6,230 (€ 950) and 10,298 (€ 1,570)	40.4% of salary plus FFr 1,750 (€ 267)
More than FFr 10,298 (€ 1,570)	57.4% of salary

The amount of the monthly benefit is established in accordance with one's average income in the last 12 months. It decreases with the length of unemployment (it

---

[6] Source: UNEDIC.
[7] Source: UNEDIC.

is reduced every 3 or 6 months - instead of every 4 months before 1997). The scale is given on Table 8.

At the end of 1996, 1,857,500 unemployed people benefited from unemployment insurance. The average allocation was FFr 4,270 (€ 651). 54% of recipients received less than FFr 4,000 (€ 610), 36% between FFr 4,000 (€ 610) and 7,000 (€ 915) and 10% more than FFr 7,000 (€ 1,067).

3.2.2 Social assistance

The *Allocation Spécifique de Solidarité* (ASS, Special Solidarity Benefit) is an unemployment benefit financed by the State. It is paid to the unemployed who have exhausted their rights to unemployment benefits, but who have worked for at least 5 years in the 10 years preceding the expiry of their last employment. ASS is granted for a period of 6 months, which can be renewed. People who are exempted from obligatory job-searching (*e.g.* because of their age) may receive ASS indefinitely for as long as their income makes them eligible. By the end of 1996, this allowance benefited 516,300 unemployed people.

3.2.3 Unemployed without coverage or social assistance

The percentage of unemployed not benefiting from unemployment insurance or assistance has increased significantly over the past few years on account of the current eligibility conditions. These conditions are particularly unfavourable towards the young. In December 1995, no less than 550,000 out of 850,000 unemployed aged 18-25 did not receive any unemployment benefit. Moreover, people under the age of 25 – except those in charge of children – have no right to the minimum subsistence allowance (*Revenu Minimum d'Insertion,* RMI). As a consequence, many young and unattached unemployed face very precarious living conditions. Based on a study by INSEE, in 1995 alone 100,000 young adults between 15 and 29 were both unemployed and unattached – twice as many as in 1982. Staff members of emergency assistance organisations confirm this tendency: more and more young adults knock at the door of their centres for the jobless.

3.3 Old age

Old age insurance benefits are based on compulsory basic schemes (more than 120), compulsory complementary schemes (more than 180), and optional supplementary schemes set up along the lines of various professional groups. Almost all basic schemes and special schemes for salaried workers of the public sector provide annuities; the complementary schemes offer additional benefits. Recently, in

February 1997, the French parliament adopted a law on pension plans that marks a decisive change in the retirement system.

3.3.1 The basic scheme

Access to the general scheme for salaried workers was modified in 1994 in order to come to terms with demographic developments. Retirement age remains fixed at 60. However, the required work period was increased from 150 to 160 trimesters while the pensionable salary is henceforth based on the best 20 (instead of 10) years. As a consequence, there will be a decrease in replacement rates. The relative standard of living of the retired will decline. In absolute terms, their standard of living will depend on the country's economic performance.

The French pensions system has limited vertical redistributive effects. For people with a high income the balance between contributions and pensions is positive. The correlation between income levels and life expectancy is not compensated for, either by progressive contributions, or by a ceiling. However, transfers are also important from men to women and between the extremities of the social hierarchy.

3.3.2 Complementary schemes

Conventional complementary schemes have been added to the basic schemes, and they are obligatory in the private sector. There are 171 different schemes, which supplement pensions up to the basic pension's ceiling allowance. They therefore do not correct the vertical distributive effects of the basic scheme. The schemes function on a national level. They do not penalise the mobility of workers, because retirement points are accumulated throughout their careers even if they change employers.

3.3.3 Pension plans

On February 20th, 1997, the French parliament adopted a law on pension plans that introduced a third stage in the retirement system: capitalisation. In the discussions preceding its passing three motives were apparent: the ageing of the French population, unemployment, and the anticipated decline in the present schemes' return. Pension plans are not compulsory and are not – for the moment – considered as a substitute for present schemes. The financial stakes are enormous. The annual fluctuations (estimated between FFr 30 and 50 billion) encourage financial institutions like insurance companies, banks, and pension funds to offer personalised pension schemes.

The unions are opposed to any reform which, according to them, undermines the solidarity principle of pay-as-you-go systems. The question they have raised is the following: should the right to a decent pension benefit be based on a social pact or on the individual's capacity and willingness to save for his or her old age?

3.3.4 Long-term care for dependent elderly people

To complete the section on old age, the position of the dependent population should be mentioned. Until 1995, there was no specific programme for the dependent elderly. They were considered as disabled and were entitled to the same benefits as all other disabled people. Dependency in old age, however, calls for specific services and benefits. In 1997, after two years of experiments, a special allowance for dependent people was put into place. It permits the elderly to remain at home under good conditions by financing regular visits by professional carers. It is means-tested.

3.4 Family allowance

The expenses of the *Caisse Nationale d'Allocations Familiales* reached FFr 236.8 billion (€ 36.1 billion) in 1995. The family allowances are directed to numerous families, young families, and lone parents. In 1995, FFr 154.6 billion (€ 23.57 billion) were devoted to family allowances. They benefited 5,831,000 families with 12.35 million children. The CNAF also pays housing benefits and the minimum subsistence allowance, RMI.

Over the last few years, priority has been given to poor families. 42.8% of benefits paid are means-tested. At the same time, there has been a tendency to reinforce the allowances paid at the child's birth instead of those paid for the duration of the parental care. For the amounts involved see Table 9.

Table 9: The amounts of the monthly allowances for the duration of parental care, on January 1st, 1997.

Number of children	Monthly allowance
2 children	FFr 675 (€ 103)
3 children	FFr 1,539 (€ 235)
4 children	FFr 2,404 (€ 366)
5 children	FFr 3,268 (€ 498)
Each additional child	FFr 864 (€ 132)

The system results in an increase of family allowances with the number of children along with a progressive decrease of these allowances with the family's income. In combination with the income tax system (which takes the number of children into account) the final result is especially unfavourable for the middle class.

4 Basic level of social security arrangements

Since the beginning of the 1970s, the terms of the various social insurance schemes have clearly improved. During the same period, the number of minimum benefits, aimed at people with no or insufficient claims on social insurance benefits, has increased. Nowadays, nearly 2,500,000 people receive a minimum benefit of some sort, among them disabled people, lone parents, long-term unemployed on *Allocation Spécifique de Solidarité*, and receivers of RMI.

4.1 Means-tested benefits

4.1.1 National Solidarity Funds

The *Fonds National de Solidarité* (FNS, National Solidarity Funds) ensures a minimum income for elderly people of 65 and over (or 60 in the event of inability to work) with low incomes. This allowances supplements their income up to the level of the minimum old age pension.

On December 31st, 1994, the FNS allocation was paid to 1,000,000 people, *i.e.* 11.6% of all people over 65. Thanks to the ongoing improvement of the old age pension (complete career, higher reference wages), the number of claimants has been in decline for at least a decade (minus 37% in 10 years). In 1994, most beneficiaries were female (70%), very old and widowed. Women over 75 constituted 50% of the total number of beneficiaries.

4.1.2 Allocation to disabled adults

The allocation for disabled adults (AAH, *Allocation Adulte Handicapé*) was put into place by the Government in 1975. It is granted to people over 20 and under 60 years of age who have a permanent disability of at least 80%, or alternatively of between 50 and 80%, and who are certified unable to work by a special commission. The benefit is means-tested and differentiated according to the degree of disability. In 1996, almost 610,000 people benefitted from the AAH, 60% of whom at full rate.

4.1.3 Lone parents

Since 1976, the allocation for lone parents (API, *Allocation Parent Isolé*) has been attributed to widowed, separated or abandoned parents who take care of one or more children. It is also granted to pregnant single women. The definition of 'lone parent' raises difficulties: is the allocation intended for parents who are unmarried and unattached or for parents who have to raise one or more children single-handedly? The law offers no clear answer.

The allocation for lone parents is paid for 12 consecutive months and may be extended until the youngest of the children reaches the age of three. The API also gives access to health and maternity insurance. In December 1993, this allowance supported 149,000 people.

4.1.4 Minimum subsistence allowance

The minimum subsistence allowance (RMI, *Revenu Minimum d'Insertion*) was created in 1988 to fight the spread of extreme poverty. The RMI is intended for people whose meagre income prevents them from attaining a degree of social autonomy. RMI is available to those 25 years old and over (18 if they have at least one child), provided that their income (including family allowances *minus* any rent subvention) does not exceed the amount of the allowance. RMI takes into account the individual's state of life and the number of children (see Table 10).

Table 10: Minimum subsistence income RMI (January 1997).

	One person	Persons living together
No children	FFr 2,402.99 (€ 366)	FFr 3,604.48 (€ 550)
1 child	FFr 3,604.48 (€ 550)	FFr 4,325.37 (€ 659)
2 children	FFr 4,325.37 (€ 659)	FFr 5,046.26 (€ 769)
Per additional child	plus FFr 961.19 (€ 147)	plus FFr 961.19 (€ 147)

Payment of RMI depends on one more condition: beneficiaries have to participate in programmes aimed at their reintegration in the labour market. Priority is given to return to work but not exclusively so. Poverty is recognised as a many-sided phenomenon. This is why the programmes on offer are personalised and try to take into account each individual's circumstances and development. However, the efforts towards reintegration meet with very little success.

At the end of 1996, 946,010 people benefited from RMI. Including spouses and children in charge, an estimated 1,800,000 people depend on this kind of allowance. Nearly 49% of all claimants are less than 35 years of age. On June 30th, 1995, of all young people between 25 and 35 years, 4.2% received RMI.

4.2 Calculating the minimum income

Means-tested benefits have no uniform calculation method as to the method of means-testing, the amount of the benefits, or the implementation of periodical improvements. Table 11 shows that disabled people receive the higher amounts. The maximum of their allowance is around FFr 3,000-3,500 (€ 457-534) for one individual, that is around 50% of the wage of a full-time non-skilled worker (minimum hourly wage) or 30%-40% of the average income of households. The guaranteed amount of ASS and RMI benefits is lower: 20 and 30% of the average income respectively. However, RMI may be topped up by additional allowances (family, housing) that are not subject to a means-test.

Table 11: Ceiling of resources and level of social assistance benefits (January 1997).

Type of benefit			*Maximum monthly amount*
Assistance for old age people	Single	• ceiling of income	FFr 3,516.08 (€ 536)
(FNS)		• benefit	FFr 3,433.08 (€ 523)
	Couple	• ceiling of income	FFr 6,158.83 (€ 939)
		• benefit	FFr 6,158.83 (€ 939)
Single parent (API)		• benefit	FFr 3,163 (€ 482) plus FFr 1,054 (€ 161) for each child
Allocation for adult disabled (AAH)		• benefit	FFr 3,433.08 (€ 523) (full rate)
Minimum subsistence income	Single	• ceiling of income	FFr 2,402.99 (€ 366)
(RMI)		• benefit	FFr 2,402.99 (€ 366)
	Couple	• ceiling of income	FFr 3,604.48 (€ 550) plus FFr 712 (€ 109) for each additional person (FFr 950 or € 145 from third child)
Long-term Unemployment	Single	• ceiling of resources	FFr 5,180.70 (€ 790)
Benefit (AAS)	Couple	• ceiling of resources	FFr 8,141.10 (€ 1,241)

According to a study by the association CERC, after 1983 all minimum wages have been eroded in terms of purchasing-power. This decline has particularly affected the position of the jobless, since the purchasing-power of ASS benefits dropped by 13% between 1986 and 1997. As far as API and RMI are concerned, their benefits have kept abreast with the rise in prices since 1988.

After the social unrest of the winof ter 1997, provoked by the alarming situation of the jobless, the whole field of minimum allowances has been given closer attention. Some allowances were increased. However, the discussion remains open: how to improve minimum allowances and, at the same time, to encourage people to participate in the labour market ?

5 Households and individuals

All insurance allowances are granted on an individual basis. Generally speaking, household composition and income do not affect the individual's entitlement.

As far as health insurance is concerned, coverage includes dependants (spouses and children). Since 1993 the notion of dependency has been extended to people who live with an insured person: family members (*e.g.* a student too old to apply for a scholarship) and live-in partners (including same-sex relationships).

As regards family allowances, the evaluation of family situations remains a serious problem, notably where lone parents are concerned. This is a fuzzy area in legislation.

6 Action in the European sector: European Unity and its consequences

The restrictions placed on public deficits by the Maastricht Treaty has pushed the French Government to control the deficits of the social security regimes. Considerable efforts have been made, especially in the area of health expenditures. The Government wants to slow down the growth rate of medical consumption which is sustained by social security arrangements. At the same time, changes in the contributions system (different rates, higher ceilings, *etc.*) have generated new resources for social expenditures. They have also permitted a relative decrease in the contributions paid by employers and employees, which was compensated for by the *contribution sociale généralisée* (CSG) and other specific taxation. Until recently, France was one of the countries in the European Union where the share of contributions in the social protection system was highest, but it now approaches the European average.

At the same time, the restraints on public deficits have either delayed the introduction of new allowances or limited their ambitions. For instance, the new allowance in favour of old dependent people is much less ambitious and generous than was foreseen in the preliminary studies: the initial proposals proved to be costly. More generally, the maximum level of minimum incomes remains low.

7 Conclusion

In France, as in the other European countries, social security plays a fundamental role in the redistributive process. Over the last decade, however, the system has been confronted with severe budget constraints. As a consequence, the question of poverty and exclusion from the labour market has received no satisfactory answers. Despite the extension and improvement of various benefits, a substantial segment of the French population has to make ends meet on a very low income. This situation may be partly attributed to a persistent ambiguity in the system in the sense that its original universal ambition has given way to a system largely based on paid professions and occupations. As a consequence, full-time workers continue to enjoy adequate social protection in the event of unemployment or illness, but the system is unable to offer a satisfactory solution to long-term unemployment, severe poverty and social marginalisation.

The phenomenon of social marginalisation, which is at the heart of the political debate in France, is nothing but a logical consequence of this flaw in its social security system. Deprived of a secure income, people are drawn into a descending spiral in which their problems accumulate: bad food, bad housing, bad health, and increasing isolation.

Unfortunately, the French system has tackled its problems with *ad hoc* measures. Several new benefits have been targeted towards specific groups, but without coherence. It is therefore inevitable that RMI, in spite of its low level, will continue to play a crucial role in mitigating the consequences of severe poverty. Optimists argue that RMI foreshadows a change in the social contract: since the right to work cannot be guaranteed for all, the right to an income and to fundamental goods such as health and housing will have to be based upon citizenship rather that on participation in the labour market. It is unlikely, and undesirable, that the French social security system should be heading towards privatisation since this would surely aggravate the spread of social marginalisation which is, at the moment, its main problem.

V Germany

Josef Schmid

1 Introduction – crisis and reform

The social security systems of the Federal Republic of Germany have come under massive pressure, as have those of all the western European countries. Changes in the general political, economical and social conditions have intensified the inherent 'contradictions of the modern welfare state'.[1] On the one hand there is the need for an increase in financial efforts, because there are more than four million people unemployed. On the other hand the national debt in excess of 1.5 trillion Deutschmark (DM, or € 0.87 trillion), severely impedes the political scope for manoeuvring. In addition, a string of further important challenges awaits, such as the problems in financing the pensions, given the altered demographic structure, the erosion of the social and moral foundations of societal solidarity, as well as the slackening of the care that, beforehand, had been provided for within the boundaries of the family. The latter phenomenon inspired the introduction of the nursing care insurance in 1994, which is intended to close this gap in the provision of care. Apart from specific socio-political questions, the future of Germany is at stake: its political and economic structure, its competitiveness, its social quality. Moreover, a considerable burden has been added to the social security system by the aftermath of the German unification.

In the past decades, many political attempts have been made to introduce reforms in order to correct the mismatch between the social security system and its socio-economic context. Along with the change of government in 1982, a neo-liberal 'change of direction' was announced, aiming at a cutback of financial transfers, a strengthening of individual responsibility, and deregulation. It was, however, only partially realised. As a consequence, the era of Chancellor Kohl brought many

---

[1] C. Offe, *Disorganized Capitalism*, Cambridge: Polity, 1985; Martin Rhodes, 'The Welfare State: Internal Challenges, External Constraints', in: M. Rhodes, P. Heywood, and V. Wright (Eds.), *Developments in West European Politics* (London: Macmillan, 1997), p. 57-74. See also: F.-X. Kaufmann, *Herausforderungen des Sozialstaates* [Challenges of the Welfare State], Frankfurt: Suhrkamp, 1997, and D. Döring (Ed.), *Sozialstaat in der Globalisierung* [The Welfare State in the Globalisation Process], Frankfurt: Suhrkamp 1999.

changes but displayed a considerable continuity in social policy.[2] However, scientific analyses produce controversial results. Some suggest continuity because the basic institutional structures have remained virtually unchanged and social contributions have remained persistently high. Others point out that numerous smaller cuts and measures add up to a qualitative transformation which will have far-reaching consequences in the near future.

The Schröder administration has been in office since the end of 1998. It comprises the *Sozialdemokratische Partei Deutschlands* (SPD, Social Democratic Party of Germany) and *die Grüne* (Green Party). It revoked some of the cuts in the social net made by its predecessor. It also announced far-reaching reforms concerning pensions, the public health service and labour market policy. However, a fundamental change in social policy is not to be expected even now, because the Government will encounter many problems if it tries to introduce its reforms too quickly. It will have to confront the sluggishness of the political system and the social security system.[3] There is enough going on within social security, however, to make predictions on its future development hazardous. For that reason, the following account will concentrate on the *status quo.*

2 The German welfare state model – an overview

2.1 History and typology

The German model of social security has a history that spans more than a hundred years. From the days of Bismarck and through the various changes of political regimes, essential characteristics have remained constant. Above all, it was conceived as an insurance for employees and not as a universal support for all citizens. According to a popular classification by Esping-Andersen,[4] Germany is a conservative welfare state. In this type
• social rights are tied to class and status

---

[2] J. Schmid, 'Mehrfache Desillusionierung und Ambivalenz. Eine sozialpolitische Bilanz [Multiple Disillusionment and Ambivalence. An evaluation of social policies]', in: G. Wewer (Ed.), *Bilanz der Ära Kohl* [An evaluation of the Kohl era] (Opladen: Leske und Budrich, 1998), p. 89-111.

[3] This position is postulated from a historical and institutionalist perspective in the comparative welfare state research, *e.g.* M.G. Schmidt, *Sozialpolitik* [Social policies], Opladen: Leske und Budrich, 1998, and J. Schmid, 'Wohlfahrtsstaaten im internationalen Vergleich: One Bad Way? [An international comparison of welfare states: One Bad Way?]', in: J. Lüdtke and S. Lamnek (Eds.), *Sozialpolitik zwischen Globalisierung und Hedonismus* [Social policies between globalisation and hedonism] (Opladen: Leske und Budrich, 1999), p. 93-114.

[4] G. Esping Andersen, *The Three Worlds of Welfare Capitalism,* Cambridge: Politiy 1990.

- social inequality and status differentiation are relatively great, and
- tendencies toward social segmentation (especially between labourers, employees and the poor) are recognisable.

Constitutionally, Germany is conceived as a *Sozialstaat* (social state). Its moral horizon is composed of diverse values, such as economic security, liberty, equality, and justice. These values give shape to its social security system. In Article 20, paragraph 1, and Article 28, paragraph 1 of the *Grundgesetz* (constitutional law), the so-called *Sozialstaatsgebot* (welfare state rule) defines the Federal Republic as a 'social and federal' or 'social and constitutional' state. These stipulations belong to the unalterable principles of the constitution.[5]

Apart from these legal norms, there exist a number of guiding principles that reflect certain notions on political order and social ethics. These principles are important because they provide orientation and legitimisation to the actors in the field of social security. One of these principles is the triad of liberty, equality and solidarity (or social justice). It establishes and regulates a complex mesh of reciprocal duties and considerations. It also helps distinguishing between collective and individual responsibilities. Finally, it constitutes the ethical foundation for redistributive measures and examples of barter justice.

Within social security, responsibilities are allotted in accordance with the principle of *subsidiarity*, which implies 'giving priority to the lower unit'. It defines the relation between individual responsibility and collective responsibility and, also, the relation between lower and higher executive organisations. It explains, for instance, why in the management of social security, 'lower' welfare unions are given pre-eminence over 'higher' municipal or State agencies. It also explains why these welfare unions are supported by public means.

2.2 Organising principles

Complementary to the *Grundgesetz,* the German social security system is shaped and organised in accordance with three principles:[6]
- the principle of insurance

---

[5] For a systematic debate about the normative base, the structures and benefits of the German system of social security see: H. Lampert, *Lehrbuch der Sozialpolitik* [Manual of social policy], Berlin: Springer 1994, L.F. Neumann and K. Schaper, *Die Sozialordnung der Bundesrepublik Deutschland* [The social system of the Federal Republic of Germany], Frankfurt a.M.: Campus, 1990, and N. Blüm and H. F. Zacher (Eds.), *40 Jahre Sozialstaat Bundesrepublik Deutschland* [The welfare state of Federal Republic of Germany over the last forty years], Baden-Baden: Nomos, 1989. A short overview provides M. Wilson, 'The German Welfare State. A conservative regime in crisis', in: A. Cochrane and J. Clarke (Eds.), *Comparing Welfare States* (London: Sage 1993), p. 141-168.
[6] These are ideal typical principles, which can hardly be applied in their pure form. In the social security system of the Federal Republic mixed forms dominate.

• the principle of provision
• the principle of care.

The principle of social insurance implies the protection of the majority of citizens against social contingencies. Therefore, in contrast to individual or private insurance, social insurance is compulsory. Individual contributions, with the exception of contributions to pension insurance, are not only calculated according to the principle of equivalence but also according to social criteria. According to the principle of equivalence contributions are calculated in relation to the costs of a potential claims settlement. However, in social health insurance family members who are not gainfully employed are co-insured without further costs. Co-insured people are entitled to the same provisions as the insured, independent of the amount of contribution paid (which is wage-related). Social insurance is thus based on the principle of solidarity. This aspect is reinforced by the fact that the state grants subsidies when the funds available for social insurances from contributions are not sufficient.

In the case of the provision principle there is no contribution, and therefore no mutuality. Benefits are financed from tax revenues. Entitlement to benefits is based on services previously rendered. These benefits include:

• benefits for civil servants (illness, disability and age), and
• benefits both for the war-disabled and for surviving dependants.

The care principle, which is reflected in the *Bundessozialhilfegesetz* (Federal Social Security Act) of 1961, acknowledges that not only group-specific emergency situations but also specific individual emergency situations must be taken into account and, if possible, rectified by suitable supportive measures. Therefore, entitlement to benefits and the actual granting of benefits are geared to individual circumstances. However, care is only supplementary. In other words, it is provided when relatives who are liable to provide maintenance are not able to do so. Because it is financed from taxation, this type of care is, in effect, a socially motivated transfer leading to a correction of the income distribution.

2.3 General problems and deficits

The social security system functions on the basis of the triad of wage labour, regular employment and full employment. On the one hand, this triad is the financial basis of the system, on the other hand it supplies the criteria for the granting of benefits. If this basis fails, fewer people pay and financial deficits arise, and the provision of benefits falters. This is especially true during protracted periods of mass unemployment. It is also true if one considers the lack of employment opportunities for women. In these cases there is the danger of impoverishment and lack of care. Other social disadvantages then accumulate. Conversely, the reliance on the triad of wage labour, regular employment and full employment may lead to a surplus of support for those who do not need it and a preferential treatment for the well-to-do as, for instance, in the case of housing subsidies and children's allowance.

Further shortcomings in the provision of benefits are the result of the organisational fragmentation into different insurance systems. This fragmentation is the result of historical development. Some of the these systems have taken on a life of their own and are partially to blame for blocking reforms. Moreover, they are dominated by the principle of causality, which implies that services are established on a legal basis and on organisational competence, and not according to specified goals (principle of finality).

Finally, German social security is confronted with the consequences of German unification. The old social security system of the *Deutsche Demokratische Republik* (DDR, German Democratic Republic), which was based on full employment through planned economy and a comprehensive social policy, was abolished and the social system of the Federal Republic was transferred to eastern Germany. This led to massive practical and administrative problems, especially in respect to the *Sozialleistungsrecht* (legislation of social benefits). The financial burden was enormous. According to estimates by the *Bundesministerium für Arbeit und Sozialordnung* (Federal Ministry of Labour and Social Affairs between 1992 and 1996 no less than DM 230 billion (€ 117.6 billion) of the unemployment and pension insurance funds flowed from the old into the new federal states.[7] In addition, extensive financial transfers are taking place which are financed through taxes. In view of the considerable structural economic deficits and weaknesses as well as the necessary investments in the public infrastructure of eastern Germany, these transfers will only take effect in the long run. Along with the general loss of competitiveness of Germany, these burdens severely limit the margins for distributive policies.

3 The social security system in Germany

3.1 Extent, financing and benefits

The German social security system is both one of the oldest and one of the most expensive in the world. Looking at the total expenditure (social budget) one can

---

[7] See A. Meusch, 'Stichwort Soziale Sicherheit [Keyword Social Security]', in: Werner Weidenfeld and Karl-Rudolf Korte (Eds.), *Handbuch zur deutschen Einheit* [Manual on German Unification] (Frankfurt a.M.: Campus 1993), p. 695-709; W. Schmähl (Ed.), *Sozialpolitik im Prozeß der deutschen Vereinigung* [Social policies and the process of German Unification], Frankfurt a.M.: Campus, 1992.

see the structure and importance of social policy in the FRG and its dramatic rise in the last decades.

Figure 1: Social budget of the Federal Republic of Germany, 1960-1998.

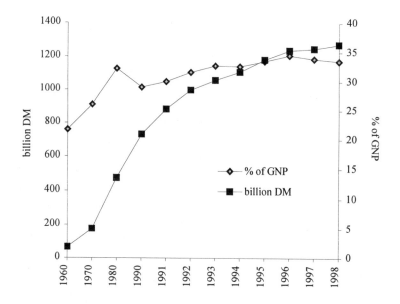

In absolute terms, the expenditure on social security has multiplied by twenty in forty years. In relative terms, the share of social security expenses of the GDP has risen from 21.7 % in 1960 to 33.5 % in 1998.

The shares of the different institutions contributing to the social budget (1998) are as follows:
• the insured: 30.9%
• the employers: 33.4%
• the public purse: 34.4% (*e.g.* DM 102.7 billion for the pension insurance)
• others: 1.3%.
These figures show an important structural characteristic of the German social security system. The main benefits are financed by the compulsory insurance schemes, most of which are funded by (continually increasing) wage-related contributions.

German social security is divided into the four classical types of insurance. Because of the historical context, they came into being in an order which differs from the usual order in other countries:

• health insurance (1883)
• accident insurance (1884)
• pension insurance (1889)
• unemployment insurance (1927)

In 1994 legislation was passed on nursing care insurance, making this insurance a compulsory part of the social insurance system. The relevance of the different types of insurance in terms of expenditures is indicated in table 1.

Table 1: Expenditures on social security in the Federal Republic of Germany, 1998.[8]

Category	million DM	million €	% of social budget	% of GDP
Social budget	1,272,058	650,393	100	33.5
1 *Social security (general system)*	836,394	427,641	65.8	22
1.1 Pension insurance	398,294	203,644	31.3	10.5
1.1.1 • workers' pension insurance	199,111	101,804	15.7	5.2
1.1.2 • employees' pension insurance	172,256	88,073	13.5	4.5
1.1.3 • miners' pension insurance	26,927	13,768	2.1	0.7
1.2 Nursing care insurance	30,659	15,676	2.4	0.8
1.3 Health insurance	245,909	125,731	19.3	6.5
1.4 Accident insurance	20,952	10,713	1.6	0.6
1.5 Employment promotion	133,287	68,149	10.5	30.5
1.6 Child benefit	137	70	0.0	0.0
1.7 Educational maintenance grant	7,156	3,659	0.6	0.2
2 *Special Systems*	10,016	5,121	0.8	0.3
2.1 Old-age benefits for farmers	6,810	3,482	0.5	0.2
2.2 Pension schemes	3,205	1,639	0.3	0.1
3 *Civil service system*	92,683	47,388	7.3	2.4
3.1 Pensions	63,836	32,639	5	1.7
3.2 Family allowance	13,364	6,833	1.1	0.4
3.3 Grants	15,483	7,916	1.2	0.4
4 *Employer's contribution*	89,594	45,809	7	2.4
4.1 Sick pay	42,901	21,935	3.4	1.1
4.2 Company pension schemes	27,786	14,207	2.2	0.7
4.3 Supplementary pensions	14,647	7,489	1.2	0.4
4.4 Other employers' contribution	4,260	2,178	0.3	0.1
5 *Compensations*	15,626	7,989	1.2	0.4
5.1 Social compensation	10,972	5,610	0.9	0.3
5.2 Equalisation of burdens	339	173	0.0	0.0
5.3 Indemnification	4,003	2,047	0.3	0.1

[8] Source: *Sozialbudget 1998* [Social budget 1998], Bonn: Bundesministerium für Arbeit und Sozial-ordnung (Federal Ministery of Labour and Social Policy), 1999.

5.4 Other compensation	312	160	0.0	0.0
6 *Social help and services*	103,610	52,975	8.1	2.7
6.1 Social assistance	50,137	25,635	3.9	1.3
6.2 Juvenile welfare	30,940	15,819	2.4	0.8
6.3 Training grants	1,646	842	0.1	0.0
6.4 Rent allowances	7,556	3,863	0.6	0.2
6.5 Public health service	3,341	1,708	0.3	0.1
6.6 Asset formation	9,990	5,108	0.8	0.3
7 *Indirect payments*	124,135	63,469	9.8	3.3
7.1 Fiscal measures	74,335	38,007	5.9	2.0
7.2 Housing subsidies	49,800	25,462	3.9	1.3

Social insurance provides income equalisation and/or non-cash benefits
• if a defined contingency occurs, for example a person is given a medical certificate of incapacity to work
• the person is a member of the insurance and
• contributions have been paid regularly.

Insurance benefits in the case of pensions are determined primarily by the principle of equivalence, according to which large contributions mean large benefits and *vice-versa*. The principle of equivalence, however, is supplemented by the principle of solidarity. For example, pension insurance benefits are granted to surviving dependants. Sometimes periods of contribution exemption are granted (as for education) and, in some cases, reduced contributions are taken into full account. Another constitutive feature of social insurance is that it is based on the causation principle. According to this benefits are granted when the contingency arises from clearly defined causes.

The benefits of social insurance can be divided into cash benefits, which have the function of a substitute income, and non-cash benefits and services. For example, in the case of pensions and unemployment, cash benefits dominate, but in health insurance income benefits account for about 8% of total expenditure, while the costs of non-cash benefits account for the remaining 92%. Thus health insurance finances doctors' fees, medical treatment and nursing care provided by private suppliers.

3.2 Maintaining living standards

3.2.1 Pension insurance

The German pension system was introduced in 1889. In 1957, it was radically redesigned by the *Rentenreform* (Act on the Revised Regulation of Pension insurance for Workers and Act on the Revised Regulation of Pension insurance for Salaried Staff). In 1972, there was a further important pension reform when a flexible retirement age was introduced. The *Rentenreformgesetz* (Pension Reform Act) of 18 December 1989 was aimed at securing funding for pensions in the long term, because in the coming decades the ratio of pensioners to pension insurance contributors is bound to develop unfavourably due to the increasing life expectancy and the lowering of the pension age. The new measures aimed at a reduction of expenditure and on prolonging the average working lifetime. At the same time, however, new entitlements were introduced for women raising small children.

German pension insurance is based on a contributions system (*Umlageverfahren*) as opposed to capitalisation. Some other features are also characteristic of the current system:
• the old age, disability and surviving dependants' pensions are meant to secure an adequate income. Pensions are therefore index-linked, which involves an quasi-automatic and legally fixed adjustment of pensions to current net wages and price levels annually
• pension insurance of workers is adjusted to match that of salaried staff
• rehabilitation measures (restoration of health and fitness for work) are given precedence over other measures.

There are three factors that determine the amount of a pension, as one can see below (Table 2).

Table 2: The pension formula.[9]

P	*Personal earnings points* Insured income (up to the contribution assessment limit) for each calendar year, divided by the average income of all insured persons, then totalled over all years during which contributions have been paid, and multiplied by the age factor.
T	*Pension type factor* A factor depending on the intended purpose of the pension.
C	*Current pension value* The monthly pension that an average earner would receive after paying contributions for one calendar year (currently DM 47.65 (€ 24.36) in western Germany and DM 40.87 (€ 20.90) in eastern Germany).
P x T x C = Monthly pension	

The group of insured persons is divided into those who are liable to compulsory insurance and those who take out voluntary insurance. The largest group of compulsorily insured persons are employees, including apprentices and trainees. In pension insurance, as opposed to health insurance, the level of income has no influence on the obligation to join the compulsory insurance for employees.

[9] Source: *Social Security at a glance*, Bonn: Bundesministerium für Arbeit und Sozialordnung, 1999 (www.bma.bundesregierung.de).

Pension insurance institutions include twenty-three state insurance institutions, the *Bundesknappschaft* (Federal Miners' Insurance), *the Bundesbahnversicherung-sanstalt* (Railway Employees' Insurance Fund), the *See-Unfallversicherung* (Seamen's Social Security) and the *Bundesversicherungsanstalt* (Federal Insurance Office for Salaried Employees). The money for pension insurance comes mainly from contributions. In 1996, these were set at 19.2% of earned income, half being paid by the employer and half by the employee. In addition, the state grants subsidies to pension insurance, and the *Bundesanstalt für Arbeit* (Federal Employment Office) pays contributions for recipients of wage compensation payments.[10]

Pension insurance distinguishes three categories of benefits: rehabilitation, pensions, and health insurance contributions of pensioners. These categories of benefits have the following order of precedence: if the capacity to work or to exercise one's profession is reduced or prematurely lost, then vocational rehabilitation is of primary importance. In the usual case or, in other words, if working life ceases because pensionable age has been reached, (partial) compensation is made for the absence of an earned income by the granting of a pension.

3.2.2 Health insurance

The *Gesetz, betreffend die Krankenversicherung der Arbeiter* (Law on Workers' Health Insurance) of 1883 was the first protection of this kind and took the form of a statutory health insurance. Since then, it has been further elaborated upon: material benefits and the social coverage were widened. With the *Kassenarztrecht* (Law on Associations of Statutory Health Insurance Funds and Substitute Private Health Insurance, 1955) the structural foundations of the system – especially the dominance of physicians and their associations – were laid. Since the end of the 1970s most political efforts have been aimed at cost-reduction; yet they have brought no lasting success in preventing the rise of expenditure to the extent required. Even the *Gesundheitsreformgesetz* (Law on the Structural Reform in the Health Service, 1988) did not achieve the expected success of contribution stability.

Finally, on 21 December 1992, the much disputed *Gesundheitsstrukturgesetz* ('Health Structure Law' or Law on Safeguarding and Structurally Improving Statutory Health Insurance) was passed. Two measures were taken:
• the acceptable increase in the total amount of fees for medical and dental services for 1993-1995 was limited to the growth rate of the income of the insurance members

---

[10] See *e.g.* D. Döring, 'Is the German Welfare State Sustainable?', in: P. Koslowski and A. Follesdal (Eds.), *Restructuring the Welfare State. Theory and Reform of Social Policy* (Berlin: Springer, 1997), p. 38-61, or Friedrich-Ebert-Stiftung, *Social Security in the International Development Cooperation*, Bonn 1997, chapter 2, and the literature mentioned in footnote 5.

• a check on market access to the outpatient sector was introduced. As of 1999, licences to practise within the public health service are granted according to statutory ratios based on forecasts of demand.

These measures improved control over statutory health insurance but did not eliminate its shortcomings altogether[11].

The German health system is highly fragmented. At present, there are over 1,200 financially and organisationally independent health insurance funds. The local health insurance funds, the craft guild health insurance funds, the farmers' health insurance schemes, the company health insurance schemes and the alternative health insurance schemes are particularly worth mentioning. As a rule, the various funds and schemes are amalgamated into associations at federal and state level.

Health insurances are financed primarily through contributions, employees and employers each paying half. This covers the group of obligatorily insured persons, *i.e.* employees whose regular earned income does not exceed the contribution assessment limit which, as a rule, is fixed annually. Furthermore, there are contributions from pensioners and the pension insurances, students and other people entitled to insurance. For those in receipt of unemployment benefits, payments are made by the Federal Labour Office. In principle, the contribution rate is variable and is oriented according to the expenditures of the funds.

Health insurance funds are self-administering. General meetings and boards of the local health insurance funds, for example, are composed of employers and members' representatives on a basis of parity. The principle of self-administration does not, however, guarantee unlimited autonomy. The legislature specifies the framework of benefits, influences the financing and is responsible for the legal basis of the health insurance funds.

3.2.3 Unemployment insurance

As a branch of social security, unemployment insurance was introduced forty years later than other important schemes. It was newly constituted in 1952 by setting up, under public law, a *Bundesanstalt für Arbeit* (Federal Office for Employment Placement and an Unemployment Insurance). In 1969, under the Grand Coalition Government (of CDU and SPD), the unemployment insurance system was reformed towards more active labour market policies and training schemes.

Besides the Ministry of Labour, the main institution is the Federal Employment Office in Nürnberg and its regional and local offices. The unemployment insurance is also self-administering.

Contributions to the unemployment insurance have to be paid by employees with a regular employment contract or in professional training, and by their employers.

---

[11] For a broader debate see N. Bandelow, *Gesundheitspolitik* [Health Policies], Opladen 1998.

At present, the contribution rate stands at 6.5%. Civil servants, school pupils, students in higher education, and employees who work less than 18 hours a week are not obliged to pay. The contribution rate is fixed by the Federal Government in view of the current financial situation of the Federal Employment Office. If the Federal Employment Office incurs a deficit, then the Federal Government is obliged to cover this by means of loans and subsidies.

The amount of unemployment benefits is based on the average weekly pay on which contributions were levied in the last 52 weeks before becoming eligible to claim (the assessment period). Unemployment benefit is 67% of net earnings (for married people with at least one child, and 60% for others). Unemployment assistance for people not covered by the benefits above is 57% of net earnings for families with a child for whom tax relief can be claimed, and 53% for others.

3.2.4 Accident insurance

Accident insurance was introduced in 1884. Many of today's accident regulations are based on the *Unfallversicherungsgesetz* (Reich Insurance Code) of 1911. In February 1993, the revised *Reichsversicherungsordnung, 1. und 3. Buch* (Accident Insurance Revision Law) came into force. Other important steps concerning accident insurance are the *Gesetz über Betriebsärzte und Fachkräfte für Arbeitssicherheit* (Law on Company Doctors and Specialists in Industrial Safety, 1976, in the amended version of April 12th, 1993) and the *Berufskrankheiten-Verordnung* (Regulation on Professional Diseases, 1976, as amended on December 18th, 1992).

The most important aim is the prevention of industrial accidents (Reich Insurance Code, Section 146). Therefore, the professional associations have adopted a series of regulations for the prevention of accidents:
• institutions, regulations and measures to which companies have to conform
• codes of conduct to be respected by the insured
• a mandatory medical examination of insured persons before starting to work, if the work involves any substantial risk of accident or health hazards.

Responsibility for employees in the private sector rests with the professional associations. The Federal Employment Office is responsible for the unemployed. Funding takes place through contributions which, in this case, are paid by the firms. The contribution rate depends on the likelihood of accidents and on the total of wages and salaries in a particular enterprise.

Benefits granted by accident insurance can be divided into two basic types:
• benefits for accident prevention and
• benefits to cover actual accidents.

3.2.5 Nursing care insurance

The *Gesetz zur Absicherung des Risikos der Pflegebedürftigkeit* (Nursing care insurance) is the most recently established system of social security. It was passed on April 29th, 1994, and came into force in several stages. The payment of contributions began in January 1995. Benefits covering home nursing became available from April 1st 1995; benefits covering inpatient care from July 1st 1996.

Nursing care insurance is compulsory, with contributions of 1.7% of salary. Institutionally and organisationally, it is integrated within the health insurance system on the principle that 'nursing care insurance comes after health insurance'.

If someone requires long-term care he or she will be assigned one of three care levels in order to determine the benefits to be received:

Care Level I is classed as 'considerable need of care'. Help is needed at least once a day with personal hygiene, eating, or with a minimum of two activities out of one or more types of activity; help is also needed several times a week with household chores.

Care Level II is classed as 'severe need of care'. Help is needed at least three times a day with personal hygiene, eating or getting around. In addition, help is needed several times a week with household chores.

Care Level III is classed as 'extreme need of care'. Round-the-clock help is needed every day, help with personal hygiene, eating or getting around, as well as help several times a week with household chores.

Table 3: The home care benefits system.[12]

Home care benefits	Category I	Category II	Category III
Monthly long-term care allowance	DM 400 (€ 205)	DM 800 (€ 409)	DM 1,300 (€ 665)
Maximum monthly total for non-cash long-term care benefits	DM 750 (€ 383)	DM 1,800 (€ 920)	DM 2,800 (€ 1,432)
Maximum for hardship cases	–	–	DM 3,750 (€ 1,917)

[12] Source: *Social Security at a glance,* Bonn: Bundesministerium für Arbeit und Sozialordnung, 1999 (www.bma.bundesregierung.de).

3.3   Other fields of social support

3.3.1   Supplementary benefit

Supplementary benefit was introduced in the Federal Republic in 1961. The term 'supplementary benefit' is synonymous with such emotionally charged terms as 'welfare' and 'poor relief' which was the current term at the beginning of this century. Supplementary benefit is granted in cases of (mainly individual) hardship if no other social benefit or family support is available. This benefit is not aimed at any specific groups; every citizen in need is entitled to it.

Since the mid-1970s the number of recipients and the amount of spending on supplementary benefits has risen drastically. There are three main reasons for this development:
• the increased unemployment rate (especially long-term unemployment)
• the increased number of elderly people and people in need of nursing care and
• the increased number of re-settlers and asylum seekers.
The number of people receiving supplementary benefits in Germany in 1998 was 2.9 million (excluding asylum seekers), compared to 1.49 million in 1970. More details are shown in the figure below.

Table 4: The supplementary benefits system: number of persons (x 1,000) and expenditure (x 1,000,000).[13]

Supplementary benefits	1997 Persons	DM	€	1998 Persons	DM	€
Benefits to help in subsistence	2,893			2,908		
Benefits to help in particular situations	1,411	44,546	22,776	...	45,043	23,030
(Of this help to nursing care)	(328)			...		
Asylum seekers receiving regular benefits	487	5,188	2,653	416	4,379	2,239
Total	4,791	49,734	25,429	...	49,422	25,269

Increasing poverty and correspondingly increasing expenditures for social assistance, combined with debates on 'black sheep' exploiting the social security system, are at the centre of the German political arena. The efforts towards reform should be dominated by two considerations:
• supplementary benefits must cover real needs and guarantee a humane living standard

---

[13] Source: *Bundesamt für Statistik* (Federal Agency for Statistics) (www.statistik-bund.de).

• so far, social assistance has been a passive measure: it should, however, be transformed into an activating instrument towards participation in the labour market.

Supplementary benefits are given mainly by local authorities. In addition, independent welfare organisations give help to people who are unable to support themselves by their own means. They also deliver a variety of social services – not only for the poor. Supplementary benefits are financed from taxes.

Supplementary benefits can be divided into two types:
• benefits to help in subsistence and
• benefits to help in particular situations.

The first type includes, for example, benefits for food, living accommodation, personal hygiene and heating. Usually, these benefits are granted as monthly cash payments. Help in particular situations can be claimed by people who have sufficient income to support themselves but need assistance to meet extra costs for such matters as training, preventive health care, assistance during sickness or help in rehabilitation.

The amount paid to a family in need depends on the number of family members and on their respective ages.[14] Any other source of family income will also be taken into account. At present, the standard payment for the head of a household in western Germany averages DM 539 (€ 276); the standard payment for his or her spouse is 80% of this amount. Depending upon their age, children will receive between 50 and 90% of the payment made to the head of household.[15] If one takes a standard situation of a family consisting of a single grown-up and two children, several benefits accumulate to nearly DM 2,400 (€ 1,227) per month (in 1998).

3.3.2 Families and children

Families with children can claim benefits according to the number of children: DM 250 (€ 128) each for the first and second child; DM 300 (€ 153) for the third child, and DM 350 (€ 179) for the fourth and each further child. Child benefit is paid regardless of parents' income. Besides this, under the new system of family compensation, child benefit takes the form of tax relief or a tax allowance for children.[16]

---

[14] The amount depends on local conditions, too. For further details see: *Social Security at a glance*, Bonn: Bundesministerium für Arbeit und Sozialordnung, 1999.

[15] Certain groups of people who have additional needs can receive supplementary payments (*Mehrbedarfszuschlag*) ranging from 20 to 60 per cent of the respective standard payments.

[16] This is typical for the German family policy, where many forms of assistance take the indirect way via tax reductions for spouses and children. Another way of support for this social clientele is participation in the benefits of the social security without paying own contributions.

Another measure to be mentioned is the child-raising allowance of up to DM 600 (€ 307) per month for each child. Child-raising allowance is as yet subject to income limits.

There are several other measures to support families and children; of the most important are grants for students and pupils (*Bundesausbildungs-Förderungs-Gesetz*, Federal Law on the Promotion of Educational Facilities).

4 One year of social politics – the new Government

Immediately after taking up office, the cabinet of the SPD and the Green Party under Chancellor Schröder passed a law introducing corrections in social insurance and improvements of the protection of the rights of employees. Furthermore the new Government took decisive steps to fight unemployment and to regulate the labour market. The main measures of the first year are as follows.[17]

4.1 Measures in social legislation

The suspension of the demographic factor. When the new Government came to power, the pension reform law of 1999 (*Rentenreformgesetz*, 1999) was still valid. This law, which had been passed by the former Kohl Government, had incorporated the 'demographic factor' into the pension formula. This would have led to a permanent slowing down of the increase in pensions and would have lowered the pension level measurably. In its amendment of this law, the new Government suspended the 'demographic factor' until the end of the year 2000 in order to find an arrangement that would be politically and socially more justifiable.

The suspension of the reduction in pensions (legislated by the former Kohl Government). By means of the pension reform law of 1999, normal pensions resulting from the inability to hold a job, as well as pensions resulting from the inability to work were to be replaced by a pension determined by the reduction in earning capacity (*Erwerbsminderungsrente*). This would have led to undue harshness, especially since the status of the labour market was to play no further part after such a pension had been granted.

---

[17] Compiled of several issues of *Sozialpolitische Informationen* [Social policy information], published by the *Bundesministerium für Arbeit und Sozialordnung* and the publication of the Federal Government *Auf den Weg gebracht. Die ersten Entscheidungen zur Bekämpfung der Arbeitslosigkeit und zur Wiederherstellung sozialer Gerechtigkeit* [Putting people on the way. First decisions in the fight against unemployment and for a restoration of social justice], Bonn 1999.

The first stage of the ecological tax reform. The revenue from the first stage of the ecological tax reform was used to lower the quota for the pension insurance by 0.8% from 20.3% to 19.5% (beginning April 1st, 1999).[18] Other measures concerning the changes in the labour market and their negative consequences for the social security system were also implemented.

4.2 Measures in labour legislation

Protection against dismissal of employees. The new Government retracted the incursions made by the previous Government into the general protection of employees against dismissal. The law for protection against dismissal again applies to all businesses with more than five employees.

The law for maintenance of payments. For the social security of employees, the re-implementation of the continuation of wage payment in case of illness was of utmost importance. Previously, the amount which had be paid in the event of repeated illness had been reduced. The new Government's decision eased the social hardship caused by this reduction, especially for the chronically ill, the pregnant and the disabled.

The minimum wage on building sites. In its law amendment, the new Government also changed the *Arbeitnehmer-Entsendegesetz* (Law regulating migrants), which combats the lowering of social standards and the practice of wage-dumping on German building sites. A regulation was put into place that specifies obligatory adherence to proper labour conditions in accordance with the collective labour agreement for the building trade.[19]

Fictitious self-employment. In the last several years, the spreading practice of fictitious self-employment has undermined the social security of those who, as a result of this trick, did not work under normal labour agreements. On 1 January 1999, a new rule was introduced which is supposed to enable social security bodies to decide more easily whether a dependent labour relation exists or not. If, after checking a case under suspicion, clarification is not reached, the meeting of two out four criteria of conjecture is sufficient to surmise dependency.

Limited employment: Through the rearrangement of limited employment, every dependent employee is now integrated into the pension insurance system. Before, people earning few than 630 DM stayed outside of the social security system.

---

[18] Long-term model calculations published in a *Prognos* report of 1995 on the development of pension insurance show figures of between 26.3 and 28.7% for the year 2040. This shows the relevance of these measures.

[19] The ordnance authorisation is an additional means. It supplements the existing practice of stating a general obligation. The supplement was necessary because various problems prevented the effective realisation of the *Arbeitnehmer-Entsendegesetz.*

Among other things, the corresponding law specifies that, starting from 1 April 1999, the employer has to pay a lump-sum toward the national pension insurance (12%) for every employee who works solely in limited employment, as well as a lump-sum (10%) toward national health insurance, should the employee be insured there. Under this new ruling, every employee acquires the legal claim to a pension as of the first Mark earned, as well as being provided with security against invalidity.

These measures, including the establishment of the pension quota of 19.5%, had the effect that the fluctuation reserve, amounting to one month's expenses of the pension system, was reached for the first time since 1994. The restoration of this 'solvency reserve' has created new faith in the national annuity insurance system.

Table 5: Development of the contribution rates (on January 1st of each year).[20]

	Pension insurance	*Unemployment insurance*
1991	17.7%	6.8%
1992	17.7%	6.3%
1993	17.5%	6.5%
1994	19.2%	6.5%
1995	18.6%	6.5%
1996	19.2%	6.5%
1997	20.3%	6.5%
1998	20.3%	6.5%
1999	20.3%	6.5%
1999, April 1st	19.5%	6.5%
2000	19.3%	6.5%
2001[21]	19.1%	6.5%

The reduction of youth unemployment. As promised in the coalition agreement, the new Federal Government quickly went into the offensive against youth unemployment. By the end of the year 1999, roughly 219,000 young people were registered, who had been involved in the programme for the reduction of youth unemployment. In June 1999, the Federal Government decided to extend the immediate programme by a year. The designated grant toward the *Bundesanstalt für Arbeit* (Federal Employment Office) allows for expenses of up to DM 2 billion (€ 1.02 billion) for both new and old measures taken by the programme in the year 2000. Of this amount, DM 200 million (€ 102 million) stems from the *European Social Fund* (ESF).

---

[20] *Bundesministerium für Arbeit und Sozialordnung:* several sources.
[21] The development of the contribution rates in 2001 is estimated.

The reform of labour market policy. The extensive revision legislation is intended to re-conceptualise labour market policy and amalgamate labour market policy and structural economic policy. In addition, the instruments are to be evaluated and further developed, in order to re-integrate the long-term unemployed into the labour process more quickly. Efficiency, flexibility and accuracy are to be the trademarks of future labour market policy, which aim to activate according to the slogan 'From Safety Net to Trampoline'.[22]

4.3 Legislation concerning labour safety

Labour safety rules. Safety rules ensure the safety and health of employees during work, but labour safety is also important for the economic development of businesses. To make labour safety efforts fully effective, businesses should be offered flexible rules and regulations that are geared to their interests and needs. More than ever before, employers rely on professional support by experts in labour safety. This also applies to smaller businesses. In the past years, a legislative foundation has been laid to ensure that all businesses are controlled where safety and health are concerned. This is the aim of the accident prevention rules that have been incorporated in the labour safety law.

Alliance for labour protection. Through the initiative by the federal ministry of labour an 'alliance for labour protection' was agreed upon in the building industry. This alliance is a body in which social partners (trade unions and business associations) and those who are actually affected work together in the common interest of preventing work accidents and occupational diseases. For example, in a joint effort of social partners, producers associations and trade associations, a trade ruling concerning cement and cement products low on chromates was achieved within the building industry, to combat the dreaded 'mason's scabies'.

4.4 The realisation of the European guidelines

Regulation of part-time work. The high demand for part-time work still confronts a comparatively low supply. According to calculations by the *Institut für Arbeitsmarkt- und Berufsforschung* (Institute for Labour Market and Job Research), a million new jobs could emerge in the long term if the wish of many employees for reduced working hours were resolutely honoured. The SPD/Green Government has announced proposals to put this suggestion into practice. The guidelines for legislative action in this area have already been established by a guideline set up by the European Union. The goal of this guideline is to raise the acceptance of

---

[22] R. Cox, *From Safety Net to Trampoline*, WiP Occasional Paper No. 2, Tübingen (www.uni-tüebin-gen.de/uni/spi/polwihp.htm).

part-time work and thus to contribute to the reduction of unemployment. It pro-
hibits the discrimination of part-time work and aims to make the change from full-
time to part-time work – or vice versa – easier. The same applies to contracts with
a time limit.

Business decision participation. According to the new Government, new steps are
also necessary to expand employee participation. This applies to decision-making
on a national as well as a European level. Europe is growing together economically. National borders have long since stopped being obstacles for businesses
operating on a Europe-wide and even global scale. The realisation of a European
Corporation (as a legal framework for firms) that is under consideration, could be
used as an example for more flexible national rules. Although there has, as yet,
been no political agreement reached in Brussels, fourteen members have reached a
compromise.

5 The influence of the European integration and possible trends

The above mentioned examples of current activities by the new Federal Government prove the significance of the European Union for social security. The
authority of the European Union in social and labour market policy has been
strengthened through the Maastricht Treaty. The various political levels are becoming more intertwined. Complex arrangements of policy formulation and implementation are coming about that concern national actors and programmes as
well.[23] There are several conceivable scenarios, with different implications.

Analogous to the history of the nation states, there is the possibility that a further
expansion of socio-political activities will occur, as well as the harmonisation of
benefits and structures in the member states. In the long run, this path would lead
to the development of a European Welfare State.

Another possibility is that the present level of European integration will lead to a
blockade of socio-political activities. As a result of the present political and economic entwining, the nation states suffer a certain loss of sovereignty, without the

---

[23] For labour market policy see *e.g.* Ch. Roth and J. Schmid, 'European Labour Market Policy and
National Regimes of Implementation', in: P. Klemmer (Ed.), *Preventive Labour Market Policy in
Europe. Experiences and Learning Perspectives* (London 2000, in print), and for welfare associations
see: J. Schmid, 'Europäische Integration und die Zukunft der kirchlichen Wohlfahrtsverbände in
Deutschland [European integration and the future of the welfare organisations of the Churches]', in: K.
Gabriel (Ed.), *Herausforderungen kirchlicher Wohlfahrtsverbände. Perspektiven im Spannungsfeld
von Wertbindung, Ökonomie und Politik* [Challenges for the welfare organisations of the Churches.
Perspectives and tensions between values, economics and politics] (Berlin: Springer, 2000, in print).

European Union actually gaining anything of equivalence. This undermines the existing barriers against the 'social dumping syndrome' and could lead to considerable cuts in the social security systems.

Finally, one can consider the Western European countries, along with their different welfare state models, as laboratories for socio-political possibilities. In this context, socio-political reforms are deliberately based on trans-national processes of diffusion and imitation, that are driven ahead by the – admittedly unplanned – political, economic and informational growing together of Europe.[24]

6 Perspectives of social security

Over and above the current measures, two concepts are emerging within the German discussion. Both these concepts amount to a fundamental institutional reorganisation of social security

On the one hand, *welfare pluralism* is propagated which implies an addition to the national bureaucratic or market support structures. Terms such as 'welfare mix', 'third sector', 'non-profit organisations', 'new subsidiarity' and also the most recent American contributions toward the notions of communitarism and civil society, pose an analogy to this concept. Specifically, this concept is about respecting and supporting a fully differentiated socio-political level of representation between the market and the state, as well as the resuscitation of self-help, honorary posts and public *spirit*.

On the other hand, *basic social security* for every citizen is the next focus within the socio-political debate. Guaranteed minimum income can take different forms. One possibility is a basic pension, which fends off poverty in old age by decoupling pensions from gainful employment. Alternatively, guaranteed minimum income can be conceived as a 'negative income tax' which lets citizens who have an average or high income carry the same tax burden as before, but grants an income increase to those with lower incomes or no income. This increase, which is limited by a threshold amount, is enough to cover the necessities of life with or without wage labour.[25]

Calculations concerning the expenditure for such an alternative form of security have shown the following: 'After balancing all of the financial components of a

---

[24] Concerning the aspect of diffusion or respectively the applicability of solutions from other countries *e.g.* R.G. Heinze, J. Schmid, and Ch. Strünck, *Vom Wohlfahrtsstaat zum Wettbewerbsstaat* [From welfare state to competition state], Opladen: Leske und Budrich, 1999.

[25] On recent debates see: Heinze, *Vom Wohlfahrtsstaat zum Wettbewerbsstaat*, and Schmid, 'Wohlfahrtsstaaten im internationalen Vergleich'.

negative income tax, the net amount of costs to be expected under the assumed general conditions are – depending on the final design – somewhere in the vicinity of DM 65 billion (€ 33.2 billion) to DM 173 billion (€ 88.5 billion). A part of the cost would already arise by realising the verdict by the constitutional court concerning tax exemption on the subsistence level'.[26]

In Germany, these issues have attracted keen attention and fervent discussions. It must be pointed out that this has much to do with the structure and self-image of the German state as a 'social security state'.[27] This model of the social security state, organised through insurances for permanently employed persons, demonstrates its strength through high benefits and a dynamic development, yet it also displays shortcomings with regard to people who simply do not have a 'normal' biography. Besides the long-term unemployed, this applies especially to women who are unemployed or only sporadically employed, youngsters with no work experience, and the poor. Unfortunately, it is exactly these problem groups which, in the wake of economic and social-structural changes, are going to increase in number. This prospect gives extra pungency to the questions of the stability and continuity of the German welfare state which were raised at the beginning of this contribution.

---

[26] V. Meinhart, D. Teichmann, and G. Wagner, "Bürgergeld': Kein sozial- und arbeitsmarktpolitischer deus ex machina ['Civil allowance': no deus ex machina for social and labour market problems]', in: *WSI-Mitteilungen*, 47 (1994), p. 630. Also: Neumann and Schaper, *Die Sozialordnung der Bundesrepublik Deutschland*, p. 224*ff.*

[27] B. Riedmüller and Th. Olk (Eds.), *Grenzen des Sozialversicherungsstaates* [The limits of the social insurance State], Opladen: Westdeutscher Verlag, 1994.

VI Greece

Angelos Stergiou

1 An outline of the Greek system

In Greece, social security, established by the Constitution of 1975/86 and organised on the basis of public law, manifests itself in three basic forms: the national insurance schemes, national assistance and the national health service. Of these, national insurance is the primary foundation for social protection.[1] Legislation has gradually developed, without a coherent overall framework. The level of social security protection is low compared to the countries of northern Europe.[2] In Greece, only 16.5% of GDP is devoted to social security, while the European average stands at over 28% of GDP. Although the Greek system may not appear a high-performer, it nevertheless stands in the European tradition which considers social protection to be an essential component of social interaction.

1.1 The structures: impossible to unify?

The Greek system is based on the Bismarckian model, where employment forms the basis for social protection. At the same time, coverage has steadily expanded towards unprotected categories of the population.[3] In addition to this tendency towards universality, various measures have been taken to guarantee a minimum income (for example: a minimum pension). One could therefore say that in a historical sense the Greek system – as well as other systems of the same type – has not remained faithful to the Bismarckian concept.

The problem of the system's fragmentation has its roots in history. In the general movement which led to the institution of national insurance, Greece did not lag behind. At the end of the nineteenth century, the first social security funds were set up. However, they were confined to a few well-defined categories of workers in a particular company or branch of the economy. Generally speaking, only

---

[1] See K. Kremalis, 'Social insurance law', in: K.D. Kerameus and Ph.J. Kozyris (Eds.), *Introduction to Greek Law* (Deventer, Boston: Kluwer, 1993), p. 257.

[2] See M. Ferrera, 'The 'southern model' of welfare in social Europe', in: *Journal of European Social Policy*, 6 (1996), p. 1.

[3] For example: granting a pension to uninsured persons aged at least 65 by Act 1296/82; and extension of health insurance to the long-term unemployed by Act 2434/96, *etc.*

highly organised trades and occupations possessed social coverage: sailors, civil servants, miners and the military. In 1922 the foundations were laid for social security legislation. A new act encouraged the setting up of special social security funds. As ideas on social security evolved, there grew a political will to grant social protection to the entire population, and to unify the existing funds. In 1937, a general system for wage-earners was instituted, *Idrima Koinonikon Asfaliseon* (IKA, National Insurance Institute),[4] but this was not enough. Since all attempts at unification met with trade union resistance, unification was not followed by the absorption of the special funds for certain occupational categories into the general system. Groups which enjoyed a more profitable system fought for its preservation. Moreover, the system may well be described as a variety of clientism since a series of retirement systems have been created, with widely divergent benefit levels and working methods, on the basis of political barter. The structure of social security is fragmented and many systems are founded on occupational or social allegiances. The wide variety of special insurance systems for socioeconomic categories, and even for individual companies and certain types of benefits, still remains the characteristic feature of the Greek system. There are around 350 funds which come under the supervision of six ministries. Some systems cover no more than a few thousand individuals. Today, Greece has a complex patchwork of systems, which poses problems as to efficiency and equity.

Despite harmonisation measures taken in 1992, the diversity has persisted and the special systems – which mainly cover bank and state enterprise personnel – have retained their autonomy. This irrational fragmentation adds to administrative expenses and leads to inequalities (for individuals who were insured before 1 January 1993) in the matter of pensionable age, the calculation of entitlements, and the term of insurance. For certain categories of workers – bank officials, employees of state enterprises – the system is very generous. Salaried workers and people equated with them are covered by the general system for wage-earners (IKA),[5] which covers around 40% of all insured persons. In practice, however, IKA is a mop-up system for poorly paid workers. The agricultural system *Organismos Georgikon Asfaliseon* (OGA, Institute for Agricultural Insurance) covers 33% of insured persons, while the State insures its own civil servants.

In 1930, supplementary pension systems appeared for categories of highly unionised wage-earners. These supplementary systems developed particularly after the Second World War. Their implementation in a branch of industry or at company level aimed at broader coverage. Originally born of private non-profit initiative, they have gradually acquired some characteristics of public systems (for example:

---

[4] By Act 6296/34.

[5] In principle, the functioning of this insurance institution is regulated by statutory order 1846/51.

compulsory affiliation, pay-as-you-earn funding).[6] These systems, of which there are about 60, have developed independently from the public pensions and have complicated the Greek system of social security even more.[7] At the same time, the State has instituted a general system of compulsory supplementary pensions (IKA/TEAM, *Tamio Epikourikis Asfalis Misthoton,* Additional Insurance Fund for Employees) for people who are not covered by any of the special supplementary systems. It will be obvious that a supplementary system without the characteristics suited to this type of protection – voluntary affiliation, capital funding, financial autonomy – has no grounds for existence. This is why it is necessary to clarify the respective roles of the basic and supplementary retirement pensions. The fragmentation of the Greek system is aggravated by the existence of some 95 contingency funds. Membership of these funds, which pay out a lump sum at the time of actual retirement, is also compulsory. The contingency funds apply to nearly 17% of the active population, in particular well-organised occupational groups: self-employed, bank employees, *etc.*

Since 1992, instead of attempting to achieve an organisational unification which would probably arouse opposition from trade unions and pressure groups, the legislature has undertaken[8] a harmonisation of the current systems of old age insurance. Since it is very difficult to tackle the vested social interests in this field, the Government has realistically confined itself to harmonising the level of benefits, entitlement conditions, and contributions. In this way, the special systems have been drawn closer to the general system, which is the least advanced in some respects. More favourable conditions for entitlement are eliminated from the special systems. Consequently, no one will have any interest in preserving their own special system. The introduction of these reforms has been spread out over time. While respecting the rights which are now in the process of being acquired, the law makes a distinction between individuals who were insured before 1 January 1993, and those who were newly insured after that date.

The political will to achieve organisational unification has recently resurfaced. One of the intentions of the socialist Government (in power since 1996) is to re-classify all occupations into seven categories: wage-earners, farmers, civil servants, wage-earners in the public sector, bank employees, scientists, and craftsmen-shopkeepers. The manner in which this project should be tackled will be the subject of broad social debate. However, it remains to be seen whether the Government's ambitions will go any further than good intentions.

---

[6] The total number of participants in supplementary retirement systems is around 3,360,000. See *Europe Sociale,* (1994), no. 3, p. 51.

[7] For some of the supplementary systems the replacement rate after retirement is very high (80%).

[8] By Act 2084/92.

1.2 Financing: need for expansion

In spite of significant achievements, one cannot fail to observe that the development of national insurance schemes has been painfully slow. It was not until 1980 that the level of benefits was improved and the Greek social security system was extended and made more comprehensive, both geographically and socially. In 1983 coverage was finally extended to the majority of all wage-earners, albeit without a simultaneous unification.[9] In general, Greek social policies seem to follow the same cycle as other European countries, but delayed: growth – slow-down – control. The restoration of democracy in 1974 put an end to the austerity of the dictatorship (during which time pensions remained blocked) and brought about a new if moderate social impetus.[10] In the course of the 1980s, despite the economic crisis, Greece also saw expenditures for social protection rise. The victory of the socialists, in 1981, prompted improvements in the level of benefits[11] while postponing the price to be paid to the following decade, however.[12] As a result, these improvements, made with no provision to cover the costs, eventually widened the gap between receipts and expenditures.

Today, a twofold crisis affects the Greek system of social security. The crisis is due both to the same events which tend to unbalance all social security systems (for example: the coming of age of the systems[13]) and to reasons inherent in the national situation (for example: large number of subsystems, poor management of funds). Among the chronic illnesses of the system, there is the falling birth rate. This decrease in fertility now fluctuates at levels below the threshold of 2.1 which ensures the replacement of each generation (1.4). For this reason, a large imbalance is expected between the group of people under 45 and of those over 45 by the year 2025.[14] A clear-cut development is emerging: the number of pensioners is increasing at a rate more rapid than that of contributions. The ratio of contributors to pensioners has dropped from 3.2 in 1980 to 2.2 in 1995. At the same time, the slow-down of economic growth has caused a decrease in the receipts of the insurance bodies. At the heart of the growing concern is the increase in the proportion of GDP which is devoted to pensions. For example, for old age, in 1995, the gen-

---

[9] By Act 1305/1982.

[10] J.-P. Dumont, *L'impact de la crise économique sur les systèmes de protection sociale* [The impact of the economic crisis on social protection systems] (Paris 1987), p. 43.

[11] The minimum pensions underwent drastic revaluations. See J.-P. Dumont, *Les systèmes étrangers de sécurité sociale* [Foreign systems of social security] (Paris 1988), p. 94.

[12] *Ibid.*, p. 13.

[13] See A. Walker, 'Les politiques de retraites dans la communauté européene [Pensions policies in the European Community]', in: *Revue française des affaires sociales* [French Review of Social Affairs], 45 (1991), p. 113.

[14] European Commission, *La situation démographique dans l'Union européenne* [The demographic situation in the European Union] (Luxembourg 1995), p. 15.

eral system for wage-earners (IKA) had a deficit of 40 billion Greek Drachma (GRD) (€ 120 million). According to the social budget for 1996, the situation gets even worse: the deficit has since swollen to GRD 85.1 billion (€ 255.5 million). The total deficit for seven social security funds amounted to 3% of GDP.

To face up to the financing crisis, from 1990 onwards, Greece has resorted to austerity measures. More precisely, in 1990-1992, the Greek Government took measures which were difficult to put into practice, politically speaking, because they challenged vested interests, especially those of persons insured under special systems. We should also note the growing number of reforms aimed at progressively raising the retirement age, limiting the purchasing power of pensions by changing the indexation method (abolition of index-linking with salaries), and increasing the contributions. In general, the tendency of replacement rates is one of decline.[15] However, these measures have not had any immediate effect. The crushing deficits continue to weigh on the future of social security. Today, the impact of ideologies is less apparent. Austerity is the rule. Apart from political rhetoric, all parties accept the necessity of exerting controls on social expenditures, but this consensus bodes ill for the future level of benefits.

Greece is one of the countries which use insurance financing. In fact, financing basically comes from contributions from employers and employees. The State participates in the financing *a posteriori* when it intervenes to cover the deficit of the institutions. In 1992, the Greek Government adopted two important measures which affect all insurance bodies as far as newly insured persons are concerned, *i.e.* those insured since 1 January 1993:[16]
• the institutionalisation of the public contribution into tripartite financing, in which the State bears one third; and
• the introduction of standardised contribution rates for old age insurance for all social security funds.

The contributions for old age insurance (the general system for wage-earners) were pegged at 6.67% for employees (deducted from their salary by their employer) and 13.33% for employers, both for already insured individuals and for new participants since 1 January 1993. Contributions for health insurance are fixed, for the already insured group, at 5.10% for employers and 2.55% for wage-earners. As to the newly insured group, the percentages are the same with the State contributing another 3.80%. For supplementary (compulsory) insurance, the contribution is 3% for employers and wage-earners respectively. For newly insured persons, there is no ceiling for contributions.[17] Finally, fraud and economic imperatives have led to a wide expansion of the base for contributions. Starting

---

[15] For the effects of recent reforms see *European Economy*, (1996), no. 3, p. 35-36 and 70-71.
[16] Act 2084/1992.
[17] Article 22, section 2 of Act 2084/1992.

from 1992,[18] contributions are due on all types of income.[19] Contributions represent 30.7% of the tax receipts and 12.4% of GDP.[20] A further increase in contributions is out of question since Greece finds itself in a median position compared to the other countries of Europe.[21] If charges become too high, they will affect the country's competitiveness[22] and encourage its parallel economy, the importance of which is already assessed at 40% of GDP.

In the financing of social security, the role played by taxes is small: 20% of total receipts. No Government has ever contemplated alternative financing (utilisation of VAT, *etc.*). Funding by taxation seems to offer a solution to the problem of the financial imbalances. The creation of a tax for social security purposes, to be imposed on all incomes, would seem to be as fair as it is efficacious. Moreover, it is necessary to establish some consistency between the method of financing and the nature of the expenditures.[23] The expenditures of solidarity must be financed by taxation. The State must take responsibility for the expenditures of social protection which are based on the principle of national solidarity.[24]

1.3 The risks covered: silence surrounds the 'new risks'

In Greece, there are national insurance schemes to cover all the classic risks: sickness, maternity, disablement, death, old age, widowhood, unemployment and family expenses. However, their current set-up seems no longer capable of covering all contingencies.[25] Sometimes the Government abandons its caution and faces up to new risks. In this way, technological innovation has been included as a risk in the insurance policies of press media workers (printers and technicians).[26] The costs of artificial insemination are also reimbursed. Since 1989, the law protects workers against the insolvency of their employer: salaries for the three last months before bankruptcy are insured, by the intermediary of the *Organismos Apascholisis Ergatikou Dinamikou* (OAED, Institute for Employment of the Labour Force

---

[18] According to Act 2084/1992 (article 22, section 2).

[19] Similarly, according to case law, all amounts paid to workers in compensation for, or on the occasion of, work are reckoned to be the basis for contributions.

[20] J.-P. Dumont, *Les systèmes de protection sociale en Europe* [Social protection systems in Europe] (Paris 1995), p. 190.

[21] The share of employers in the financing of social security is 41.2% of the total receipts for social security and 5% of GDP (1992). See Dumont, *Les systèmes de protection social en Europe*, p. 203.

[22] However, one should not take too strict a view on this point.

[23] See M. Hirsch, *Les enjeux de la protection sociale* [Issues in social security] (Paris 1994), p. 53.

[24] See the provisions of Act 2084/1992.

[25] In general, for changes in this, see P. Rosanvallon, *La nouvelle question sociale. Repenser l'Etat-providence* [The new social question. Re-thinking the Welfare State] (Paris 1995), p. 27.

[26] According to Act 1186/1981.

(OAED).[27] On this point, Greek legislation has been made to conform to directive 80/987 of the European Economic Community dated October 20th, 1980.

To a certain extent, the Government is not unaware of the effects of divorce. An uninsured divorced woman, aged at least 35, has the right to retain the health insurance of her ex-husband if she pays the contributions.[28] In general, married women do not acquire rights of their own. They are treated as if they were their husband's responsibility. The presence of the wife in the home is not recognised by social security. In the event of divorce, legislation does not provide for the apportionment of rights. This situation is a flagrant example of the inequalities experienced by women when they do not work outside the home. However, among the themes of the social dialogue (1997) is the partition of rights and entitlements when a couple separates. Natural disasters are covered by the OGA (system for farmers) if they affect agricultural production. Agricultural production is insured against certain well-defined natural risks, such as hail and frost, which threaten agricultural income. Moreover, public compensation is made to victims of terrorist acts.[29] The State taking charge of reimbursement of damage caused by terrorism seems legitimate. However, no provisions are made for taking charge of dependants. Although the traditional support of older relatives is declining, especially in urban regions,[30] the responsibility for elderly persons is still very much the concern of the family. Similarly, the new risk involved in the changing methods of employment is not covered.[31] Originally, social insurance schemes were designed from the point of view of regular full-time employment. As a result, they are ill suited to any non-standard forms of employment.[32] In general, the system does not offer sufficient protection to part-time workers.[33] In order to integrate these in the system of social security, it will be necessary to make certain adjustments.

---

[27] Act 1836/1989, presidential decree 1/1991. For OAED, see section 2.6.

[28] Article 30 of Act 1469/1984.

[29] Act 1879/1990, completed by Act 1977/1991.

[30] D. Ziomas, in: *Europe Sociale,* (1993), no. 1, p. 57.

[31] See M.-T. Join-Lambert, 'Les 'nouveaux risques' [The 'new risks']', in: *Droit social. Textes et documents annotés concernant les rapports professionnels et l'organisation de la production* [Social law. Texts and annotated documents concerning labour relations and the organisation of production], (1995), no. 9-10, p. 779-784.

[32] With regard to unemployment insurance, the conditions for the minimum duration of participation are more favourable for workers in the hotel business.

[33] See European Foundation for the improvement of living and working conditions, *New forms of work. Labour law and social security aspects in the European Community* (Luxembourg 1988), p. 115-127.

1.4 The place of fixed rate benefits in the Greek system

In Greece, benefits are calculated in relation to a person's previous income from work. The only exceptions are the flat-rate pensions paid by OGA, which until recently were not dependent upon previous contributions. The retirement pension awarded to each small farmer at the age of 65, if he has been farming for 25 years,[34] is a fixed amount and is very low (around GRD 25,000 or € 75).[35] A new contributory system, in which the pensions are based on the contributions paid, was introduced in 1997.[36] The Government has planned a transitional period for the introduction of this system.

Furthermore, one could class among the fixed-rate benefits all specific allowances paid to disabled persons. These are non-contributory benefits intended to help certain categories of disabled persons to take responsibility for their keep. The allowances vary with the nature of the handicap and are awarded to eight categories of disabled persons:
• the blind
• deaf-mute persons
• persons suffering from paraplegia or quadriplegia
• the disabled
• people suffering from sickle-cell anaemia
• persons suffering from mental illnesses
• persons over 60 with a serious disability requiring the aid of another person
• invalids aged 0-59 who need the assistance of another person, and
• persons suffering from cerebral palsy aged 18 and up.

These allowances do not depend on a person's means. When the disabled person is hospitalised or lives in an institution, payment is suspended. With the exception of those who suffer from sickle-cell anaemia or cerebral palsy, the disabled in the categories mentioned above may not be in receipt of a benefit awarded by an insurance body. The protection offered to the disabled is limited to payments which are insufficient to enable them to become independent. The assistance is segregative and does not encourage disabled persons to integrate more fully into society. The State tends to acquit itself of its obligation towards the disabled with financial aid which is frequently elementary. The problem is to integrate the disabled into paid employment, to facilitate their participation in school, in architecture, in leisure activities, in culture, in means of communication, in everyday life. In 1982,[37] an allowance was introduced for persons suffering from quadriplegia or paraplegia who were insured with insurance bodies or in receipt of old age, disablement and

---

[34] Moreover, he must have been farming for the 10 years prior to submitting his application.

[35] In Greece, farmers make up around 30% of the population.

[36] By Act 2458/1997.

[37] By Act 1140/1981 (article 42, section 1), amended by article 16 of Act 2042/92.

survivor's pensions, and for their family members. This special allowance, a fixed amount (around GRD 100,000 or € 300 per month), is paid for as long as the person is deemed to be quadriplegic or paraplegic. The payment of the allowance is dependent upon a minimum number of days or years of contributions and upon a rate of disablement of around 67%, to be determined by a medical committee. The heterogeneous nature of this benefit stands out, since it blends elements of national assistance and elements of insurance.

Finally, all allowances which guarantee a minimum income to some of the most disadvantaged categories – this guarantee does not extend to all citizens[38] – and which are subsidised by the State, are granted as a lump sum. The amounts are fixed for each category on a monthly basis: GRD 25,000 (€ 75) for the elderly (at least 65 years of age) without national insurance cover, GRD 12,000 (€ 36) for homeless children, GRD 36,000-50,000 (€ 108-150) for one-parent families, and GRD 15,000-60,000 (€ 45-180) for the poor.

1.5 Seeking social consensus

Greek social security is in crisis. The moment of choice has arrived. The question is to find out how the Greek system can be adapted to current economic and social conditions. The present socialist Government (in power since the elections of 1996) seems to be convinced of the necessity of structural reform. Desperate cases call for desperate remedies: minor adjustments of the system will not suffice. Instead, an institutional, functional and financial rationalisation seems in order.[39] According to G. Perrin, rationalisation constitutes a powerful tool to achieve administrative simplification and to improve social equity.[40] The socialists want to use the current social dialogue to reform the system of social security. This dialogue, although not institutionalised at national level, is an attempt to achieve within the country a minimum of social consensus on a number of issues concerning work and social security. However, since the beginning, a clash of views has been apparent.

While debates on the future of social security in Greece are taking place the Organisation for Economic Cooperation and Development (OECD) and the International Monetary Fund (IMF) lobby in favour of increased austerity. The OECD

---

[38] Here, the guaranteed minimum income is understood as a national assistance benefit.

[39] See G. Perrin, 'Rationalisation et humanisation: deux objectifs prioritaires pour une réforme de la sécurité sociale [Rationalisation and humanisation: two priorities of social security reform]', in: *Travail et Société* [Labour and Society], 6 (1981), no. 4, p. 409.

[40] G. Perrin, 'L'avenir du droit de la sécurité sociale [The future of social security law]', in: *Mélanges A. Bernstein* [Miscellany for A. Bernstein] (Lausanne 1989), p. 461.

urges that retirement age be postponed and contributions raised.[41] Although the trade organisations are not inclined to make concessions, it is nonetheless a perfect opportunity for the Greek trade union movement to demonstrate its capacity for constructive intervention. The question remains what will be the limits of social consensus. It seems likely that the system will become more contributory (which will involve a distinct division into contributory and non-contributory, and between insurance expenditures and solidarity expenditures) and more selective (for non-contributory benefits). Reforms for the sole purpose of reducing social expenditures should be avoided. Rather, all efforts should be aimed at achieving greater social equity, without dismantling social security.

Recently, attention has focused on the *Spraou Report* (October 1997) on the relation between economy and the pensions system. This report introduced a new approach into the public debate, an approach which seems unwise in view of a turnaround of the Greek system. The report rejects the suggestion that the system should move toward a pure form of capital funding, which would imply that, during the transitional period, one generation would have to carry a double burden. Instead, the report suggests a measured dose of capital funding, a mixed triple system which relies only in part on the accumulation of funds and savings.

2 Maintaining reasonable living standards

The Greek social security system aims to preserve the standard of living for workers when certain social risks materialise. The national insurance system is founded on work and on the prior payment of contributions.[42] Thus, active employment is a condition to obtain social benefits. This is very inconvenient for those who do not work or who have no steady employment.

2.1 Health insurance: an ongoing debate on the unification of health services and the effectiveness of the system

In Greece, health expenditures, representing around 15% of social outgoings, are below the average for the countries of the Union. Despite significant progress in

---

[41] *OECD economic surveys. Greece. Special feature social security. Pensions and health care*, Paris 1997.

[42] See I. Karakatsanis and G. Amitsis, 'Droit de la protection sociale [Social protection law]', in: *Semaine sociale Lamy*, no. 712 (26.9.94), p. 45-52.

the past decade,[43] health services continue to be of mediocre quality and unevenly distributed throughout the country.

Protection against the risk of illness is basically insured in the context of health insurance.[44] However, the level of protection is unequal and varies greatly. There are many funds – around 35[45] – which in certain cases constitute a distinct branch within a general system, as is the case for IKA. Some of them even have their own hospitals and medical centres (IKA and OGA). The funds provide highly divergent reimbursements. The inequalities between the various systems are obvious: for example, expenditures for employees of the agricultural bank (special system) are as high as GRD 154,000 (€ 462) per insured person, whereas for IKA (general system) they are only GRD 53,949 (€ 162) per insured person.

Only wage-earners may claim sickness benefits.[46] Entitlement to benefits in cash depends on the duration of prior employment. A person covered by national insurance[47] must prove that he or she has worked for at least 100 days in the course of a period of reference – during the year preceding the official notification to IKA of

---

[43] On the high growth of expenditures in the field of health care in Greece, see Dumont, *Les systèmes de protection sociale en Europe*, p. 45.

[44] The extension of health insurance has succeeded in providing protection for almost the entire population (the rate of coverage stands at 98% of the population). The most destitute, who are still not covered by health insurance, are provided for by national assistance. In 1982, the socialist government implemented a national health service (ESY), which constitutes an attempt at a rational organisation of the distribution of medical care at a national level (Act 1397/83). Among the measures implemented, are the reorganisation of the hospitals, the creation of centres for primary care, and the hiring of full-time salaried doctors. This ambitious programme was later checked by economic difficulties. Since the outset, the institution of a national heath service has aroused lively opposition on the part of doctors (making it difficult to arrive at consensus with the medical field), on the part of the funds which grant higher benefits to those insured, and on the part of the private sector. The objective of unifying the various health services was not achieved. Unification still remains a source of tension.

[45] IKA, OGA and TEVE (*Tamio Epagelmation kai Biotechnon Ellados,* Insurance Fund for Professionals and Craftsmen) cover 87.27% of those insured.

[46] Health insurance provides benefits in cash and in kind. The benefits in kind basically cover medical fees, costs of hospitalisation, medicines and paraclinical examinations. For benefits in kind (general system of wage-earners, IKA) it is necessary to have completed 50 days of work during the year prior to the date of notification of a person's illness or during the previous fifteen-month period. The distributive nature shows itself in the requirement of a short duration of membership, which is easy to fulfil. People insured by IKA may not choose their own doctor. Medical care is provided by IKA's community clinics or by the health centres of the national health service. As for pharmaceuticals, patients must pay a patient's (proportional) contribution of around 25% (article 19 of Act 1902/90). In the case of some long-term and expensive illnesses, the rate is lower (for example, 10% for Parkinson's disease). Control measures are called for to reduce the overconsumption of medicines (GRD 47,100 or € 141.44 per person in 1995; expenditures on drugs make up 2.8% of GDP and 40% of health care expenditures).

[47] Legislation sets the condition of incapacity for work (a stoppage of work of more than 3 days counting from the notification of the illness) as a result of a physical or mental illness.

the illness or during the preceding fifteen-month period.[48] Workers may receive cash benefits for a limited period, ranging from 182 to 720 days. After the expiry of the maximum period, they may receive a disability pension if the reduction in their earning capacity has become permanent (disability constitutes another branch of social security).

If an employee has worked for more than one year with the same employer he continues to receive his full salary – sickness benefit plus the portion paid by the employer – in the event of illness lasting one month or less. After that, his income falls back to 50% of the reference salary for the class of insurance to which he belongs; there are 28 salary classes. Benefits are increased by 10% for each dependant. This increase is calculated over the basic amount of the allowance.

2.2 Maternity: more or less satisfactory protection

Maternity is insured as a sickness benefit. Sickness benefits are only awarded to women who work. Consequently, only they receive a maternity allowance for a period of 112 working days starting 56 days before the estimated date of birth and ending 56 days after birth. For a woman who has worked for a certain length of time, cash benefits are at the same level as her previous salary. To receive a maternity allowance, an insured person must have completed at least 200 days of work in the course of the two years prior to the estimated date of birth. In order to become entitled to benefits in kind, women insured by IKA must prove that they have been participants for a period equal to 50 days of work. IKA pays a lump sum of 30 times their current basic daily wage to cover medical fees involved in birth and confinement, provided these do not take place in a hospital at the expense of the insurance body. On the whole there are many differences in the extent to which maternity is covered by the various funds.

2.3 Old age insurance: a recent reinforcement to its contributory nature

At 68% of the total of social benefits, retirement pensions represent the largest segment within the Greek social security system. The retirement system is composed of a multitude of schemes which offer an unequal level of protection. In some special systems, pensioners receive a high proportion of the salary they enjoyed before retiring. Among the employees who were insured before 1 January 1993, some are much better off than others. Under the general system of wage-earners (IKA), the normal age of retirement is 65 for men and 60 for women. The required duration of employment is 4,500 days or 15 years. Numerous possibilities

---

[48] Not counting the days of work within the last quarter.

for early retirement are provided:[49] starting from the age of 60 (55 for women) in the case of heavy or unhealthy work;[50] from the age of 62 (57 for women) for those who have been insured for at least 10,000 days; from the age of 58 for those who have been insured for at least 10,500 days;[51] from the age of 55 for mothers, *etc.* The special systems for wage-earners (for example: the schemes of employees of banks and public enterprises) and the specific system for the civil service turn out to be the most favourable.

In 1992, confronted with many difficulties, Greece decided to overhaul its pension system. For want of organisational unity, the Greek Government harmonised the insurance conditions for all new insured persons, starting from 1 January 1993. Since 1992,[52] all pensions systems have been aligned with the general system for wage-earners (which is the least favourable system). Employees insured under special systems were particularly affected by the postponement of their retirement age and by the extension of the required period of contribution payments. More precisely, the age of retirement has become the same for all insured persons, both men and women: 65. Moreover, an affiliation term of at least 4,500 days or 15 years of work is required.[53] For insured working mothers of young or disabled children, the age at which full pension entitlement starts is 55 and the required duration of work and affiliation is 6,000 days or 20 years. A lowering of the retirement age to 55 years is provided for mothers who have (at the age of 50) at least 3 children and for wage-earners in mines, quarries, underground railways and production plants of the public electricity company. A partial pension is possible from the age of 60, on the condition that the person has fulfilled the minimum period of participation (4,500 days of work). The pension is reduced by 6% for each year that retirement is advanced.

The pension awarded by the general system for wage-earners (IKA) is composed of a basic pension and supplements. For persons insured before 1 January 1993, the basic pension is a percentage of the salary of one of the 28 classes of insurance (more precisely: of the estimated salary corresponding to the class in which the insured person belongs). In this way, the system effects some redistribution in favour of poorly paid workers. On the whole, the rules for pension calculation have the effect of loosening the link between contributions paid and the level of the pension received. Again, the system, which works as an insurance scheme, takes into account the duration of the working life during which contributions

---

[49] The average effective retirement age is therefore 61 years.

[50] The list of occupations which are considered taxing is rather long but not always justified by the facts.

[51] Starting from January 1st, 1998, the retirement age has been progressively postponed from 58 to 60 years.

[52] By Act 2084/1992.

[53] Wage-earners doing heavy and unhealthy work can claim a retirement pension at the full rate from the age of 60.

were paid. People with more than 4,500 days of work receive an increase of 1% for each period of 300 days in excess of 4,500, calculated on the basis of 25 times the estimated daily wage for their class of insurance. The system becomes more contributory as the period of reference used for the calculation of the pension is extended. Since 1991, the law[54] has provided for the calculation of retirement pension on the basis of average salaries of the last five years instead of two years (revalued on the commencing date of the pension).[55] An increase is provided for each minor child and for the spouse. The calculation of the pension is different for those insured after 1 January 1993. The amount of the pension is 1.714% of the remuneration which serves as the basis for each year of contributions (each year corresponding to 300 days of work). The remuneration serving as the basis is found by dividing the total salary received during the five years prior to the year of the application by the number of months worked in the course of the same period.[56] For those insured after 1 January 1993, the pension may not exceed four times the monthly average GDP *per capita* in 1991, increased by the rate of increase for civil service pensions.[57]

Traditionally, the State has been involved in establishing compulsory supplementary pensions schemes.[58] As we have seen, the number of supplementary social security funds at the level of branches or companies increased particularly between 1950 and 1970. In 1979, the Government created a general supplementary system (TEAM), without doing away with the existing funds. This new fund was later integrated into IKA. As a result, all wage-earners who until then had been excluded became compulsorily covered by the supplementary retirement fund IKA-TEAM.[59] Similarly, all those insured under IKA or any other main insurance fund, are compulsorily subject to IKA-TEAM (provided that they are not affiliated to another supplementary fund).[60] The financing of IKA-TEAM is accomplished by a contribution of 6%, shared equally between employer and insured employee. The amount of the supplementary pension depends on the previous salary and on the duration of participation. Starting from January 1st, 1998, supplementary pensions corresponding to a duration of affiliation of 35 years or 10,500 days may not

---

[54] Act 1976/91 (article 13; also article 28, section 1 of Act 2084/92).

[55] People insured before January 1st, 1993, who have completed 35 years (or 10,500 days) of work cannot receive a pension in excess of 80% of the gross salaries used for the calculation of retirement pension (revalued salaries for the past five years). Moreover, the pension may not exceed four times the monthly average GDP *per capita* in 1991 as readjusted to the rate of increase of retirement pensions for the civil service (article 51, section 1 of Act 2084/1992).

[56] Article 28 of Act 2084/92.

[57] Article 29, section 1 of Act 2084/92.

[58] See *Europe Sociale* (1994), supplement no. 3: *Les régimes complémentaires de retraite dans l'Union Européenne* [Additional pensions schemes in the European Union].

[59] The supplementary social security fund for wage-earners (TEAM) was instituted by Act 997/79.

[60] Article 56 of Act 1140/1981.

exceed 20% of the standard remuneration.[61] This ceiling will cause a serious reduction in the level of pensions. However, it is likely that the implementation of this measure will be suspended for some time.

It is permitted to combine a pension with paid work as long as the salary is less than 50 times the minimum daily wage.[62] The employment of pensioners is a thorny and complex issue. On the one hand, most retirement pensions are modest or very small; on the other hand, it is important that retired persons leave the labour market in order to make room for the next generation. However, a total ban might well encourage work in the black economy or cause the social marginalisation of many pensioners.

2.4 Disablement: access must be brought under control

One characteristic of the Greek system is the high number of disablement pensions: around 20% of the pensions paid by IKA alone are disablement pensions. This is basically due to a laxness on the part of the authorities. The growth of the number of disablement pensions has been stimulated by the practice of taking social considerations into account when defining disablement.[63] In fact, in many cases disablement pensions have been substituted for old age pensions. Since 1990, attempts have been made to curb this phenomenon[64] by reducing the discretion of the competent bodies in assessing disablement. The Government has also established stricter conditions for the award of disablement pensions. At the same time, to discourage people from applying for disablement pensions, it has reduced the amount of these pensions.

Disablement involves a reduction in earning capacity. In general, the handicap is assessed in relation to the degree of occupational disability. Nearly all relevant texts are based on the residual work capacity, on the difficulty of finding, keeping and having access to employment or remuneration. Social security funds are called upon to decide on the basis of the assessment of the degree of disablement by a medical committee. Disablement insurance covers only the insured individu-

---

[61] Article 54 of Act 2084/92.

[62] Article 70 of Act 2084/92.

[63] See L. Copeland, 'Tendances du développement des régimes de pensions d'invalidité: une perspective internationale [Tendencies in the development of inability pensions schemes: an international perspective]', in: *Revue Internationale de Sécurité Sociale* [International Review of Social Security], 35 (1981), no. 3, p. 264-267.

[64] Several countries are worried about the growth of the number of disabled persons. For attempts to control this phenomenon, see H. Bolderson and D. Mabbett, 'Maîtrise des coûts des régimes complexes de sécurité sociale: les limites du ciblage [Controlling the costs of complex social security systems: the limits of determining eligibility]', in: *Revue Internationale de Sécurité Sociale* [International Review of Social Security], 49 (1996), no. 1, p. 15-16.

als themselves; their family does not benefit. An insured person must prove that he or she has participated for at least 1,500 days (or of 5 years of work), of which 600 days (or two years) were during the five years preceding the year in which the disablement arose. Alternatively, the insured person may prove that he or she has worked for at least 4,500 days (or 15 years).[65] The amount of the pension is proportionate to the disablement rate and calculated on the basis of the old age pension: 1/2 of the old age pension for a disablement rate of 50% (partial disablement), and 3/4 of the pension for a disablement rate of 67% (ordinary disablement).[66] A rate of 80% (serious disablement) gives entitlement to a full pension. The disablement pension is increased for insured persons whose state of health demands permanent surveillance by another person.

In Greece, there is no specific cover for work accidents. Industrial accident insurance does not constitute a separate branch. After an industrial injury or an occupational illness, the insured person may receive a disablement pension (or his or her family members a survivors' pension). The nature of the accident or occupational illness does not affect the level of the benefit but only the duration of the insurance.[67] The victim of an industrial injury is covered without a minimum condition of previous work.[68] One single day of contributions is sufficient.

2.5 Survivors' insurance: necessary adjustments

Survivors' insurance guarantees the payment of a pension. This pension is awarded if the deceased has been insured for at least 1,500 days of work (of which 300 are in the course of the five years preceding the year of decease) or 4,500 days of work (in the course of his entire working life). The amount of the pension paid to the surviving spouse corresponds to 50% of the retirement pension of the deceased or 50% of the pension which would have been paid to him if he had been recognised as 80% disabled at the time of his death.[69]

---

[65] Disabled persons under the age of 21 must have completed a period of participation of 300 days or one year of work; beyond the age of 21, this period is increased by 120 days or 5 months of work per year up to 1,500 days or 5 years of work.

[66] Insured persons who fit the definition of the second category (ordinary disablement) may claim the pension at the full rate if they have completed a duration of affiliation of 6,000 days or 20 years (article 27 of Act 1902/90, article 12 of Act 1976/91).

[67] For the tendency to abolish the specific nature of the compensation for work accidents, see G. Dorion, *La modernisation de la réparation des accidents du travail et des maladies professionnelle* [The modernisation of compensation for work accidents and professional diseases] (Paris 1991), p. 39.

[68] By contrast, for occupational illnesses, the law does require having completed a certain period of affiliation.

[69] The pension is around 60% of the net average salary.

For persons who were insured before 1 January 1993, the pension paid to their widows is subject to no extra conditions.[70] By contrast, widowers receive survivor's pension only if they are disabled or if they have no income. Recently, the Council of State ruled that this discrimination is contrary to the equality of the sexes which is guaranteed by article 4, section 2 of the Constitution.[71] This was corrected by extending various advantages from one sex to the other in judicial decisions. The surviving spouse of new members (after 1 January 1993) may claim a survivor's pension only if he or she is disabled at a rate of at least 67% or if he or she does not have sufficient income (the monthly income may not exceed 40 times the applicable daily wage of a worker, increased by 20% per covered child). This adjustment seems more in keeping with the evolution of the situation of women in Greece. The sole objective of a survivor's pension must be to help a surviving spouse with no income in overcoming the difficulties of widowhood. The granting of survivor's pensions is thus dependent on the economic situation of the survivors.

2.6 Unemployment: new priorities

It is difficult to estimate the volume of unemployment in Greece on account of the large parallel economy and the durability of family ties. Nevertheless, it seems certain that unemployment affects around 10% of the active population.[72] Furthermore, there is a striking increase in unemployment among youngsters, qualified people, and women. More precisely, the unemployment rate among young people under the age of 25 increased to 28% (1994). The unemployment rate of women has increased disturbingly: in 1993, 58.8% of job applicants were female.[73] Obviously, statistical data are limited to registered unemployment only. There is a large amount of unregistered unemployment, particularly in agriculture.

Unemployment insurance comes under the OAED,[74] which provides a replacement income. The benefits depend on the duration of affiliation before the loss of employment. Age is irrelevant. For a person to be eligible, he or she must be without work and must be seeking a position. Since 1985,[75] benefits are paid to wage-earners who are involuntarily unemployed as a result of redundancy or the

---

[70] However, they must have been married for at least six months.

[71] Ruling 2435/1997. See Ruling of the Auditor General 1273/96.

[72] According to official estimates, unemployment is currently falling. See *MISSOC-Info*, (1997), no. 1.

[73] While their part in the active population is only 37%. See *MISSOC-Info*, (1997), no. 1.

[74] The *Institute for Employment of the Labour Force* (OAED) is a statutory body; its principal mission is to register and to link the supply to the demand for work. See J. Lixouriotis, 'Promotion et réglementation de la création de possibilités d'emplois en Grèce [Promoting and regulating the creation of employment opportunities in Greece]', in: *XIV World Congress of Labour Law and Social Security* (Seoul 1994), p. 313-344.

[75] According to Act 1545/1985 (article 3).

termination of a temporary job. They must remain available to accept an employment offer through the OAED in the branch of their specialisation, or to follow a course of occupational training. The scheme is financed by wage-earners (at a rate of 1.33%) and employers (at a rate of 2.67%). The benefits, which are paid for a maximum of one year, are linked to previous remunerations (40%-50% of the last salary), with an increase of 10% for each dependent person (up to a maximum of 70%). The minimum benefit is 2/3 of the basic daily wage.

There is a separate system of benefits for young people under 29 years of age who are looking for their first job.[76] Fixed allowances are paid for a period of five months after their registration with OAED. This is the only case of benefits being paid to applicants who have had no prior employment. In Greece, the Government has made no provision for long-term unemployment, which can lead to permanent social exclusion. The long-term unemployed who are over 55 (who have completed 3,000 days of insurance) are only entitled to health insurance benefits in kind.[77] They may enjoy these benefits for two years or until their retirement. Two additional systems have been instituted by an agreement between employers and employees of various sectors of the economy. They were also funded by contributions of employers and employees. The first was a programme for vocational training ELKEPE (*Eidikos Logariasmos Programmaton Epagelmatikis Katartisis kai Ekpedeusis*, Special Fund for Professonal Training Programmes) and the second a special unemployment fund EKLA (*Eidikos Koinos Logariasmos Anergias*, Special Unemployment Fund). EKLA offered supplementary benefits to the long-term unemployed, as well as programmes for their reintegration into the labour process. Since 1996 these two systems have been united in a system called *Logariasmos gia tin Apascholisi kai tin Epagelmatiki Katartisi* (LAEK, Fund for Employment and Professional Training).[78] LAEK is part of the OAED.

Finally, active measures are taken for the promotion of employment. OAED has put into operation a new policy for this purpose: vocational training courses in conjunction with business and industry, the creation of numerous trainee places in companies,[79] the promotion of occupational and geographic mobility among workers, the introduction of special incentives for the recruitment of young unemployed persons, the development of programmes to fight unemployment in priority regions, the implementation of local employment programmes,[80] and the crea-

---

[76] Act 1545/85.

[77] Article 10 of Act 2434/96.

[78] Act 2434/96.

[79] The State awards subsidies to companies to encourage the integration of certain categories into the labour market: the disabled, unemployed youths, repatriates, *etc.* See Lixouriotis, 'Promotion et réglementation de la création de possibilités d'emplois en Grèce', p. 326.

[80] Article 21 of Act 1836/1989.

tion of community service jobs.[81] However, this is only the beginning of a reorientation from unemployment insurance to employability insurance.

2.7 Family policy: rather ungenerous

Family allowances are linked to some form of work: only wage-earners – more precisely: each person who works as a subordinate – enjoy family allowances paid by the *Dianemitikos Logariasmos Oikogeniakon Epidomaton Misthoton* (DLOEM, Redistributive Fund for Family Allowances for Wage-earner*s*), a fund separate from OAED. This fund is financed from contributions by employer and employee (both at the rate of 1%). In order to be entitled, one must have been a member for a period of at least 50 days during the preceding year. The amount of the benefit increases with the number of children; it decreases as the net family income during the preceding year rises. Family allowance is only paid for children under the age of 18. However, for children in higher education the allowance is paid until the age of 24.[82] For all other occupational categories, there is no form of compensation for the costs of raising a first and second child.

Because of its confinement to wage-earners and contributory financing the current system is outmoded and inegalitarian. Unquestionably, family allowances ought to be a matter of national solidarity. Moreover, expenditures devoted to the family only account for 1% of GDP. The family is clearly not among the priorities of the Greek Government. It is evident that the collective responsibility for children must be strengthened. No system of social security can afford to ignore this.

Since 1990, family policy in Greece has begun to focus on raising the national birth-rate. Large families are actively encouraged. For instance, the system steps up its support of the family from the third child onward. Presently, there are three 'non-contributory' allowances for large families:[83] the allowance for the third child (up to the age of 6, GRD 40,000 or € 120), the allowance for the mother of a large family (a family is considered to be large starting from the fourth child), as well as the pension for the mother of a large family. Means-testing has been recently introduced,[84] but its selectivity is very moderate since the law fixes fairly high ceilings for the award of family allowance.

---

[81] Article 28 of Act 1262/1982.
[82] The allowance is paid on a permanent basis for children who become disabled after having reached the age of 18.
[83] Article 63 of Act 1892/199.
[84] By article 39 of Act 2459/1997.

2.8 The privatisation of social security protection

Although neo-liberal ideas seem to be gaining favour in a part of the Greek electoral body (especially the middle classes and the well-to-do), there have been no privatisation measures in the strict sense (a transfer of public tasks to private organisations).[85] Nonetheless, a certain encouragement of the private sector is taking place simply by limiting the protection offered by the public system. Since 1990, Governments of every political colour have pursued an austerity policy which tends to curb social expenditures. The purchasing power of pensions has been curtailed and eligibility conditions have been tightened. This indirectly encourages insurance companies to step in. Besides, it should be added that collective labour agreements are seldom used to secure a degree of social protection. In a narrow legal context,[86] collective agreements are used only to institute supplementary insurance for employees against certain risks (particularly the risk of accidents) through the intermediary of private life insurance companies.

2.9 Legal protection against arbitrariness

In Greece, social protection arrangements are such that the administration has hardly any leeway in establishing the eligibility of an applicant or in determining the level of benefits. The rules of entitlement to social security are written down and of a public nature; they are imposed on the implementation bodies. Since the rights and obligations of insured persons are determined by law and regulations, social security funds have to pay benefits without the authority to make any closer assessment. The rules cannot be altered even if all parties consent. Moreover, alas, the mills of justice grind very slowly: it takes about two years to reach a decision. This ignores the fact that people need social benefits for their daily bread. The procedure ought to be more rapid. Finally, there is no comprehensive social security law, legislation being scattered over a whole series of texts.[87] This makes it difficult to inform the public as to its rights and entitlements.

---

[85] See A. Euzéby and J. Van Langendonck, 'Néo-libéralisme et protection sociale: la question de la privatisation dans les pays de la CEE [Neo-liberalism and social protection: the issue of privatisation in EEC countries]', in: *Droit social. Textes et documents annotés concernant les rapports professionnels et l'organisation de la production,* (1989), p. 256.

[86] Article 2, section 3 of Act 1897/91.

[87] See K. Kremalis (Ed.), *Health and Assistance. Simplification and systematisation of social protection rules,* Athens: University Research Institute of Social Insurance, 1996.

3 The guarantee of a minimum income

In Greece, there is no general mechanism to guarantee a minimum income and to ensure that benefits are sufficient to live in accordance with human dignity. The phenomenon of social marginalisation is spreading.[88] It is estimated that, at present, around 22% of the Greek population live in poor households.[89] Therefore, creating some sort of minimum income guarantee for all residents must be a priority for Greek social security policy. Recently, some degree of political consensus seems to have been reached on the expediency of a 'national pension' for all residents of Greece. This universal pension would represent the basic pension level and would be financed through taxation.

Nonetheless, there are certain categorical provisions which have the same effects as a guaranteed minimum income. These provisions apply to categories such as elderly persons with no national insurance cover, the disabled, one-parent families, and the poor.[90] Protection is offered either in the form of 'non-contributory' benefits (comparable to a kind of general social assistance) or in the context of national assistance which generally plays a supplementary role in domains where social security does not intervene[91] – by awarding, for example, allowances to people who find it impossible to cope with their everyday needs.[92] In actual fact, the differences between these several types of protection are becoming blurred, giving rise to more universal forms. To determine the amounts involved in these fragmented provisions, the Greek Government refers to arbitrary indicators. The diversity of these indicators betrays their opportunistic or *ad hoc* nature. Actually, they are not indicators at all. On the whole, the guaranteed amounts are determined administratively, and re-evaluated regularly.

3.1 Guarantee of a minimum pension

The minimum pension, which expresses the integration of the idea of national assistance into social security, is not subject to conditions as regards income. 62% of the pension beneficiaries under the general system of wage-earners (IKA) re-

---

[88] See National Centre for Social Research – Commission of the European Communities, *EC Observatory on national policies to combat social exclusion. Consolidated Report Greece*, Athens 1992.

[89] In Greece, one finds poverty of a socially integrated type. This type of poverty fits in with Mediterranean societies. See *Problèmes économiques* [Economic problems], 50 (1997), no. 2,508 (February 19th, 1997), p. 9.

[90] See G. Amitsis, 'Rapport National: Grèce', in: *Les problèmes juridiques de la réglementation et de la mise en oeuvre d'un revenu minimum pour chacun. XIII Congrès Mondial de Droit du Travail et de la Sécurité Sociale* [Legal problems of the regulation and introduction of a universal minimum income. XIII World Congress of Labour Law and Social Security] (Athens 1991), p. 243-262.

[91] In Greece, national assistance is secondary to social insurance and family solidarity.

[92] According to statutory order 57/1973.

ceive only a minimum pension. Its amount depends on the date on which participation commenced. For members who entered after 1 January 1993, the amount of
the pension cannot be less than the retirement pension deducted from the average
monthly GNP *per capita* in 1991, which is readjusted according to the rates of
increase in civil service retirement pensions (calculated on the basis of estimated
monthly salary and 15 years of participation).[93] For participants who entered before 1 January 1993, the minimum pension is equal to the minimum pension for
1990 (GRD 62,360 or € 187) which is readjusted starting from 1 January 1991
according to the rate of increase for retired civil servants.[94] The link with the civil
service pensions does not constitute an objective indicator, since their adjustment
is at the discretion of the State.[95] The level of the minimum pension is not enough
to give adequate protection to the beneficiaries. In 1997, the minimum pension
amounted to around GRD 100,000 (€ 300) – no more than a mere 8% of the net
average salary in industry.[96]

3.2 Social solidarity allowance for retired persons

The solidarity allowance for retired persons *Epidoma Kinonikis Allilegiis Misthoton* (EKAS, Solidarity Benefit for Pensioners)[97] is paid to retired persons over
60 years of age whose income is below a certain threshold (in 1998: a total
amount received in pension below GRD 1,680,000 per year, or € 5,045).[98] This
'non-contributory' allowance, which reinforces the basic income of the neediest
retired persons and is a matter of national solidarity, amounts to between
GRD 3,000 (€ 9) and GRD 12,000 (€ 36) per month. Initially, its amount was
fixed without the use of an indicator. Since then it has been adjusted annually by
ministerial order in accordance with the consumer price index.[99] The introduction
of the EKAS allowance represents an attempt to separate 'contributory' from
'non-contributory' in the field of pensions.

---

[93] Article 29, section 3 of Act 2084/92.

[94] Article 29, section 3 of Act 1902/1990.

[95] For insured persons in other funds (with the exception of IKA) according to article 21 of Act
2434/96, since 1 January 1997 the revaluation of the minimum pension, which takes place on an annual
basis, is based by law on the consumer price index. Indexation is not automatic. It takes place following a ruling by the Ministry of National Economy. For the year of 1997, this index was fixed at 4.5%
(ministerial order 1478/590/97/14.1.97).

[96] Commission des Communautés européennes, *La protection social en Europe* [Social protection in
Europe] (Luxembourg 1993), p. 55.

[97] Instituted by Act 2434/96, article 20.

[98] Moreover, the income of the household must be less than GRD 3,050,000 or € 9,159 per year.

[99] Article 20, section 5 of Act 2434/96.

3.3 The fixed-rate OGA pension for non-insured persons aged 65 and older

People of 65 years and older without national insurance cover receive a pension at a single rate, fixed monthly, of around GRD 25,000 (€ 75).[100] It is a minimum guaranteed income for elderly persons, subsidised by the national budget. The amount is very small, and is fixed without reference to any appropriate indicator. It is subject only to budgetary exigencies.

4 Households and individuals

In a system of social insurance schemes, benefits are calculated on an individual basis. Entitlement to benefits depends basically on the payment of contributions. Taking into account the income of a household is not compatible with the idea behind social insurance. However, the size of the family does affect the amount of certain social benefits. For example, insured persons receive higher sickness benefits and pensions if they have a spouse and children.[101] Recently, there is a tendency to subject non-contributory benefits to an income condition. As a result, the income of a household influences the amount of the benefit. As we have seen, this is the case with family allowances paid to large families. Generally, the Government adopts a neutral attitude toward the composition of families. However, the absence of any affirmative action in favour of less fortunate families (such as one-parent families) seems to imply a preference for the traditional family. In Greece, lone parents and their children are particularly vulnerable to set-backs and are badly in need of extra protection.

5 European perspectives

The criteria established by the treaty of Maastricht will drastically change the landscape of social security in Greece. Every attempt at reform will aim at achieving financial equilibrium within the system in order to alleviate the huge deficit of the national budget. If the public deficit is blamed on social security it is likely that the perspective of the single market will have a negative impact on the

---

[100] Act 1296/82.

[101] In the case of IKA, the pension rates are increased if an insured person supports his non-working wife (1/2 of minimum salary) and his children (20% of the pension for the first, 15% for the second and 10% for the third child). Moreover, the dependants of the person covered by national insurance may claim benefits in kind from the health insurance cover.

level of benefits. Checks on social expenditures will curb the expansion of the benefits.[102] However, in our opinion it is not necessary to restrict spending to save social security. Maastricht does not have to lead to the dismantling of the system. There is more room to manoeuvre in the shape of rationalisation. The best solution is to adapt the social security system to the new ways of life,[103] such as the disappearance of the salary-based model,[104] and the radical changes taking place in family life.

On the other hand, the convergence of European social security systems and the need to adjust to the requirements of the European Community charter of social rights, will encourage the introduction of new benefits. If Greece is to take this road, it will have to adopt, first of all, a general guaranteed minimum income[105] to combat marginalisation and social exclusion. For the time being, such measures will encounter financial obstacles. For all its good intentions, the European Commission cannot possibly guarantee that all member states will recognise the right of the individual to a minimum income and act upon it effectively.[106]

6 Conclusion

In Greece, everyone agrees that the social security system faces serious problems and that there is a pressing need for comprehensive reform. If no reform gets under way the viability of the present system will be threatened. If an attempt is to be successful, it must tackle the huge institutional heterogeneity and socioeconomic vested interests. However, the basic principles which have inspired the creation of the system must not be called into question: its public and social nature, the solidarity between generations, and the principle of share and share alike. Ultimately, the way in which social security evolves will depend on political choices, since at the heart of the debate on social security is the problem of the breadth to be covered by social benefits, and the issue of the distribution of the national wealth. It is up to politicians to translate the concept of social justice into practice.

---

[102] The provisions of Acts 1909/90, 1976/91, 2084/92 bear out just such an attempt.

[103] See BIT, *La sécurité sociale à l'horizon 2000* [Social security in view of the year 2000], Geneva 1984.

[104] See J.-P. Fitoussi and P. Rosanvallon, *Le nouvel âge des inégalités* [The new age of inequality] (Paris 1996), p. 81.

[105] See A. Sissouras and G. Amitsis, 'Social security policy', in: P. Kazakos and P.C. Ioakimidis (Eds.), *Greece and EC membership evaluated* (London, New York 1994), p. 257.

[106] See L. Betten, 'Marché interne et Union monetaire. Reexaminer le cas pour l'harmonisation de la sécurité dans l'Union Européenne [Internal market and monetary Union. Re-examining the case for a harmonisation of social security within the European Union]', in: *5th European Regional Congress for Labour Law and Social Security* (Leiden 1996), p. 11.

VII Ireland

Mel Cousins

1 Introduction

1.1 Historical roots and legal basis

The foundations of the Irish social welfare system (as the social security system is known) were laid when Ireland was a part of the United Kingdom. The first national system of income maintenance payments was established in the Poor Law (Ireland) Act of 1838. Subsequent United Kingdom legislation in relation to workmen's compensation (1898), old age pensions (1908) and national insurance (1911) also applied to Ireland. Following Independence in 1922, a number of additional schemes were introduced including unemployment assistance (1933), widows' and orphans' pensions (1935) and children's allowance (1943). In 1947 a new Department of Social Welfare was established to be responsible for the planning and administration of social welfare. It was recently renamed the Department of Social, Community and Family Affairs. In 1952 the existing social insurance schemes were brought together into one unified system of social insurance.

The current legal basis for the social welfare system is set out in the Social Welfare (Consolidation) Act of 1993 and in a series of Ministerial Regulations made under that legislation.[1] The 1993 Act is amended on at least an annual basis.

1.2 Structure and financing

The Irish social welfare system can broadly be divided into three categories of payment:

• social insurance or contributory payments;
• social assistance or means-tested payments; and a
• universal child benefit payable in respect of all children (and unrelated to employment or income).

---

[1] For an annotated version of the legislation, see R. Clark, *Annotated guide to social welfare law*, London 1995.

The Irish social welfare system is primarily a system of income support payments. Only a very limited number of health-related services are provided under the social insurance system, and the main public health care provision is by way of a separate national health scheme operated under the auspices of the Irish Department of Health and Children. Social insurance is funded by contributions paid by employers and employees and, to a limited extent, the State. Both social assistance and child benefit payments are funded out of general taxation.

Figure 1: Social welfare expenditure as % of GNP 1986-1998.[2]

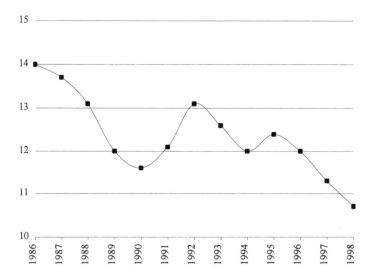

In 1998 total social welfare expenditure will amount to an estimated 4,800 million Irish Pounds (IR£) (€ 10,337 million).[3] This will account for over one third of current Government expenditure and 10.7% of GNP (Gross National Product). The funding of this expenditure in 1996 came from the State (59%), employer's contributions to the Social Insurance Fund (28%), employee's contributions (11%) and contributions from the self-employed (2%). The social insurance scheme operates on a pay-as-you-go basis but, for the first time in recent decades, due to the growth in employment in the Irish economy, income under the social insurance scheme has slightly exceeded outgoings. Total expenditure has declined

---

[2] Source: Department of Social Welfare, *Statistical Information on Social Welfare Services* (various years); *Estimates of Public Expenditure* (1998).

[3] *Estimates of public expenditure 1998*, Dublin: Stationery Office, 1998.

significantly over the last twelve years as a percentage of GNP, from 14% in 1986 to an estimated 10.7% in 1998:

1.3 Social insurance and social assistance

The social insurance scheme applies to all private sector employees earning over a certain minimum payment each week (currently IR£ 30 or € 38). Employees are insured against the risks of old age and retirement, disability, unemployment, invalidity, occupational injuries, survivorship, maternity and limited medical benefits. Full social insurance cover has recently been extended to the civil and public service in respect of new employees since 1995, but existing civil and public servants are only covered for a limited range of benefits on the basis that they have existing occupational pensions. Social insurance also covers the self-employed since 1988 but only in respect of a very limited range of long-term benefits. About one and a half million people are insured under the social insurance scheme. The social assistance scheme provides benefits in respect of the traditional insurance categories – though generally at a lower level – and also provides payments for lone parents, a residual welfare allowance for persons whose means are insufficient to meet their needs, an allowance for carers and a means-tested payment for low income families in employment.

In terms of the volume of expenditure, there has been a switch over the last decade, away from social insurance and towards social assistance spending (see Figure 2). There were a number of reasons for this development. Firstly, the high level of unemployment – and in particular long-term unemployment – experienced in Ireland in this period, meant that more people were forced to rely on the means-tested unemployment assistance payment rather than on the short-term insurance-based unemployment benefit. Secondly, contribution requirements for a range of benefits were made more stringent in the late 1980s and early 1990s, meaning that fewer people qualified for insurance benefits.

In 1985, over half of all expenditure was on social insurance. By 1993 more was being spent on social assistance than on social insurance, and in 1997 45% of all expenditure was on social assistance as compared with only 43% on social insurance.[4] This trend may reverse in coming years as self-employed persons, who came into insurance in 1988, will begin to qualify for social insurance pensions. Also, the declining level of unemployment means that fewer people are claiming social assistance-based unemployment payments.

---

[4] In 1995, the figures for both are approximately equal, but this is distorted by the fact that the social insurance figure given here includes IR£ 200 million (€ 254 million) in arrears of payments relating to the period 1986-1995 arising from the implementation of the European Union equality directive.

Figure 2: Structure of social welfare spending, 1985, 1990, 1997.[5]

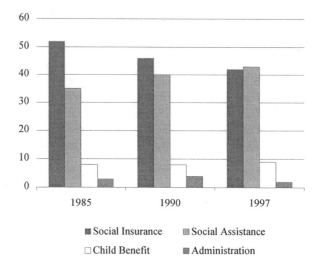

- ■ Social Insurance   ■ Social Assistance
- □ Child Benefit   ■ Administration

In 1996, almost one and a half million people out of a total population of 3.6 million were in receipt of a social welfare payment (excluding the universal child benefit). Unlike social security payments in most European countries, almost all social welfare payments are flat-rated, with increases in respect of adult and child dependants. A limited pay-related scheme which was introduced in the 1960s was phased out and eventually abolished in recent years. Only maternity benefit is currently income-related.

1.4 Organisation

The Irish social welfare system is highly centralised. All aspects of planning, implementation and delivery are the responsibility of the Department of Social, Community and Family Affairs, with the exception of the residual welfare allowance for people whose means are insufficient to meet their needs (which is delivered on behalf of the Department by the regional health boards). As set out above, there is only one social insurance scheme, although this is broken down into over ten subcategories of people concerned, the most important being private sector employees earning over IR£ 30 (€ 38) per week (69% of all insured), civil and

---

[5] Source: Department of Social Welfare, *Statistical Information on Social Welfare Services* (various years); *Estimates of Public Expenditure* (1998).

public servants (11% in three different subcategories) and the self-employed (10%). In contrast to social welfare systems in other European Catholic countries, the Irish case is notable for the absence of a corporatist welfare system, involving different insurance schemes for different categories of workers and tripartite management by employers, employees and the State.[6]

1.5 Appeals

People who are dissatisfied with a decision in relation to a social welfare payment are entitled to appeal to the Social Welfare Appeals Office. This is an independent administrative office of the Department of Social, Community and Family Affairs. The office is directed by the Chief Appeals Officer who publishes an annual report. The appeals officers are all officers of the Department of Social, Community and Family Affairs although they are fully independent of the Department in the performance of their functions. There has been considerable reform of the appeals system in recent years and there is no doubt that it has improved significantly. Criticisms have been made of the fact that the appeals officers are departmental officials and their degree of independence from the Department is sometimes questioned. However, the overall success rate of social welfare appeals is high compared with many other European countries.

2 Maintaining living standards

2.1 The objectives of the social welfare system

As payments under the Irish social welfare system are, with the exception of maternity benefit, flat-rated, the Irish system does not aim to provide a replacement income which would maintain the income of a person in receipt of the average industrial wage anywhere near the level of earnings which that person would have received prior to ceasing work. Thus, for example, comparative studies show that in 1993, the basic Irish old age pension replaced only 42% of the average net earnings of a manual worker in manufacturing industry, compared with a European Community average (for the then twelve countries) of 75%.[7] Rather, the aim of the social welfare system is to provide a minimum level of payment so as to

---

[6] W. Korpi, *Welfare state development in Europe since 1930: Ireland in comparative perspective,* Dublin: Economic and Social Research Institute ESRI, 1992.

[7] European Commission, *Social protection in Europe 1993,* Luxembourg: Office of Official Publications of the European Union, 1994.

ensure that persons affected by certain contingencies do not fall into poverty. Accordingly, for example, arrangements to maintain the standard of living in old age are almost entirely dependent on occupational or personal pensions. A recent survey of comparative replacement rates (*i.e.* the proportion of earnings out of work in comparison with those in work) indicates that, while Ireland has a very low basic pension, the inclusion of typical occupational benefits brings Ireland above the average replacement rate.[8] However, less than 50% of the Irish workforce are covered by occupational pension schemes.[9]

2.2 Pay-related short-term benefits

Historically, the State system has always focused on providing basic minimum standards rather than pay-related benefits. Pay-related benefits for short-term payments (*e.g.* unemployment and disability) were introduced in the late 1960s, but – as was mentioned above – have been phased out and abolished in more recent years.

The introduction of pay-related benefits for short-term payments to some extent mirrored similar developments in the United Kingdom. It also reflected a belief in the principle that persons who were out of work should be in a financial position which would allow them to look for appropriate work even if this, to some extent, increased the duration of unemployment. This must be seen in the context of the comparatively low unemployment levels at the time. In response to rising unemployment in the 1980s, of course, as in many other countries this approach fell into disfavour. It was replaced by a concern with keeping replacement ratios as low as possible. This approach was reflected in the reduction and eventual abolition of pay-related benefits for short-term payments. However, a concern with what are perceived as high replacement ratios remains a major issue in Irish social policy. While Irish social welfare payments are flat-rate, the fact that persons with dependants receive dependency increases, combined with the operation of benefits in relation to housing and health services, can mean that a proportion of unemployed people still have what are seen as comparatively high replacement ratios. The extent to which this occurs in practice and the extent to which it is actually a problem are subjects of considerable controversy. Nonetheless, the emphasis amongst social policy makers is on ensuring that replacement ratios do not rise. Accordingly, there would appear to be little likelihood that any system of pay-related benefits for short-term claimants would be introduced in the foreseeable future.

---

[8] *National pensions policy initiative: consultation document*, Dublin: Department of Social Welfare / Pensions Board, 1997.

[9] G. Hughes and B. Whelan, *Occupational and personal pension coverage 1995*, Dublin: Economic and Social Research Institute ESRI, 1996.

Private unemployment insurance *per se* is not readily available on the market. However, some private protection exists in the form of loan and mortgage protection policies whereby people who become unemployed will have their loan or mortgage paid for them by the insurance company. Private and occupational pensions in relation to disability and invalidity are more common, although (as we have seen) a large proportion of the population are not covered by occupational pensions of any kind.

2.3 Pay-related retirement pensions

The introduction of a statutory pay-related pension for retired people has been discussed on a number of occasions. Towards the end of the 1970s it appeared possible that a statutory pay-related system would be introduced, following similar developments in the United Kingdom. However, the second oil shock in 1979 and public finance problems relating to national policy decisions intervened before the introduction of any such system. Effectively it was ruled out throughout the 1980s.

Recent upturns in the Irish economy have again led to discussions of this issue. A recent Consultation Document published by the Irish Department of Social Welfare and the Irish Pensions Board,[10] has set out a number of possibilities for improving protection for retired persons. The options discussed included:
• improvements to existing pension schemes
• the introduction of a State earnings-related pension
• making occupational pension cover mandatory
• encouraging industry-wide schemes
• ncouraging personal retirement accounts
• the improvement of basic statutory pensions, or
• a combination of some of these options.

At the time of writing, no official decision has been taken in relation to which option will be pursued. General policy trends would suggest that the introduction of a statutory earnings-related pension scheme is somewhat unlikely, and it seems more likely that one of the alternative options of improving occupational coverage will be chosen. The coverage of occupational and personal pensions has increased rapidly up to the mid-1980s. However, a recent study indicates that there has been little change in the situation since then with just under half of all persons in employment having pension coverage, and only 7% of those not economically active.[11]

---

[10] *Ibid.*
[11] *Ibid.*

To a large extent, groups representing welfare claimants and anti-poverty organisations have focused on raising basic social welfare rates as opposed to the introduction of pay-related benefits, which would be seen as being of comparatively little benefit to the worst off.

2.4 Unemployment policy

One of the key challenges facing the social welfare system in recent years has been the very high level of unemployment – peaking at 300,000 people in 1993. Unemployment has subsequently declined rapidly to 240,000 in early 1998. Since the early 1990s, the Department of Social, Community and Family Affairs has put more emphasis on the employment support (as opposed to pure income support) aspects of its functions. A range of active labour market measures have been introduced to support unemployed people in taking up employment or education opportunities, and in-work benefits for low income families have been extended. In 1992, only 1% of the total unemployment payments related to such 'active' measures, whereas this has increased to 15% of the unemployment budget in 1998.

3 The level of basic social security arrangements

3.1 Indexation and level of payments

Irish social welfare rates are generally increased on an annual basis. There is no legislative provision as to the level of increase. Historically, no explicit policy has been set as to the appropriate manner or level of increase in social welfare rates and these have varied over time. However, analyses of the rates of increase in the post-war period up to the late 1970s and early 1980s show that successive Governments have implicitly adopted a policy of increasing the main social welfare payments in line with changes in average gross industrial earnings.[12]

The then existing rates of social welfare payments were considered by a Government appointed Commission on Social Welfare in the mid-1980s.[13] This Commission adopted a number of different ways of assessing the level of the then social welfare rates. The Commission found that rates were seriously inadequate and recommended significant increases. They recommended that rates should gener-

---

[12] G. Hughes, *Payroll tax incidence, the direct tax burden and the rate of return on state pension contributions in Ireland,* Dublin: Economic and Social Research Institute ESRI, 1985.

[13] Commission on Social Welfare, *Report,* Dublin: Stationery Office, 1986.

ally be increased in accordance with the *Consumer Price Index* (CPI), but this should be reviewed every five years. This recommendation should be seen in the context of the fact that, at that time, consumer prices were increasing more rapidly than earnings. Since the publication of the report of the Commission on Social Welfare, Governments have generally adopted a policy of increasing benefits in line with or above the rate of the CPI. Significantly higher increases have been adopted in relation to the lower rates of social welfare (*e.g.* unemployment payments), and it has recently been agreed by the Government and the Social Partners that the minimum rates recommended by the Commission on Social Welfare will be implemented by the year 2000.[14] This is a policy agreement and does not have any legal status. However, by 1998, 94% of payments will be above the rates recommended by the Commission.

The current Government – elected in mid-1997 – has given a commitment in its programme for Government to increase social insurance-based old age pensions to IR£ 100 (€ 127) per week by 2002. This commitment would involve significantly higher increases going to pensioners than they have received in recent years. It may also mark a change in policy, with higher increases being targeted at persons over pensions age and, therefore, largely outside the labour market.

3.2 Trends 1987-1994

Examination of trends between 1987 and 1994 shows that average net earnings for an industrial worker have increased by 40% to 43% over this period, compared to an increase of 21.3% in the CPI. High earners would appear to have increases above this level and it is estimated that average personal disposable income per head increased by about 55%.[15] All social welfare rates have increased by amounts above the CPI over the same period with old age and survivors' pensions increasing by 29-30%. In line with the recommendations of the Commission on Social Welfare, the lower rates (*e.g.* unemployment assistance) increased much more rapidly, up to 73%. Average increases in respect of children increased by 46%. However, adult dependency increases have been significantly lower, ranging from 22% for dependants of old age pensioners to 33% in the case of unemployment assistance. This partly reflected the fact that the Commission on Social Welfare recommended that adult dependant payments should represent 0.6 of the full adult payment, whereas several dependency increases represented from 0.65 to 0.72 of the then personal rate. Partly, it reflected a political desire to devote resources to the 'headline' increases.

---

[14] *Ireland, Partnership 2000,* Dublin: Stationery Office, 1996.
[15] T. Callan *et al., Poverty in the 1990's,* Dublin (ESRI) 1996.

3.3 Reviewing the level of payments

As set out above, and unlike the practice in many other European countries, there is no statutory provision setting out the manner in which social welfare rates should be set or increased over time. Decisions in this regard have tended to be made on a somewhat *ad hoc* basis and without any clearly expressed basis in policy. Indeed, there has been relatively little discussion of the basis upon which social welfare rates should be established or set, even amongst organisations representing claimants and anti-poverty groups. This has been largely because of the adoption by such organisations of the target rates established by the Commission on Social Welfare in 1986.

While the Commission used a number of different methods in arriving at its target rates, the methodology involved has been criticised in a recent review of social welfare rates.[16] The fact that the minimum rates recommended by the Commission are now close to being achieved, combined with the fact that Ireland's GNP and average earnings are now increasing much more rapidly than the cost of living, may give rise to more detailed discussion of these issues in coming years. In 1994, the then Minister for Social Welfare commissioned a review of the appropriate rates of social welfare payment by the Economic and Social Research Institute.[17] This report outlined a number of different methods of assessing income adequacy and examined the implications of increasing rates to different levels in terms of cost, impact on poverty and on work incentives. However, it carefully refrained from recommending any particular level of income as the appropriate one.

4 Household and individual

4.1 Household or individual?

The extent to which payments are made on an individual basis or, in contrast, the extent to which household circumstances are taken into account, varies from one type of payment to another.[18] In general, most social insurance payments are paid on an individual basis. However, the household circumstances are taken into account to the extent that increases in respect of adult and child dependants are pay-

---

[16] T. Callan, B. Nolan, and C. Whelan, *A review of the Commission on Social Welfare's Minimum Adequate Income,* Dublin: Economic and Social Research Institute ESRI, 1996.

[17] *Ibid.*

[18] See M. Cousins, *The Irish social welfare system: law and social policy* (Dublin 1995), ch. 4: 'The treatment of households'.

able in certain circumstances. In the case of social assistance or means-tested payments, household circumstances are generally taken into account. However, the precise way in which this occurs varies from payment to payment. In the case of most means-tested payments, the means of a spouse or partner are taken into account in assessing a claimant's means. In general, children's means are never taken into account in assessing a parent's income, but, in a number of cases, the means of parents may be taken into account in assessing the income of children who are living with the parents. This does not apply in the case of children living outside the family home. In 1996, adult dependency payments[19] were made in respect of 150,000 persons, about 95% of whom are women. As set out in the previous section, adult dependants have received much lower rates of increase in payments in recent years than have persons claiming in their own right.

Given the dependency based nature of much of the Irish social welfare system, the question of the balance between household and individual has been one of the key questions in recent social policy debates. The introduction of equality in social welfare, required by the European Union Directive on Equal Treatment in Matters of Social Security, gave rise to considerable controversy in Ireland and required important changes in the structure of the welfare system. It has been argued that – while some aspects of the implementation of the Directive have been positive and have facilitated women's participation in the paid labour force – the effect of the retention of the concept of dependency and the resulting continued disincentive for many women to enter the labour force means that the system has, to a large extent, retained a dependency based approach rather than representing a major move towards individualisation of benefits.[20] It has also been argued that this approach is dominated by the view that, given the already very high levels of Irish unemployment, there is little point in facilitating the entrance of married women into the labour force combined with the somewhat weakened ethos that the woman's place is in the home. Given the current booming labour market, however, the number of married women in the labour force is increasing significantly and this, combined with a drop in the levels of unemployment, may lead to significant reductions in the numbers of people in receipt of dependency payments over time.

---

[19] In 1997, the 'adult dependant' was renamed as a 'qualified adult'. However, the underlying concept of dependency was not changed.

[20] Cousins, *The Irish social welfare system*, ch. 7: 'The Implementation of the EU Equality Directive: Individualisation or Dependency'.

4.2 Recent studies

The issue of the treatment of households in the Irish social welfare system has been considered in a number of recent reports.[21] However, the conclusions of these reports have generally been disappointingly weak and there is an absence of a clear policy direction in relation to the choices between dependency and individualisation. While a number of organisations have called for individualisation of benefits, these proposals have generally been at a very rhetorical level and have not worked out the difficult questions as to how to move to an individualised system of payment without adverse social policy consequences. For example, the Expert Working Group on the integration of the tax and social welfare system carried out a computer modelling exercise on a totally independent system of tax and social welfare. This showed that the system would be extremely costly, and would not be well targeted in terms of addressing financial need. It would also involve re-distribution from single people and dual-earner couples to single-earner married couples. And it could have undesirable social effects, such as encouraging couples to transfer ownership of assets from the non-earning spouse to the earning spouse.

While the present dependency-based model is not appropriate to changing socio-economic structures and while it tends to discourage women's participation in the labour force, much more detailed consideration is needed in order to establish alternative proposals. An interdepartmental committee chaired by the Department of Social, Community and Family Affairs is currently carrying out research on this issue with a view to developing proposal for future policy development.

5 European unity and its consequences

It is not at all clear that there will in fact be a *convergence* of national social security systems in Europe in the short term. The social protection issues relevant in the Irish context are often quite different from those in other European countries. Ireland has, for example, a much younger population and a much higher proportion of children. Therefore, pension problems are much less of an issue at this time. Nor is it clear that there has been any intentional convergence of the Irish social welfare system towards a European model in recent years, and there is little evidence that the Irish social policy makers have paid a blind bit of notice to the

---

[21] Review Group on the Treatment of Households in the Social Welfare Code, *Report,* Dublin: Stationery Office, 1991; Expert Working Group on the Integration of the Tax and Social Welfare Systems, *Integrating tax and social welfare,* Dublin: Stationery Office, 1996.

European Union recommendations on Minimum Income or the Convergence of Social Protection Policies.

The most obvious area in which Irish social welfare policy *has* been affected by external factors is in relation to the rate of social insurance contributions, where there is continuous pressure from Irish manufacturers in competition with the United Kingdom to lower the levels of Irish social insurance contributions. This has been reflected in a number of reductions in Irish social insurance charges over the last number of years.[22] Given the lower levels of trade with other European countries and the lesser importance of wage costs in much of that trade, there has been much less pressure in relation to convergence with social policy trends in other European countries. In addition, although the numbers are increasing, labour mobility between Ireland and European Union countries other than the United Kingdom has traditionally been quite low. While these factors are likely to become increasingly important in the future, it is not necessarily obvious that convergence of national social security systems will be more marked in the coming five to ten years than it has been in the past five to ten. Given that the levels of Irish social welfare payments are generally comparatively low in European terms (although overall expenditure is quite high because of the high levels of unemployment and inactivity) it is not clear that convergence, if it was to take place, would hold significant dangers for the quality of social welfare in this country.

In relation to *Economic and Monetary Union*, Ireland intends to be one of the countries which will enter the EMU when it is originally established. With a view to that aim and because it suited its policy of keeping borrowing levels low, the Irish Department of Finance has been pointing to the importance of achieving EMU guidelines for a number of years now, and this has been accepted by successive Governments. Originally, there was considerable concern amongst anti-poverty organisations that this would give rise to consequential difficulties for social policy spending. However, because of the very rapid rate of growth in the Irish economy, with a consequent buoyancy in tax revenues, this has not, in fact, created significant problems. It is predicted that Ireland's economy will continue to grow at a high rate over the next decade and if this is, in fact, the case, compliance with the EMU criteria probably will not create problems for social welfare spending. At a macro-economic level, most Irish economic commentators would see European unity as a good thing for the Irish economy generally as it assisted in enforcing careful management of the public finances while at the same time providing significant financial support to the Irish economy by way of the Structural Funds. In so far as this is the case, it obviously has indirect beneficial implications for social welfare policy generally.

An area in which *European Union law* has had direct implications for Irish social welfare policy is in relation to the introduction of equality for men and women.

---

[22] *Social Insurance in Ireland*, Dublin: Department of Social Welfare, 1996.

Again, the outcome here would generally be seen as being positive in that the Irish Government was forced to introduce equality legislation at least a number of years before they would otherwise have done so. It should, however, be pointed out that the Government has subsequently introduced equality in relation to a number of areas of family payments where this is not required by European Union law, and it seems likely that Equal Treatment legislation would have been introduced at some stage by a domestic Government even in the absence of any European Union obligation in this regard. The other area in which European Union law has a direct impact in Ireland is in relation to Free Movement of Workers. Given that many Irish people emigrate to the United Kingdom to work and return here following retirement, a significant number of persons living in the Republic of Ireland (75,000 in 1995) are in receipt of United Kingdom retirement and widows' pensions. However, similar bilateral provisions did exist between Ireland and the United Kingdom prior to joining the EEC as it then was.

6 Conclusion and comments

The basis of the Irish social welfare system was established when Ireland was part of the United Kingdom, and Ireland's colonial and postcolonial status has had an important influence on the development of the Irish system. The Irish system has aimed to provide a basic minimum level of support for people out of the workforce rather than aiming for high levels of income replacement. However, one should not overemphasise comparisons with the United Kingdom model.

In the first place, the Irish system applied to a workforce which remained heavily agricultural until the 1960s and still retains a much higher level of agricultural employment than the United Kingdom. Accordingly, the social insurance system in Ireland applied in a very different context and, given that insurance was only extended to the self-employed in 1988, affected a much smaller proportion of the workforce. In contrast to the Beveridgean model, the unification of the Irish social insurance system which took place in the 1950s was explicitly *not* solidaristic.[23] More recently, the Irish and United Kingdom systems have tended to diverge in many ways with the neo-liberal approach to policy adopted in the United Kingdom not being followed in Ireland. In contrast to the 1950s (and to the United Kingdom Government's review of social security in the 1980s), the Government appointed Commission on Social Welfare which reported in 1986 *was* explicitly solidaristic in its approach. While no Government ever explicitly responded to the recommendations of the Commission, in practice many of its key recommendations have been adopted, with significant increases in many rates of payment and

---

[23] Cousins, *The Irish social welfare system*, p. 20.

the extension of social insurance to the self-employed and civil and public servants.

Figure 3: Distribution of cash and tax benefits, 1987.[24]

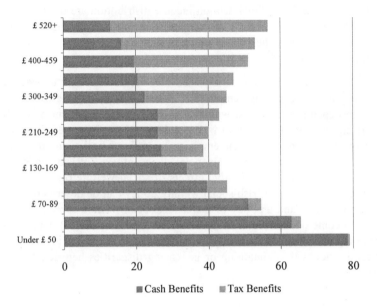

Research indicates that income inequality and poverty remained fairly constant in the period 1980 to 1987, and that poverty has declined in the period from 1987 to 1994.[25] A comparative study of income distribution suggests that, while Ireland's income is distributed comparatively unequally compared to richer countries, it is not particularly unequal compared to countries with similar or lower levels of GDP *per capita*.[26] However, Irish studies have suggested strong class based inequalities in terms of income redistribution. For example, it has been found that in 1973 and 1980 farmers benefited significantly from direct transfers from the State (not including indirect transfers by way of price supports), and that because of the

---

[24] Source: Central Statistics Office, *Redistributive Effect of State Taxes and Benefits.*

[25] Central Statistics Office, *Redistributive effects of state taxes and benefits on household incomes in 1987,* Dublin: Stationery Office, 1995; Calan *et al., Poverty in the 1990's.* While the total number falling below a poverty line drawn at 50% or 60% of average household income has actually risen between 1987 and 1994, the numbers falling below a 40% line have dropped, and measurements of the 'depth' of poverty show a drop in that period.

[26] T. Callan and B. Nolan, 'Income distribution and redistribution: Ireland in comparative perspective', in: J. Goldthorpe and C. Whelan (Eds.), *The development of industrial society in Ireland,* Oxford 1992.

low levels of direct taxes which they paid, all farm categories regardless of their income levels received substantially more in income transfers than they paid by way of taxation.[27] At the same time, the middle classes benefit from the largely unseen support of tax expenditures in relation to house purchase, health care costs and personal and occupational pensions.

Unfortunately, the fact that official data on income distribution are only available up to 1987 and that no analysis on a social class basis has been published, means that we cannot yet analyze the impact of the social welfare system in terms of redistribution over the period of the last decade.

Official social welfare policy over this period has been solidaristic in the sense that both policy and practice have emphasised the need to protect the living standards of those dependent on social welfare. As we have seen, all social welfare rates have risen faster than the cost of living and some have increased faster than earnings. However, there is also an emphasis in official policy in 'rewarding work' and a recurrent concern with financial disincentives. Official policy has shown little interest in the redistributive effects of social welfare (or other) policies. Thus the extent to which Irish social welfare policy can be described as solidaristic is quite limited and a policy of increasing social welfare support to those in the lowest income deciles (so as to decrease the depth of poverty) is not – in a rapidly growing economy – necessarily inconsistent with increases in overall income inequality nor with maintaining or increasing disparities between different social classes.

---

[27] R. Breen *et al., Understanding contemporary Ireland,* Dublin 1990.

VIII Italy

Gian Guido Balandi and Simonetta Renga

1 Introduction

1.1 The Italian social security system

Article 38 of the Constitution is the fundamental basis of the Italian social security system. This article states: 'Any citizen who is unable to work and without the means regarded as necessary to live on has a right to maintenance and social assistance. Workers have a right to means adequate to the necessities of their lives in the event of accident at work, sickness, invalidity, old age, involuntary unemployment. Those who are invalid or have mental disorders have a right to education and professional training. The objectives of this article are pursued by bodies and institutions set up or integrated by the State. Private assistance is free'.

The Italian social security system is essentially based on social insurance principles in relation to old age and retirement pensions (survivors' pensions included), and benefits in the event of invalidity, sickness, accidents at work, occupational diseases and unemployment. The system is strictly linked to the payment of contributions by workers and employers. Therefore, eligibility and, in many cases, the benefit level depend on the occupational status of the claimant. Family benefits and childcare allowances (maternity benefits) are also granted to the working population, as we shall see. However, there are some benefits which are available to all citizens. These are: the *Assegno sociale* (Social Assistance Benefit, formerly: *Pensione sociale,* Social Pension), for citizens over 65 whose income is below a certain level; the *Pensione d'invalidità civile* (Civil Invalidity Pension), for all invalid citizens aged between 18 and 65 years; and the *Indennità di accompagnamento* (Disabled Mobility Allowance), for the disabled. Recently, occupational pensions have also been regulated. They cannot, however, as yet be regarded as a main benefit in our system.

1.2 A brief sketch of the main benefits paid by the social security system

1.2.1 Old age pensions

In Italy, the whole field of pensions schemes has recently been reformed.[1] However, the old system is still operative for those workers who had a contribution record of 18 years or more at the time the reform was enacted, *i.e.* on December 31st, 1995. Those workers who had paid contributions for less than 18 years will have their pensions calculated according to the old rules in relation to the contributions paid until December 31st, 1995, while the new rules will be applied with respect to contributions paid after that date. As regards their pensionable age the old rules will be applied. The new scheme takes full effect for those workers who, on the December 31st, 1995, did not yet have a contribution record. Pensions under the old system are paid to those workers who:
• have a contribution record of 15 years, if they had paid contributions for at least 15 years on December 31st, 1992
• have a contribution record of 20 years, if they had paid contributions for less than 15 years on December 31st, 1992. There is, however, a transitory period for the application of this rule
• are 60 (women) or 65 (men) years of age. The pensionable age is lower for a transitory period of two years. More precisely: it is set at 58/63 years until June 30th, 1998, and at 59/64 years until December 31st, 1999).

The pension is earnings-related. It is calculated as a percentage of the average salaries of the last 10 years of work for those who were already employed on December 31st, 1992, and as a percentage of the average working-life salaries for those who have been employed after December 31st, 1992. The amount of the pension also depends on one's insurance record: a worker with 40 years of insurance receives 80% of his or her former salary.

Pensions under the new system are paid to workers who meet all the following conditions:
• the claimant has paid contributions for at least 5 years
• the claimant is 57 years of age or, alternatively, has paid contributions for at least 40 years
• the amount of the claimant's pension is not less than 1.2 times the amount of the *Assegno sociale* (about 9,594,000 Italian Lire or € 4,955 a year) or, alternatively, the claimant's age is at least 65 years.

---

[1] By Act no. 335/1995. See also *decreto legislativo* of December 12th, 1992, no. 503 and *decreto legislativo* of August 11th, 1993, no. 374.

The pensionable age is therefore flexible within a period of 8 years, from 57 to 65, equal for men and women. The pension is calculated in relation to the contributions paid and to the age of retirement.

Under the old system, there was also a so-called *Pensione di anzianità* (Retirement pension). This pension is due to disappear in 2008. At present, it is paid to those workers who are at least 55 years old and have a contribution record of 35 years, or alternatively just 37 years' worth of contributions. These requirements will increase gradually up to 57 years of age by 2006, or 40 years' worth of contribution by 2008. The old age pensions scheme is financed through workers' and employers' contributions, as well as through State participation.

Assegno sociale (formerly *Pensione sociale*) is a social assistance benefit paid as of right to citizens over 65 years of age whose income is below the amount of L. 7,995,000[2] (€ 4,129) per annum. The income of the spouse is also taken into account to determine entitlement to benefits, but in this case the threshold is doubled. The amount of pension is reduced in relation to the income of the recipients; if he or she is married, the spouse's income is also taken into account. The amount of the pension is L. 7,995,000 (€ 4,129) a year.

1.2.2 Invalidity benefits

There are three kinds of invalidity benefits in Italy: the *Pensione d'invalidità* (Invalidity Benefits Scheme), the *Pensione d'invalidità civile* (Civil Invalidity Pension) and the *Indennità di accompagnamento* (Disabled Mobility Allowance). Under the Invalidity Benefits Scheme,[3] the law regards as 'invalid' a person afflicted by a permanent reduction of up to 1/3 of his or her capacity to work in jobs which fit his or her professional aptitudes, owing to physical or mental defects. A person is considered 'unable to work' if, as a consequence of infirmity or a physical or mental defect, he or she is totally and permanently unable to carry out any work.

Entitlement to invalidity benefits depends on the fulfilment of contributions and insurance conditions, that is: 5 years of insurance; and 5 years of contributions, three of which during the last 5 years preceding the application. An 'invalid' person has a right to the so-called *Assegno ordinario d'invalidità* (Regular Invalidity Allowance). The benefit is calculated in the same way as the old age pension. Once the pensionable age is reached, the benefit is converted into an old age pension, provided that the claimant fulfils the relevant requirements. Otherwise he or she is left with the original benefit. A person regarded as 'unable to work' has the right to a disability pension, the amount of which is the same as the *Assegno ordinario d'invalidità* plus an extra amount targeted to top up the pension to the level

---

[2] All the amounts of benefits and thresholds refer to 1999.
[3] Act of June 12th, 1984, no. 222.

it would have been, had the pensionable age been reached. Again, the disability pension is calculated according to the same criteria as the old age pension. The changes regarding the latter, which have been described above, also affect, therefore, the former. Contributions are paid by both employers and employees but the scheme also relies on public funds. Finally, if the invalidity or inability has been caused by an occupational accident or disease, entitlement to benefit is not conditioned by contribution requirements.

The invalidity pension, *Pensione d'invalidità civile,* is a public assistance benefit for those invalid persons aged 18 to 65, who have a permanent reduction in their capacity to work of at least 74%, and who do not fulfil insurance requirements.[4] The benefit, paid as of a right, amounts to about L. 350,000 (or € 181) a month *plus* one fictitious 13th month. No benefit is granted if the applicant's own income exceeds a certain level. *Indennità di accompagnamento* is an allowance paid to all those invalid persons in need of continuous care as a result of a 100% inability to work. This benefit is not dependent on income requirements and is paid also to the recipients of other invalidity benefits. The amount of this benefit is around L. 800,000 (or € 413) a month.

1.2.3 Benefits in the event of occupational accidents and diseases

This insurance scheme is operative in relation to dangerous activities. In the industrial sector work carried out through automatic machines, or work carried out in plants where these machines are installed, is considered dangerous. Moreover, 28 specific activities – such as construction, draining, loading and unloading, including activities subsidiary and complementary to these main categories of dangerous work – have also been declared dangerous by the law, independent of the presence of automatic machines.[5] This definition of dangerous work covers the great majority of dependent workers. In the agricultural sector, practically all activities are regarded as dangerous. The insurance protection covers all employees who carry out manual activity, all workers employed in plants where there are automatic machines, as well as works superintendents, home workers and those employed in housework. The concept of manual activity is thus interpreted in a very broad sense.

In the event of temporary total inability to carry out the job for which one has been employed, the insurance provides for a daily allowance equivalent to 60% of the wages received in the last 12 months of work. This percentage is increased to 75% when the inability lasts for over 90 days. Temporary partial inability to carry out one's job is not covered by the insurance. Permanent inability to work – total or partial – is compensated for by a benefit equal to the employee's wage at the

---

[4] Act of March 3rd, 1971, no. 118.
[5] See *decreto del Presidente della Repubblica* of June 30th, 1965, no. 1124.

time of the accident, if the degree of inability is over 79%. When the degree of inability is below 80%, the benefit is proportionally reduced. Degrees of inability under 11% are not covered by the insurance. If it is not possible to determine an employee's wage because of a lack of continuity in his or her work record, the amount of the benefit is calculated on the basis of legal criteria. In any event, the relevant wages (effective or legal) are bound by law to a minimum and a maximum. In the event of a 100% inability, the recipient has a right to an extra allowance when he or she is in need of another person's care.

In order to be covered by the insurance, occupational diseases must be included in a specific legal list. Alternatively, the claimant must prove that the disease was caused by the job carried out. The scheme is financed entirely by the employers. No contribution or insurance requirements are made upon workers. Precarious workers are therefore included in the scheme. Medical assistance is provided by the National Health Service.

1.2.4 Survivors' pensions

Survivors' pensions are granted to the pensioner's spouse, sons and daughters, and under certain conditions to his or her parents, brothers and sisters. Benefits are provided in the event of the pensioner was entitled to old age and invalidity pensions. Sons and daughters of the pensioner (and equivalent persons) become entitled to the benefit if they are under 18 years of age, or students under 26 years of age and unemployed, or invalid. The right to survivors' benefits is conditional on the pensioner having been responsible for the maintenance of his or her relative. The surviving spouse has a right to 60% of the original pension; each son and daughter has a right to 20% of the original pension if their right concurs with the spouse's, otherwise they are entitled to 40% of the original pension. The total amount of survivors' pensions can never exceed the original pension.

In the event of an accident at work or an occupational disease, the workers' relatives are entitled to special pensions: to *Rendita ai superstiti* (Survivors' Special Pension) provided under the accidents at work and occupational disease insurance, and to *Pensione privilegiata ai superstiti* (Survivors' Privileged Pension) provided under the old age and invalidity scheme. When the insured worker dies before having fulfilled the contributions requirements for a pension, his or her relatives have a right to a lump sum if their income is below a certain amount. A lump sum is also paid to the worker's spouse when he or she loses the entitlement to survivor's pension as the result of a re-marriage.

The pension is reduced when the income of the recipient exceeds a certain amount. There are three income thresholds, ranging from L. 27,000,000 (or € 13,944) to L. 36,000,000 (or € 18,592) to L. 45,000,000 (or € 23,241). If the recipient's income passes these tresholds the pension is reduced by 15%, 40% and 50% respectively. There is no reduction, however, if the recipient has dependent children.

1.2.5 Sickness benefits

Statutory sickness benefits are paid for a period of 180 days a year; those who are sick for a period longer than 180 days are not covered as regards income protection. The amount of the benefit usually equals 50% of the workers' average daily earnings, but it can be increased according to the duration of illness. The statutory benefit is supplemented, through collective agreements, by the employer so as to reach an amount very close to the workers' usual earnings. There is no definition of sickness for the purpose of these benefits: the state of illness is proved by the claimant through a medical certificate, which has to be sent to the institute paying the benefit, the *Istituto nazionale per la previdenza sociale* (INPS, National Institute for Social Security). Contributions are paid by both employees and employers.[6]

1.2.6 Maternity benefits

There is compulsory parental leave for women during a two month period before birth and a three month period after birth.[7] Furthermore, women have the right to:
• six months (optional) leave during the child's first year of age
• days off to care for children under three years of age when they fall ill
• two paid hours off for feeding children under one year old (the two hours' wage is paid by the social security system).

During the compulsory parental leave, women are entitled to a daily benefit called *Indennità di maternità* (Maternity Benefit). This benefit is equal to 80% of the daily medium global wage earned in the last month's work. During the optional parental leave, women are also entitled to *Indennità di maternità*; the amount of benefit is, however, reduced to 30% of the daily wages. Benefits are not conditioned by insurance and contributions requirements. The scheme is financed by contributions to sickness benefits (see above). Women on *Indennità di maternità* also have a right to fictitious contributions, necessary for determining entitlement to pensions and the amount of pensions (*e.g.* fictitious contributions). The recent reform of pensions has extended the right to fictitious contributions for paid leave.[8]

Indennità di maternità is paid to subordinate employees, workers on *Indennità di mobilità* (Unemployed Mobility Allowance),[9] workers on short-time earning

---

[6] See Act of February 29th, 1980, no. 33; Act of December 23rd, 1978, no. 833; Act of April 23rd, 1981, no. 155; and Act of November 11th, 1983, no. 638.

[7] See Act of December 30th, 1971, no. 1204.

[8] *Cf.* Act no. 335/1995.

[9] Act no. 223/1991: the periods of parental leave are not taken into account to determine *Indennità di mobilità* duration.

funds[10] or unemployed (provided the leave period starts within a certain period from the last working day), and self-employed workers. The provisions of the *Indennità di maternità* have been extended to adoptive mothers.[11] Optional leave and the relevant benefit, as well as time off for childcare, are now also granted to fathers, both natural and adoptive, as an alternative to optional leave for the mother. In exceptional cases, such as the mother's severe infirmity, the father has a right to parental leave during the three month period after birth and to the relevant benefits.[12] Legislation also provides:

• the crediting of fictitious contributions for 170 days for each child in the case of parental leave for reasons of education or assistance to children aged up to 6 years, for the purpose of entitlement to the new contributory pension benefits[13]

• for women, a credit as regards the age of retirement under the reformed system of 4 months per child, with a maximum of 12 months.[14]

Finally, the law permits women to pay contributions towards their retirement pensions for periods of inactivity due to pregnancy and childcare.[15]

1.2.7 Family benefits and additions for dependants

Additions for dependants are granted in the Italian social security system through the *Assegno per il nucleo familiare* (Family Benefit). This is a general family benefit. It was introduced in 1988,[16] and has brought under unified legislation all family supplements and additions to benefits of the private and public sectors. The concept of family includes: legally married spouses; children under 18 years of age (or incapable of work); sisters and brothers; and grandchildren under 18 (or incapable of work, orphaned and with no income). The benefit is also paid to lone-parent families. The *Assegno per il nucleo familiare* is paid to employees, to the unemployed (as an addition to unemployment benefits and to *Indennità di mobilità*), to employees on short-time earning funds, to pensioners, to recipients of occupational accidents and disease benefits, to recipients of sickness benefits, to employees on parental leave and to women during maternity leave. Part-time workers are entitled to full weekly family benefits when they work at least 24 hours a week, working hours of different employment relationships being aggre-

---

[10] The Short-time earning funds pay 80% of their former income to workers who have been suspended from work or whose working time has been reduced as a result of a company crisis.

[11] *Corte costituzionale* no. 332/1988.

[12] *Corte costituzionale* no. 1/1987 and no. 341/1991.

[13] Act no. 335/1995.

[14] See Act no. 335/1995. Act no. 448/1198 has also provided for a maternity lump sum. This is paid to all mothers whose income is below a certain amount and who are not entitled to other maternity benefits.

[15] *Decreto legislativovo* no. 503/1992 (article 14).

[16] By Act of May 13th, 1988, no. 15.

gated. Part-time employees working less than 24 hours a week are entitled to family benefits in proportion to the number of days spent at work, regardless of the number of hours worked per day.[17] These additions aim to provide a minimum income for the family as a whole.

The amount of the benefit is determined on the basis of the size of the family and the level of taxable family income. There is a scale of benefits in the form of fixed amounts corresponding to different levels of family income and family size. For any number of children exceeding seven the benefit amount remains fixed. If the family income from subordinate work, or from social security benefits related to subordinate work, totals less than 70% of the total family income, no benefits are granted. Also, no benefits are granted when the family income mainly stems from self-employment, from business activities or from capital. Benefits are calculated for the whole family and paid to the applicant only once for the same family. As the benefit is included in the taxable income, it is usual for the parent earning a lower income to apply for it. The financing of family benefits is based on both employers' contributions and public assistance contributions.

Finally, insured persons with invalid dependants are granted a credit of fictitious contributions towards their right to pension under the new contributory system. The amount of the credit ranges from 25 days per year to a maximum of 24 months. The credit can be granted to both spouses in the family.[18]

1.2.8 Unemployment benefits

Italian social security includes three kinds of unemployment benefits: short-time earning funds, *Indennità di mobilità,* and unemployment insurance benefits. The employees of the industrial, agricultural, building and commercial sectors – and of some other specific sectors or companies determined by law[19] – have a right to *short-time earning funds,* if they are suspended from work or if their working time has been reduced as a result of a company crisis. In some cases one is required to have been employed by the affected firm for at least 90 days in order to qualify for short-time earning funds. Short-time benefits are calculated in relation to former income: their amount is equivalent to 80% of this former income for each working hour lost between zero and the contractual working time, but not for working time exceeding 40 hours a week. The relevant income is that fixed by the collective agreements of the time when the employee was put on short-time. The benefit can last from 3 months to 4 years, depending on the nature of the crisis that the firm is

---

[17] Act no. 863/1984, article 5 VI c.

[18] Act no. 335/1995.

[19] Such as the newspaper sector, political parties, travel agencies, transport companies and craft companies which have as their major customer an industrial firm in crisis.

in. The scheme is financed primarily through public funds. However, contributions are also paid by employers and (to a much lesser extent) by employees.[20]

Within the same sectors which are covered by the short-time earning funds, workers who become involuntarily unemployed have a right to a special unemployment benefit called *Indennità di mobilità,* or 'mobility allowance'.[21] However, this benefit is reserved for those workers who have been employed for at least 12 months by the firm affected by redundancies. Of these 12 months, at least 6 months must have been spent working normally. The benefit is calculated on the basis of the employee's former income, *i.e.* the salary fixed by collective agreements at the time when he or she lost his or her job. For the first 12 months the benefit is equivalent to 80% of the former income. It is subsequently reduced to about 64%. The benefit duration is 12 months, increased to 24 for workers of 40 years and over, and to 36 months for workers of 50 years and over. In the south of Italy, an extra 12 months are added. The mobility allowance is financed by public funds and employers' contributions.

Unemployment insurance is a general benefit paid to workers involuntarily unemployed who have been affiliated for at least two years and who have paid contributions for at least one year during the two years preceding their application for a benefit. Workers who are not covered by the short-time earning funds and by the *Indennità di mobilità* have only this benefit to fall back on in the event of unemployment. Contributions are paid by the employers; the scheme is also financed through public funds. The benefit amounts to 30% of the employee's medium wage during the three months preceding unemployment. The benefit duration is 180 days.[22]

Once the benefits paid under these three schemes expire, unemployed workers have no other income protection on which to fall back.

2 Maintaining living standards

2.1 Living standards of formerly employed workers

The living standards of formerly employed workers are maintained under a number of schemes, which have already been extensively discussed above. As for the

---

[20] See Act of May 20th, 1975, no. 164; and Act of July 23rd, 1991, no. 223.

[21] See Act of July 23rd, 1991, no. 223.

[22] See *regio decreto* of December 30th, 1923, no. 3158; *regio decreto* of December 7th, 1924, no. 2270; *regio decreto legge* of October 4th, 1935, no. 1827; *regio decreto legge* of April 14th, 1939, no. 636 and Act of May 20th, 1988, no. 160.

old age and inability pension schemes, under the old rules (see above) the pension is earnings-related and calculated as a percentage of the average salaries of the last 10 years of work for those who were already employed on December 31st, 1992, and as a percentage of the average working life salaries for those who were employed after that date. The amount of pension depends also on the insurance record: a worker who has been affiliated for 40 years receives 80% of his or her former salary. It can be said therefore that the living standard is more or less maintained. Under the new rules the situation is quite different. The pension is calculated, in fact, in relation to the contributions paid. The new scheme's capacity to maintain the workers' previous living standard depends, therefore, very much on the claimant's contribution record. It must be considered, however, that the contributions are calculated as a percentage of one's salary. Employees who earn more pay higher contributions and receive higher pensions. One's former living standard is thus reproduced. The same considerations are valid for the inability pensions. These benefits are, in fact, calculated according to the same criteria as the old age pension.

The occupational accidents and disease scheme can also be regarded as one of those which maintain the workers' living standards. As mentioned earlier, it provides a daily allowance equal to 60% of the wages of the last 12 months' work in the event of temporary absolute inability to carry out the job for which the worker had been employed. The percentage is, however, increased to 75% when the inability lasts for over 90 days. If the degree of inability is over 79%, permanent inability to work, absolute or partial, is compensated by a benefit equivalent to the employee's wage at the time of the accident. If the inability degree is less than 80%, the benefit is reduced proportionally. The short-time earning funds maintain the workers' living standards too: its benefits equal 80% of the former salary. However, the situation is different where the *Indennità di mobilità* is concerned. Here benefits amount to 80% of the former income only for the first 12 months; after that, it drops to a mere 64%. Moreover, the benefit is of a limited duration, as we have seen.

Unemployment insurance (30% of the previous wage for 180 days) and statutory sickness benefits (50% of the workers' daily average earnings) cannot be said to maintain the workers' living standards. Sickness benefits, in particular, are supplemented, through collective agreements, by the employer so as to reach an amount very close to the workers' previous earnings. The childcare benefit called *Indennità di maternità* is able to maintain the workers' living standards only in relation to compulsory maternity leave, when it is equivalent to 80% of the daily medium global wage earned in the last month's work.

2.2 A shift from public to private security schemes

In Italy, a shift is taking place from public to private schemes, due to the financial crisis caused by high public expenditure. The recent pensions reform from an earnings-related system to strictly contributions-related is a case in point. It calls for private pensions to supplement public pensions, the amounts of benefits in which are going to decrease. Supplementary pensions have recently been regulated in the Italian income security system. Legislative interventions have gradually favoured the creation of private funds through fiscal concessions.[23]

In the general frame envisaged by the legislator, the risks to be covered by private arrangements are the same as in the public system, *i.e.* old age, invalidity, and death. As yet, however, the schemes which were actually set up only concern old age pensions. Participation is voluntary. Both entitlement to benefits and the level of benefits are strictly linked to the amount of contributions paid, in accordance with common insurance principles. The law has set minimum age conditions – the pensionable age has to be the same as that fixed by the compulsory insurance to which the worker belongs – and minimum insurance periods to be fulfilled in order to gain entitlement to benefits. Finally, the law has provided a complex system of direct and indirect controls on the management of funds for the sake of their designated purpose.

2.3 Social security and family responsibilities

As we have already mentioned, family responsibilities surrounding child bearing and caring are compensated through the *Indennità di maternità*. This benefit also provides the credit of fictitious contributions towards pensions. Under the new contributory pension system this provision has been extended to parental leave for the purpose of education and assistance to children aged up to 6 years. Moreover, women are granted a credit, as regards their age of retirement, of 4 months per child (with a maximum of 12 months).[24] Women are also enabled to pay contributions towards their pensions for periods of inactivity due to pregnancy and childcare.[25] Nevertheless, the care of children remains inadequately covered by the *Indennità di maternità* as far as benefits, amounts and duration are concerned.

All those situations of need arising from the care of the dependants, such as the elderly and disabled, are not covered in the Italian system. Moreover, any caring activity can spoil the contribution record of claimants in relation to all insurance schemes, especially since the introduction of the new pension scheme, which is

---

[23] See *decreto legislativo* of April 21st, 1993, no. 124; *decreto legislativo* of December 30th, 1993, no. 585; Act of August 8th, 1995, no. 335.

[24] See Act no. 335/1995.

[25] *Decreto legislativo* no. 503/1992, article 14.

based on insurance principles. In general terms, a social security system essentially based upon the employment status of the claimants strongly penalises those persons who are in a situation of need and do not have a good employment record. As the care of the family is mainly entrusted to women, this can result in their exclusion from the labour market and consequently from contributory benefits. In Italy this means that they have to fall back on *Assegno sociale* or on a very small civil invalidity benefit. The only provision that addresses these situations is the above-mentioned pensions credit for insured people with invalid dependants.[26]

There are no provisions in the Italian social security system for the consequences of divorce. Lone parents are entitled, however, to the family benefit *Assegno per il nucleo familiare*. Finally, natural disasters which cause a suspension of work or a reduction in working time are addressed by short-time earning funds.

3 The level of basic social security arrangements

3.1 Benefits geared to provide a minimum income

Within the Italian social security system only three benefits provide a minimum income. The first of these is the *Integrazione al minimo*, which supplements old age and invalidity pensions under the 'earnings-based' pension schemes. This benefit has been abolished as regards pensions paid under the new rules: its role in the system should be now played by the *Assegno sociale*.[27] However, the *Integrazione al minimo* is still operative in relation to pensions paid under the old scheme. It is, in effect, a supplement which tops up pensions if they remain under a certain minimum level according to normal calculation criteria. The minimum pension provided by the invalidity and old age schemes is about L. 700,000 (or € 362) per month. In order to be entitled to this supplement pensioners must meet the minimum insurance and contributions requirements for old age and invalidity benefits. No supplement is granted if a single pensioner's annual income amounts to more than about L. 18,000,000 (or € 9,296), or if a pensioner's annual income plus that of his or her spouse amounts to more than about L. 36,000,000 (or € 18,592). For invalidity pensions these limits are set at about L. 9,200,000 (or € 4,751) and at about L. 13,900,000 (or € 7,179).

Secondly, there is the *Assegno sociale,* which is a social assistance benefit paid as of right to citizens over 65 years of age whose annual income is below the amount of L. 7,995,000 (or € 4,129). The income of the spouse is also taken into account

---

[26] Act no. 335/1995.
[27] By Act no. 335/1995.

to determine entitlement to benefits, but in this case the threshold is simply doubled. The maximum amount of the pension is L. 7,995,000 (or € 4,129) a year; this amount is reduced in relation to the income of the recipients. Thirdly, the invalidity pension *Pensione d'invalidità civile*, as we have already mentioned, is a public assistance benefit for invalids between 18 to 65 who do not fulfil insurance requirements. The benefit, paid as of a right, amounts to about L. 350,000 (or € 181) a month for 13 months a year. No pension is paid if the applicant's own income is over a certain level.

At the national level, the Italian social security system has no other benefits which provide a minimum income. In some regions local legislation provides social assistance for people with no income, mainly the long-term unemployed whose right to unemployment benefits has expired and who face a particularly hard situation. However these various local benefits are generally very low.[28]

3.2 The level of benefits

The level of the benefits just described is fixed by the relevant legislation with no specific reference to any poverty line indicator whatsoever. Their amounts are clearly very low, and as such far below the minimum required to live decently, as envisaged by article 38 of the Italian Constitution. The criteria used to fix the benefit amount are strongly influenced by budget constraints, which is why the benefits are so low. This low amount is, however, automatically adjusted each year to the changes in prices. These changes are calculated through a specific index, called ISTAT, which monitors changes in the prices of the main goods bought by the families.

4 Household and individual

The only benefit in the Italian social security system which is specifically awarded to the household is the *Assegno per il nucleo familiare* (see above). All the other social security benefits are granted to individuals. The household income is, however, relevant where the *Assegno sociale* and the *Integrazione al minimo* are concerned. As we have already said, the *Assegno sociale* is a social assistance benefit. It has a threshold which is doubled for claimants with a spouse. The spouse's income is also taken into account in calculating the exact amount of the benefit. The *Integrazione al minimo* for old-style old age and invalidity pensions is a sup-

---

[28] Art. 59 of Act no. 449/1997 has provided for a minimum income benefit to be paid to those who have an income lower than L. 500,000 a month and who cannot work for physical, psychical or social reasons. This benefit is experimental and it is paid at a local level.

plement which tops up insufficient pensions. Here also, the pensioner's income plus that of his or her spouse is taken into account to determine entitlement.

5 Judicial remedies

In Italy, a specific procedure is followed in cases concerning social security. This procedure takes place at two levels: the administrative and the judicial. The administrative level is the compulsory first step for the claimant in order to have the agency's decision reviewed. The object of the administrative proceedings is the decision taken regarding the benefit, which is re-examined in all its aspects: in other words, the administrative commission in charge of the case is not conditioned in its ruling by the claimant's specific suit. That is to say that administration is given the power of entirely changing its decisions before being brought before a court. The claimant has a term to present his or her suit, but it is not a compulsory one. In fact, in the administrative proceedings concerning social security no preclusions whatsoever are taken into account.

After having experienced the administrative procedure, the dissatisfied claimant can start a civil process. Proceedings in the matter of labour law and social security legislation are regulated by a special procedure, which theoretically aims at the characteristics of an oral process, concentrated and uninterrupted. This procedure has been conceived as very flexible: during the process new facts may be introduced (which is inadmissable in ordinary civil processes where the case is definitively set by the suit presented at the beginning of the action). Moreover, if the claimant loses his case he is not required to pay all the proceedings expenses (nor those of the successful opposing party), unless his claim was blatantly baseless or temerarious. Unfortunately, there are no facilities for the payment of legal assistance.[29] In practice, even processes of this kind are very slow. They are never completed in a single session or hearing, and they can last from two to four years. This is because the theoretical principles underlying this special procedure are not implemented through specific rules. Moreover, the number of processes is very high while the courts are badly understaffed.

Another obstacle to legal security in this area is represented by the complexity and obscurity of social security legislation, which, among other things, is affected by very frequent modifications. This may cause different interpretations of the same provision (which may even result in the withdrawal of social security benefits), an increase in litigation, and a growing complexity of the social system, which becomes more and more difficult to disentangle, not just for laymen and their lawyers but even for the legislator and the administrators themselves.

---

[29] It should be mentioned, however, that trade unions provide their member with free legal assistance.

6 European unity and its consequences

For some people, the possible convergence of national social security systems in Europe is a dream; for others a nightmare. Realistically, the outcome is likely to be a mixture of both. Most recent literature stresses both the importance and the variability of political consensus on the actual organisation of social security. This is one of the most important observations which can be made at the moment. The European Union is moving towards a greater homogeneity in social and economic conditions, but the point at which this will be reflected in a real European consensus on welfare organisation is still far away. The popular approach to these themes is also still largely influenced by considerations and emotions which stem from the culture and history of each national system.

Legal, economic and social literature have convincingly illustrated the differences between Beveridgean and Bismarckian patterns, between social insurance and social assistance, etc. Actually, in many of the European legal systems these two models are at present more or less inextricably interwoven. According to A. Laurent, 'This partial merger of both entities – social security and social assistance – is testimony to the consolidation of the notion of social security as such'.[30] This state of affairs, however, does not solve the problem of the social perception of the existence of two different models of social relief, which may constitute a serious obstacle to European harmonisation. At least, the 'Eurocrats' who compiled the Programme of Action for implementing fundamental social rights, in 1989, took this problem seriously enough to reckon that European harmonisation *"n'était ni souhaitable, ni souhaitée, le Danois, par exemple, refusant d'être assaisonnés à la sauce Bismarckienne et les Allemands ne voulant pas entendre, chez eux, l'anglais de Beveridge"*.[31]

In any case, the Italian system of social security could profit from some aspects of modernisation, and at the same time be endangered by the introduction of institutions or practices alien to its history. A more comprehensive and simplified system of protection in the event of industrial accidents and occupational diseases – the Italian system is still inspired by the patterns of the original Act of 1898 – would be welcome. A heavy prevalence of private pension schemes, typical of some northern countries, could, however, accelerate the crisis of Italian public pensions schemes, with undesirable social effects.

As regards the financial conditions to be met in order to be allowed to take part in the EMU in 1999, they have exerted, they exert, and they will exert a formidable pressure on the Italian social security system. Almost every day, right wing politi-

---

[30] D. Pieters, *Introduction into the Basic Principles of Social Security* (Deventer 1993), p. 6.

[31] "...is neither desirable nor desired as long as, for example, the Danes refuse to be seasoned with a Bismarckian sauce and the Germans do not want to hear Beveridgean English within their walls". A. Laurent, 'Rapport introductif', in: *Social Security and Europe 1992* (Deventer 1990), p. 1-30, esp. p. 3.

cal parties – now in the opposition – attack the public pension scheme, emphasis-ing the necessity of cutting it in order to be admitted into the club of the EMU countries. The second best target of this political pressure is the National Health Service.

As has been explained above, pensions legislation was reformed in 1995.[32] This reform has deeply changed the structure of the public pension scheme. In order to make these changes socially acceptable the Government has provided a long tran-sitory period during which a large (but annually decreasing) number of the old rules is kept in force. Confronted with the 'Maastricht constraints' (as they are known to the general public), the reformers of 1995[33] admit that it may become necessary to accelerate some elements of the new legislation, but not before hav-ing thoroughly checked its functioning. Much criticism is aimed at the so-called 'seniority pensions' (or early retirement pensions). Currently, the 'old' law offers early retirement to employees in the public sector who have contributed for a mere 20 or 25 years, regardless of their actual age. Employees in the private sector, on the other hand, must have contributed for at least 37 years (35 years in the original scheme, and still rising) to become entitled to early retirement. Under the new law this preferential treatment of public sector employees will be gradually abolished in about ten years, but in the meantime several tens of thousands of them apply for early retirement each year. The savings which could be realised by an abrupt and drastic rise in the requirements for early retirement (or, as some would have it, a complete repeal of all early retirement arrangements) would probably not be worth the social disruption that would follow. Therefore, the insistence on cutting re-tirement pensions appears to be mainly motivated by domestic political strife. Nevertheless, this issue may well reflect a wider economic and social project. The most important outcome of a sharp intervention in the retirement arrangements for, generally speaking, people between 50 and 60 years of age would be the dis-ruption of another section of the labour market, with far-reaching effects on sala-ries and on the social protection enjoyed by workers: a further step towards a complete deregulation of the labour market.

It is very difficult to give a simple answer to the question of whether or not Euro-pean unity would be good for Italian social security. Generally speaking, much will depend on the shape which European unity will take and, more precisely, on the question of whether supremacy will be given to political considerations or to monetary policies. If politics prevail, one may assume that a democratic body will discuss and decide – under a political responsibility – the future of social security for the whole Union. If, however, monetary policies get the upper hand, grave dangers to the social security systems of all European countries may loom ahead.

---

[32] Act of August 8th, 1995, no. 335.

[33] *I.e.* T. Treu, then Minister of Labour (and present Minister of Transports) and L. Dini, then Prime Minister (and present Minister of Foreign Affairs).

IX The Netherlands

Irene Asscher-Vonk, Frans Pennings, Cees Sparrius, and Lei Delsen

1 Introduction

The Dutch social security system aims at providing income for citizens who do not or no longer participate in the labour process as a consequence of sickness, disability, unemployment or old age.[1] They are provided with a substitute income. Under certain circumstances, citizens may also claim supplementary income if their income, either from work or from social insurance benefits, is insufficient to meet the general costs of living, or in the event of exceptional costs (children, specific medical expenses). The system has additional aims. It aims to prevent people from becoming permanently excluded from the labour market due to, for instance, disability or unemployment. It also aims at re-integrating disabled and unemployed persons into the labour market.

The Dutch social security system is embodied in a series of Acts and in civil law arrangements which are often part of collective and binding labour agreements. It grants a right to assistance in cash or in kind to a precisely defined group of persons if certain specified circumstances affect them.[2] Not all risks are covered. There is, for instance, no legal provision for the loss of income due to the care for invalid family members. Such provisions can be based on private arrangements between employers and employees, on private insurance or on private savings. In the Netherlands, these forms of non-coverage in social security are often ignored in discussions on social security. However, in this contribution attention is also focused on *statutory* social security.

The main responsibility for decision-making on social security rests firmly with the legislature. In fact, it is the legislator who determines the extent of social security, the financial resources involved, and the way in which it is financed from contributions and taxes. Moreover, the Government itself administers some of the social security regulations. It is also responsible for the implementation by others.

---

[1] For this paragraph, extensive use was made of F.M. Noordam, *Inleiding sociale-zekerheidsrecht* [An introduction to social security law] (Deventer 1996), p. 23-24.

[2] M.G. Levenbach, 'Sociale zekerheid [Social security]', in: *Sociaal Maandblad* [Social Monthly], 2(1947), p. 260-264. According to L.J.M. de Leede, *Sociaal bestuursrecht* [Social administrative law] (Alphen aan den Rijn 1985), part 6.2, this description has met with general agreement.

Typical for the Dutch system is the involvement of the social partners – employees' and employers' organisations – in preparing, formulating and implementing policy. The Government's responsibility for financing and for implementation has been under discussion over the past few years. Increasingly these responsibilities are being shifted towards private parties, in this case the employers. As a consequence, new forms of private social security law have come into being.[3] An example of this development concerns the responsibility for the financing and implementing of sickness benefits, which was recently laid in the hands of the employers (privatisation). In addition, there has been some discussion on whether or not the legislature should withdraw from its decision-making position with regard to certain risks, *e.g.* the pensions awarded to surviving relatives. Until recently, the *Algemene Weduwen- en Wezenwet* (AWW, General Widows and Orphans Act) provided widows and orphans with a basic pension. In the new *Algemene Nabestaandenwet* (ANW, General Surviving Relatives Act) benefits have become means-tested and restricted to certain categories, such as disabled and older persons. As a result, those who wish to be covered but do not meet these requirements have to take out private insurance.

1.1 A note on the history of social security in the Netherlands

In the first half of the twentieth century, the need for some sort of social security provisions was especially felt with regard to the risks connected with wage labour. This resulted in provisions against the loss of income in the *Ongevallenwet* (Accidents Act; 1901), in the *Invaliditeitswet* and the *Ziektewet* (Invalidity Act and Sickness Act; both adopted in 1913)[4] and in the *Ziekenfondsbesluit* (Health Insurance Decree; 1941). The risk of unemployment was covered only to the extent that the Government subsidised trade union and local community schemes. Unemployment benefits had no statutory basis until the *Werkloosheidswet* (WW, Unemployment Act) of 1949.[5] The costs of child rearing were met by the *Kinderbijslagwet* (Child Allowance Act) of 1939.[6]

After the Second World War the coverage and the benefit levels of the then existing social insurance schemes were substantially improved. General national insurances were established for certain risks which until then had been covered for employees only.[7] As a result, the *Algemene Ouderdomswet* (AOW, General Old Age Act; 1956), the General Widows and Orphans Act of 1959, the *Algemene Kinderbijslagwet* (General Child Allowance Act; 1963) and the *Algemene Ar-*

[3] *Ibid.*, p. 158 e.v.
[4] However, the Invalidity Act did not come into effect before 1919, the Sickness Act not before 1930.
[5] The Unemployment Act came into effect between November 1st, 1949, and July 1st, 1952.
[6] The Child Benefit Act came into effect only in 1941.
[7] De Leede, *Sociaal bestuursrecht*, p. 17.

beidsongeschiktheidswet (AAW, General Disability Act; 1976) were introduced. The *Algemene Wet Bijzondere Ziektekosten* (AWBZ, General Exceptional Medical Expenses Act; 1968) takes care of exceptional expenses. The *Algemene Bijstandswet* (ABW, General Social Assistance Act; 1963) introduced social assistance benefits to which claimants had a legal right.

From the 1980s onward the expansion of social security arrangements began to stagnate and public social security retreated in favour of private law arrangements and voluntary schemes. An example of this trend is the *Wet uitbreiding loondoorbetalingsverplichting werkgever* (WULBZ, Act on the Extension of the Mandatory Continuation of Payment of Wages by the Employer, 1996), an operation which robbed the Sickness Benefits Act of all meaning except in cases of maternity, and which placed all responsibility for the payment of salaries during sickness on the shoulders of the employer for as long as the employee has a contract with the employer. In fact, the collective insurance against the loss of income due to sickness was replaced by the employers' obligation to continue the payment of wages in case of sickness.

1.2 Risks covered

The risk of old age is covered by a three-tier system. The bottom tier is formed by the *Algemene Ouderdomswet* (AOW), which has already been mentioned. This Act provides benefits on the level of the social minimum, *i.e.* the net minimum wage for a couple and 70% of this for a single person. The second tier is formed by collective pensions that are not statutory in character. They are provided for by pension funds which are organised per industry or profession. Over 70% of the pension schemes pay 70% of the last earned wage and 25% of them pay 70% of the average pay – including the bottom tier – after a full working career. Employers, and sometimes also employees, pay contributions towards these funds. Lastly, a growing number of people make private arrangements – the third tier – in order to bridge the difference between the combined pensions of AOW and pension fund (which often do not reach the full 70% of the last income earned) and their former income.

At present, article 7:629 of the *Burgerlijk Wetboek* (Civil Code) stipulates that in the event of *sickness* – including (industrial) accidents or infirmity – employees with a regular employment contract are paid 70% of their normal wages by their employer for a maximum of 52 weeks. The actual amount paid has a maximum (the same applies to social security benefits) but may never be less than the statutory minimum wage. The employer is free to take out a private insurance against the costs of this obligation. According to the Sickness Act, employees who cannot claim continued payment by their employer (*e.g.* employees whose employment has been terminated) are also granted 70% of their wages for a maximum of 52 weeks. The costs involved in this safety net are financed from contributions by employers and employees. Employees are insured against loss of income due to prolonged disability by the *Wet op de Arbeidsongeschiktheidsverzekering* (WAO, Disability Insurance Act; 1966).[8] Benefits are paid when the disability has lasted for longer than the 52 weeks covered by the Civil Code or the Sickness Act. WAO-benefits are related to previously earned wages. The current system is highly complicated. We can summarise it by saying that persons are paid 70% of their former wage (in the event of complete disability) if they are under 33 years of age. If a person has retained a degree of earning capacity the benefit level is related to the difference between the formerly earned income and the earning capacity. The benefit is paid at this level for a limited time only, depending on the age of the claimant. After this period the benefit level becomes age-dependent. Benefits are granted for as long as the disability continues, but only until the age of 65 (when old age-pensions take over). WAO-benefits are payable to employees only. The self-employed are compulsorily insured (on a minimum level) by the *Wet arbeidsongeschiktheidsverzekering zelfstandigen* (WAZ, Disability Insurance Act for the Self-Employed). Persons who have been disabled for some time when reaching the age of 17 receive a benefit from the *Wet arbeidsongeschiktheidsvoorziening jonggehandicapten* (*Wajong*, Disability Benefits Act for the Young Disabled).

Employees are insured against the loss of income due to unemployment by the Unemployment Act. Employees may claim a benefit of, initially, 70% of their former wages under certain conditions concerning their employment history. The duration of this benefit depends on their age. After this benefit expires, beneficiaries receive a minimum benefit for two years if they meet four out of five specified conditions concerning their employment history. If beneficiaries meet some but not all conditions, they are entitled to a flat-rate benefit for six months. Unemployment benefits are financed from contributions paid by employers and employees. Supplementing the Unemployment Act, the *Wet Inkomensvoorziening Oudere en Gedeeltelijk Arbeidsongeschikte Werknemers* (IOAW, Act on the Provision of Income for Older and Partially Disabled Employees; 1986) and the *Wet Inkomensvoorziening Oudere en Gedeeltelijk Arbeidsongeschikte Zelfstandigen* (IOAZ, Act on the Provision of Income for Older and Partially Disabled Self-Employed; 1987) grant a minimum but not earnings-tested benefit to older or partially disabled unemployed persons who are not or no longer entitled to unemployment benefit. The IOAW and IOAZ are financed from general funds (tax money).

According to the General Child Benefit Act *child benefits* are not related to the parents' income but to the child's age. Child benefits are financed from public funds. The General Old Age Act grants a flat-rate pension to every resident over 65 years old. It is financed from contributions paid by all residents. Benefits for surviving relatives are regulated in the General Surviving Relatives Act, which

---

[8] The Disability Insurance Act replaced the Accidents Act and the Invalidity Act.

recently replaced the General Widows and Orphans Act. The new Act grants a flat-rate benefit to certain categories of widows and widowers and is means-tested. The Act also grants a flat-rate benefit to orphans.

Whenever an individual or a family 'legally residing in the Netherlands' is unable to meet the costs of living, the General Assistance Act helps out with a basic social assistance benefit, *e.g.* if a person receives a benefit which is altogether insufficient, if a person is not entitled to any of the benefits mentioned above, or after expiry of these benefits. The amount of assistance benefit is fixed by law and regulations. A person's financial means and social circumstances (children, marriage, housemates) are taken into account. Social assistance benefits are paid out of Government and local community funds. They are the social security system's final safety net.

Finally, the *Toeslagenwet* (Supplementary Benefits Act; 1987) supplements the insurance benefits for unemployment, sickness or disability. It is intended to bring the income of the claimant of these benefits up to the level of the General Assistance Act. The claimant's capital (savings *etc.*) is not relevant either to entitlement or to the level of this benefit.

1.3 Administration

The administration of social security and social assistance has undergone changes in recent years, and there are more changes to come. Formerly, the administration was in the hands of special bodies, each linked to a specific sector of industry. These bodies were governed jointly by trade unions and employers' associations. Since 1997, however, a central body, the *Landelijk Instituut Sociale Verzekeringen* (*Lisv*, National Institute for Social Insurances) has been the appointed administrator. The actual implementation of the insurance schemes is performed by so-called *uvi*'s (*Uitvoeringsinstellingen*, Executive Institutions). These *uvi*'s perform all administrative tasks on behalf of the *Lisv*.

Not only the administrative bodies have changed. There is also a shift in the goals at which the system aims. The importance of reintegrating clients into the labour market is stressed more than ever before. New ideas have been developed concerning the co-operation between the social security administration and various employment bodies. Close co-operation between the two could make the administration more efficient and more client-oriented. This would bring the goal of reintegration nearer. Suggestions for even more privatisation of social security are also being discussed. At this moment it is debated whether private institutions, such as insurance companies, could be assigned a role in the administration of statutory social security. Some experts believe that competition by private companies would increase the system's efficiency, especially where the reintegration efforts are concerned. Other experts argue that the solution to the problem of inactivity, which in the Netherlands is concentrated with older workers and long-term unemployed, lies in an active reintegration policy.

2 Maintaining living standards

2.1 Supporting the formerly employed

As we saw in section 1 the Dutch social security system aims at maintaining the standard of living of the unemployed, the sick or disabled and the elderly. In general, benefits stand at a level of 70% of the previously earned income in case of full disablement, full unemployment or sickness. There is, however, a maximum. At the moment, the gross maximum is GLD 4,658 Dutch Guilders (GLD) (€ 2,114) per month. Because benefits are subject to taxes and social security contributions this amounts to a net monthly benefit of GLD 3,500 (€ 1,588). Benefits are not paid unconditionally, as we will see. The actual conditions depend on the type of benefit in question.

In order to qualify for the 70% unemployment benefit a person must have worked in 26 weeks of 39 weeks preceding unemployment, regardless of the actual number of hours worked.[9] He or she must also have been employed for at least four years during the past five years, with an annual minimum of fifty-two days for which wages have been received. The years a person has cared for a child under the age of six, belonging to his or her household, are considered as years the person has been employed. If the child is between 6 and 12 years of age, the years of care are considered years of employment for 50%. If a person cannot meet the second condition, he or she can claim a benefit of 70% of the *minimum* wage, which equals about GLD 1,100 (€ 499) net per month.[10] Once these conditions are met, the duration of the benefit depends on the age of the claimant. Depending on the outcome of a rather complicated calculation, it ranges from six months to five years. On the basis of collective agreements or redundancy payment schemes, employers sometimes supplement the benefits of their former employees up to 100% of their previous wages.

In 1993 the disability benefit system was thoroughly revised. Benefits now stand at a maximum 70% of previous wages but this maximum is only granted to persons over the age of 33 who are fully disabled. In order to determine the extent of

---

[9] Special rules apply in some circumstances, such as sickness, to prolong the period containing the 26 week period, or, in the case of holidays, to combine periods of no work with periods of work.

[10] The qualifying conditions were seriously tightened by March 1st, 1995. Previously, the only condition was that one had worked for 26 weeks within a period of 52 weeks.

a person's disability, an estimate is made of his or her remaining 'earning-capacity'. This is done in the abstract, *i.e.* regardless of any actual job openings. Since this procedure has been tightened considerably, many people have lost their benefit or part of it after a reassessment of their situation. Payment of a wage-related benefit is always limited in time, ranging from six months to six years. After this period expires, benefits amount to 70% of an income level which is, dependent on the age of the claimant, somewhere between the minimum wage and the claimant's previous wages. To determine the exact amount the age of the claimant is also taken into account. This complicated system was introduced in 1993. For the majority of employees, however, the impact of these changes has been cushioned by provisions made in collective agreements or by private insurance schemes. If they ever become partly or fully disabled, the level of their benefit will remain linked to their former wages.

As mentioned above, sick employees remain entitled to 70% of their normal wages, to be paid by their employer for 52 weeks. Again, the benefit is limited by a maximum. Special provisions apply when a person's employment comes to an end during his or her sickness period and also in the event of maternity: pregnant women and new mothers are entitled to 100% of their normal wages, provided their normal earnings do not exceed the maximum benefit level. Employees are prevented from starting new fifty-two weeks' periods indefinitely by the simple expedient of going to work for a few days and then falling ill again: they must have worked for at least four weeks before a new period commences. As in the case of disability benefits, the statutory sickness benefit is supplemented on a large scale by provisions made in collective agreements. As a result, the vast majority of employees receive 100% of their normal wages in the event of sickness.

The General Old Age Act grants a (modest) flat-rate old-age pension to every resident over 65 years of age. Supplementary employees' pension funds (which cover 87% of all employees) provide additional retirement pay. Pension rights have to be built up in the years before retirement age, so the actual amount of one's pension depends on the number of years worked. Optimum pension is 70% of the last earned wages, but only about a quarter of the employees reaches this level. However, since social security contributions and income tax are much lower for pensioners than for workers, the net level of pensions is higher than it seems. Old-age pensions are paid indefinitely.

2.2 A shift from public law to civil law?

Wage-related unemployment and disability benefits are financed from contributions paid by employers and employees. Both these contributions and the insurances they support are obligatory by law. Sickness payments are mainly paid by employers. These, too, are mandatory. Although the State does not finance any of these arrangements, they are under public law in the sense that they are prescribed by law. Some other social security arrangements are of a civil law character. This is the case with supplementary wage-related old-age pension schemes, which are negotiated and financed by employers and employees. The same goes for the supplementary provisions specified in collective agreements.

In the past five years the Dutch Government has investigated all sectors of social security for opportunities to extend the role of private arrangements. One practical result was the reduction of the Sickness Act to workers who have no employer (anymore), but even under the revised Act the law stipulates employers' obligations and employees' rights. Recently, an amendment of the Disability Insurance Act (WAO) was brought about. Employers are free to opt out of this Act and bear the risk themselves or to insure their employees with a private insurance company against the risk of disability. After five years of disability the (former) employees of these employers are again relegated to the public law arrangements. However, even in this example of privatisation it is the law which lays down the framework: the policy conditions of the private insurance are identical to those of the public insurance. One may conclude that so far privatisation, *i.e.* the shift from public law arrangements to civil law arrangements, is not a very radical operation. The role of private organisations remains to a very large extent under the control of public law. At the moment, there are no other projects for privatisation in the political pipeline. Since the economy seems to be doing very well and the number of beneficiaries is decreasing, the Government feels no need for new reforms.

In general, privatisation projects have not changed the situation of most employees in any considerable way since the new 'privatised' schemes tend to follow the former or existing public ones. However, the privatising operation undoubtedly also had adverse effects. In some sectors of industry employers have tried to get rid of employees who are frequently ill. Although there is some protection against dismissal during sickness, this protection is not watertight. Sickness does not prevent loss of employment in the event of a company reorganisation, during a trial period, in the event of dismissal for urgent reasons, or if the labour contract is dissolved by the court. Employers are also reluctant to take on employees with any physical deficiency which might lead to financial claims. The fear that privatisation will widen the gap between the healthy and the less-than-healthy seems well justified. While the healthy enjoy the perks of a booming economy, the less-than-healthy seem doomed to remain in relative poverty.

2.3 Coverage of special risks

Generally some risks are covered, adequately or inadequately, by the present social security systems: unemployment, sickness, disability, old age. However, life entails other risks which are less likely to be covered. Divorce, natural disasters, maternity or the care for children or sick relatives can cause considerable financial difficulties.

In the Netherlands, the consequences of *divorce* are not covered by any earnings-related social security arrangement. It is usual for one spouse (usually the wife) to claim alimony from the other. If there is no alimony involved or if the alimony is insufficient to pay the costs of living, a divorced person may qualify for a social assistance benefit. Single mothers living on social assistance – provided under the General Assistance Act – are a common phenomenon in the Netherlands too. Proposals have been made to improve their situation, but so far no agreement has been reached. Politicians are afraid to burn their fingers. The problem is, among other things, how to avoid abuse. It could be tempting to wriggle out of financial responsibilities if one's former partner was taken care of by social security.[11]

There is no general social security provision against *natural disasters*. However, employees who find themselves temporarily out of work due to, for instance, bad weather or frost, may claim unemployment benefit, even if they do not meet all the usual conditions. So far, there seems to be no special need for a more generic coverage of natural disasters.

Only in the case of *maternity*, and for employees only, are earnings-related benefits provided. Under the Sickness Act, the coverage for pregnant employees or those who have recently given birth is generous. For a maximum of 16 weeks within the period starting six weeks before delivery and ending twelve weeks afterwards, they receive 100% of their normal income (but not more than the current maximum benefit level). Extension of this period is possible for medical reasons related to the pregnancy. After this period, however, there is no general coverage. Civil law entitles female and male employees to unpaid parental leave for the number of hours that corresponds with thirteen of their normal working weeks. Each week their leave may amount to a maximum of half their normal working hours. Employees are entitled to parental leave for a child under 7. Collective agreements and schemes for civil servants sometimes contain provisions for paid leave for a certain period. These provisions are, however, infrequent. Many people feel that the present provisions are insufficient, but the question of who will pay for better leave conditions, remains as yet unanswered.

The care for sick relatives does not come under any social security protection, except in very rare cases. This is felt to be a serious flaw in the social security system. It can be argued, of course, that the State cannot protect its citizens against all conceivable risks. The organisational and financial investments involved would be awesome. Moreover, some risks depend very much on the sensible or foolish behaviour of the citizens themselves. This makes it difficult to devise adequate provisions which do not invite abuse. There is a debate going on how new forms

---

[11] It should be mentioned that social assistance paid to a divorced person can be claimed back from the former spouse. These claims are, however, subject to restrictions.

of leave should be financed. In this debate, attention is given to the possible introduction of a special social insurance.[12]

In general, the gaps in the Dutch social security system are neither alarming nor
exceptional. The existing provisions fall short in two areas. First, compared with
provisions existing in neighbouring countries, maternity and paternity leave is
poorly provided for. Until recently, women were expected to stop working as soon
as their first baby was born in order to devote themselves fully to its care. The
influence of this tradition is still strong. Secondly, the fact that there is no provision for people nursing sick or disabled relatives is galling, the more so because in
recent years drastic cutbacks have been made in home care facilities. In both cases
financing is, of course, the key problem.

2.4 Legal protection

If a person finds a decision taken by a benefit administration unacceptable – or in
the absence of any decision at all – he or she must first ask the issuing body for a
reconsideration. This procedure is prescribed in the law on administrative procedures. In many cases this is enough to settle the dispute to the claimant's satisfaction. If not, the claimant can take the next step and appeal to the District Court.
There is, apart from some time limits and the payment of a fee (GLD 50) no limitation to these procedures. No legal advisor is required and there are no precondi-
tions for appeal.

At present there are no obvious gaps in the possibilities for appeal against decisions taken by the benefit administrations. Since sickness payment is paid by the
employer, an employee has to go to the cantonal court for a civil law procedure in
case there is a conflict. If necessary, a subsequent appeal can be made to the district court according to civil law procedure. There are some disadvantages to civil
law procedures like this. One disadvantage is that the burden of proof lies more
heavily on the claimant than in administrative procedures. Another disadvantage is
that in a civil procedure the employee opposes his employer: the resulting ill-
feeling may even lead to severance of the employment contract. A third disadvantage is that if a civil judge feels that the claimant's case is manifestly unrea-
sonable he is more likely to make him responsible for the costs of the procedure.
Consequently, proceedings are rare.[13] Employees with a temporary or a flexible

---

[12] M. Westerveld, 'Verzorging verzekerd? – Een pleidooi voor een nieuw soort werknemersverzekering
[Care insured, care assured? – A plea for a new kind of employees' insurance]', in: *Nemesis.
Tijdschrift over Vrouwen en Recht* [Nemesis. Journal on Women and Law], 11 (1995), no. 6, p. 140-
146.

[13] P.E. Minderhoud, I.P. Asscher-Vonk, and T. Havinga, 'Procederen inzake weigering loondoorbe-
taling bij ziekte: een zeer zeldzaam verschijnsel [Litigation about continued payment of wages in case

contract face another problem: in the event of sickness they may face the prospect of becoming involved in two lawsuits simultaneously: a civil law action against an unwilling employer (who will argue that the contract has expired, and that the benefit organisation should pay) and an administrative law action against the benefit administration (which will argue that the contract is still valid and that the employer should pay) – with the risk of losing on both counts.

3 The level of basic social security arrangements

3.1 Indicators

In the Netherlands, the minimum level of benefits (the so-called 'social minimum') is linked to the legal minimum wage, the age of the beneficiary, and his or her family situation. Since January 2000, the minimum wage for an adult in full-time employment amounts to GLD 2,406.30 per month plus a holiday allowance of 8%. This is considered to be sufficient to maintain a family of two parents and two children. Consequently, the minimum benefit for married couples and for persons living together is 100% of the legal minimum wage.[14] The minimum benefit for single persons with a child is 90%, for singles without a child 70% of the social minimum. According to the General Assistance Act, singles with a child receive a lower social minimum of 70% when they share a house with someone else. Singles without a child sharing a house receive 50% of the social minimum. However, it is left to the discretion of the municipalities which implement this Act to grant single housemates an extra allowance to bridge the gap, completely or partially, with the benefit received by singles living alone.

For persons younger than 23 a lower social minimum applies, because their legal minimum wage is lower too. Moreover, parents are obliged to support children under 21. Irrespective of age, a lower social minimum applies to schoolchildren and students (whose State grant does not cover their costs of living).

3.2 Adaptation mechanism

According to the *Wet Koppeling met Mogelijkheid van Afwijking* (WKA, Act on Linkage with Optional Deviation, 1991), beneficiaries are indirectly entitled to

---

of illness: a rare occurence]', in: *SMA. Tijdschrift over arbeid en sociale zekerheid* [SMA. Labour and social security review], 54 (1999), no. 3, p. 145-153.

[14] As a consequence of a difference in tax rates, the net amount of minimum benefits results in 2% less than the legal minimum wage.

share in the rise of wages. Benefits are readjusted on the basis of an estimate of the average wages in all sectors of the economy. On January 1st, half of this readjustment is implemented; on July 1st (the date of the annual increase in housing rents) the other half. The difference between the estimated development and the actual development is taken into account when the next readjustment is due on January 1st of the following year. This readjustment cycle can, however, be broken if wages should rise disproportionately to labour productivity and prices and an adverse effect on employment is to be expected; also, if increasing numbers of beneficiaries were to cause a considerable increase in the total cost of social security, and make an increase in tax or social security contributions necessary. During the 1980s the cycle was almost permanently broken, *i.e.* the legal minimum wage was 'frozen'. Until 1988, this policy was motivated by the Government's wish to limit expenses in the collective sector, and, by doing so, to improve the unfavourable socio-economic situation.[15] In 1988[16] and 1989[17] a reduction in unemployment was the primary reason. The effect of this 'delinkage' between benefits and minimum wages was somewhat mitigated by a decrease in tax and social security contributions. In the 1990s a different criterion was introduced, namely the 'I/A-ratio' between 'inactive' social security beneficiaries and 'active' working persons.[18] At present this ratio is calculated at 82.6 to 100, but it used to be higher. In 1992-1995 this criterion came into play. In 1992 the 'optional deviation' was invoked to limit the increase of the minimum wage (and thus of social security benefits) to 3% instead of 3.6%. In 1993-1995 the minimum wage and the social security benefits were not readjusted to wage movements but, again, the effect was mitigated by lower taxes and contributions. Since 1995 the I/A-ratio has improved considerably and in 1996 the 'linkage' was fully restored.[19]

At first sight it would seem that, in this matter, economic considerations easily prevailed over social considerations. This, however, is an unfair criticism. Limiting expenses in the collective sector and controlling the number of beneficiaries has a positive, if indirect, effect on reducing unemployment. This is a social aim, too. However, 'delinkage' policies imply that the Government feels that the social

---

[15] Sociaal-Economische Raad (Socio-Economic Council), *Advies Bijzondere Verhoging Minimumloon* [Advice on a special raise of the minimum wage] (The Hague 1990. Publication no. 90/25), p. 8.

[16] Consideration accompanying the Act of December 21st, 1988, in: *Staatsblad van het Koninkrijk der Nederlanden* [Law gazette of the Kingdom of the Netherlands], 1988, 625. Below the *Staatsblad* is referred to as: *Stb.*

[17] Explanatory Memorandum accompanying the Decree of December 20th, 1991 (*Stb.* 1991, 726), p. 1.

[18] See: Explanatory Memorandum accompanying the Act on Linking with Grounds for Deviation, in: *Bijlagen van het Verslag der Handelingen van de Tweede Kamer der Staten-Generaal* [Annex to the Parliamentary Proceedings] II (1990-1991), no. 22 012, no. 3, p. 25-26.

[19] *Annex to the Parliamentary Proceedings,* II (1995-1996), no. 24 515, no. 2, p. 3; *Annex to the Parliamentary Proceedings,* II (1995-1996), no. 24 515, no. 2, p. 6; Decree of December 22nd, 1993 (*Stb.* 1993, 768), p. 1; Explanatory Memorandum accompanying the Decree of December 19th, 1994 (*Stb.* 1994, 902), p. 1.

aim of increasing employment has priority over the social aim of income protection. The price for this choice has been paid by the people receiving benefits. Between 1981 and 1995 people on an unemployment or social assistance benefit lost 9.5% of their purchasing power. People with a disability benefit even lost 17.5%.[20] Whether this loss is acceptable depends on the categories involved. For beneficiaries who have a real prospect of finding a job, this loss is acceptable because indirectly it may help them to find a job (and to boost their purchasing power). For those who have no realistic prospect of ever finding a job, the loss of purchasing power is only acceptable if it helps the system to pay their benefits even in times of recession. However, it is a matter of social justice that in times of economic growth these beneficiaries benefit, too.

3.3 Fighting poverty

To know whether poverty is effectively prevented in the Netherlands, it is important to know what is meant exactly by 'poverty', since poverty has not only a financial but also a social and a cultural dimension. These three dimensions are expressed in the definition used by the European Union: 'Poor people are those persons, families or groups of persons whose means (materially, culturally and socially) are thus limited that they are excluded from the minimally acceptable patterns of living in the Member States in which they reside'.[21]

At the end of 1995, approximately 830,000 Dutch households received an income at or below the accepted social minimum level.[22] In the past twenty-five years the purchasing power of these households has fluctuated considerably. After an increase in the second half of the 1970s, it decreased in the first half of the 1980s.[23] From 1985 onward, it improved again but this improvement was undone in the first half of the 1990s.[24] It can be imagined that these movements have caused much uncertainty amongst those who depend on benefits. Generally speaking, the current social minimum is sufficient to cover the usual recurring costs of living, but insufficient to build up a modest reserve for incidental expenses. Therefore, the financial situation of those who depend on a minimum benefit more or less permanently, is precarious at best. The category of people in this situation is by no means a reflection of the Dutch population as a whole. Women (especially single mothers), the elderly, the under-educated, the disabled and members of ethnic minority groups are clearly over-represented. Since poverty should not be defined

---

[20] Centraal Bureau voor de Statistiek (Central Bureau for Statistics), *Statistisch Jaarboek 1997* [Statistical Yearbook 1997], (1997), p. 312.

[21] *Annex to the Parliamentary Proceedings*, II (1995-1996), no. 24 515, no. 2, p. 3.

[22] *Annex to the Parliamentary Proceedings*, II (1995-1996), no. 24 515, no. 2, p. 6.

[23] Sociaal-Economische Raad, *Advies Bijzondere Verhoging Minimumloon*, p. 37.

[24] *Annex to the Parliamentary Proceedings*, II (1996-1997), no. 25 002, no. 2, p. 7.

in financial terms only, the social and cultural position of people on minimum benefits, *i.e.* their capacity to take part in the social and cultural life of their surrounding society, should also be considered. According to research undertaken by the *Sociaal en Cultureel Planbureau* (Social and Cultural Planning Bureau) it seems that social and cultural development follows financial developments with some delay. In 1974-1983 a strong improvement of the socio-cultural situation of the lowest income groups was registered. This was followed by an equally strong deterioration in the middle of the 1980s which was only partially undone afterwards.[25] Here too, the situation is problematic.

Since the middle of the 1980s, pressure groups of beneficiaries, academics,[26] representatives of churches and trade unions, and directors of municipal social service departments have tried repeatedly to bring these problems to the attention of the Government and parliament. It was not before the previous cabinet period (1994-1998), that these efforts seemed to meet with some success. The increased attention of politicians for these problems led, among other things, to a Government policy memorandum entitled *De andere kant van Nederland* (The other side of the Netherlands).[27] In it, five policy aims were laid down: the promotion of social participation (by creating employment), income support, the reduction of living costs (by raising rent subsidies), debt clearance and reducing the under-utilisation of available social provisions. Among these, income support is chiefly a responsibility of municipalities since they implement the General Assistance Act. The Government has allowed the municipalities more freedom to conduct their own income support policy, *e.g.* by granting extra allowances to whole categories of people without checking their actual individual needs or by offering social and cultural provisions at a reduced fee. At the national level, single elderly people with an income at or just above the social minimum level receive income support through a special tax deduction. As regards debt clearance, a multidisciplinary approach was introduced in which municipal finance companies, social services and welfare organisations closely co-operate. This approach is to be backed up by a Bill proposing the enforcement of debt repayment by the intervention of a judge.[28] Finally, the under-utilisation of existing provisions will be tackled by

---

[25] Sociaal en Cultureel Planbureau (Social and Cultural Planning Office), *Sociale en Culturele Verkenningen 1995* [Social and Cultural Explorations 1995] (Rijswijk 1995), p. 60.

[26] G. Engbersen and R.E. van der Veen, *Moderne armoede. Overleven op het sociaal minimum. Een onderzoek onder 120 Rotterdamse huishoudens* [Modern poverty. Surviving at the social minimum. A survey of 120 Rotterdam households], Leiden 1987; G. Engbersen, *Publieke bijstandsgeheimen: het ontstaan van een onderklasse in Nederland* [Public assistance secrets. The making of an underclass in the Netherlands], Leiden 1990. Thesis University of Leiden; G. Engbersen, J.S. Timmer, and J.W.A.M. van der Sluis, *Unlisted numbers. The making of a Dutch underclass*, Leiden 1990; G. Oude Engberink and B. Post, *Grenzen van de armoede. Risico's en risicogroepen op het sociaal minimum* [The limits of poverty. Risks and risk groups at the social minimum], Rotterdam 1994.

[27] *Annex to the Parliamentary Proceedings*, II (1995-1996), no. 24 515, no. 2.

[28] *Annex to the Parliamentary Proceedings*, I (1995-1996), no. 22 969, no. 34.

streamlining regulations and by extra efforts in public information. It should be noted that in the policies laid down in *De andere kant van Nederland,* social security seems to play a far less prominent part than in the European Union Recommendations of 1992.[29] The explanation lies in the Dutch Government's contention that it is not social security but the promotion of employment opportunities which constitutes the most important instrument in fighting poverty. However, despite the good intentions of *De andere kant van Nederland* and its vigorous approach, the reality of its policy leaves something to be desired. There are still organisational flaws and blind spots. For example, it is dubious whether improvement will be achieved for the elderly, the disabled and members of ethnic minority groups, who are still in a weak position on the labour market. The financial and social situation of youngsters also deserves more attention than it gets. The minimum wage for people under 23 is low compared with other European Union countries. Unemployed school-leavers – many of them from underprivileged social backgrounds – depend in principle on support from their parents until their twenty-first birthday. Available benefits do not exceed the level of child allowance – which is not enough to live on. Finally, student grants were drastically reduced during the first half of the 1990s, forcing the majority of the 157,000 students to work their way through university with part-time jobs. *De andere kant van Nederland* did not even address the income position of students.[30]

3.4 The country's performance in social security

On the whole, the Dutch social security system will have little difficulty in matching the criteria of the European Union Recommendations. Dutch social security still provides good coverage. The Government's social security and anti-poverty policies are well-intentioned and seem, on the whole, effective and sufficient. According to a 1994 Eurostat publication, the percentage of poor families in the Netherlands, compared with other countries of the European Union, was quite low (see Table 1). In 1997, however, a different European survey claimed that in 1993 the percentage of poor families (14%) was higher than in Belgium (13%) and Germany (13%).[31]

---

[29] 'Council Recommendation of 24 June 1992 on common criteria concerning sufficient resources and social assistance in social protection systems' (92/441/EEC, published in: *Official Journal of the European Communities,* L 245, August 26th, 1992, p. 46-48); 'Council Recommendation of 27 July 1992 on the convergence of social protection objectives and policies' (92/ 442/EEC, published in: Official Journal of the European Communities, L 245, August 26th, 1992, p. 49-52).

[30] *Annex to the Parliamentary Proceedings,* II (1995-1996), no. 24 515, no. 2, p. 6.

[31] European Commission, *Social protection in Europe 1997. Modernising social protection and adapting systems to change,* Luxembourg: Office for Official Publications of the European Communities, 1998.

Table 1: Poverty in Europe in the late 1980s (in poor households as % of the total number of households).[32]

Country	Percentage	Country	Percentage
Portugal	26.5	France	14.9
Italy	22.0	Germany	12.0
Greece	20.8	Luxembourg	9.2
Spain	17.5	Belgium	6.6
United Kingdom	17.0	Netherlands	6.2
Ireland	16.4	Denmark	4.2

In spite of the Dutch system's sound overall performance there are still deficiencies. Some of those are to be found in the realm of organisation and implementation; others are more directly caused by deliberate policy. The fact that benefit conditions have been made considerably less attractive in recent years has had little effect on workers with a long and steady employment record. Many of them have a strong legal position which is set down in employment contracts for an indefinite period of time. For these employees no radical changes have taken place; cutbacks on benefits, if any, have been supplemented by the employers. For people with a less robust position on the labour market, however, developments have not been so benign. Persons with physical or mental handicaps find it ever more difficult to obtain work and to remain at work. As a consequence, they are less likely to qualify for long-term benefits. Persons who have been irregularly employed also have difficulties in qualifying for benefits, especially for unemployment benefit. Although both Government and parliament have tried hard to cover all foreseeable problems caused by privatisations in social security, they have not entirely succeeded. The Dutch labour market is a relatively 'free' market. For instance, authorities have few, if any, instruments to coerce employers who refuse to recruit employees with a health risk; employers can hardly be expected to do so voluntarily, since they have been saddled with much of the financial risk. Likewise, in general, employers are never forced to renew a contract indefinitely. Legal employment protection cannot always protect disabled or sickly employees against dismissal if their employer is determined to get rid of them.

In addition, mention should be made of the self-employed, of people who have never worked, and people who have to take care of partners or relatives. For them, no earnings-related benefit or hardly any benefit at all exists. At best, they have to resort to modest flat-rate benefits. An answer to the above-mentioned deficiencies would be an even greater emphasis on employers' responsibilities in terms of labour law. It is time for a modernisation of labour law and of the social security

---

[32] Source: Eurostat, *Poverty Statistics in the late 1980s*, Luxembourg 1994. Poverty is defined as: spending below 50% of the median spending level for all households, *i.e.* the level of spending which is not reached by 50% of all households and which is exceeded by the other 50%.

system in order to extend facilities and coverage to 'new risks', such as the care for sick or disabled relatives.

4 Household or individual

4.1 Regulations

The concepts of 'family' and 'household' play an important role in the General Assistance Act. They are relevant to decide if a claimant has a right to benefit: married people and cohabitants do not have an individual right to assistance but a *shared* right. The concepts are also important for the level of benefit. While there are certain obligations attached to receiving a social assistance benefit, the presence of a live-in partner and the presence and age of children determine exactly *which* obligations.[33]

To determine if there is a rightful claim to a social assistance benefit, the costs of living of the cohabitants are compared with the total of their financial means. To determine the level of benefit, a distinction is made between married persons, single persons and single parents. Benefits for married persons amount to the net minimum wage; singles receive 50% and single parents 70% of the net minimum wage. The General Assistance Act stipulates that the municipality will grant an extra allowance to singles or to single parents who cannot share the costs of living with someone else. In the case of a married couple, the General Assistance Act requires that both of them seek employment as best as they can. For parents who have full-time care for one or more children under the age of five, this obligation does not apply. For parents who share the care for their child(ren) there may be an obligation to seek part-time employment. However, everyone may be temporarily exempted from this obligation for social, medical or other compelling reasons.

The allowances payable under the Supplementary Benefits Act also depend on the family income. Members of the younger generation, however, do no longer receive a supplement for their partner. Since 1990, a married person or cohabitant whose spouse or partner was born after December 31st, 1971, does not have a right to supplementary benefits, unless there are children in his or her household.[34] The amount of the supplementary benefit also depends on the size of the family. Both partners have an obligation to seek employment.

---

[33] *Cf.* W.H.A.C.M. Bouwens, *Onderhoudsplicht en bijstand* [Liability for maintenance and social assistance] (Nijmegen 1996), p. 108 ff.

[34] J.H.P.G. Wielders, *De 1990-maatregel* [The 1990-measure], Nijmegen 1996.

The pension granted by the General Old Age Act is not dependent on individual circumstances. This act, however, also provides for extra allowances and these do depend on a beneficiary's marital status and on the income of his or her partner. The General Old Age Act does not impose any obligations on the beneficiary or on the spouse except to provide information on their marital status and income.

To claim a benefit under the General Surviving Relatives Act a person must be a surviving family member of the deceased. In addition, he or she has to take care of a child or to be disabled. The family situation of the claimant does not influence the level of benefit. Half-orphans receive 20% of the net minimum wage. Therefore, a surviving parent with a child under 18 is, in principle, entitled to 90% of the net minimum wage. All family members are required to provide information necessary for ascertaining the claim to this benefit. Finally, the General Child Benefits Act stipulates that a child, when younger than 16, must belong to the household of the receiving parent. For children under 18 it is required that the receiving parent maintains the child to a considerable degree; alimony from a former spouse and contributions by a housemate are regarded as contributions to this end. There used to be a differentiation in the level of child benefits according to the size of the family but this is no longer the case. For each child one receives the same amount.

To sum up, it may be said that the social circumstances of the claimant are taken into account to establish whether there is a rightful claim to a minimum level benefit and to determine the exact level of benefit. A means-test may be applied to the income of the claimant and cohabitant. The presence of children determines the amount of benefits at the minimum level. Their presence is one of the alternative ways to become entitled to a benefit under the General Surviving Relatives Act. The usual obligation to seek new work may be temporarily suspended if there are young children to be taken care of. The General Disability Act, which also provides for a minimum level benefit, is an exception since it ignores the social situation of the person involved. The reason is that it primarily provides for loss of income, not for covering general needs.

Taking the social circumstances of the claimant into account (and especially his or her marital status) is traditional in Dutch social security.[35] Reference to a person's marital status may, however, amount to indirect discrimination of women. Some justification may be found in the fact that social assistance benefits are intended to protect persons at a minimum level.[36] Because of European Community rules on equal treatment of men and women, references to family or marital status are no longer found in any Dutch legislation granting benefits above the minimum level.

---

[35] L.H. van den Heuvel and I.P. Asscher-Vonk, *Vrouw en sociale verzekering* [Woman and social insurance], The Hague 1974.

[36] Case law in: *European Court of Justice,* 11 June 1987, Teuling, and 13 December 1989, Ruzius-Wilbrink.

4.2 The concepts of marriage, family and household

How are terms like 'married', 'family' or 'household' defined? In various social security Acts the term 'married persons' is frequently used. In general, being formally married is not enough: sharing a household is an additional (or better: *essential*) requirement for being considered 'married' under the terms of these Acts. Consequently, married persons who are permanently separated are regarded as 'unmarried', even if their separation is not voluntary but due to, for instance, long-term admission into a psychiatric ward or a nursing home.[37] In the General Assistance Act this train of thought also implies that unmarried persons living in one house and sharing a household are treated as married. This equal treatment also applies to persons of the same sex and even to next of kin living together, *e.g.* grandparents and grandchildren, or brothers and sisters. People are considered to be 'sharing a household' if they live in the same house and share the costs of the household in one way or another. Very similar provisions can be found in the Supplementary Benefits Act, the General Old Age Act, and the General Surviving Relatives Act.

The equal treatment of married persons and persons living together without being married is almost completely implemented in various social security acts on minimum benefits.

5 European unity and its consequences

How will the progress of European integration effect the social security system of the Netherlands? Social protection expenditure in the Netherlands as a percentage of Gross Domestic Product (GDP) is among the highest in the European Union. Employers' and employees' contributions are also relatively high.[38] It is inevitable that any Dutch Government will feel the pressure to adjust to 'cheaper' countries within the EMU. However, there are reasons to believe that the effect on the Dutch system will not be so dramatic. In fact, the success of the so-called 'Polder Model' (consensus model) can, to a large extent, be attributed to this to this negative policy competition since the early 1980s. The most important impact of the EMU on Dutch social security will be through its effect on the national budget and on the Government's spending policy.[39] Like all EMU member states, the Netherlands have lost the ability to print money to finance spending. The country has

---

[37] Bouwens, *Onderhoudsplicht en bijstand,* p. 108-109, see also footnote 72.

[38] European Commission, *Social protection in Europe 1993,* Luxembourg: Office of Official Publications of the European Union, 1994.

[39] P. de Grauwe, *The economics of monetary integration,* Oxford 1992.

also lost its sovereign borrower status, for the EMU convergence requirements lay down very tight conditions for membership, with fixed limits on national budgetary deficits and borrowing. At present, GDP growth in the Netherlands is higher than in Germany and well above the European average. Employment, too, has grown considerably while in neighbouring Germany it has actually decreased. The Government budget has displayed a remarkably favourable development. The Netherlands had little difficulty in fulfilling the EMU convergence criteria. The Netherlands seem to prove that meeting the EMU convergence criteria is compatible with maintaining social policies and achieving dramatic job growth.[40] No wonder Germany and other European countries have come to regard Dutch economic policies and structural readjustments as a model.

Nowadays, the Netherlands reaps the fruits of the Government's early decision to carry out necessary cutbacks and readjustments. Policies for gradually reducing the budget deficit were introduced in the first half of the 1980s under pressure of autonomous internal economic considerations. In the field of social security reduction in benefits and 'delinkage' between benefits and wages were also introduced in the 1980s, together with strong measures to reduce the number of beneficiaries by introducing higher thresholds and by promoting the outflow out of the system. It is because these measures have already been taken, that the (transition to) the EMU will probably have little visible effect on Dutch social security. However, the level of Dutch social security is not guaranteed indefinitely. Should the rate of economic growth decrease, the Stability Pact will become tighter. Consequently, further changes in the social security system may be needed to retain competitiveness. The Dutch employment record also merits some critical comment. Although an impressive quantitative improvement has been achieved, the quality of the newly created jobs is disputable. Much of the employment growth consists of small part-time jobs (less than 12 hours per week) and flexible jobs (temporary jobs, stand-by jobs and agency work). In fact, in 1993 and 1994 the number of full-time jobs *decreased*. Moreover, in spite of the overall favourable development long-term unemployment has remained high. Eventually this will result in the permanent social exclusion and impoverishment of certain categories in society. The growth of part-time jobs and flexible jobs, although in itself satisfactory, may also result in dependence and impoverishment for households and individuals with no additional sources of income.[41] These developments will boost expenditure on social assistance. The growing number of senior citizens will add to this effect.

---

[40] Delsen and De Jong, *The German and Dutch economies.*
[41] *Ibidem.*

X Spain

Eugenio M. Recio and Pilar Núñez-Cortés

1 Introduction

1.1 Historical development

Social security was first introduced in Spain in 1853, inspired by the Bismarck model, with the creation of some non-compulsory insurance schemes, including those against accidents at work. In 1919 the first compulsory insurance scheme, for the retirement of wage-earners, was introduced. More insurance schemes followed – again non-compulsory – for instance for maternity leave and for the support of large families. In 1932 compulsory coverage of accidents at work was introduced, funded by employers.

After the Spanish Civil War (1938) other compulsory schemes appeared. The wage-earners' retirement insurance scheme was transformed into the old age pension (1939). It was again changed into the compulsory old age and invalidity insurance scheme in 1947. More insurance schemes came into existence until 1963, when an attempt was made to unify the system with the *Ley de Bases de la Seguridad Social* (Basic Social Security Law). Three years later, the *Ley de Seguridad Social* (Social Security Law) gave effect to the Basic Law. Social security was now designed as a compulsory system of national solidarity aimed at covering individual risks. Social insurance ceased to be exclusively for wage-earners and attempts were made to cover all citizens. Thus Spain changed over from a Bismarckian system to a Beveridgean universal type of welfare state. However, this change took place only in principle, because its practical application did not take effect before 1986 and 1990; moreover, social security was still basically financed by means of contributions by employers and workers. However, the State took on responsibility for financing part of social welfare expenditure out of general tax revenue and for covering any deficits which might appear. As a result, the social security system became a redistributive system.

In 1974 the *Texto Refundido de la Ley General de la Seguridad Social* (Revised Social Security Law) was passed, ratifying earlier regulations regarding financing and coverage.[1] The purpose of these regulations was to match insurance contribu-

---

[1] For example: those of Law 24 of June 21st, 1972.

tions to real salaries, in order to increase revenue and to make contributions cover a greater share of the costs. Most of these regulations are still in force. Other laws introduced reforms of an administrative nature in order to manage the system,[2] and to improve services.[3] Furthermore, mention should be made of the following changes:

• In 1986 the *Ley General de Sanidad* (General Health Care Law) was passed, which made health care universal, in accordance with the Basic Law of 1963 and with articles 41 and 43 of the Spanish Constitution of 1978. The General Health Care Law created the *Servicio Nacional de la Salud* (SNS, National Health Service) as an umbrella organisation for all health care services provided by the Spanish national and regional Governments. As of 1989 it was to be financed essentially by public funds.

• In 1990,[4] the system of social protection was extended to the entire population, and non-contributory benefits were established. Thus the implementation of the Beveridge model of welfare was completed.

• In 1994,[5] a third Revised General Social Security Act was approved, which included and updated all regulations in effect at that time.

• In 1994,[6] a set of fiscal, administrative and social measures was approved, introducing significant new reforms regarding temporary disability.

• Lastly, since 1997, pension amounts are set according to a new law[7] which modifies the financing of the social security arrangements and which also introduces new measures in order to achieve a better proportion between contributions and the level of retirement pensions. The purchasing power of pensions will be adjusted to inflation by means of an automatic annual revaluation.

1.2 Structure

The historical development of the public system of social security in Spain has given rise to a complex situation, because it has created a general system of social security alongside an array of special systems for various professional groups: farmers, the self-employed, seafarers, civil servants, domestic helpers, *etc.* As a result the same risk can be covered on different levels, depending on the systems to which workers belong. Furthermore, there are complementary systems such as

---

[2] Royal Decree-Law 36 of November 10th, 1978.

[3] Law 26 of July 31st, 1985.

[4] By Law 26 of December 20th, 1990.

[5] By Royal Decree 1 of June 20th, 1994.

[6] By Law 42 of December 30th, 1994.

[7] By Law 24 of July 15th, 1997, on the *Consolidación y Racionalización del Sistema de Seguridad Social* (Act on the Consolidation and Rationalisation of the Social Security System).

social work (which is still developing rapidly), the remains of a former labour movement protection in some sectors of economic activity, and the private pension schemes of companies for their labour forces. As will be seen later in more detail, under these systems workers are insured against the risks of old age in retirement, invalidity, illness, occupational injuries, unemployment, maternity leave, widowhood, widowerhood or orphanhood. Benefits can take the place of income, and they can be in cash or in kind. To a lesser degree they aim to reintegrate disabled and unemployed persons into the labour market.

1.3 Financing

The system of financing social security became more and more complex as time went by. Initially, contributions from employers and workers predominated, and State funding through general taxation was merely complementary. However, when unemployment insurance was extended in 1980 and health care in 1986, the revenue accruing from the tax and duty system became more and more important for the financing of most social security expenditure. From the beginning, financing has been based on the so-called 'pay as you go'-system. However, because of the general ageing of the population brought about by demographic trends, and the high level of structural unemployment, the Government is studying the possibility of introducing a capitalisation system, as other countries have begun to do.

In 1997, Spain's total social security expenditure amounted to 15% of GDP, social spending *per capita* amounted to 459,503 Spanish Pesetas (Ptas) (€ 2,762).[8]

2 Risks covered and maintaining living standards

Spanish social security does not cover all situations of social need, but only those which are expressly defined as such by law. The risks of illness, death, disability or unemployment in themselves are not fully covered, but only part of their economic consequences: loss of income and increased expenses. The fact that most of these benefits are linked to being in salaried or professional occupations, and that most work-related social security schemes do not require beneficiaries to prove that they are in a situation of genuine need, means that social security in Spain still overwhelmingly benefits wage-earners and professionals.

---

[8] This amount contains more than social *security* expenditure in the narrow sense of the word. It also includes public social spending on education, housing and social services.

2.1 The pension system

There are many types of public pension in Spain: retired civil servants' pensions, special veterans' pensions, *etc.* The most important, however, are statutory social security benefits, which are paid out under nine sub-systems and cover the following contingencies: retirement, disability, widowhood, and other contingencies (orphanhood, the need for family support etc.) covered by contributory schemes. There are non-contributory schemes, too.

2.1.1 Contributory insurance schemes

The contributory *Sistema Público de Pensiones* (SPP, Public Pension System) goes mainly towards protecting the aged. Retirement pensions are lifelong pensions payable to people over the age of 65, who have ceased working and have paid retirement insurance contributions for at least 15 years. The pensions are paid until the pensioner's death and may be suspended only if the pensioner accepts any form of employment.

The public pension system in general and old age pensions in particular were affected by institutional reform in 1978.[9] Benefits were also revalued at the end of the 1970s, although galloping inflation soon neutralised the effects of any increase. At the beginning of the 1980s maximum contributions were increased, so that they accounted for a greater share of the financing system. Attempts were also made to increase the level of benefits by institutionalising a system whereby pensions would be pegged to the Consumer Price Index and revalued accordingly every year. Another important step towards reforming the SPP involved gradually increasing minimum benefits in order to bring the minimum family benefit up to the level of the minimum wage. Other benefits were also increased, ensuring that all pensioners in similar circumstances received equal payments. In 1989 new measures for the revaluation of benefits were adopted, and in 1990 and 1994 they were ratified in agreements signed between the national organisations of employers and employees. When non-contributory pensions were introduced in 1990, the social security system's entire financial structure was changed: contributory pensions are now essentially financed by contributions while their non-contributory counterparts are financed through taxes.

Retirement pensions vary, although the State budget and laws on pension revaluations set minimum amounts every year. Minimum pensions for 1997 are 64,505 Ptas monthly (€ 388) for pensioners with dependent spouses, and 54,825 Ptas (€ 330) for unmarried pensioners. For the sake of comparison, it should be mentioned here that in 1997 the minimum wage is 66,630 Ptas (€ 400) per month. The maximum payable to people meeting all the requirements and, in addition, having

---

[9] Dictated by Decree-Law 36/1978.

a dependant, amounted to 284,198 Ptas (€ 1,708) monthly. To sum up, an analysis of the Spanish public contributory pensions system reveals that despite efforts made in past decades, when increases in benefits outstripped the economy's annual growth rates, benefit levels continue to be low in comparison with the cost of living.

2.1.2 Non-contributory schemes

In 1990 legislation on non-contributory benefits[10] extended social security coverage to include everyone over the age of 65 and people between the ages of 18 and 65 who are more than 65% disabled. Help for the disabled will be discussed in a later section, and therefore this section will be limited to a discussion of help for the elderly. Non-contributory pensions amount to 36,510 Ptas (€ 219) per month regardless of whether or not the pensioner has a dependent spouse.

2.1.3 Pension plans

Article 41, chapter 3 of the Spanish Constitution stipulates that 'the public powers shall maintain a public social security system for all citizens, which guarantees social assistance and benefits in cases of need, particularly when caused by unemployment. Supplementary assistance and benefits shall guarantee economic sufficiency to senior citizens by means of adequate and periodically updated pensions'. However, the fact that collective bargaining and certain employment contracts increasingly include private pension arrangements that involve more than what would be considered 'supplementary' benefits in the public social security system, demonstrates that the public system does not offer adequate protection. Starting with employers' supplementary pension payments, Spain has moved toward a system of employer-contracted insurance coverage, and eventually, in 1987, to pension schemes which are regulated by law.[11] More recently, in 1995, legislation on the regulation and supervision of private insurance policies,[12] has amended the 1987 law. Workers' interests are protected by guaranteeing that, in the event of employer insolvency, pension commitments will be met, even if workers lose their jobs.

Pension schemes entitle beneficiaries to receive income or capital in the event of retirement, of disability or of the death of a spouse. They stipulate the workers' obligation to contribute to the schemes. They also outline how the assets necessary for due recognition of these rights must be accumulated and managed. Private pension scheme benefits supplement, but do not replace, public social security

---

[10] By Law 26 of December 20th, 1990.
[11] By Law 8 of June 8th, 1987.
[12] By Law 30 of November 8th, 1995.

pensions. Employer-financed pension schemes are also a parallel system of social protection.

2.2 Illness and disability

2.2.1 General considerations

Until 1986, insurance against illness was part of the compulsory public system of social security for wage-earners, financed principally through contributions by employers and employees. With the creation of the National Health Service, the insurance against illness was extended to all citizens. As of 1989 it was to be financed essentially from public funds from general taxation. Other publicly-funded health care systems – among them *Mutualidad General de Funcionarios Civiles del Estado* (MUFACE), and the *Mutuas de Accidentes de Trabajo* (an employers' mutual covering industrial accidents) – which are managed either privately or as public-private partnerships, will also eventually be included in the SNS. The SNS covers:
• medical care (in cases of general or occupational illness, childbirth and industrial or other accidents) and rehabilitation (when required in the above cases); and
• economic assistance in cases of temporary disability and of childbirth.

As far as economic assistance is concerned, no difference exists between benefits on a contributory or a non-contributory basis.

2.2.2 Temporary disability

Temporary disability, as a situation of need, occurs when a wage-earner loses his income because of health problems caused by ordinary or occupational illness, by an industrial or another accident, or by any physical or mental ailment. Temporary disability is considered to exist as long as medical care is being received from the social security system and the wage-earner is unable to work. In cases of temporary disability due to an industrial accident or occupational illness the benefit payable is 75% of the basis for regulation, *i.e.* the mean wage he or she was earning before. In cases of ordinary and non-industrial accidents the amount is 60% of the basic wage between the 4th and 20th day of sick leave, and 75% from the 21st day onward. These benefits are payable for a maximum of 12 months and are renewable for an additional six months when there is a reasonable assumption that during this time the worker will be given a medical discharge on the grounds of complete recovery. Should the disability persist at the end of this period, the beneficiary will be medically examined within the space of three months in order to determine whether the disability can be considered permanent.

2.2.3 Permanent disability

Social security pays permanent disability benefits when the maximum period for temporary disability comes to an end and the wage-earner continues to need medical care and is expected to be permanently unable to work. Spanish social security distinguishes four different categories of permanent disability:
• partial disability to resume one's customary occupation
• total disability to resume one's customary occupation
• full disability, making a person incapable of any work; and
• major disability involving physical or functional disability that prevents the disabled person from performing, without assistance, such basic actions as getting dressed, moving, eating *etc.*

Invalids are entitled to one or more – flat-rate or lifetime – pensions, depending on the category of permanent disability:
• invalids who are partially disabled are paid a flat-rate equivalent to 24 months' basic salary
• invalids who are totally disabled are paid a lifetime pension amounting to 55% of the basic salary, provided the disability is caused by ordinary illness. In exceptional cases when the beneficiary is under the age of 60, this pension may be replaced by payment of a flat-rate benefit
• invalids unable to work at any occupation or profession due to full disability are entitled to a lifetime pension that is the equivalent of 100% of their basic pay
• pensions for major disability amount to 100% of their basic salary plus a 50% supplement payable to the invalid's care-giver.

According to OECD statistics,[13] spending on public health in Spain increased from 2.3% of GDP in 1960 to 6.3% in 1989. Both figures were below the OECD averages (3.8% in 1960 and 7.6% in 1989), although Spain's increase for the entire period was slightly higher than the average (4% as opposed to an OECD average of 3.8%).

2.2.4 Provisions for the disabled

People who are unable to work due to chronic illness not arising from work, are covered by the *Ley de Integración Social de los Minusválidos* (LISMI, Law on Social Integration of the Disabled),[14] which is not part of the social security system. Social services for the disabled have not as yet been organised into a single unified system. At the moment they are delivered by a public-private partnership consisting of the *Organización Nacional de Ciegos de España* (ONCE, National Organisation for the Blind, created by Decree on December 13, 1938), and the

---

[13] OECD, *Health Data Bank, Health Affairs. Fall-Spring 1989* (1991)
[14] Of April 7th, 1982.

Servicio de Recuperación y Rehabilitación de Minusválidos Físicos y Psíquicos (SEREM, Service for the Recovery and Rehabilitation of the Physically and Mentally Disabled, created by Decree on February 21, 1974). In accordance with the LISMI, since 1985 the State has not only provided health care but also a minimum guaranteed income to people who are more than 65% disabled and whose income is less than 75% of the minimum wage.

2.3 Unemployment

2.3.1 The development of unemployment insurance

Spain's system of unemployment protection was created by law in 1961. In 1963 it was included into the Social Security Law. The 1980 the *Ley Básica de Empleo* (LBE, Basic Employment Law) took a new approach to the issue. It can be said to be the origin of the current Spanish system of unemployment protection. Unemployment insurance was made a separate system, completely independent of the general social security system. Responsibility for its management it was shifted from the National Social Security Institute to the *Instituto Nacional de Empleo* (INEM, National Employment Institute), which had been created in 1978. However, with the passage of the LBE the percentage of unemployed covered dropped from 50% to less than 30%.

The year 1983 saw the enactment of the *Ley de Protección por Desempleo* (LPD, Unemployment Protection Law). With minor amendments being made in 1989, 1992 and 1993, this law basically remains in effect today. The LPD aimed to bring the level of unemployment coverage back up to pre-LBE levels. A year later, the Government and the national organisations of employers and workers signed the *Acuerdo Económico y Social* (AES, Economic and Social Agreement). The Government undertook to increase coverage to a minimum of 48% of the unemployed. The terms of contributory and welfare benefits were improved, and it was stipulated that, for as long as the worker remained jobless, INEM would make full payments to the social security system, *i.e.* both employer and worker contributions. In the following years two improvements to the LPD were made. First, a general strike in December 1988 led to the introduction in 1989 of urgent social measures which increased welfare benefits coverage.[15] A year later, new regulations on unemployment benefits for temporary agricultural labourers were laid down in an attempt to bring their unemployment benefits closer in line with the general system of welfare benefits.[16] Having mortgaged the future of the public sector with these improvements, the Government then thought again and reduced contributory benefits, while attempting to cushion the effect by providing some

---

[15] By Royal Decree-Law of March 3rd, 1989.
[16] By Royal Decree 1387/1990.

sort of welfare coverage.[17] Tax measures and measures concerning the reform of the legal regime of public administration and unemployment protection[18] reduced the net amounts of contributory and social welfare benefits and enacted other labour market reforms, such as an improvement of the current training contract, the introduction of an apprenticeship contract, and the equation of unemployment benefits with earned income as far as income tax is concerned.

2.3.2 Unemployment benefits

Unemployment benefits replace the previously earned wages of workers who are officially unemployed – totally or partially. They guarantee a minimum level of subsistence. The general system (*Régimen general*) includes (contributory) unemployment benefits and social welfare support, while a special system (*Régimen especial*) is responsible for income support paid to seasonal farm workers.

Unemployment benefits paid out under the general system are linked to the amount of contributions paid by the worker and the length of time that contributions have been paid. Benefits also include payment of the employers' share of social security contributions and 35% of the worker's contribution. In order to be eligible for these benefits a worker must
• be registered as unemployed with the general or special social security system
• have paid contributions for a minimum of 360 days within the six years prior to becoming unemployed; and
• be under legal retirement age, unless (a) the worker is ineligible for retirement (due to failure to have paid contributions for the required length of time), or (b) the cause of unemployment is a Government authorised layoff or reduction of working hours.

Benefits are payable for a minimum of 120 days (when contributions have been paid for only 360 days) and a maximum of 720 days (when contributions have been paid for at least 2,160 days). Unemployment benefit levels vary in accordance with the beneficiary's situation: they depend on the current minimum wage, and on payment of social security contributions for medical care, family protection (when applicable) and retirement. INEM has set maximum unemployment benefits for 1997 at 171,017 Ptas (€ 1,028) per month for people over the age of 18, and minimum benefits at 58,300 Ptas (€ 349). This is a 2.6% increase over previous year's maximum benefit. It amounts to 75% of the minimum wage for people with no dependent children and 100% for people with one or more dependent children.

---

[17] Law 22 of April 8th, 1992.
[18] In Law 22/1993, popularly known as the 'companion law', included in the 1994 Budget. A 'companion law' is a law passed at the same time as the annual Budget. However, formal requirements for its passing are different from those of the Budget Act.

On expiry of the (contributory) unemployment benefit, the unemployed are entitled to social welfare support. Other requirements for entitlement to welfare support include ineligibility for contributory unemployment benefits (due to failure to meet the required conditions), family responsibilities and/or old age. Moreover, applicants for social welfare support must be registered as job-seekers. They may not have turned down any reasonable job offers, may not have refused to take part in job promotion or professional training or recycling programmes, and may not have an income exceeding 75% of the minimum wage. Social welfare support is paid for 6 months and may generally be renewed for up to 18 months. When age and family responsibility so warrant, welfare support can be extended to 21 months or, in the case of workers over the age of 52, until legal retirement age.

The social security sub-system known as the special system is very limited in its scope. It applies only to temporary farm labourers who are covered by the Farm Labourers sub-system (*Régimen agrario*) and are registered with social security offices in the autonomous regions of Andalusia and Extremadura.

2.4 Family assistance

2.4.1 Childbirth and parental leave

The social security system pays salaried wage-earners, regardless of gender, the equivalent of 100% of their latest basic salary during leave of absence on grounds of childbirth, adoption or pre-adoption custody, and medical care in cases of pregnancy and childbirth. Women giving birth are entitled to sixteen consecutive weeks of paid leave, or up to eighteen weeks in the case of multiple births. Should the beneficiary still require medical care and be unable to work at the end of that time, she will be covered on grounds of temporary disability due to ordinary sickness.

2.4.2 Family allowances for dependent children

Benefits protecting the children under a worker's care consist of an annual allowance of 36,000 Ptas (€ 216) for each child under eighteen years old or seriously disabled to the extent of 65% or more.[19] Entitlement to this allowance is restricted to workers who are included in the social security system and whose annual income is below a specific amount which is set annually by the State Budget Law (currently around 1,100,000 Ptas or € 6,611). The same allowance is granted, on the same conditions, to non-contributors who reside legally on Spanish territory.

---

[19] These beneftis werde introduced by Law 26/90.

2.4.3 Death and surviving dependants

These benefits are intended to alleviate the straitened circumstances of surviving dependants. The surviving dependent spouse is entitled to a pension of 45% of the deceased's base salary at time of death. This pension is payable for life or until such time as the surviving spouse remarries. Each child of a deceased wage-earner is entitled to the equivalent of 20% of the wage-earner's basic wage at the time of death. These pensions are payable until the orphan's eighteenth birthday. Moreover, regardless of the cause of death, surviving dependants are entitled to a supplementary funeral grant, which amounts to a flat-rate sum of 5,000 Ptas (€ 30) payable immediately to cover the costs of burying the deceased.

2.5 Coverage of other special risks: divorce

Article 32.2 of the Spanish Constitution states that the Law will regulate the grounds for marriage separation and dissolution and their effects. This constitutional precept was put into effect in 1981, establishing that the effects of divorce include the following:[20]
• there is obligatory maintenance of children subject to parental authority and also of those older children who live in the family home without resources of their own
• alimony may be granted to either of the ex-spouses if his or her resources are insufficient for survival
• compensatory alimony may be granted to either of the ex-spouses if the divorce has caused an economic imbalance *vis-à-vis* the other spouse.

Maintenance cannot be waived but alimony can be waived if both ex-spouses agree to an alternative financial arrangement. Obligations regarding maintenance and alimony are assumed by one of the ex-spouses; failure to comply may result in prosecution. None of these obligations will be assumed by the State: the State does not provide social cover for the person who has to pay alimony, nor for the person who has a right to alimony but does not receive it. On the other hand, the State may grant, as part of social welfare, financial assistance to divorced women who carry the financial burden of their family alone. As a consequence, the majority of those receiving a social wage are women with family members under their sole charge.

The law also states that widows' or widowers' pensions should be paid to the legitimate spouse in proportion to the length of time he/she has lived with the deceased.[21] Therefore, if the deceased had two legitimate wives, both will receive a widow's pension from the social security system – the amount depending on the length of time each lived with the deceased.

---

[20] By Law 30/81, in particular section 81 and subsequent sections regulating separation and divorce.
[21] Law 30/1981, section 10.

3 The level of basic social security arrangements

3.1 Indicators

In Spain the following indicators are used to determine the levels of basic social security arrangements and protection:

• The minimum wage (*Salario Mínimo Interprofesional,* SMI) is used to determine the levels of unemployment benefits, housing aid and educational grants. In 1980 the minimum wage amounted to 37.5% of the average wage. By 1991 it had dropped to 27.65%. The average wage is understood to mean the gross bulk wage, according to national accounts, divided by the wage-earning population. The minimum wage for 1997 is 66,630 Ptas (€ 400) per month, or the equivalent of 30.6% of the current average wage.
• The *Instituto Nacional de Estadística* (INE, National Statistics Institute) uses the 'equivalent average spending level' (*Gasto Medio Equivalente,* GME) as a further indicator to guide decisions about benefit levels. According to the 1990-1991 survey on family budgets, the GME at that time amounted to 852,640 Ptas per year (€ 5,124). The poverty line is also defined in terms of average spending. It would be more accurate to draw the poverty line in terms of income, but – due to the difficulty in obtaining information – spending is used as a criterion instead. Households spending 50% or 60% of the national average rank as poor. The poorest households spend less than 40% of the national average.
• Family income is the indicator used to determine the *Renta Mínima de Inserción* (RMI) or income support (see below).
• The extent of social security protection is usually measured by comparing the average benefit with GDP *per capita*.

3.2 Fighting poverty

In order to protect citizens from poverty or insufficient income, Spain has gradually introduced specific systems to cover various segments of the population. As a result, protection against poverty is highly fragmented and poorly coordinated.

In the 1980s the Spanish welfare state was extended to include virtually the entire population, but its impact on society is unequal. While working members of the population could supplement their level of protection with private arrangements, a considerable effort was made to provide a series of public welfare benefits to ensure a level of subsistence for the poorest segment of the eligible population. It has been ruled that supplements be paid when social security retirement and dependent spouses' pensions are insufficient. These supplements are semi-contributory, and they are payable to those who have paid their social security contributions in the past. Moreover, for people who are no longer entitled to receive contributory benefits, welfare support is available. In Spain welfare support is known as the *Renta Mínima de Inserción* (RMI) or social salary, following the lead taken by France in 1988. RMI is payable for a maximum of 3 years. This period can be extended, but the procedure is fairly complex and some people may end up being deprived of this benefit. Welfare support is paid by regional Governments and in most cases eligibility is contingent upon having been resident for a certain time in the region concerned. It happens that a change of residence can cause people to forfeit their right to welfare support from the region where they formerly resided without their being able to meet the residence requirement for support from the new region.

In 1989, the Basque Country was the first to introduce RMI as part of a global plan to fight poverty. All other regions, with the exception of the Balearic Islands, have since followed suit. In some cases, the programmes are only symbolic, but most of them have involved public action against social marginalisation and extreme poverty. Almost five years of experience have finally made Spain's public institutions aware of the true state of poverty and the problems involved in fighting it.

An estimated 36,383 people received income support in 1992. This is the equivalent of 0.19% of the population between the ages of 25 and 64 and 0.32% of all Spanish households. Unfortunately, there is little coordination among state, regional and municipal policies. As a result the system has become increasingly disperse, not to say fragmented, in terms of production and delivery of social services. The result of all social spending has had a limited effect on reducing poverty. In fact, rather than reducing poverty, it has simply contained it:

• Between 1985 and 1992 the percentage of families living below the 50% poverty line (as explained in section 3.1.) increased from 19.5% to 19.7%. During this same period the percentage of poor people among the population dropped from 20.5% to 18.9%.[22]
• In a survey carried out by the *Fundación FOESSA*, in 1994[23] – in response to the question 'How do you make it to the end of the month on your income?' – 27.7% of the respondents replied that they had trouble making it; 33.8% said that they had some trouble and only 37.1% said that it was easy for them to make it through the month. Chief among those who said they had trouble were unemployed people

---

[22] Fundación FOESSA, *V Informe Sociológico sobre la situación social en España. Sociedad para todos en el año 2000* [Sociological report on the social situation in Spain. A society for all in the year 2000] (Madrid 1994), p. 1489. Please note that the first percentages, which register an increase from 19.5% to 19.7%, refer to families or households, while the subsequent percentages, which show a decrease from 20.5% to 18.9%, refer to individuals. This means that, although the number of poor households registered in 1992 was higher, the number of members of these households was lower and, consequently, the percentage of poor individuals was lower in 1992 than in 1995.

[23] Questionnaire, question no. 51, in: *ibid.*, p. 2300, comment on p. 1485.

who are actively seeking jobs, followed by unemployed people who are not looking for work. Retired people have no more trouble than the national average in making it to the end of the month.

Apart from its dubious effectiveness, social policy development caused a good deal of conflict between 1985 and 1993, with a constant struggle to strike a balance between universal human rights and the need to contain spending. This has resulted in a deepening of the poverty of households beneath the 40% poverty line. There has also been a struggle between increased social costs and attempts to contain the public deficit. Problems have been aggravated by the high incidence of fraud.

4 Household or individual

The *Ley de Medidas Fiscales, Administrativas y de Orden Social o Ley de Acompañamiento* (Law on Fiscal Administrative and Public Policy Measures, or Companion Law),[24] which was included in the 1997 Budget, has introduced a new concept of the household, modifying the concept which had been in effect until then for income tax purposes. Under the new law the household may consist of:
• a married couple not legally separated with (a) any number of children aged under 18, other than those who live independently from their parents with the consent of the latter; and (b) any number of disabled children aged over 18 who are legally under parental authority
• a father or a mother with any number of children who fulfil the requirements outlined above.

No one may form part of two households simultaneously.

Unlike the LISMI regulations on benefits for the disabled (see section 2.2.4), the law on non-contributory social security allowances (1990) stipulates that benefits depend upon household income.[25] Although RMI, or welfare support benefits (see section 3.2), are payable on an individual basis, the household continues to be used as a frame of reference. Thus, benefits depend on households or families more than on individuals. Individuals are not eligible for these benefits if they live with others who enjoy an income. In order to be eligible for welfare support, individual income must be less than a certain amount, which varies depending on the size of the household. The minimum is between 30,000 and 40,000 Ptas (between € 180 and € 240) per month. Small amounts are added to these figures for every additional member of the family. In some cases, there is no ceiling; in others, the

---

[24] Law 13/1996 of December 30th, 1996.
[25] Law 26/90.

ceiling consists of an income equivalent to the amount of the minimum wage. Welfare support is payable for between 3 months and 3 years. In some cases it may be extended, but the procedure is fairly complicated. Welfare support is quite strictly and explicitly linked to serious efforts at finding employment.

5 Legal protection

The following recourse may be taken when decisions of administrative agencies violate individual rights.

5.1 Administrative action

In the event of an appeal against a specific decision, a preliminary complaint must be filed with the administrative agency responsible for the decision. This must be done within thirty days following notification of this decision. Should there be no specific decision, the complainant may request that one be made: this request is the equivalent of a preliminary complaint. In either case, the competent administrative authority (the director of the provincial branch of the Social Security Institute) must make a resolution on the preliminary complaint or application within 45 days. Should no specific resolution have been made at the end of this time, the complaint is considered to have been dismissed, and the complainant may resort to legal action before the Court of Social Affairs.

5.2 Complaints: court action, the Government Ombudsman

Conflicts and iniquities in the area of labour relationships are handled under social jurisdiction, in the first instance by the *Juzgados de lo Social* (Social Courts) and on appeal by the *Salas de lo Social de los Tribunales Superiores de Justicia de las Comunidades Autónomas* (Social Courts of the Higher Tribunals of the Autonomous Communities) and the *Tribunal Supremo* (High Court), the latter being responsible for appeals against decisions by Social Courts. Compared with normal civil jurisdiction, social jurisdiction is faster, more agile and cheaper, with fewer formalities and tighter deadlines. Traditionally, this jurisdiction gives special protection to the workers. It was set up to protect the weaker party in labour relationships, in consideration of the fact that employers have more means at their disposal to keep up a legal fight. All the same, if a company is within its rights, and can prove this, it will receive a favourable decision by the tribunal.

Legal protection of fundamental rights and liberties in the field of labour relationships (equality, strikes, trade unions, *etc.*) is provided by appeal to the *Tribunal Constitucional* (Constitutional Tribunal).

Citizens have a right to submit complaints to the *Ombudsman*. However, since the Ombudsman has no executive power, he cannot restore their rights but merely admonish other bodies to make amends.

6 From public to private arrangements

The survey carried out in 1994 by the *Fundación FOESSA*,[26] revealed that 47.6% of all Spanish households receive some sort of Government economic benefit. This percentage equals 5,634,000 people. Of these, 2,071,356 receive benefits from two different sources and 343,256 from three.

In the not-too-distant future private insurance schemes will perhaps become an alternative to contributory public assistance and individuals will be able to opt for the system of their choice. However, this development may be blocked by the fact that the public social security system needs to continue collecting funds in order to finance current, let alone future, benefit payments. Nevertheless, the public sector is already signing agreements with private institutions, primarily in the fields of education and health care, in order to facilitate private production of State-financed services. A private volunteer movement is also beginning to flourish. Members of a variety of associations and foundations are now undertaking tasks formerly regarded as public services.[27] Privatisation would be beneficial in bringing social services to segments of society hitherto ignored by the State. Budget constraints prevent the public administration from expanding its social services, which are not always delivered efficiently anyway. Moreover, and perhaps this is its greatest advantage of privatisation, it could stimulate greater solidarity in society. Public provision of services can lull people into the falsely complacent belief that solidarity is simply a matter of paying taxes. According to the *Fundación FOESSA* survey of 1994, 78.6% of the population feel that 'there are people who really need State aid and do not get it', and 42% feel that 'Government social spending undermines social solidarity'.[28] The authors of the report predict that the new welfare system in Spain will be mixed: the State will continue to be at the hub but regional and local Governments will play an increasingly important role, as will volunteer associations, provided that they avoid becoming overly dependent on State financing.[29] Lastly, higher income groups will purchase the services they need on the open market, thus relieving the pressure on public services.

---

[26] Questionnaire question no. 47, in: Fundación FOESSA, *V Informe Sociológico*, p. 2287.

[27] *Ibid.*, p. 1833. The *Fundación FOESSA* survey is an interesting source of information about this movement. In addition to presenting an institutional balance sheet that illustrates the movement's theoretical framework, the report also contains the results of an empirical survey on volunteer services.

[28] Questionnaire question no. 54, in: *ibid.*, p. 2300, comment on p. 1492.

[29] *Ibid.*, p. 1493.

During the long years of the Franco dictatorship the role of the State became so deeply rooted that Spain's civil society, though increasingly dynamic, is not yet strong enough to take over from the public administration as the supplier of social services. However, it seems as though it will only be possible to maintain the welfare state in Spain if welfare services are decentralised and made available to all segments of society. This, of course, will require better coordination, closer cooperation and greater participation on the part of all agents involved.

7 European unity and its consequences

The obligation to rationalise its social security system will provide Spain with its greatest opportunity. As discussed in detail in our study of the welfare state,[30] the main problem in Spain is that social security benefits have been generously increased without ensuring adequate financing. As a result, social spending financed by specific taxes, which are the basis of social security budgets, has been enhanced with transfers from the public budget, whose income comes from general taxes. Increased social spending has therefore led to increased public spending, and to an increased public deficit which fails to meet the requirements of the *Agreement on Stability and Growth* signed by the countries participating in the Economic and Monetary Union (EMU). Benefits can only be improved if tax revenue increases. However, increasing the tax burden is a dangerous course. It would be excessively costly for the business community, could discourage individuals from striving to increase their earnings and could lead to a serious recession in Spain. The entire system must be restructured. This will not be possible without social consensus, which will be difficult to achieve: citizens want benefits that equal those in other European Union countries but are unwilling to bear an equal tax burden.

To meet the EMU conditions, Spain's public spending needs thorough restructuring and a more realistic approach to social security benefits. One cannot overlook the fact that the country's high rate of unemployment makes it difficult to finance the social security system through employers and workers' contributions alone. Demographic change in recent years has increased the cost of pensions. Health care has recently been extended to the entire population. Health care spending and unemployment benefits account for the lion's share of the increased cost of social protection in Spain.

---

[30] E.M. Recio *et al.*, *El Estado del Bienestar* [The Welfare State], Barcelona: Generalitat de Catalunya (Regional Government of Catalonia), 1996. Collecció Textos i Documentos, no. 14 (Collection of Texts and Documents, no. 14).

Ultimately, the effects of European unity will depend on the prosperity of Spain's businesses and economy. Although Spain has made a considerable effort, levels of productivity and competitiveness are still far below the European Community average. Moreover, we do not feel that the subject of social security can be considered separately from other aspects of social policy and labour law. Further efforts should be made to define the 1989 European Community Charter of the Fundamental Social Rights of Workers (the so-called 'Social Charter') and the corresponding appendix to the 1991 Maastricht Treaty (the Agreement on Social Policy, or 'Social Chapter'). In our opinion, efficient measures should be introduced to ensure minimum working conditions (*i.e.* material and financial circumstances: safety, health, wages, *etc*). If the conditions established are those that are considered acceptable minima in the majority of European Union countries, workers in countries like Spain will benefit while employers will suffer. If the minimum conditions are reduced to the level of conditions in Spain and in similar countries, employers in the richer countries will benefit while their employees will suffer. Eventually, compulsory minimum working conditions should be on a level acceptable to all countries of the European Union. However, for less developed countries like Spain these conditions should, for the time being, have the status of goals. These countries should only be obliged to actually implement these conditions once their economies have sufficiently converged with those of the wealthier member states.

Bibliography

In addition to the references given in footnotes, we refer to:

M. Aguilar *et al.*, 'El Salario Social de las Comunidades Autónomas [Social wages in the Autonomous Regions]', in: Fundación FOESSA, *V Informe Sociológico sobre la situación social en España. Sociedad para todos en el año 2000* [Sociological report on the social situation in Spain. A society for all in the year 2000] (Madrid 1994), p. 1525-1549.

J.M. Almansa Pastor, *Derecho de la Seguridad Social* [Social security law], Madrid 1995.

M. Alonso Olea and J.L. Tortuero Plaza, *Instituciones de la Serguridad Social* [Social security institutions], Madrid 1997.

J.F. Blanco Lahoz, J. López Candia, and M.A. Monparler, *Curso de Seguridad Social* [A course in social security], Valencia 1995.

D. Casado, 'Acción Social y Servicios Sociales [Social action and social services]', in: Fundación FOESSA, *V Informe Sociológico sobre la situación social en España. Sociedad para todos en el año 2000* [Sociological report on the social situation in Spain. A society for all in the year 2000] (Madrid 1994), p. 1737-1880.

Legislación social básica. [Basic social legislation], Madrid: Civitas, 1997.

Ministerio del Trabajo y Asuntos Sociales (Ministry of Labour and Social Affairs), *Sistema Público de Servicios Sociales Básicos. Plan Concertado de Prestaciones Básicas en Corporaciones Locales. Memoria Anual 1994 / Previsiones 1995* [The public system of basic social services. Outline of the provision of basic benefits by local organisations. Annual report for 1994 / Prospects for 1995], Madrid 1996.

Ministerio del Trabajo y Asuntos Sociales, *Guía laboral y de asuntos sociales 1997* [Handbook of Labour Affairs and Social Affairs 1997], Madrid 1997.

Organisation for Economic Cooperation and Development (OECD), *Health Data Bank, Health Affairs. Fall-Spring 1989*, Paris 1991.

E.M. Recio, 'El Gobierno local ante el desarrollo y las perspectivas del Estado del Bienestar [Local Government and the development and prospects of the welfare state]', in: Fundación Carles Pi i Sunyer, *Informe sobre el Gobierno local en España* [Report on local Government in Spain] (Barcelona 1997), p. 93-108.

G. Rodríguez Cabrero, 'Política de Rentas [Interest policies]', in: Fundación FOESSA, *V Informe Sociológico sobre la situación social en España. Sociedad para todos en el año 2000* [Sociological report on the social situation in Spain. A society for all in the year 2000] (Madrid 1994), p. 1411-1549.

A. Rodríguez Castedo, 'Los Servicios Sociales: hacia una sociedad más justa y solidaria [Social services: towards a more just and solidary society]', in: *Temas para el Debate* [Issues for debate], 24 (1996), p. 57-61.

XI United Kingdom

Hannah Reed and Simon Deakin

1 Introduction

What is to become of the welfare state is a basic question within social and political policy – a question, which has dominated the political agenda in the UK for some time. In the past opinion has been divided between incremental change to the benefit system and more radical reform to the balance between cash benefits and services, means-testing and universality. The last two decades have witnessed substantial change in the welfare in the UK. Motives for reform have been diverse: to reduce the benefits bill, to reduce the length of time spent on benefit, to create incentives for people to move from welfare to work and to improve quality of services. At different times, different strategies have been adopted, but much of the discussion in the UK has been based on snapshots, leading to decisions, which later have proved inadequate or inappropriate.

On entering power in 1997, the Labour Government committed itself to a comprehensive review of social security. The objective was to survey the welfare system in its entirety, assessing its strengths and weaknesses and laying out a political and intellectual framework for its future development and reform, based on the 'third way' for welfare. The Green Paper *New Ambitions for our country: A New Contract for Welfare* identified key principles which would steer future reform. These principles focused on key themes: work as the best form of welfare; the maintenance of high quality services; promoting partnership between public and private sector providers; tackling poverty and social exclusion, particularly among children and families; and reducing fraud within the welfare system.[1] This paper seeks to assess the practical implications of the 'third way' for the welfare system. It asks: to what extent does the 'third way' offer a real alternative to previous welfare policy? To what extent does it vary the existing balance between cash benefits and services, means-testing and universality; and to what extent has Government policy succeeded to date in putting its guiding principles into action?

---

[1] Department of Social Security, *New Ambitions for our country: A New Contract for Welfare*, Cm 3805, London: HMSO, March 1998.

2 General overview and developing trends

The modern British system of social security dates from the legislative reforms of 1946/47. These were based largely on the Beveridge Report (1942) and established the principle that all those in active employment should be entitled, by virtue of contributions paid into a social insurance fund, to protection against major interruptions in employment and to provision in retirement. Supplementary social assistance was also made available for those in need but who were not entitled to contributory benefits. Unlike models developed in other European states, the British welfare system did not provide for earnings-related benefits; instead, flat-rate benefits were paid in return for flat-rate contributions. During the 1960s and 1970s this was to change as earnings-related supplements for unemployment and sickness benefit were introduced and the *State Earnings-Related Pension Scheme* (SERPS) was established.

Throughout the 1980s and early 1990s, the social security system in Britain became the subject of extensive reform under a series of Conservative Governments. The main objectives for the change were to reduce public expenditure on welfare provision and to sharpen the incentives for the unemployed to re-enter the labour market. In the process, the value of contributory benefits was reduced through the removal of earnings-related supplements in 1982 and the linking of benefits to prices as opposed to wages, which have risen faster. Further reforms were made to the rules on eligibility for benefits for the unemployed, reducing entitlement to benefit and imposing stringent 'job search' duties on claimants. Changes were also made to the tax-benefit system which aim to reduce the disincentives for workers returning to the labour market and to encourage employers to offer, and potential employees to accept, lower paid employment. More generally, means-tested benefits were targeted away from the unemployed and towards those in low paid employment, in particular through the introduction of *Family Credit* in 1988.

Throughout this period, the British system became orientated more clearly towards a form of provision based on the criterion of need, rather than on individuals' social insurance contributions while in employment. Although certain social insurance benefits remain formally in place, the link between benefits and earnings has been broken for many purposes. Universal benefits, paid regardless of need or contribution and financed out of general taxation, have traditionally played a relatively small role in the system, and, with the significant exception of *Child Benefit,* continue to do so. On the other hand, certain services (in particular health and education) are provided by the state on a universal basis, that is to say, free at the point of supply. These forms of welfare provision are not generally regarded as part of the social security system, and are outside the scope of the present paper.

Since the 1970s, then, the British system could be said to have become more 'residual' in character, in contrast both to the universalism of the Scandinavian systems and the broadly-based social insurance systems of the continent.[2] However, the changes made to social security in the 1980s did not succeed in the aim of reversing the growth of public expenditure on social welfare; during the 1980s, expenditure on social security in Britain *increased* as a proportion of GDP, largely because of the costs associated with continuing high levels of unemployment.

2.1 A third way for welfare

The election of the new Labour Government in 1997 guaranteed that welfare reform would continue to have a high profile within the social policy and political arenas. The proposed programme for welfare reform stood at the forefront of the Government's quest to re-think the social democratic vision for the welfare state and to devise a 'third way' for social policy. On entering power, the Government made clear its commitment to a 'root and branch' reform of the welfare system, setting in train a series of major programmes of reform, notably active labour market policies, in the form of the *New Deal* and the establishment of a *Social Exclusion Unit* at the centre of Government. Substantial inroads were also made towards realigning the tax and benefits systems to reduce the financial disincentives for people returning to work. Each of these policy initiatives embodied an approach to welfare, which focuses on work as the key route out of poverty and social exclusion.

It is still very early to assess what effects the Government's 'third way' approach may have on the welfare system, in part because the precise direction for the 'third way' remains to be defined. As one leading commentator has suggested at a concrete level, 'the Government has in fact left its options very wide, without giving many clues as to where the 'third way' will actually take us'.[3] One definition of the 'third way', as articulated in terms of welfare, is contained in the Green Paper, *New Ambitions for our country: A New Contract for Welfare*.[4] This conceived the 'third way' as a path between neo-liberal and traditional social democratic routes:

'The welfare state now faces a choice of futures. A privatised future [...] the status quo; or the Government's third way – promoting opportunity instead of dependence, with a welfare state providing for the mass of people, but in new ways fit for the modern world.'[5]

What is most certain is that the Government's adopted approach for welfare, marks a watershed from previous social democratic approaches to welfare. The Government's joint offensive on jobs and welfare are no longer framed 'in terms of job creation and demand side intervention', but rather in the new language of combating 'depend-

---

[2] G. Esping-Anderson, *The Three Worlds of Welfare Capitalism,* Cambridge: Polity, 1990.

[3] J. Hills, *Thatcherism, New Labour and the Welfare State* (London: Centre for Analysis of Social Exclusion, London School of Economics, 1998. CASE-paper CASE/13), p. 33.

[4] DSS, *New Ambitions for our country.*

[5] DSS, *New Ambitions for our country.*

ency', enforcing rights and responsibilities' and – above all – incentivising work'.[6] This transition in policy forms part of the Government's response to rapidly shifting economic conditions. Advocates of the 'third way' perceive the globalisation of markets and the rapidly changing nature of consumer demand as having had a significant impact on the ability of national Governments to shape their own macro-economic policy, on the kinds of flexibility and skills required of workers in changing labour markets, and on Governments' capacity to redistribute income.[7] This changing perspective explains the reasoning behind the Government's welfare reform programme, including the emphasis on supply side measures for tackling unemployment; the focus on lack of education and skills as the primary causes of poverty; and the reluctance to pursue more transparent forms of income distribution.

As a result, the Government has set about devising a new formulation for the social democratic project, a primary goal for which is the creation of lifelong equality of opportunity. Within this new framework emphasis is placed on tackling the primary causes of poverty through investment in education and training, increased attachment to the labour market and increased capacity to earn, rather than through redistribution by means of the benefits system. Associated with this approach are such policies as the New Deal, the realignment in tax and benefits systems, the introduction of *Individual Learning Accounts* and the implementation of the *National Minimum Wage*.

Alongside this new conception of equality of opportunity, the Government has also sought to redefine the debate on poverty in terms of social exclusion and inclusion. Once again, as with the debates on equality of opportunity, paid work is identified as the principal route out of social exclusion. Emphasis, however, is also placed on the importance of fostering social capital and the development of local solutions for multi-dimensional forms of exclusion, generated through local ownership and participation.[8] Accompanying the increased focus on the refurbishment of civil society and neighbourhood renewal, is a redefinition of the role of the individual within the welfare system, with a growing emphasis on obligations on individuals to match rights.

The final theme underlying the Government's changing approach to welfare is a rethinking of the roles of the state and the market, the public and private sectors in the provision of welfare. Throughout the 1980s and early 1990s, in response to rising expenditure and concern for likely future expenditure increases brought about by demographic factors, a major effort was made by successive Conservative Govern-

---

[6] J. Peck and N. Theodore, *Between Welfare and Work: Workfare and the Re-regulation of Contingent Labour Markets*. Paper presented at the 20th International Working Party on Labour Market Segmentation, July 9-14, 1998, Arco, Trento, Italy.

[7] C. Oppenheim, 'Welfare Reform and the Labour Market: a 'third way'?', in: *Benefits. A Journal of Social Security Research, Policy and Practice,*(1999), no. 25, April/May, p. 1-5.

[8] Social Exclusion Unit, *Bringing Britain Together. A national strategy for neighbourhood renewal*, Cm 4045, London: HMSO, 1998.

ments to shift responsibility for the provision of welfare away from the state and into the private sector. This took the form of active encouragement for individuals to opt out of the state-run social insurance scheme, in favour of private and occupational provision of various kinds. These efforts focused particularly on pension provision and sick pay, although they did not extend to unemployment benefits.

The election of the new Labour Government has not stemmed the tide towards increased private welfare provision in the UK, although it appears that the Government is taking a more pragmatic approach than its predecessors in determining whether welfare should be delivered or financed by the public or private sector. Emphasis is placed on partnership between public and private sector providers and the introduction of protection for individuals to prevent them from being discouraged from making private provision. Nevertheless the on-going expansion in private sector provision, particularly in the areas of pensions and sick pay, signals a potentially fundamental transformation in the system of social security and of the state's role within it, with the state's principal role now that of regulator, rather than provider. These developments raise important issues concerning the effectiveness of regulation and the implications for equity and solidarity of the shift to private provision.

2.2 Legal, administrative and financial foundation

The law on social security in Britain consists of a complex network of interlocking statutes, secondary legislation, and case law.[9] Since 1988, responsibility for the development of social security policy has rested with the Department of Social Security,[10] although from the late 1980s the system was administered by six 'New Steps' Agencies. The stated aim of creating these agencies was to improve both the efficiency with which public services were provided and responsiveness to consumer demand. The principal agencies included the *Benefits Agency*, which administers benefits payments; the *War Pensions Agency*; the *Child Support Agency*; and the *Contributions Agency*, which is responsible for the National Insurance scheme. In April 1999, the Contributions Agency and responsibility for National Insurance policy was transferred to the Inland Revenue, the aim being to simplify tax and National Insurance processes for businesses and to facilitate a greater alignment of tax and

---

[9] The principal Acts of Parliament include the *Social Security Contributions and Benefits Act 1992*, the *Social Security Administration Act 1992*, the *Pensions Scheme Act 1993*, the *Pensions Act 1995*, the *Jobseekers Act 1995* and the *Social Security Act 1998*. At the time of writing the *Welfare Reform and Pensions Bill* is being considered by the UK Parliament. We do not make detailed references to statutory sources in the text below; Ogus, Barendt and Wikeley provides a detailed account of the legal structure of the social security system: A. Ogus, E. Barendt, and N. Wikeley, *The Law of Social Security*, London: Butterworths, 1995 (4th ed.). See also J. Mesher and P. Wood, *Income-Related Benefits: The Legislation*, London: Sweet and Maxwell, 1994.

[10] For a detailed narrative of the history of the administration of social security in Britain see Ogus, Barendt, and Wikeley, *The Law of Social Security*, ch. 1.

National Insurance Contributions (NIC) rules in the longer term. In addition, local authorities administer benefits relating to accommodation needs and local taxation.

In the Green Paper *New ambitions for our country: A New Contract for Welfare,* the Government announced its intention to streamline the administration of benefits, by developing a *Single Gateway to Welfare.*[11] The approach adopted in a subsequent green paper on the Single Gateway to Welfare[12] was to bring together the Employment Service, responsible for assisting job seekers to find work or training, the Benefits Agency and other welfare providers, including local authorities, to a single point of contact for benefit recipients. It proposed that new claimants of working age, with limited exceptions should be required to attend a work-focused interview with a personal adviser as a condition of receiving benefit.

In any one year spending on social security benefits in Britain represents the largest single outlay for Government. In 1998/99 the total social security spending amounted to 99.349 billion Pounds Sterling (£), accounting for nearly 30% of all planned Government expenditure[13]. Over the last 15 years, spending on social security as a proportion of GDP has grown, having risen from 9% in 1979/80 to 13% in 1994/5, although in recent years there has been a slight decline in spending, accounting for slightly over 11% of GDP in 1998/99. Concern over the growth in the cost of welfare, arising in particular from the increase in the proportion of elderly people and single parents in the population, has been at the forefront of Government deliberations.

Social welfare provision in Britain can be divided up into four broad categories:

• The *Jobseeker's Allowance* (JSA) (the main social security provision for the unemployed) which comes in two forms: contributory JSA, which is replaced after 6 months with an income-based JSA
• Other social insurance or contributory benefits, which are based on an individual's National Insurance Contribution record
• Social assistance which is means-tested and paid according to need, and
• Universal benefits, which are neither contribution nor income related.

The source of funding for social welfare varies according to the category of benefit. Contributory benefits are paid for out of the National Insurance Fund, which is financed from contributions from employers and employees and the self-employed, and to a limited extent by the State, while means-tested and universal benefits are funded from general taxation.[14] For the first time in 1992/93, expenditure on non-contributory benefits exceeded that for contributory benefits. By 1998/99 contribu-

---

[11] DSS, *New Ambitions for our country.*

[12] Department for Education and Employment (DfEE) and DSS, *A New Contract for Welfare: the gateway to work,* Cm 4102, London: HMSO, 1998.

[13] DSS, *Social Security. Departmental Report 1999,* London: HMSO, 1999.

[14] Statutory sick pay and Statutory Maternity Pay, since 1994 and 1992 respectively, have been partly payable by employers (see below).

tory benefits accounted for 47% of benefit expenditure (just over £ 45 million), 70% of which was taken up by the payment of the basic state pension. As a result in 1998/99 over half of the social security programme was funded by the State from general taxation, about a quarter by employers' National Insurance Contributions and a fifth by contributions from employees and the self-employed.[15]

2.3 Coverage

The social security net in Britain is, in principle, spread very wide. The system continues to provide some protection against the main interruptions from work, caused by unemployment, sickness, disability, industrial accidents, or maternity, and also makes provision for retirement. Limited provision is made, in the form of the Invalid Care Allowance, for those who are unable to work because they care for someone who is sick or disabled. No special provision however is made for such social risks as divorce[16] or natural disaster, although individuals may be entitled to general welfare benefits, provided certain criteria are met. In addition to the social welfare for those out of work, since 1970, in-work benefits have been provided for families who are employed in low-paid work or who have children. This first took the form of the *Family Income supplement,* which was replaced in 1988 by Family Credit. From October 1999, in-work benefits have been revised, with the introduction of the *Working Families Tax Credit* and the *Childcare Tax Credit.*

The principal beneficiaries of social security fall into four broad categories: people of working age, who need financial support while they are unable to support themselves through work; families, in recognition of the additional costs of raising children; disabled people; and retired people. In recent years there has been a shift in welfare expenditure away from people of working age who are unable to support themselves through work towards benefits for the disabled and the elderly. While welfare spending on the unemployed fell from 26% of all welfare expenditure in 1993/94 to 21% in 1998/99, welfare spending on the disabled and the elderly increased from 22% to 25% and from 44% to 47% respectively over the same period. This trend, which can largely be explained by the decline in unemployment levels, appears set to continue. In the 1999 Budget, the Government indicated that additional spending between 1998/99 and 2001/02 was to be focused in areas of greatest need: support for children (an additional £ 0.9 billion), the disabled (an additional £ 1.7 billion) and pensioners (an additional £ 2.8 billion). By 2001/02 the Government predicts that less than 20% of all benefit expenditure will be paid to the unemployed, just over 8% to families, 26% to disabled people and just under 47% to people over working age.

---

[15] DSS, *Social Security. Departmental Report 1999.*
[16] The *Welfare Reform and Pensions Bill 1998-99* makes provision for pension splitting arrangements in the case of divorce.

An indicator of the effectiveness with which benefits are being focused on those in most need is the distribution of benefit expenditure across different income groups. Research undertaken by the Family Resources Survey showed that in 1996/7, 82% of all social security expenditure went to 63% of people in households with less than average income.[17] Benefits which are not income-related are inevitably spread up the income distribution, but there is still a bias towards low-income households. The bottom 40% of households receive 77% of all income-related expenditure (or 26% of all benefit expenditure) and around 50% of non-income related expenditure (33% of all benefit expenditure).

The welfare system in Britain is also comprehensive in its coverage, in the sense that no specific category of workers is excluded from it, although entitlement may vary according to circumstances. For example, although the self-employed are covered in most respects, they are not protected against unemployment, industrial injury, or sickness. Changes made in 1977 also enabled married women to qualify in their own right for full contributory benefits, having previously been limited to reduced benefits for reduced contributions. The system is also comprehensive in the sense that employers, employees and the self-employed are all required to pay contributions into the National Insurance fund. The main exception to the rules on compulsory contributions applies to those employees whose earnings fall below the lower earnings limit, as determined annually by the Secretary of State. In 1998/99 the lower earnings limit was £ 66 per week. All workers whose average weekly earnings fall below this level are not only exempt from paying contributions, but more importantly are excluded from receiving contributory benefits (although they may still be entitled to in-work means-tested benefits). Employers are also exempt from paying National Insurance Contributions for workers earning less than the lower earning limit, thereby creating an incentive for low paid employment. In addition, the self-employed, whose net income is expected to be low, *i.e.* less than £ 3,770 in 1999/2000, can apply for a small earnings exemption from paying contributions.

On entering Government, new Labour indicated that it intended to revise National Insurance Contributions and the way in which they interact with work. The changes were to form part of a wider package of policies designed to promote work. The Government adopted a three-pronged approach aimed at encouraging employers to hire more staff, making work pay for employees and promoting self-employment. First, changes were made to reduce the level of National Insurance Contributions employers pay for employees earning less than £ 450 a week and to make the system easier and cheaper for employers to administer. To this end, from April 1999 the starting point for employers' contributions have been aligned with the single person's allowance for income tax (£ 81 a week), which has had the effect of increasing by over 25% the level of earnings at which employers start to pay National Insurance Contributions. The Government have also simplified the administration of benefits by

---

[17] DSS, *Social Security Departmental Report 1999.*

replacing the complex system of four different employers' contributions rates with a single rate of 12.2% per year.[18] New penalties have also been introduced for people who fail to pay contributions.

Secondly, the Government also sought to reduce the burden of National Insurance Contributions on employees, in particular the low paid, by abolishing the 2% entry fee payable by all employees on reaching the lower earnings limit and by aligning the threshold for employees' National Insurance Contributions with the single person's tax allowance over a two year period. From April 2000 employees will no longer pay National Insurance Contributions on earnings below £ 76 per week, and below £ 87 a week from April 2001. As a result approximately 900,000 employees will no longer be required to pay National Insurance Contributions. Nevertheless, their benefit entitlement is to be protected by means of a zero rate of National Insurance Contribution on earnings between £ 64 – the lower earnings limit at the time the changes were first introduced – and the new threshold for National Insurance Contributions. However the Government has failed to extend these benefits to the estimated 2.5 million employees already earning less than £ 64 a week, who are excluded from contributory benefits.[19] Thirdly, measures have been introduced to reduce the burden of National Insurance Contributions on the self-employed with low earnings, by realigning the National Insurance and tax systems and making it easier and cheaper for the self-employed to administer the system. The aim of these policies is to encourage the start-up of self employed businesses.

2.4 Levels of contribution

The contributory system in Britain has never been funded on a strictly actuarial basis, but rather has operated on a pay-as-you-go basis, with benefits being paid out of contributions received each year. Beveridge originally advocated an approach to funding under which flat-rated benefits were paid in return for flat-rated contributions. However, as a result of the funding difficulties under this system, combined with the disproportionate burden which it placed on the low paid, the contributions system unavoidably evolved to include earnings-related contributions. The shift towards earnings-related contributions in 1975 took place at the same time as the introduction of the State Earnings-Related Pensions Scheme (SERPS). While the earnings-related supplements for short-term benefits were abolished in 1980, earnings-related contributions were retained. Indeed, the principle of capacity to pay as a basis of funding was further extended with the introduction of contributions liability for the self employed on business related profits, and, in 1985, the scaling of contributions according to earnings and the removal of the upper limit for contributions for em-

---

[18] The 12.2% contributions rate applies to all employers who have contracted out of the *State Earning Pensions Related Scheme* (SERPS).

[19] E. Maclennan, *Low Paid and Excluded*, London: TUC, 1998.

ployers.[20] Although employers' and employees' contributions are earnings-related, the short-term contributory benefits (principally, unemployment benefits, now the contributory Jobseeker's Allowance) are paid on a flat rate basis, thereby removing the direct link between earnings and contributions and reinforcing the sense in which contributions are a form of 'social security taxation'.[21] All social assistance benefits, with the exception of Child Benefit, which is universal and paid at a fixed rate, are means-tested and therefore paid according to need.

3 Maintaining living standards

As noted earlier, the British social security system continues to cover individuals who have either reached retirement age or who are facing an interruption from work caused by unemployment, sickness or maternity related reasons from the risk of loss of income. As the majority of benefits in Britain are not related to earnings, but are flat-rate, the extent to which social security provision compensates claimants for loss of income is limited, especially in comparison with the practices in other European countries.

3.1 Pensions

Pension reform is probably one of the most contentious areas in the social security debate, not least because it is one of the largest areas of welfare expenditure. In terms of the number of recipients and of total expenditure, retirement pensions continue to represent the most significant of benefits in Britain. In 1998, over ten and a half million people were in receipt of retirement pensions, with spending on the basic retirement pensions accounting for £ 33.5 billion of expenditure and on state earnings-related elements £ 3.2 billion. Pension reform is also a contentious policy area due to the significant number of new challenges it presents for policy makers.

Patterns of risk, cost and reward in pensions are constantly shifting. Increased life expectancy, the issue of the ageing population and the potential problems which it poses for funding of the welfare system, continue to be a subject of heated debate. By 1991 about 16% of the population was already aged 65 or over and this figure is forecast to rise to 24% by 2041.[22] By 2040, the Government has predicted that there will be around 30% fewer people of working age per person over state pension age

---

[20] The upper earnings limit is determined annually by the Secretary of State and for 1999/2000 it is set at £ 500.00 per week. Employees are not required to pay contributions on earnings exceeding the upper earnings limit.

[21] D. Williams, *Social Security Taxation*, London: Sweet and Maxwell, 1982.

[22] J. Hills, *The Future of Welfare*, York: Joseph Rowntree Foundation, 1993.

than is currently the case. Broadly speaking, while there are over three people of working age to support every pensioner now, by 2040 there will closer to two.[23] There is also evidence that life expectancy varies according to income levels, the average gap between life expectancy between the poorest and most affluent neighbourhoods being eight years.[24] In addition, there are also new risks to be faced if expected welfare levels failed to be met in terms of the provision of long-term care.

When William Beveridge first laid the foundations of the pensions system fifty years ago, the system was constructed on the male breadwinner model of full employment, under which men undertook the paid work and women did the non-paid work of caring, at least once they had had children. The composition of the labour force has now changed considerably, with women accounting for half the workforce in some localities, and working mothers becoming the norm, with the exception of lone parents. Changes in the labour market brought about by changing technology and in particular the growth in atypical employment in some sectors has resulted in an increase in job insecurity and mobility. This means that pension provision based on employment with a single employer throughout the course of working life is no longer thought to be appropriate.

Furthermore, in Beveridge's time it was not uncommon for men to live for only one or two years beyond retirement. Living for a long period after retirement was therefore something to be insured against, rather than a predictable event to be saved for, increasingly out of personal savings and earnings. Policy makers, however, should be wary of concluding that all retirement income can be met through efficient individual savings. There will always be individuals who cannot afford to save, or whose incomes are too low or irregular to build up decent second-tier pensions, and others whose pensions will not produce the expected reward expected.

Faced by these challenges, previous Governments responded by encouraging a growth in the diversity of pension provision in Britain, with an increased role for occupational and private pension schemes and a diminution in state provision. The latter is demonstrated by the decline in the relative value of the basic state pension in relation to wages and the gradual dismantling of SERPS. The effects of these changes on pensioners' income levels are varied. Over the last 20 years average pensioner incomes have risen in real terms by over 60%, more rapidly than for the rest of the population. This trend is due to a number of different factors, in particular the growth in the numbers of people in receipt of second pensions and retiring with sufficient income to avoid claiming income related benefits. Occupational pensions have played a particularly important role. Twice as many pensioners currently receive an occupational pension than 30 years ago. Nevertheless many pensioners have only small occupational pensions. Many recently retired pensioners are in receipt of a

---

[23] DSS, *A New Contract for Welfare: Partnership in Pensions*, Cm 4179, London: HMSO, 1998.

[24] J. McCormick, 'Prospects for Pension Reform', in: J. McCormick and C. Oppenheim (Eds.), *Welfare in Working Order* (London: Institute for Public Policy Research (IPPR), 1998), p. 175-249.

second state pension, benefiting from the provisions of the original State Earning Related Pensions Scheme, as established in 1978, before the level of benefits was reduced in the 1980s.

This increase in pensioner income has, however, been accompanied by a marked growth in income inequality and poverty amongst pensioners. Since 1981, the income gap between high and low-incomed pensioners has grown, with the incomes of the poorest pensioners having risen by 21% in real terms as compared with 60% for the richest 20%.[25] In 1996/97 the poorest 20% of single pensioners received an average income of £ 68 a week, before paying housing costs. This compares with the richest fifth of single pensioners receiving average weekly incomes of £ 205. As a result, by 1998 1.7 million pensioners being in receipt of income support, another 1.3 million receiving Council Tax benefit and almost 1 million pensioners receiving assistance with housing costs.

Since entering office, new Labour has published its proposals for a package of pension reforms. It is far too early to assess the effects of these proposals on the pension system and on income levels of pensioners, largely due to the fact that the majority of proposals have not as yet been given legislative effect.[26] The Government's Green Paper *Contract for welfare: Partnership in Pensions*, however, signalled the likely direction of future reform, which contains three main elements.[27] Firstly, the document articulated the continuing role of the State in reducing poverty amongst pensioners and in securing a decent income in retirement, especially for low and moderate earners and carers and the disabled with broken work records. Secondly, it sought to encourage more people to take out funded schemes, by increasing the diversity of pension provision and reducing the costs of contracting out. Thirdly, it also emphasised the need for limits to be placed on public expenditure. Although the package of reform outlined by the Government is intended to increase public spending on pensions in real terms, it also aims to reduce from 60% to 40% the proportion of pensioner incomes coming from the state, while correspondingly raising from 40% to 60% the proportion coming from private pensions. As a result, public spending on pensions has been forecast to decline as a share of GDP from the current 5.4% to 4.5% in 2050.[28] The remainder of this section will seek to outline in more detail how the Government proposes to change existing pension provision.

Pension provision in Britain is currently made up of three tiers. The first tier is made up of the *Basic State Pension;* the second tier is a mix of state and mainly private provision, which are additional to the basic state pension (this tier includes SERPS), occupational and personal pensions); and the third tier comprises other voluntary

---

[25] DSS, *A New Contract for Welfare.*

[26] At the time of writing the *Welfare Reform and Pensions Bill,* which contains the government's proposals on stakeholder pensions and other related matters, is still being considered within Parliament.

[27] DSS, *A New Contract for Welfare.*

[28] DSS, *A New Contract for Welfare,* p. 8.

private provision. People are already compelled in the UK to save towards a pension. As noted earlier, all employees and self-employed people, except the lowest paid, are required to pay National Insurance Contributions, which give entitlement to the basic state pension. The basic state pension is a flat-rated, as opposed to earnings-related benefit. From April 1999, the standard basic pension for an adequately insured man or women is £ 66.75 per week, while a wife relying on her husband's contribution is paid £ 39.95. Further payments are available in cases of invalidity or where the claimant is in need of care assistance, and a small increment is also paid to those who reach the age of 80.

While the Basic State Pension provides the foundation for pension provision in the UK, it has two major limitations. The first main drawback is the declining relative value of the basic state retirement pension. When introduced in 1946 it was envisaged that the retirement pension should meet the basic subsistence needs of retired people. Since the early 1980s, the value of the basic pension has gradually declined, when it ceased to be up-rated with earnings, but rather was linked to prices, which have risen more slowly. Originally having represented around a fifth of male average gross earnings, by 1993 it had declined to around 15% of this figure. The value of the Basic State Pension has now fallen below income-related supplements, offering 10% less than Income Support for the oldest single pensioners.[29] As a consequence, a significant proportion of pensioners rely on means-tested assistance from the state.

Secondly, the Basic State Pension is a contributory benefit, rather than a universal entitlement related to age. Entitlement to the basic state retirement pension is dependent on two main conditions. First, the claimant must have reached pensionable age, which is currently 60 for women and 65 for men. Following developments in European law, the state pension age is due to be equalised at 65 for both men and women from April 2020, the change being gradually phased in over a 10 year period between 2010 and 2020.[30] Second, a claimant will only be entitled to the basic retirement pension if he or she has paid or has been credited with enough National Insurance Contributions. Usually a man will need 44 years of contributions and a woman 39 in order to qualify for a full basic pension.[31] While many women and a declining number of men are unable to meet these requirements due to care responsibilities or periods of unemployment, the state currently provides for contribution credits to fill these gaps and to secure full pension entitlements.[32] Nevertheless, low pay continues to prove a persistent barrier to many individuals being able to contribute towards the Basic State Pension. Approximately 2.5 million currently earn less than the lower

---

[29] McCormick, 'Prospects for Pension Reform'.

[30] *Pensions Act 1995.*

[31] A married woman, widow or widower can claim on the contributory record of his or her spouse or deceased spouse. Similarly, a divorced person can also claim on the contributory record of a former spouse, provided he or she has not re-married before reaching the pensionable age.

[32] Contribution credits are paid to the basic state pension for the registered unemployed, those claiming incapacity benefit and invalid care allowance.

earning limit, and are therefore not required to pay National Insurance Contributions towards the Basic State Pension.[33] The introduction of the national minimum wage will help some of these individuals benefit from the Basic State Pension, yet is likely that a core group of workers will not have the consistency and level of earnings necessary to accrue the Basic State Pension.

The future status of the Basic State Pension is still under discussion, the main issue being that of affordability. There appears little doubt that a universal Basic State Pension paid at a level at or above Income Support can be sustained by current pay-as-you go arrangements.[34] However, the issue of reinstating or indeed retaining the real value of the basic state pension, relative to average earnings, is far more difficult and contentious. Nevertheless, if the Government is committed to narrowing the margin of income inequality between pensioners, then reform of the basic state pension is essential. It is arguable that the basic state pension is the only element of pension provision which is capable of playing a redistributive role from higher income groups to lower income groups and from men and women across the lifecycle.

In response, the Government has introduced a minimum income guarantee for pensioners from April 1999 of £ 75.00 a week for single pensioners and £ 116.60 a week for couples. Single pensioners between 75 and 79 will receive £ 77.39 a week and couples will receive £ 119.85. In effect the Government boosted pensioners' entitlement to Income Support, increasing it by three times the amount they would have normally been entitled to under usual Income Support up-rating rules. It also extended the scope of Income Support entitlement to include a further 65,000 pensioners, whose incomes were just above Income Support levels. Further the Government, 'as resources allow', has committed itself to increase the minimum income guarantee year by year, although over the longer term the aim is that they should rise 'in line with earnings'.[35]

In addition to making contributions towards the Basic State Pension, employees are required to pay towards a second-tier pension – SERPS – unless they have contracted out to benefit from alternative provision, either in the form of an occupational pension or a private pension. When introduced in 1975, SERPS was intended to provide a pension equivalent to around one quarter of a claimant's average pre-retirement earnings between the lower and upper earnings limits (see above for details). Reforms introduced since 1986 have severely curtailed the level of protection provided. Married women have been worst affected by these changes, most notably through the abolition of the 'twenty year' rule. Under this rule pensions were calculated using the twenty best years of a claimant's working life, which enabled women to gain good pension provision regardless of irregular or discontinuous working patterns caused by child-rearing or family responsibilities. Pensions are now calculated on the basis of a

---

[33] Maclennan, *Low Paid and Excluded.*
[34] McCormick, 'Prospects for Pension Reform'.
[35] DSS, *A New Contract for Welfare.*

full working life. Years when a claimant was unable to take regular employment due to responsibilities at home are still disregarded when calculating the average lifetime earnings, but this does not apply to time spent in part time employment. The impact of this rule has been compounded by the changes to the state pensions age for women from 60 to 65. Not only will women have to wait an extra five years to receive the Basic State Pension, but if for those five years they are in low or no employment, this will also depress the value of their SERPS entitlement. More generally, the value of SERPS entitlement has been eroded by revisions made to the pension formula, with the effect that pensions are now based on 20% of a claimant's average earnings, as opposed to 25%, and by changes to indexation of earnings introduced in 1996.[36]

In addition to reducing the value of and tightening the qualification rules for state pension provision, during the mid 1980s to mid 1990s successive Conservative Governments sought to encourage individuals to contract out of SERPS, by advancing alternative forms of pension provision. While there is no statutory obligation on employers to provide an occupational pension scheme, incentives have been created for employers to 'contract out' of the state system and set up their own pension arrangements. These primarily take the form of rebates on both employers' and employees' National Insurance Contributions, which are diverted into the occupational schemes. In order to achieve contracted-out status, occupational schemes originally had to meet certain conditions, most notably having to provide employees with a guaranteed minimum pension (GMP), equivalent to the benefits received under SERPS. Where the level of the GMP was lower than SERPS, the difference used to be made up by SERPS. In effect, then, SERPS operated as a kind of statutory floor of rights for private, occupational schemes. The link between SERPS and occupational pensions was eroded in 1995, when GMPs were abolished, and replaced by a weaker reference scheme. While the pensions paid out under the reference scheme should in most instances be as good as SERPS or GMPs, some will not. Groups most notably at risk include those who leave pension schemes early as a result of a change in job and members of pension funds which become insolvent.[37]

Most occupational schemes in Britain are 'salary related' and offer the employee pensions based on his or her average salary and length of service. Since the Social Security Act 1986 came into force (in 1988), however, it has been possible for employers to operate money-purchase occupational schemes.[38] Under such schemes

---

[36] R. Nobles, 'The Pensions Act 1995', in: *Modern Law Review*, 59 (1996), no. 2, p. 241-259.

[37] *Ibid.*

[38] Occupational pension schemes in the UK can be established either on a 'salary-related' (or 'defined benefit') basis, where the pension received depends on the employee's salary and service history (*e.g.*, a scheme might pay a pension of 1/60 of final salary of each year of service), or on a 'money-purchase' (or 'defined contribution') basis, where the contributions and any rebate are invested. On retirement the pension savings are used to buy an annuity; the pension received depends on the investment performance and the annuity rates available at retirement. Hybrid schemes or 'mixed benefit' schemes also exist. All personal pensions are provided on an money-purchase basis.

employers continue to make minimum contributions, but the scheme need not guarantee any particular outcome for the employee. Rather, the pension is based solely on the returns from investments, although the nature of the investments is regulated. In addition to such occupational schemes, employees may also set up their own personal pension schemes.

By 1998, of the 35 million people of working age in the Great Britain, 10.5 million are in occupational pension schemes, around 10 million personal pensions are held and over 7 million belong to SERPS. Second pensions are not however available to everyone. Occupational pension schemes are not an option for 35% of employees, as their employers do not provide such a scheme. In addition, while employees are required to pay into a second pension, the self-employed are not. The only pension option available to the self-employed is a private pension, or other savings and investments. It is unusual however for such schemes to offer benefits equivalent to either SERPS or to employer-run occupational schemes. Personal pensions can also be less accessible to the lower paid and those who change jobs regularly.

On entering Government, new Labour identified that there were clear gaps in the current provision of second-tier pensions within the UK, as well as a growing lack of confidence and trust in private and occupational pension arrangements. The Green Paper on Pension reform outlined a detailed package of reform. Central to the Government's programme was the proposal to develop a stakeholder pension, which would encourage more moderate earners to invest in funded pension schemes and therefore save for retirement.[39] The underlying objective for the scheme was to devise a second-tier pension which avoided the shortcomings of current private pensions, and which accommodated the changing nature of the labour market, including the greater flexibility and mobility of labour. The stakeholder pension schemes will be open to everyone, but are targeted at those earning £ 9,000 to £ 20,000 and who are not currently in an occupational pension scheme. Employers who do not offer an occupational scheme will be required to identify an occupational pension scheme and to facilitate access to it for their employees. While the schemes will only be able to offer money-purchase benefits, their members will be able to take advantage of lower charges and a simpler tax regime as compared with existing private pensions. The schemes will also be required to have an approved governance structure and meet minimum standards for charges. The schemes will also be required to register. In addition, there will be no penalties if individuals stop contributing for a period of time, thereby assisting individuals who do not have sufficient consistency in employment currently to benefit from personal pension arrangements.

In addition to proposals on stakeholder pensions, the Government's Green Paper on Pension reform also outlined proposals for a Second State Pension to replace SERPS.

---

[39] At the time of writing, the *Welfare Reform and Pensions Bill* is under consideration in Parliament.

If implemented,[40] the Second State Pension would have two clear advantages over current pension provision. Firstly, the scheme would seek to assist individuals for whom second pensions are not currently an option, because of low earnings, or because they have caring responsibilities or are disabled. While SERPS is currently only available to those who have earnings above the lower earnings level and are therefore liable for National Insurance Contributions, the new scheme would make provision for contribution credits for some individuals who have earnings below that level or no earnings at all. The Green Paper suggests that those who care for elderly or disabled people, or those with children aged 5 or under would be entitled to credits. Disabled people would also be entitled to credits, provided they can demonstrate an attachment to the labour market, through a contributions test. It appears that contribution credits, however, will not extend to the unemployed. In addition, the Government has also published proposals for strengthening the regulatory framework of occupational pension schemes.

3.2 Active labour market policies and benefits for the unemployed

3.2.1 Welfare to work

Welfare to Work, which encompasses a range of policies targeted at promoting work and getting the long-term unemployed back into employment, rests at the centre of the new Labour Government's welfare reform programme. The challenge facing the Government is how to tackle the problems of persistent structural unemployment, at the same time as devising policies that respond to the changing socio-economic conditions which, over the last twenty years, have made entering work more risky. The growth of insecure and atypical employment, the inadequacy of childcare provision and the extension of means-tested benefits have all served to create barriers to entering the labour market. In response, the Government has sought to devise a framework of policies designed to remove barriers to employment and secure sustainable transitions into work, by improving the employability of individuals and creating opportunities to participate in a wider range of forms of paid work or education and training. The dominant theme running throughout the proposals is the centrality of employment as a tool both to foster equality of opportunity and to tackle social exclusion and poverty.

There are three main elements to the Government's Welfare to Work: active labour market policies, primarily involving the New Deal and the establishment of Employment Zones; changes to the delivery of benefits and the creation of a Single Work-

---

[40] At the time of writing the government has not set a timetable for introducing the *Second State Pension.*

Focused Gateway to the welfare system; and increasing incentives to work, by introducing a range of measures designed to make work pay, including the realignment of tax and benefits systems and the introduction of in-work benefits. A range of other policies, not dealt with in this paper, has also accompanied these measures. These include the commitment to life-long learning, through Individual Learning Accounts and measures to introduce family friendly policies and to increase employment security.

3.2.2 The New Deal

The New Deal, which is Britain's first dedicated Welfare to Work scheme, bringing resources to bear on long-term unemployment among targeted groups, forms the centrepiece of the Government's policy agenda. The £ 5 billion dedicated to this end represents, by a considerable margin, the Government's largest spending commitment to date. The New Deal is geared towards enhancing labour market attachment, most directly through the use of employer subsidies, but also through opportunities in voluntary, on environmental and in educational options. The schemes seek to increase the contact between the unemployed or economically inactive and the world of work. The objectives are to reduce prejudice against unemployed people, reduce the costs of recruitment for employers, and to increase the skills and confidence of unemployed people who enter the workplace directly, without having first to overcome the hurdle of an employment interview.

The majority of the funding for Welfare to Work, £ 3.5 billion, has been used to develop the New Deal for the Young Unemployed, which is focused on getting 250,000 young people aged 18 to 25, who have been unemployed for more than six months, into work. All are offered counselling and guidance by Employment Service Advisers and independent advice as part of the 'gateway' to the New Deal. The purpose of the 'Gateway' is to prepare young people for jobs over a four-month period, before moving onto one of the New Deal options, of which there are five.[41] These include employment in the private or public sector with a wage subsidy of £ 60 a week; work experience for 'benefits plus' £ 15 a week in the voluntary sector or as part of the Environmental Task Force; access to full-time education or training on an approved course; and a self employment option. The first three options last for six months on a full-time basis and are accompanied by a day release scheme for an accredited educational or training qualification. The fourth option may last up to 12 months. A similar New Deal programme has also been developed for the long-term unemployed (those who have been out of work for over twelve months). Participation in the New Deal is in effect compulsory for all young people and long-term unemployed who are eligible. Refusal to participate in any of the prescribed options can lead to a reduction in or removal of benefit entitlement, mirroring the rules for general job seekers under

---

[41] Young people with particular disadvantages or special needs can access New Deal options without having to wait six months.

the Jobseekers Act (see below). The element of compulsion applied to the New Deal is set to increase, with the Government recently announcing that it intends to narrow the gateway for young people, making it clear that there is no alternative other than work.

One significant feature of the New Deal is that it extends to those who are economically inactive as well as those who are registered unemployed. Following on from the schemes for young people and the long-term unemployed, the Government has also introduced New Deals for lone parents, disabled people and the partners of the unemployed. One the one hand, the inclusion of these groups within the New Deal may be seen as being beneficial. It acknowledges the high level of hidden unemployment which exists in the UK, demonstrates a commitment to address the associated problems of low incomes and social exclusion and seeks to extend opportunities for paid employment and access to education and training to these groups. On the other hand, this policy has proved highly controversial, attracting much criticism, not least because of the new duties, which the scheme imposes upon claimants, as a condition of benefit entitlement. The Welfare Reform and Pensions Bill proposes to introduce compulsory attendance for work focused interviews with a personal adviser, for all new benefit claimants. Participation in subsequent paid work or training options will be voluntary. Although these changes are quite modest, they have nevertheless been introduced under the rhetoric of seeking to tackle the 'something for nothing' culture and emphasising the toughness of the welfare regime.

3.2.3 Administrative changes

The Government have stated that in introducing the Welfare to Work programme their aim is to change the culture among benefit claimants, employers and public servants – with rights and responsibilities on all sides – to provide positive assistance and not just benefit payment.[42] Nevertheless the New Deal programme has been built on the foundations of the Jobseekers Act, which imposes a stringent job search test on benefit recipients and the threat of significant sanctions for failure to comply. Over the last decade a number of changes have been made to the rules on eligibility for benefits in the UK which have increased the stringency of the job search test and reduced entitlement to benefit. While social security provision in Britain has always contained an element of work discipline, during the 1980s the job search duties of unemployed claimants were significantly increased. As a result, claimants are required to show that they are 'actively seeking work', and the range of jobs which a claimant can be required to accept has been widened to include work with either lower wages or hours, or which is in a different occupation from that to which he or she was normally accustomed. Since 1988 a claimant could also have benefit reduced for failing to attend certain Government training schemes. Additional requirements were introduced in October 1996 under the Jobseekers Act 1995. Under this legisla-

---

[42] DSS, *New Ambitions for our country.*

tion, a claimant is required to enter a 'jobseeker's agreement' with a local officer of the Employment Department, which can specify not only the lowest wage for which the claimant should be willing to work, but which also imposes a duty on the claimant to comply with any job seeking direction which is reasonable. Further, failure to comply with any of the above job search conditions can be penalised not only by a reduction in, but also by the total withdrawal of, benefit for a period of up to 26 weeks.

Rather than reducing the stringency of job search requirements imposed on the unemployed, the Government has extended the element of compulsion imposed on benefit claimants, in order 'to forge an entirely new culture which puts work first'.[43] As noted earlier, those qualifying for the New Deal are under a mandatory duty to participate in the schemes, albeit that the level of compulsion varies between the different schemes. Alongside these measures, the Government is also seeking to extend the work-focused duties on a wider range of benefit claimants. The Welfare Reform and Pensions Bill contains proposals to extend the 'Single Gateway', and to bring together the Employment Service, the Benefits Agency and other welfare providers at a single point of contact for benefit recipients. It provides for regulations to be drawn up requiring most claimants of working age to attend a work-focused interview with a personal adviser, as part of the claim process. Existing claimants and future claimants may be called for an interview after their eligibility for benefit has been established.

Under the provisions of the Bill all new and existing benefits claimants will be required to attend a work-focused interview. Failure to attend may result in sanctions, including a delay in benefits payments or a small reduction in the aggregate benefit paid, although this would be refundable once the interview had been attended. The requirements of the Single Gateway will apply primarily to those in receipt of income replacement benefits, such as Income Support, Housing Benefit, Council Tax Benefit, Incapacity Benefit, Severe Disablement Benefit and Invalid Care Allowance, the intention clearly being to encourage people into work, in order to reduce benefit payments. The Single Gateway would also apply to Widows Benefits and the new Bereavement Benefits, although the reasoning behind these proposals is not clear. It would not however extend to those receiving benefits designed to assist in the additional costs associated with being disabled.

3.2.4 Making work pay

The final component of the Government's Welfare to Work strategy focuses on reforming the tax and benefit systems with a view to removing the financial disincentives which act as barriers to people entering work. The centre piece of the Government's polices in this area has been the introduction of the Working Families Tax

---

[43] DfEE and DSS, *A New Contract for Welfare*, p. 1.

Credit, which replaces family credit as the main benefit payable to those in work. The Working Families Tax Credit increases the benefits payable to those in work and is also accompanied by a Childcare Tax Credit, which covers 70% of childcare costs for low and middle income families.

In addition, the Government has also introduced measures aimed at reducing the tax burden carried by those on lower incomes. This has been achieved through a reduction in the level of National Insurance Contributions payable by employees and the self-employed, particularly those on low incomes, as outlined above. In April 1999 the Government also introduced a 10% rate of income tax, which together with the Working Families Tax Credit has reduced the marginal rates of tax faced by those at the lower end of the labour market. Another significant component of the Government's strategy for making work pay has been the introduction of a national minimum wage. These measures have also been accompanied by policies aimed at improving parental rights to leave from work, which has formed part of the Government's fairness at work proposals.[44]

3.2.5 Assessment

In developing its Welfare to Work strategy, the Government had a number of clear objectives in mind. These included enabling people to move from out-of-work benefits and into employment; improving employability; increasing the opportunities, particularly for disadvantaged groups, to take up paid employment, education or training; increasing social inclusion and maintaining a sustainable social security budget. It is still premature to assess to what extent the policy changes have succeeded in meeting any or all of these objectives, although a number of clear trends are emerging.

The New Deal has clearly been geared towards increasing labour market participation, not only for the long-term unemployed, but also for those who are economically inactive. It represents a substantial investment in the work experiences and skills of the long-term unemployed in order to make people more work-ready and to broaden the range of jobs open to them. As such it has made an important contribution towards improving employability, particularly of the young and is also making inroads among lone parents and the disabled. Nevertheless, it is still open to question whether the quality of investment into skills, training and education under the New Deal is sufficient not only to make people more 'work-ready' but also raise the level of human capital in order to secure sustainable employment. Research reveals that under earlier employment and training schemes introduced in the UK, it has proved difficult to move people from unemployment into work which offers stability, family supporting wages and the prospect of career advancement. Research reveals that between 1990 and 1995, three out of four jobs entered from unemployment were temporary,

---

[44] See the *Employment Relations Act 1999*.

part-time or self employed with low skills levels.[45] If the New Deal is to achieve more than 'churning' between unemployment and low-paid, irregular and short-term work, then ways of creating employment opportunities beyond the marginalised sectors of the labour market need to be addressed.

Another important element of the Welfare to Work strategy has been the introduction of policies aimed at realigning the tax and benefit systems, enhancing in-work benefits and improving childcare provision which have made a significant contribution towards easing transitions into work. The success of these policies in creating incentives for work has already been demonstrated by early evaluations of the New Deal for Lone Parents. This shows that between July 1997 and March 1998, the programme succeeded in reducing the number of lone parents on income support by between one and two per cent.[46] By June 1999, 21,000 lone parents had moved into work as a result of participating in the New Deal for Lone Parents, representing nearly a third of the 64,000 who have decided to participate in the scheme since July 1997. Nevertheless, while the policies appear to be successful in moving people from out-of-work benefits onto in-work work benefits, it is doubtful whether Welfare to Work will also be successful in enabling people to become completely independent of welfare support. In reality, the types of jobs, which the unemployed and the economically inactive will enter, are likely to be predominantly low paid, and as a result will need to continue to be subsidised by the state, through measures such as the Working Families Tax Credit.

3.2.6 Benefits for the unemployed

Although, traditionally, social insurance formed the cornerstone of social welfare provision for the unemployed in Britain, reforms introduced during the 1980s and 1990s mean that contributory benefits now form only an adjunct of welfare provision, having been largely superseded by means-tested benefits. By 1994 less than one in five unemployed claimants received any form of contributory benefits, the remainder relying on means-tested benefits.[47]

The role of means-tested benefits has been further extended with the introduction in October 1996 of the Jobseeker's Allowance, as a substitute for unemployment benefit and income support. Under the Jobseeker's Allowance, entitlement to contributory benefits is limited to 6 months (having previously been 12 months) after which the claimant will be entitled to a means-tested Jobseeker's Allowance, provided certain conditions are met. The reduction in the scope of contributory benefits may not necessarily have disadvantaged unemployed claimants in monetary terms. Since the

---

[45] M. White, S. Lissenburgh, and A. Bryson, *The Impact of Public Job Placing Programmes*, London: Policy Studies Institute, 1997.

[46] C. Oppenheim, 'Welfare Reform and the Labour Market: a 'third way'?', in: *Benefits: A Journal of Social Security Research, Policy and Practice*, 25 (1999), no. 25, April/May, p. 1-5.

[47] DSS, *Social Security Statistics 1996* (London: HMSO, 1996), Table C1.01.

abolition of earnings-related supplements for unemployment benefit in 1980, the value of contributory based benefits has fallen to the same level as means-tested benefits and indeed in some instances contributory allowances are lower than means-tested allowances. However, the income gap between those in employment and those out of employment did widen significantly in the 1980s. During this decade the extent to which unemployment benefit compensated for lost earnings fell by 30% for single men on average earnings and more for married men with children.[48] While this is largely due to the abolition of earning related supplements and of the child dependency additions, the failure to uprate short-term benefits in line with earnings also contributed to the declining relative value of benefits. Taxation of unemployment benefit, introduced in the early 1980s, also played a role in reducing its value for individuals with irregular working patterns.

Since April 1999, the basic personal benefit for both contributory and means-tested Jobseeker's Allowance has been £ 30.95 for those under 18,[49] £ 40.70 for 18-24 year olds, and £ 51.40 for those who are 25 or above. Contributory allowance is paid as of right to the individual and is not affected by a partner's income or the household's capital or savings. No specific provision is made for dependants, although where in the assessment of the state, the claimant and his or her household cannot manage on their contributory benefit entitlement, their income can be supplemented by means-tested benefits. If a claimant works for 16 hours or more a week, eligibility for contributory allowance ceases. If he or she works less than 16 hours, benefit entitlement is reduced by the amount equivalent to the earnings received. In contrast, entitlement to the means-tested benefit is assessed on the needs of the claimant and his or her household (the 'applicable amounts') as compared with their 'resources' derived from the household's earnings, capital or savings. For example, benefit will be withheld where the claimant or his or her married or unmarried partner has capital or savings of over £ 8,000, or be reduced where there are savings between £ 3,000 and £ 8,000. Some provision is made for dependants with additional payments for children reinstated in 1998, having been abolished in 1984. From September 1999, a couple with children will be entitled to an additional £ 25.90 following the child's 11th birthday and £ 30.95 for those over 16. Entitlement to means-tested Jobseeker's Allowance ceases not only if the claimant works 16 hours or more a week, but also where the claimant's partner works 24 hours or more a week. If either or both partners work under these prescribed limits, when assessing benefit entitlement the first £ 10 of a couple's earnings is disregarded, although any earnings in excess of that amount are taken into account of a penny-for-penny basis.

---

[48] S. Deakin and F. Wilkinson, 'Labour law, social security and economic inequality', *Cambridge Journal of Economics*, 15 (1991), p. 125-148.

[49] Those under 18 are unlikely to fulfil the National Insurance Contributions requirements to qualify for this amount.

As part of the New Deal for Partners of the Unemployed, the Government is planning to make further changes to entitlement for couples to Jobseeker's Allowance, with a view to encouraging more people to enter employment. Currently, married and heterosexual couples who claim the couple rate of income-based Jobseeker's Allowance can choose which partner claims. The partner who 'signs on' must meet the labour market conditions for payment of the benefit. The dependent partner is not required to meet these conditions unless he or she elects to 'sign on' as unemployed in order to received National Insurance credits. In 1998, of the 230,000 couples claiming income-based Jobseeker's Allowance, in 90% of cases only the male partner signed on. The Welfare Reform and Pensions Bill contains provisions requiring childless couples below a certain age to make a joint claim for Jobseeker's Allowance. The intention is to ensure that both partners in childless couples are involved in the labour market, to prevent them from becoming dependent on benefit at an early age. The measures are intended to ensure that both partners are treated as having equal rights, whilst retaining assessment on the basis of household income. The measure will also extend job search and work requirements within unemployed households. In childless couples, partners between the age of 18 and 24 who remain unemployed for six months will be placed into the New Deal for Young People. Couples with children will continue to be offered help to find work on a voluntary basis, through the New Deal for Partners of Unemployed People, although they will still be required to attend at least one work-focused interview.

In addition to the Jobseeker's Allowance, the unemployed may also qualify for a number of other means-tested benefits relating to local taxation (Council Tax Benefit), and to accommodation needs. These benefits are automatically payable to claimants in receipt of means-tested Jobseeker's Allowance or Income Support. The entitlement of those on contributory Jobseeker's Allowance depends on the 'resources' available to them. For instance the benefits will be withheld if the claimant or the claimant's partner have savings in excess of £ 16,000 or be reduced if they have savings of £ 3,000 to £ 16,000. The maximum Council Tax Benefit currently available is a 100% rebate on liability. Assistance for housing costs come in two forms: Housing Benefit, payable to those who rent accommodation in either the public or private sector and mortgage interest payments payable to owner occupiers. The rules on entitlement to Housing Benefit are extremely complex. Tenants renting from local councils and housing associations are entitled to rebates or allowances up to or equivalent to full rent.

Since January 1996 restrictions have been imposed on Housing Benefit for tenants renting from private landlords. First, tenants who were eligible for Housing Benefit prior to 1 January 1996 and who have not moved house are entitled to benefit amounting to 100% of the eligible rent. Those who made a claim for benefit after 1 January 1996 are subject to the 'local reference rent restriction', under which benefit entitlement is reduced if the rent payable is above the average rent for that type of property in that area. In such cases benefit entitlement is reduced to the average rent for the area. Those who became eligible for benefit between 2 January 1996 and 6

October 1997 are entitled to receive a top-up amounting to 50% of the difference between the average rent for the area and the rent payable. Those who become eligible for benefit after 6th October 1997 are not entitled to the top-up, although local authorities do have the discretion to pay claimants up to the full rent to prevent exceptional hardship. Secondly, all single people under the age of 60, with the exception of the severely disabled and those with dependent children, are restricted to receiving 'single room rent', which amounts to the average cost of renting one room plus facilities which are shared with others. For owner occupiers, some assistance is provided for the payment of mortgage interest rates, although with a view to reducing expenditure and to encouraging the use of private insurance to secure mortgage payments the Government has gradually reduced the level of state assistance provided for home owners who suffer a loss of work. Under regulations introduced in 1995, those who first claimed Income Support before 1 October of that year continue to have their mortgage interest rates paid in full. Those who started to claim after this date but whose mortgages were taken out before 1 October 1995 receive no assistance on mortgage payments for the first 8 weeks, for the following 18 weeks they are only covered for half their mortgage interest rate and only thereafter are their interest rates paid in full. Further, those who took out a mortgage after 1 October 1995 and who are in receipt of either means-tested Jobseeker's Allowance or Income Support (see below) receive no assistance on mortgage for the first 39 weeks. Further, the state only covers the cost of interest rates on loans or mortgages amounting to a maximum of £ 100,000.

3.3 Income support

Having been largely supplanted by the means-tested Jobseeker's Allowance, Income Support is still payable to those who are aged 60 and over or who are unable to work because they are unfit, are bringing up children on their own or caring for a disabled or sick member of their family, and do not have enough money on which to live. Unemployed claimants who are looking for work are not entitled to Income Support. Entitlement to Income Support is calculated in the same way as the means-tested Jobseekers' Allowance, in that it can be reduced on the basis of a household's income, savings or capital. For example, claimants with savings or capital in excess of £ 8,000 are excluded from benefit, and those with savings or capital over £ 3,000 are liable to have their benefit entitlement reduced. (From April 1996 the upper limit for Income Support for people living in a residential or nursing home was increased to £ 16,000, and the lower limit from £ 3,000 to £ 10,000. Eligibility to benefit also ceases where either the claimant is working 16 hours or more a week or where his or her partner is working 24 hours or more. Income Support is made up of four main parts: a personal allowance, for either an individual claimant or a couple which is payable at the same basic rate as the Jobseekers' Allowance; a personal allowance for dependent children; premium payments for certain categories of claimant whose expenses are likely to be higher due to their circumstances, for example because they are a single parent, are disabled or have a disabled child; and housing costs payments such as mortgage interest rate payments, although not water rates or residual housing costs such as maintenance or insurance which must be paid for out of the Income Support personal allowance. In addition, Income Support claimants will be entitled to Housing Benefit and Council Tax Benefit.

Income Support is intended to fill the gap which exists between an individual's or household's income and needs. When assessing entitlement to Income Support the first £ 5 of an individual's earnings, £ 10 of a couple's earnings or £ 15 of the earnings of lone parents, the disabled, carers and some pensioners are discounted, although any wages in excess of these figures are taken into account on a penny-for-penny basis. There are a number of other circumstances where deductions may be made from an individual's benefit entitlement. These cover mortgage interest payments, not covered by the state; payments relating to debts outstanding with third parties for example for water rates and gas or electricity bills; unpaid fines; social fund payments (on the Social Fund, see below, section 3); and child support maintenance.

3.4 Maternity provision

While Statutory Maternity Pay (SMP) has it origins in the national social insurance system for contributory benefits, since the mid 1980s moves were made by the Conservative Government to privatise maternity pay, shifting responsibility from the state on to employers. The statutory right to receive maternity pay from the employer was first introduced in 1975. Under the original scheme, state provision consisted of a National Insurance Maternity Allowance, based on contributions, and a non-contributory, non-means-tested lump sum Maternity Grant, which was abolished in 1987, and replaced by means-tested Social Fund Maternity Grants. Occupational schemes operated separately from the state provision, although some occupational schemes deducted the value of Maternity Allowance from Maternity Pay. Entitlement to Maternity Allowance was not affected by receipt of occupational Maternity Pay.

In its Green Paper *Reform of Social Security* in 1985 the Conservative Government expressed its intention 'wherever possible to disengage itself from activities which firms and individuals can perform perfectly well for themselves'.[50] The objective to withdraw state provision from those areas which overlapped with private employer provision, resulted in part in the introduction of the existing arrangements for Statutory Maternity Pay, which date from 1987 and also the Statutory Sick Pay scheme considered below. While the intention of the Government at the time may have been to privatise maternity provision, in practice the resulting scheme is a 'halfway house'. While employers are under a legal duty to make the relevant payments the costs of

[50] Department of Health and Social Security (DHSS), *Reform of Social Security,* Cm 9597, London: HMSO, 1985.

doing so are recoverable by way of a rebate on National Insurance Contributions. Since 1992 the level of rebate has been reduced to 92% of total costs, with the exception of small employers.

Under the scheme the employer is required to pay eligible employees Statutory Maternity Pay for six weeks at a rate of 90% of average earnings (which includes bonuses, overtime and sick pay), and for the following 12 weeks at a lower flat rate equivalent to the rate for Statutory Sick Pay, which since April 1999 has been £ 59.55. In order to be eligible for these payments a woman must have been continuously employed by the employer for at least 26 weeks up to the qualifying week which is the 15th week before the baby is due. The claimant must have stopped work due to her pregnancy or confinement, prior to which she must have given the employer at least 21 days' notice of her intended absence for reasons of pregnancy or confinement.

Perhaps the most restrictive qualifying condition for Statutory Maternity Pay is that in the 8 weeks (or two months, if paid monthly) prior to the qualifying week the claimant must have had average earnings which exceeded the lower earnings limit for National Insurance Contributions (£ 66 a week). In 1997 an estimated 2.5 million women in part-time work had earnings which were too low to qualify for Statutory Maternity Pay.[51] Those who have not been continuously employed for 26 weeks before the qualifying date, but who have worked for 26 weeks in the 66 weeks before the week of their baby's expected birth, even if they have been employed by different employers, are entitled to state Maternity Allowance. The allowance is paid at the lower rate of £ 51.70 for up to 18 weeks. Self-employed women may qualify for an even lower rate of allowance of £ 48.35. In the 1999 Budget, the Labour Government announced that it intends to expand the entitlement to state Maternity Allowance. As a result, all women who are expecting a baby from 20th August 2000 onwards and who earn £ 30 a week or more, will be entitled to Maternity Allowance. This change is predicted to benefit approximately 14,000 mothers a year. From the same date, self-employed mothers-to-be will receive a 15% increase in Maternity Allowance entitlement.

No additional provision to the basic means-tested benefits, considered elsewhere in this report, is currently available in Britain for state or private assistance for either women or men to take parental leave in order to care for children. In line with the 1992 EC Directive for Pregnant Workers, pregnant women who are still in work in the twelfth week before their baby is due to be born are entitled, provided they have given the requisite notice, to a minimum to 14 weeks' maternity leave, to all non-wage contractual rights and not to be dismissed or made redundant during the 14 weeks' leave for pregnancy or confinement related reasons. Those women who, by the 12th week before expected childbirth, have been employed either full time or part time with their existing employer are entitled to a longer period of maternity leave of

---

[51] E. Maclennan, *Below the Limit*, London: TUC, 1997.

up to 40 weeks, a maximum of 11 weeks of which must be taken before the expected date of birth and 29 weeks after the birth.

3.5 Sickness and incapacity

Although the common law has evolved to imply a term into the contract of employment providing a right to sick pay, the payment of short-term benefit for loss of income incurred through sickness has for a long time in Britain primarily been the preserve of social security. Employees with an adequate contribution record were entitled to a social insurance benefit, Sickness Benefit. In addition to this state provision many employers provided occupational sick pay, although in some instances the value of the state benefit was deducted from the sum paid by the employer. State Sickness Benefit was not however affected by the payment of occupational sick pay. As in the case of Statutory Maternity Pay, during the 1980s Conservative Government sought to privatise the provision of Sickness Benefit. In 1980 the Government sought to shift responsibility for the administration of sick pay onto employers, who it was considered could deal with it more effectively than the state.[52]

Under legislation introduced in 1982 employers were required to pay employees Statutory Sick Pay at a range of rates for the first six weeks of illness. Not only were these payments set off against the employers' contractual duties, thereby ending 'double compensation' which had previously taken place, but also the costs to the employer could be recovered in full in the form of rebates on National Insurance Contributions. During the 1980s and 1990s the scheme was gradually revised. First, the period of entitlement was extended to 28 weeks. Second, unlike Statutory Maternity Pay, the costs of the scheme were gradually transferred from the state onto employers. In 1991, the rebates payable to employers were reduced from 100% to 80%, while in 1994 the rebates were withdrawn from all but the smallest firms. Following significant disquiet from employers, legislation restored a general rebate for employers in respect of Statutory Sick Pay payments exceeding 13% of an employer's National Insurance Contributions for any one month.

From April 1997, employers have been able to opt out of the Statutory Sick Pay scheme altogether, providing that they operate an occupational sick pay scheme which provides benefits at least equal to those required by the SSP legislation. Unlike Statutory Maternity Pay, Statutory Sick Pay is not earnings-related, but is paid at a flat rate, with no additions for dependants. The current rate is £ 59.55. Entitlement to Statutory Sick Pay commences on the first day of employment; however, as in the case of SMP, eligibility for Statutory Sick Pay is limited to employees whose average weekly or monthly earnings exceed the lower earnings limit of £ 66. As a result an estimated 2.6 million workers, more than three quarters of whom are women, are

---

[52] DHSS, *Income During Sickness: A New Strategy,* Cmnd 7684, London: HMSO, 1980.

excluded from receiving Statutory Sick Pay.[53] Further, entitlement is restricted to employees or more specifically 'employed earners', but not the self-employed.[54] Temporary workers employed under contracts for three months or less are also excluded, although following a ruling of the Court of Appeal in 1996, it appears that workers employed on a series of contracts which stretch over the three month period are entitled to Statutory Sick Pay.

Statutory Sick Pay is only payable for days which are qualifying days, which usually means the days which the person would normally work. In order to claim the benefit the worker must have been sick for at least four days, three of which count as 'waiting days' for which benefit is not payable. However if a person is ill for two spells, the first of which was four days or more and the gap between the end of the first spell and the start of the second is not more than eight weeks, the person need not serve another three 'waiting days'. A period of sickness with another employer cannot be linked, although the current employers' duty to pay Statutory Sick Pay may be reduced due to previous benefit received. Employees must also notify their employers that they are absent from work due to sickness within 7 days, and thereafter once a week. Employers are also entitled to reasonable evidence to determine entitlement to Statutory Sick Pay.

The principal benefit for longer-term sickness and invalidity is Incapacity Benefit, a contributory benefit which was introduced in 1995 in place the earlier system of invalidity benefits. Incapacity benefit is paid at a series of rates, the highest of which applies when the claimant has been ill for 52 weeks, and is payable, in principle, until retirement. Disabled people may also be entitled to a range of other benefits. These include Severe Disablement Allowance, which is a non-contributory and non-means tested benefit for those who are disabled at a young age or are deemed to be 80% or more disabled; Income Support, which includes disability premiums; and Disabled Persons Tax credit.[55] They may also be entitled to Disability Living Allowance and Attendance Allowance, which are non-contributory and non- means tested benefits to assist in providing extra mobility and in meeting care costs.

On entering power, the Labour Government committed itself to reforming the provision available to disabled people. The principle underpinning their reforms was to ensure that 'those who are disabled should get the support they need to lead a fulfilling life with dignity.' In practice, the Government has been seeking to implement this principle in three principal ways: by encouraging more disabled people to enter work,

---

[53] Maclennan, *Below the Limit.*

[54] For these purposes an employed earner is a person over the age of 16 who is 'gainfully employed' either under a contract of service in an office the income from which is subject to Income Tax. By regulations, employed earners are taken to include office cleaners, agency workers, lecturers, teachers and instructors and those employed by their own husband or wife. A self-employed person is construed to mean a person in business on their own account.

[55] The *Disabled Persons Tax Credit* replaced the *Disability Working Allowance.*

by reforming the rules on Incapacity Benefit and launching the New Deal for the Disabled; by improving the support provided for severely disabled people, in particular those disabled from childhood; and by improving the civil rights of disabled people by establishing a Disability Rights Task Force and a Disability Rights Commission to protect, enforce and promote the rights of disabled people.

To this end, at the time of writing, the Government is seeking to introduce a number of controversial measures in the Welfare Reform and Pensions Bill. Firstly, the Bill seeks to reform the rules governing entitlement to Incapacity Benefit by revising the existing 'All Work Test', so that, in addition to determining entitlement to benefit, it will also provide information on people's capabilities that can be used to assist them in planning a return to work. Those in receipt of incapacity benefits will be required to take part in a Single Work-Focused Gateway interview, which is designed to help them plan a route back to work. The Bill also further strengthens the link between work and entitlement to Incapacity Benefit by specifying that the benefit should only be paid to those who have recently been in work and paid National Insurance Contributions. In addition, the Bill will require income from private and occupational pensions to be taken into account in determining the level of entitlement to Incapacity Benefit. Secondly, the Bill plans to reform the Severe Disablement Allowance, with a view to tilting entitlement in favour of the young disabled. Those who are disabled and cannot work before the age of 20 will receive Incapacity Benefit. After a year on benefit, their entitlement will be £ 80.80 a week, as opposed to £ 54.40. This change will reduce the need for these people to rely on Income Support to top up their income. In addition to these work-focused changes, the Government has also introduced a new Disability Income Guarantee for the disabled and has extended the higher rate of the mobility component of the Disability Living Allowance.

3.6 Adjudication of claims

The British social security system has an extensive system of adjudication of claims which mainly takes place through specialised tribunals, with rights of review and/or appeal to the general courts. Tribunals are capable of hearing a wide range of appeals from decisions of local benefit officers ('adjudication officers'). The most important recent reform was the establishment in 1984 of Social Security Appeal Tribunals, merging the jurisdictions of the former local insurance tribunals and the Supplementary Benefit Appeal Tribunals. The establishment of the Social Fund in 1988 (see below, section 3), replacing the previous system of single needs payments, led to the loss of a significant right of appeal to the tribunal system; social fund decisions may only be reviewed by senior civil servants and inspectors. Separate processes of appeal and review apply to decisions concerning the incidence of social insurance contributions. The Social Security Act 1998 simplified and streamlined the way decisions and appeals are handled and maintained rights of appeal to independent tribunal

4 Meeting basic income needs

There is no *universal* basic income guarantee in the British system of social security, in the sense of an income which is paid to individuals as an incident of citizenship regardless of needs or of social insurance contributions.[56] Most basic income benefits are means-tested. A major aim of policy since the early 1980s has been to 'target' these benefits more effectively to those who are in need of support. Different categories of benefit apply according to whether the claimant is employed and what type of employment they have. As noted in section 2, above, the means-tested Jobseeker's Allowance is payable to claimants who are either unemployed or who are employed for less than 16 hours per week. Claimants who are neither employed nor unemployed (in the sense of seeking work) may be eligible for Income Support. Those who are employed for 16 or more hours per week may be eligible to receive Family Credit, depending upon their household needs and upon their weekly earnings levels.

4.1 Income support and the means-tested Jobseeker's Allowance

The principal features of these benefits were explained in section 2, above. The means-tested Jobseeker's Allowance is payable to unemployed persons who have no entitlement to social insurance benefits. This situation may arise where the individual concerned has an insufficient record of contributions. Even where these conditions are met, the contributions-based job-seeker's allowance runs out automatically after six months of unemployment; after that, the claimant moves on to the means-tested allowance. The contributions-based and means-tested allowances are paid at the same basic age-related rates (see above: £ 30.95 for those under 18, £ 40.70 for 18-24 year olds and £ 51.40 for those who are 25 or above). However, the claimant's right to the means-tested JSA is dependent upon the income and employment of other household members, which is not the case with the contributions-based allowance.

Income Support is also payable according to need and is subject to a household means test. Those who qualify represent a residual category of those who do not have an income from full-time employment but are not classified as unemployed: these include those aged over 60, those who are unable to work on account of illness and disability, those bringing children up on their own or caring for a disabled or sick member of the family, or who otherwise do not have the necessary means to meet basic income needs.

In principle, Income Support represents the law's attempt to set a minimum subsistence income, or an amount below which the subsistence needs of individuals and

---

[56] For discussion see H. Parker, *Instead of the Dole. An enquiry into integration of the tax and benefit systems,* London: Routledge, 1989.

households cannot be effectively met. The amount of the benefit is calculated according to a series of allowances which are in part age-related (different allowances apply to the under-18s, those aged 18 to 24, and those aged 25 or over); the rate of benefit also differs according to whether or not claimants are single. Special allowances for dependent children are also payable, as are certain premiums in respect of lone parenthood, disability, and the receipt of age-related pensions. In 1997/98, the average weekly payment for all types of income support was £ 52.90.[57]

4.2 Benefits for those in work

These benefits are designed to supplement individual and/or household income from low-paid employment. Wage subsidies for low earners with dependent family members were introduced in 1971, in the form of Family Income Supplement. The benefit was calculated as a proportion of the difference between the gross wages received by the household and a set 'prescribed amount' of income. There was a low take-up rate for this benefit, which was thought to be a consequence, in part, of the disincentive effects caused by the loss of benefit once wages rose above a certain point. In 1985, it was replaced by family credit, which was paid net of taxes and National Insurance Contributions, and which was gradually reduced as wages rose. Family credit was in turn replaced in October 1999 by the Working Families Tax Credit, which forms a central part of the new Labour Government's strategy for 'making work pay'.

Unlike family credit, the Working Families Tax Credit, as its name suggests, is paid in the form of a tax credit, through the claimant's pay packet, as opposed to a benefit payment. The tax credit route for in-work benefits was seen as having three clear advantages for the Government: firstly, the visibility of the tax credit in the pay packet, which should serve to enhance the incentive effect; secondly, the policy represents an attempt to disassociate the benefit system from paid work and thereby to remove the sense of stigma sometimes associated with claiming benefit; thirdly, there was a clear political objective of improving the living standards of those on low incomes through more popular tax cuts than benefits increases. The main downside of policy is that payment of the credit directly through the claimant's pay packet decreases the incentive for employers to raise wages, and encourages reliance on state subsidy for maintaining the living standards of their employees. Nevertheless, the Working Families Tax Credit provides more generous financial assistance to working families and lone parents, by providing a longer taper than Family Credit, by which benefit is reduced as income rises.

To qualify, the claimant must show that he or she is normally engaged in paid employment for 16 or more hours per week, and that they are employed at the date of the claim. It must also be shown that the claimant is responsible for a child or young person living in the same household. This comprises both the case of a single person

---

[57] DSS, *Income Related Benefits Estimates of Take-up 1997/98*, London: HMSO, 1998.

who is responsible for a child or young person living with them, and the case of a couple, at least one of whom (not necessarily the claimant) is responsible for the child or young person. The basic adult tax credit amounts to £ 52.30 per family. A further credit of £ 11.05 is payable if the hours worked by the recipient (or his or her partner) exceed 30 per week. The Working Families Tax Credit is replaced at a rate of 55% of net income, compared to 70% in Family Credit. In addition, the threshold to which the taper applies will be increased from £ 80.65 under FamilyCcredit to £ 90 a week.[58]

Additional provision is also made towards childcare costs. The Working Families Tax Credit includes a Childcare Tax Credit component, which is worth 70% of eligible childcare costs of up to £ 100 a week for families with one child and £ 150 a week for families with two or more children. The qualifying age for the Childcare Tax Credit is 15, as compared to 12 under Family Credit. The maximum duration of an award of working families tax credit is 26 weeks; when that period expires, the claimant may submit another application.

Expenditure on family credit was £ 2.47 billion in 1998/99. In 1989, just after the benefit was introduced, there were 285,000 recipients; by February 1999, there were approximately 788,000 recipients of whom 388,000 had partners, and whose dependants totalled 1,578,000. At this time, the average weekly payment of Family Credit was £ 61.83 and the average weekly income from wages of Family Credit recipients was £ 116.80.[59]

Disability Working Allowance is paid as a supplement to the wages of certain low-paid workers with disabilities and operates in a similar way to Family Credit. The average weekly payment was £ 57.85 in April 1998 and there was a total of 15,106 recipients.[60]

4.3 Housing benefits

Benefits in respect of housing costs include Housing Benefit, which is payable to tenants; Council Tax Benefit, which is a form of assistance for paying council taxes which are partly levied on property; and mortgage interest payments which are met by the social security system in the case of some unemployed claimants. These were outlined in section 2, above.

---

[58] DSS, *Social Security. Departmental Report 1999.*

[59] DSS, *Family Credit Quarterly Statistics. July 1999,* London: HMSO, 1999.

[60] DSS, *Quarterly Statistics. September 1999,* London: HMSO, 1999.

4.4 Social Fund

The Social Fund was set up as one of a series of measures designed to meet the one-off and exceptional needs of people in receipt of the basic means-tested benefits. Unlike its predecessors, the Social Fund works on a different basis from other benefits in that it operates from a fixed budget and payments often form loans as opposed to grants. In practice the Social Fund is made up of two main components. First, there are mandatory benefits payable to claimants who are in receipt of certain basic means-tested benefits such as Income Support, Jobseeker's Allowance, Family Credit or Disability Allowance. These include maternity payments, under which a woman who is expecting a baby is entitled to a £ 100 payment, provided she or her partner do not have savings in excess of £ 500; funeral payments of up to £ 875 for those who are responsible for the funeral of a partner or close relative; and cold weather payments of £ 8.50 for each period of cold weather.

Second, there are a number of discretionary payments, comprising a mixture of loans and grants. These include budgeting loans designed to help claimants with direct lump sum needs, and which are repayable by direct deductions from benefit; crisis loans, which are designed to meet urgent, in particular living expenses; and community care grants payable to those moving out of institutions, (*e.g.* mental health care institutions or prison) to live in the community and to families in exceptional need.

Throughout the 1980s and early 1990s the Social Fund was the subject of significant criticism. Most notably, as many aspects of the fund are discretionary and combined with the cash limits, it could appear that the decisions of social security officers in allocating resources were arbitrary and the treatment of individuals was not uniform. Individuals were also often required to repay Social Fund loans over a short period of time, involving significant direct deductions from benefit, which constrained their ability to manage resources and meet other needs. Further, increasingly it appeared that claimants were being refused loans on the grounds that they were too poor to make the necessary repayments. Figures from the Benefits Agency revealed that the numbers refused assistance on this basis more than doubled from 44,890 in 1992/93 to 116,095 in 1993/94.[61] From April 1999 the Government introduced a number of changes to the scheme. In particular, the Government has limited the discretion of officers in determining applications for Social Fund budgeting loans, requiring that decisions are decided according to certain factual criteria.

4.5 Child benefit

Child Benefit is the only significant universal cash benefit in the British system. It was introduced in 1976 and replaced a system of tax allowances for households with

---

[61] E. Kempson, *Life on a Low Income,* York: Joseph Rowntree Foundation, 1996.

children. In its present form, it consists of a non-taxable weekly payment made to the parent (in practice, normally the mother) of the child. In April 1999 the rates of Child Benefit were £ 14.70 for the first child and £ 9.60 for each other child. The additional one parent benefit (payable to lone parents) was £ 2.10 a week, although this payment is no longer payable to those who claimed as lone parents after July 1998. Total expenditure on Child Benefit was £ 6,278 million in 1998/99.

The principle of paying a universal benefit has been the subject of continuing debate. Although it appears to contradict the aim of more effective targeting, it also avoids the low take-up and the unemployment and poverty traps which are associated with means-tested benefits such as Family Credit. For several years in the 1980s Child Benefit was not increased with price inflation when other benefits were and taxation of the benefit was discussed, although no legislation was introduced.

4.6 The system of benefit up-rating

Legislation first provided for social security benefits to be increased annually in line with inflation in 1975. Legislation of that year provided that retirement pensions and other long-term benefits were to be raised with prices or earnings, whichever was the higher. In the 1980s and 1990s, the principle that the value of social security benefits should be maintained against inflation was qualified in a number of ways. In particular, the longer-term benefits were linked to prices rather than earnings. This resulted in a gradual erosion in the value of the basic State Retirement Pension (see above, section 2). The short-term benefits (in respect of unemployment and sickness) also rose with prices rather than earnings, and certain benefits (in particular Child Benefit) were not raised at all in certain years.

At present, there is only a limited legal obligation upon the Secretary of State to raise or 'up-rate' certain benefits.[62] He or she is under a statutory duty, firstly, to review certain benefits to see if they have retained their value in relation to prices over the past year. If their value has fallen, then in the case of certain benefits only (principally the long-term social insurance benefits), an order must be laid before Parliament to restore the difference. There is no attempt to anticipate price inflation in the coming year. There is no duty, merely a power, to order an annual increase in the case of Child Benefit, the means-tested benefits, or the Jobseeker's Allowance.

---

[62] See Ogus, Barendt, and Wikeley, *The Law of Social Security*, p. 418-419.

5 Households and individuals

Social insurance benefits are paid on the basis of the contribution record of the individual concerned, but the basic rates of benefit may be supplemented according to household needs if there are dependants. Survivors' benefits (widows' and widowers' benefits) may also be paid on the basis of social insurance contributions under the relevant circumstances. The household or family, rather than the individual, is taken as the unit of assessment for the purpose of the means-tested benefits.[63] For this purpose, the family consists of the claimant, a partner of the opposite sex (who need not be a spouse of the claimant), and any dependent children who are members of the household in question. When one partner is in receipt of a means-tested benefit, the other is normally precluded from receiving that benefit for the relevant period, and the benefit in question is normally counted towards the household's income for the purpose of other benefits. The partners must separate permanently in order to be treated as separate claimants.

There are complex rules for calculating household income and capital. Earnings from employment, whether those of the claimant or of his or her partner, are normally treated as income, and thereby set off against means-tested benefits. Benefits may be forfeited altogether if earnings reach a certain level. A number of earnings 'disregards' operate so as to allow recipients to undertake part-time employment without loss of benefit entitlement, and for various other purposes. In relation to capital, a number of thresholds operate, with the effect that means-tested benefits may either be lost altogether or reduced on penny-for-penny basis.

The effect of the household means test on the rules governing entitlement to unemployment benefits was considered earlier (see section 2). Briefly, if the claimant is in receipt of the contributory Jobseeker's Allowance, no deduction is made for a partner's earnings from employment. However, where the claimant is in receipt of the means-tested allowance, his or her right to benefit is lost if their partner works for more than 24 hours per week; if the claimant's partner works for less than 24 hours per week, their earnings are set off against the claimant's benefit entitlement, subject to a £ 10 'disregard'. (It may also be noted that the claimant's entitlement is lost if he or he works for more than 16 hours per week, and that below that figure, any earnings are again set off against benefit. The £ 10 disregard applies to the earnings of the two partners together.)

The increase in reliance on the means-tested benefits has necessarily meant that the disincentive effects of the household means test are more widely felt than they were during periods when a larger proportion of the unemployed received contributory social insurance benefits.[64] In *Opportunity for all: Tackling poverty and social exclu-*

---

[63] *Ibid.*, ch. 14.

[64] See Deakin and Wilkinson, 'Labour law, social security and economic inequality'.

sion – the Labour first Annual Report on the progress of its welfare policies identified
workless households as one of the principal sources of poverty, particularly amongst
children.[65] The Report recognised that between 1979 and 1996/97 the proportion of
children living without a parent in work had doubled, with nearly one in five children
currently living in a household where no one works.[66] Furthermore, the problem of
child poverty was often concentrated among large families, lone parents and the ethnic minorities. As has been outlined throughout this report, in seeking to tackle the
primary causes of poverty, the Labour Government has placed emphasis on increased
attachment to the labour market and increased the capacity to earn, rather than
through redistribution by means of the benefits system. As a result, the Government
has chosen not to reform the way in which entitlement to means-tested benefits are
calculated for households. Instead, policies have focused on encouraging individuals
to enter paid work, through the introduction on the New Deal for Lone Parents and
for the Partners of the Unemployed. It is undoubtedly the case that paid work forms
the most effective route out of poverty. Nevertheless policy makers should be wary of
losing sight of the fact that poverty amongst people of working age is not limited to
the unemployed or economically inactive. Those returning to work through the New
Deal are most likely to enter low paid and insecure jobs and to continue to be dependent on welfare, in the form of in-work benefits. Although measures such as the
Working Families Tax Credit and the Childcare Tax Credit aim to target resources
towards families in work, the current level of these benefits may not be sufficiently
high to lift families out of poverty.

6 The impact of European integration

The process of European integration has so far had little impact on social security
policy in Britain. Outside the field of equality legislation, where Directive 79/7 has
had a major impact in particular with regard to the equalisation of pensionable ages,
the effects of directives and regulations concerning social security have been minimal. Nor has there been a significant debate on the implications of European monetary union for public expenditure levels, largely because the United Kingdom has,
except for brief periods, remained outside the European exchange rate mechanism
and its predecessors. This perspective would necessarily change if it became clear
that the UK intended to rejoin the ERM in the immediate future, or, indeed, to participate in the single currency at some point. However, separately from the European
dimension, there are strong domestic political pressures for the reduction (or at least,
stabilisation) of public expenditure levels. Both major political parties are committed
to reducing levels of personal taxation over the medium to long term, and it is widely

[65] DSS, *Opportunity for all: Tackling poverty and social exclusion,* Cm 4445, September 1999.
[66] Office of National Statistics, *Labour Force Survey,* London: HMSO, 1999.

assumed that this places limits upon public expenditure. These domestic pressures replicate, to a large extent, the effects in other systems of the Maastricht 'convergence criteria' for the single currency.

7 Conclusion and prognosis

The neoliberal reforms carried out in Britain since the early 1980s have confirmed the residual character of social security provision, with means-testing (or, 'targeting') growing in importance at the expense of both social insurance and universal benefits. The election of a new Labour Government and the commitment to a 'third way' for welfare has not altered the balance between cash benefits and services, means-testing and universality it inherited from its Conservative predecessors.

In many senses, however, the system did not conform to the general European pattern of social insurance even prior to the recent period of reform. Earnings-related contributions and benefits were only introduced on a systematic basis in the 1970s. Prior to then, the social security system had largely followed Beveridge's proposal for flat-rate benefits and flat-rate contributions (although the precise actuarial basis for social insurance benefits which he proposed was not adopted). The introduction of the State Earnings-Related Pension Scheme, which effectively began in 1977, was to have marked a major step towards a comprehensive social insurance system based on state provision. Almost immediately, however, doubts were cast on the feasibility of the new system, and the benefits it provided became less generous as a result of the Social Security Act 1986. The failure to raise the basic state pension with earnings after 1980 had a similar effect: the income of pensioners reliant on the state scheme failed to keep pace with the increase in earnings of those in employment during this period, with the result that larger numbers of the elderly became dependent on means-tested Income Support.

A similar development unfolded for the short-term benefits. The abolition of the earnings-related supplement for Unemployment Benefit in the early 1980s greatly reduced its effectiveness as an income-replacement mechanism, at the same time as new disciplinary rules were introduced with the aim of heightening the incentives of the unemployed to take up paid work, even at low rates of pay. The disciplinary emphasis was reinforced, and the element of social insurance further diluted, by the introduction of the Jobseeker's Allowance in the Jobseekers Act 1995 (implemented in 1996).

Policies introduced by the new Labour Government have not led to a significant overhaul of the welfare system, as might have been expected. Rather, their policies have led to an extension of the disciplinary rules applied to benefit recipient and an expansion of means-tested benefits. In addition, they have failed to reinstate earnings-related components to pensions or unemployment benefits. Indeed, a return to a fully comprehensive social insurance system looks unlikely. It is much more likely that, for the foreseeable future, social security in Britain will continue to operate on a combination of two elements: firstly, the promotion of private or occupational welfare, achieved through increased 'partnership' between public and private providers of welfare. In effect, this 'partnership' will lead to the displacement of state provision by private and occupational welfare. Nevertheless, private welfare will be regulated by the state, with a view to protecting individual's interests and minimising financial risks. This will be accompanied by a residual form of social assistance which, in practice, is coupled with disciplinary rules aimed at increasing labour market activity rates.

7.1 State support for private provision

This model is already emerging in the area of retirement pensions through the Government's proposals for stakeholder pensions. The underlying objective for the scheme was to devise a second-tier pension, targeted at low and moderate earners, which would accommodate the changing nature of the labour market, including the greater flexibility and mobility of labour, and at the same time offer greater security and a floor of minimum safeguards for individuals. This was to be achieved by a system of registration and requirements for approved governance structures, and regulation of minimum standards for charges. In addition, there would be no penalties if individuals were to stop contributing for a period of time, and the state would continue to support private provision in the form of tax subsidies and rebates from social insurance contributions. The scheme also envisages tighter regulation of the financial management of, and solvency requirements for, private pension providers.

A fundamental question here is the degree to which the state can meet through regulation (as opposed to direct provision) the goals of income replacement and maintenance of living standards during interruptions to work and during retirement. It may be questioned, for example, how effective the stakeholder pensions might be in avoiding the shortcomings of private pension schemes, experienced throughout the 1980s and early 1990s. These shortcomings arose primarily from the removal by the Pensions Act 1995 of both the guaranteed minimum pension requirement and of the ultimate safety net which had been provided by the State Earnings-Related Pension Scheme in the case of occupational scheme failure. Furthermore, the 1986 Social Security Act opened up alternatives to the normal defined-benefit scheme, in the form of employer-based and personal defined-contribution, or money-purchase schemes, which do not guarantee a final pension of any particular amount. In effect, the risk of financial fluctuations in securities markets is thrown largely on to the employee. Throughout the 1990s, such schemes have increased in number, in part because they are free of many of the regulations which apply to defined-benefit schemes. Nevertheless, many of the individuals (over half a million) who left occupational, defined-benefits schemes to set up personal schemes suffered financial losses as a consequence, largely because their employers ceased to pay additional contributions, over and above the minimum social insurance contributions, into their schemes. The wider effects were felt in terms of a destabilisation of the system of social insurance funding, which had to be remedied by a series of stop-gap measures aimed at protecting the National Insurance Fund.

7.2 Social assistance and work discipline

Social assistance payments represent a low, basic level of provision, which have become detached from increases in earnings. As the numbers of recipients dependent on social assistance has grown, so has the impulse to impose strict conditions on the receipt of means-tested benefits. This is most evident in the case of the means-tested benefits for the unemployed, where the goal of limiting benefit expenditure coincides with the wider economic policy aim of generating effective competition in the labour market. The jobseeker's agreement, under which the benefit recipient may be committed to accepting levels of pay not just below those in his or her previous work but also below the customary 'going rate' for the job, is the clearest manifestation of this policy. Measures, such as the Single Work-focused Gateway to Welfare, introduced by the Labour Government represents a further extension of the policy.

The tightening of the rules governing the receipt of means-tested benefits may be thought to have masked the degree to which the system continues to provide long-term basic support to groups excluded from regular employment or from other sources of subsistence. One such view is that during the 1970s and 1980s, 'the welfare system acted with increasing effectiveness as a safety net over a period of economic crisis and restructuring. The most important 'outcome' of the welfare state in the period may have been the economic gains of the 1980s'.[67] Certainly, as we have noted, social security expenditure as a proportion of GDP increased in Britain during this period, largely as a response to recession and unemployment. Neoliberal policies of market deregulation presuppose that the state is prepared to underwrite the costs of structural change through the social security system. At the same time, the 1980s and 1990s were periods of considerable growth in inequality.[68] Between 1979 and 1993 the lowest decile of households (the group most dependent on means-tested social security) saw no increase in income before housing costs are taken into account, whereas the highest decile had a rise of 45%. When housing costs are taken into account, the lowest decile had a drop in real income of 17%, compared to an increase of 62% for the highest decile.[69] While social security in Britain may have been suc-

---

[67] J. Le Grand, 'The state of welfare', in: J. Hills (Ed.) *The State of Welfare. The Welfare State in Britain since 1974* (Oxford: Clarendon Press, 1990), p. 338-360, esp. p. 350.

[68] See A. Goodman and S. Webb, 'For richer, for poorer: the changing distribution of income in the UK, 1961-91', in: *Fiscal Studies*, 15 (1994), no. 4, p. 29-62, and *Inquiry into Income and Wealth*, London: Joseph Rowntree Foundation, 1995.

[69] DSS, *Households with Below Average Incomes*, London: HMSO, 1995.

cessful in preserving social order, it has arguably been less successful in combating social exclusion.

Since entering office in 1997, the new Labour Government has kept to its commitment to introduce widespread reform to the welfare system, having produced a substantial body of consultation documents and legislative proposals. The approach adopted by new Labour marks a watershed from previous social democratic approaches to welfare. However, it marks less of a watershed from the neoliberal policy which preceded it. Many of the measures introduced since May 1997 are built upon the foundations laid by previous Governments. The main distinctive component of this part of new Labour's programme for welfare reform is the overwhelming emphasis placed on paid work as the principal route out of poverty and social exclusion, through the adoption of active market policies, combined with increased labour market discipline. The goal of 'making work pay' has involved an integrated strategy for improving work incentives, in which the national minimum wage plays an important part along with the realignment of the tax and benefit systems. The new system differs from its immediate predecessors in its acceptance of the need for a wider variety of regulatory techniques, including basic labour standards, as ways of improving the performance of the labour market. New Labour's strategy is based on the argument that equity in the operation of the welfare system is compatible with, and perhaps even the foundation of, economic efficiency. However, it is an open question whether this philosophy will produce outcomes which address long-standing concerns about fairness and income inequality. In particular, how successful it will be in tackling poverty and generating social inclusion is still to be determined.

XII European integration: Current problems and future scenarios

Lei Delsen, Nicolette van Gestel, and Joos van Vugt

1 Introduction

Since the Second World War social security systems in most Western European countries have expanded dramatically. Besides the classical contingencies of old age, unemployment and ill health, other contingencies fell successively under the coverage of social security. Moreover, social security was extended to more and more categories of the population. Economic growth paid for it all. However, since the economic recession of the mid-1970s the days of relatively carefree and optimistic expansion of social security have ended. Everywhere governments have been under pressure to cut back on their social expenditure and to reform their national social security system. However, from the national contributions one gathers that this pressure has seldom resulted in anything which resembles a wholesale reform. Fear of the unknown, politicians' vacillations, and numerous vested interests probably prevented this. As a result, real reform was postponed until well into the 1980s and, in some cases, the 1990s. Even then, change has often been the sum of numerous partial reforms instead of the result of wholesale reform. In a sense, therefore, the current debate and controversy on social security is a belated result of the reversal of the 1970s. Most issues, especially the financial ramifications of social security, have been debated at a national level. But in the last decade of the twentieth century, European developments, in particular the impending introduction of the *Economic and Monetary Union* (EMU), have begun to loom over national issues. In the contributions on national social security in this volume, the mixture of internal and European issues can be felt everywhere. However, it is not so easy to determine where European integration will eventually lead us.

When, in preparation of this publication, the Committee approached its European correspondents for the purpose of making a contribution on their national social security systems, it was motivated by interest in three major topics:

Topic 1: recent developments in the various national systems of social security (legal and financial basis, the extent of coverage, the proportion of income-related and flat-rate benefits)

Topic 2: the impact of this development on those in receipt of benefits (the financial position of unemployed, disabled or retired citizens, the level of basic social security provisions, individuals or households as the focus of social security provisions)

Topic 3: the impact of European integration on the various national systems of social security and on the living conditions of those in receipt of benefits.

They were asked to summarise the overall characteristics in regard to their national social security system: its organisational and financial basis and the scope of its arrangements. In addition, they were invited to assess its performance in maintaining an individual citizen's living standard in the face of such contingencies as sickness, unemployment, disability, and old age. Most countries have some sort of social assistance arrangement, aiming at citizens who, for some reason or other, are not eligible for regular benefits for unemployment, disability and such. It is these social assistance arrangements which, in most cases, constitute the minimum social protection provided by the State for its citizens. The authors were asked to describe this provision in their country and to assess its worth. Furthermore, they were asked if, in their national social security system, the household or the individual is the unit on which social security legislation is focused, and if there are any developments in this respect. Finally, the matter of European unity was brought up. Does the increasing European integration on economic and monetary matters, with its concomitant financial restraints and requirements, influence domestic social security? And if so, in which direction? Is the social security system in the various European countries likely to flourish or flounder under wider European influence?

In the following paragraphs we will try to describe, on the basis of the national contributions, the most important findings regarding these three topics. We will concentrate on identifying *trends* that seem to be shared by most if not all of the countries which have been reviewed. This is not an easy task in view of the numerous and divergent developments which have been described. Conclusions should be phrased with caution. National security systems are part of the economic, cultural and political structure of their country, which makes it hard to assess their evolution. For example, measures aimed at privatisation of social risks or at flexibilisation of the labour market may have different impacts in different countries. Finally, a large amount of legislation is so recent that its consequences are as yet unknown. This, too, is a reason for being modest in one's conclusions. Next, we will discuss some of the most persistent *problems* of social security in Europe which, despite many efforts, have not yet been solved: financing, long-term unemployment and the system's adaptation to atypical (temporary, flexible, and part-time) employment. Finally, we will try to see beyond the current situation to the future of European social security. We will present, and discuss, two possible *scenarios* for the adaptation or reform of social security, which may offer a solution for these and other problems.

2 Recent developments in social security

2.1 More universal flat-rate benefits

Although most European systems of social security are dominated by income-related benefits, the emphasis is shifting towards universal basic benefits which replace or supplement the income-related benefits. In most European countries (Spain, Germany, Greece, Italy, Belgium), social security has developed along the lines of the Bismarck model. The United Kingdom is an exception: since the 1940s its social security has been dominated by the Beveridge model and its universal flat-rate benefits. Ireland is another exception. Since its unification in the 1950s, Irish social security also relies mainly on flat-rate benefits, even though these are not derived from the Beveridgean principle of national solidarity. In recent years, even countries with a tradition in income-related benefits – with the possible exception of the Netherlands – tend to develop more flat-rate benefits. As a result, social security systems in Europe will refer less often to the employment history of claimants as a criterion for eligibility. Moreover, they will display growing selectivity in determining the claimant's *actual* needs (*cf.* Denmark). European social security systems seem to converge on a mixture of Beveridgean universal flat-rate low coverage and a Bismarckian supplementary system, based mainly on participation in the labour market.

2.2 Towards mixed financial responsibility

Traditionally, most national systems of social security are mainly funded from contributions by employers and employees. In most countries, direct State funding, *i.e.* out of taxes, is substantially smaller, although the sums involved may be huge. Nevertheless, the differences between various countries are substantial, from Denmark with 68.9% State funding to the Netherlands 16.4% (see Table 1).

In tune with the first trend, there has been a development towards a more mixed system of funding. In general, direct State financing seems to be on the increase in southern European countries while in most northern European countries the contribution of the State is decreasing (but still considerable). In Spain, for example, the State has taken a much larger share in social security than before (social assistance, medical costs), but since national authorities find it difficult to live up to their financial responsibilities in this respect, regional and local authorities, volunteer organisations, private insurance companies and pension funds are stepping in. In Belgium, the State finances large parts of the social security system but its share is decreasing as a result of the requirements by the EMU. In France, a shift is taking place from a largely State-financed system to the more usual system of mixed private and public financing. In Denmark, the financial share of the State in social security is not fixed but fluctuates with unemployment statistics. Generally speaking, it seems that the role of the State in mixed financial systems depends on the developmental state of the national social security system. In countries with fully developed social security systems, the State is slowly retreating, while in countries with less developed systems the State comes to the fore as a guarantor in an increasing number of social security schemes.

Table 1. The structure of social protection receipts in the European Union as a percentage of total receipts, 1996[1]

	General government contributions	Social security contributions	Social security contributions paid by employers	Social security contributions paid by protected persons	Other receipts	Total
Denmark	68.9	24.9	9.6	15.3	6.2	100
Ireland	63.0	36.1	21.9	14.2	0.9	100
Luxembourg	46.7	45.7	25.9	19.8	4.6	100
United Kingdom	48.5	39.0	24.6	14.4	12.3	100
Finland	44.6	35.0	35.0	13.2	7.2	100
Sweden	45.3	46.7	40.0	6.7	7.9	100
Portugal	42.2	42.5	26.0	16.5	15.0	100
Austria	35.7	62.2	37.4	24.6	0.6	100
Spain	27.8	67.1	52.0	15.1	2.6	100
Italy	29.6	67.3	49.3	18.0	3.1	100
Greece	30.3	61.4	38.0	23.4	8.3	100
Germany	30.0	63.5	39.1	24.4	2.4	100
Belgium	20.4	69.6	44.5	25.1	9.2	100
France	20.2	76.9	49.9	27	1.9	100
The Netherlands	16.4	59.9	23.2	36.7	16.0	100
European Union (15)	31.9	62.9	39.2	23.7	5.2	100

2.3 Cutbacks and improvements simultaneously

In the past two decades, in most European countries the social security issue has been dominated by cutbacks. In actual fact, however, total expenditure has gone up (see Table 2). Moreover, while cutbacks were being contemplated and introduced, social risks which were not covered before, were included in the social

[1] Source: Eurostat, 1999.

security system. While some social schemes were curtailed (*e.g.* old age pensions in Italy) others were extended (*e.g.* parental leave in Italy). In some countries (Ireland, Greece) benefits for some categories were actually raised.

Some member states, such as Spain and Greece, seem to be in the process of catching up with the European average by acknowledging social risks which have already been covered elsewhere. In other countries, serious if cautious efforts are being made to include 'new' risks into social security. The United Kingdom, for example, made some provision for those who are unable to work because they care for someone who is sick or disabled by the introduction of the Invalid Care Allowance. In Germany, the growing number of invalid elderly citizens led to the introduction of a special nursing care insurance in 1994. All in all, the financial crisis which has beset European social security from the 1970s onward has not brought the system to a complete standstill, let alone into a state of regression. Some provisions have been downgraded and some benefits have been decreased but efforts have been made towards improvement and modernisation, as well.

2.4 More private insurance schemes

In some EU countries, the trend towards cost control in social security has paved the way for the development of private insurance schemes, especially where sick pay and old age pensions are concerned. In the Netherlands, sick pay has been privatised in an attempt to reduce absence through illness and to encourage employers to improve working conditions. The Government has perhaps primarily intended to shift responsibility for financing and for implementation of sick pay and old age pensions towards private parties, i.e. to the employers and the employees. In the United Kingdom, employers may opt out of the Statutory Sick Pay scheme provided they operate an equivalent scheme. In both countries the State has defined the margins of privatisation.

In many European countries, private old age pension schemes are on the rise. In most cases, these private insurances supplement existing State pensions or occupational pensions which are insufficient for maintaining the pensioners' accustomed standard of living. In some countries – Belgium and the United Kingdom, for example – these private insurances are actually encouraged by the State, which is well aware of the inadequacy of its basic pensions. In Italy the crisis of public finances has inspired supplementary private insurance schemes for old age, invalidity, and death. By regulating conditions and financing, the State has taken partial responsibility for the quality and solidity of these provisions.

The trend towards privatisation is far from ubiquitous. Ireland, with its highly centralised social security system, displays no tendency towards privatisation. Some private protection does exist though in the form of loan and mortgage protection policies. Only a minority of employees is covered by a private insurance in regard to disability and invalidity. In Denmark, the welfare state seems to remain firmly universal and public in character. The debate on privatisation of the welfare state has petered out. Hardly any privatisation has been implemented. In Greece, too, no deliberate privatisation has taken place, but by limiting protection by the public system, the State nevertheless encourages private arrangements. In Spain, private insurance schemes will probably become more important in the future, but their development may be blocked by the fact that the State needs a broad basis for collecting funds to finance its own benefit payments. Interestingly enough, social services for the disabled are provided by organisations like ONCE and SE-REM, which are managed on the basis of public-private partnership.

Suggestions for more privatisation of social security are being discussed in many European countries, mostly from a pragmatic point of view. As a result, privatisation has so far not been a radical operation at all, since the role of private organisations remains, to a very large extent, under the control of public law. Nevertheless, the privatisation trend reflects a re-thinking of the relation between the State and the market or, alternatively, the public and the private sector in society. The notion that the State's possibilities are large but far from inexhaustible, has taken root. Privatisation also reflects a re-thinking of the position of the private citizen, who, more than ever before, is being thrown upon his or her own responsibility. The debate in Germany on the resuscitation of self-help and public spirit, which extends into the field of social security, has brought this re-thinking back to the public domain.

3 The impact of recent developments

3.1 More emphasis on reintegration and the obligation to work

Since the early 1990s, reintegration of beneficiaries has become a more important policy objective for all European Governments – at any rate, at the ideological level. The objectives of all models of social security can now be found in a combination of providing social protection and of encouraging people to re-enter work. As a result, the balance between rights and obligations has shifted appreciably. Emphasis has shifted towards the obligations of claimants and beneficiaries. In most of the countries described in this book, efforts have been made to strengthen the *activating* effect of the system in order to reintegrate beneficiaries more rapidly into the labour market. Sometimes this activating process involved positive incentives such as, in Belgium, a 'reintegration premium' or, in other countries, an offer of free additional training, work experience jobs, and job counselling. On the other hand, however, activating policies always involve some kind of coercion or pressure. In each country, receiving a welfare benefit entails an obligation to search for a job, although certain categories may be exempted for the time being (*e.g.* single women with young children, or individuals who are, for some reason, unemployable). In Belgium, young welfare applicants are induced to sign an integration contract which defines mutual obligation concerning training and employment. In Denmark, various benefits are to be made conditional on accepting work offers or additional training. In the United Kingdom, job search duties of the unemployed have been toughened since the 1980s. The new Labour government has maintained this course by 'narrowing the gateway for young people', leaving them hardly any other alternative than that of accepting any job offer. The Government has also proposed that welfare claimants will be compelled to attend an interview with a counsellor in order to survey their job prospects. In Greece, however, reintegration policies have only just started to become an issue.

Since governments realise that the carrot-and-stick principle will probably be most effective, efforts are also made to take the sting out of the 'poverty trap' by making the acceptance of a new job more attractive fiscally (*e.g.* in the United Kingdom). In spite of such efforts, the reintegration of women in the labour market poses substantial problems. Not only are they most likely to get caught in the poverty trap (divorced, untrained), but they often have the care of small children, parents or relatives. Since 'care' is not considered 'work', the emphasis on the obligation to work affects them the worst if there is no affordable childcare and if home help provisions are not available. If a job involves many extra costs, it is hardly financially worth the trouble to accept it.

3.2 Emphasis on basic minimum benefits

Historically, social security in Europe has moved from providing social protection on a minimum subsistence level to providing benefits which allow the claimant to more or less maintain his or her accustomed living standard. In recent years, however, a reverse tendency seems to have appeared. Social protection is being once again concentrated on fighting poverty instead of maintaining living standards. In some countries (Italy, Greece), the basic minimum benefit is pegged well below the poverty line. Although eradicating poverty is the official aim, this ambition is not always realised. In Spain and Greece, the State's financial resources are inadequate but also in other countries the number of people living on too low a basic minimum is on the rise (*e.g.* France) – many of them have not been able to pay enough contributions to social insurances or to build up an adequate pension entitlement. Both in France and the Netherlands the purchasing power of minimum benefits has decreased. In France large categories of unemployed young people are not entitled to any benefit at all. Ireland is the exception: assisted by a booming economy and a relatively 'young' population, the Irish State has raised many benefits. Poverty in Ireland has demonstrably declined.

3.3 The gap between the rich and the poor is widening

With the possible exception of Ireland, social security systems in Europe have to some extent a redistributive effect. Without complex social security provisions, the gap between the rich and the poor would undoubtedly be wider than it is now. Some countries have taken special measures to close this gap even more. Belgium, for example, introduced extra financial support for poor families and decided on a relatively expensive provision called 'bridging pension', which enables companies to allow older employees to go on a good pension and substitute young unemployed. Any measure which increases the amount of direct tax financing of social security, has a redistributive effect; unlike insurance schemes which are largely funded from contributions by the people who will eventually receive the benefits. Basic old age pensions and social assistance benefits all fall into this category. In spite of this general redistributive effect, people who depend on a basic minimum provision have not benefited (or at least not fully benefited) from the overall rise in prosperity in Europe during the past decade. For people who have been caught in the social security system for a long time and for whom the prospect of a new job and an improvement in their standard of living is bleak, this means slow impoverishment which, with all its concomitant effects, eventually results in social marginalisation. In the contributions on Germany and the Netherlands, the categories which are affected most are identifiable: women (in particular, single mothers), the elderly, the disabled, members of certain ethnic minorities, and long-term unemployed (often young people with insufficient qualifications and work experience).

4 The impact of European integration

4.1 Options for social security in Europe

What significance will European integration have on national and perhaps even European social security? In their contributions on national social security systems various authors have tried to shed light on this issue. Some have pointed out that, given the many uncertainties, several lines of development seem equally plausible. There is no way of knowing for certain what will happen in the coming decades. In his contribution on Germany, Josef Schmid summarised three options. The first option is one of an optimistic nature. European integration could lead to an expansion of social policies, as well as to the harmonisation of benefits and structures within Europe. European integration would hence stimulate efforts to reduce the differences between national systems; the same motives which have inspired social security at a national level for many decades would now inspire social security at a European level: the 'European welfare state' may be dawning. Unfortunately, the pessimistic second option is just as plausible. European monetary and political integration could entail a loss of national sovereignty of the member states. In the foreseeable future, this loss would not be compensated by an increase in authority at a European level. Social policies would be brought to a virtual standstill. Social security would deteriorate because there would be no authority, national or European, that could check the process of social dumping, *i.e.* unfair competition between national systems whereby disparities in wages, social costs, and labour conditions would be exploited to gain the upper hand. Finally, as a third possible option, Europe could become a 'laboratory' for new social policies. This could be achieved if European integration would no longer be considered a reason for adapting the existing systems but for the creation of new systems which would survive far into the twenty-first century.

4.2 European welfare state or race to the bottom?

Will European economic integration entail a convergence of social security systems in the future? There is little doubt that *some* form of convergence will take place between the various national systems of social security. It is inconceivable that a Europe which has reached such a high degree of political and economic integration, would remain as socially fragmented as it is now. However, the prospects for a concerted effort towards harmonisation of social policies and social security systems are not encouraging. In none of the European countries can a willingness to adapt in the direction of any European model be detected. In their contribution on Italy, Balandi and Renga observe that, although the European Union is moving towards a greater political and economic homogeneity, the point at which this will be reflected by a European consensus on social security is still far removed. They quote European policy-makers who, in 1989, observed that European harmonisation was 'neither desirable nor desired'.[2] Harmonisation policies will provoke serious resistance. No wonder, since all national social security systems have firm historical roots. They are interwoven with their country's political, economic and judicial systems, and reflect cultural notions on poverty, on individual responsibility, on the State, on work, on the family, and on the social roles of men and women. Many people have vested interests in their country's social security system as it is at present. Given these obstacles, it is highly unlikely that any substantial harmonisation will be achieved in a systematic or planned way. It is much more likely that instead of planned harmonisation a creeping convergence will take place. This convergence will be the result of indirect pressures rather than direct policies. G.A. Ritter argues, therefore, that direct, systematic and planned harmonisation should *not* be made the aim of European social policy. Instead, some degree of harmonisation may be approached by a

---

[2] Laurent, 'Rapport introductif'.

roundabout method. This can be achieved, legally, by laying down the basic social rights of the 1989 European Social Charter in national law, by harmonising certain aspects of national labour law regulations and by promoting regulations on health and safety at work; and economically, by extending the *European Social Fund* and European regional policy programmes which are aimed at improving the living and working conditions in the underdeveloped regions of the Union.[3] In this way, divergence between European countries can be reduced without having to resort to the complex and perhaps even impossible task of systematic harmonisation.

Table 2: Social protection expenditure in the European Union as a percentage of GDP, 1980-1996.[4]

	1980	1990	1993	1996
Belgium	28.2	26.8	29.0	30.0
Denmark	28.7	30.3	33.5	33.6
Germany	28.8	25.4	20.1	30.5
Greece	9.7	22.7	22.0	23.3
Spain	18.2	20.4	24.4	22.4
France	25.4	27.7	31.2	30.8
Ireland	20.6	19.1	20.8	18.9
Italy	19.4	24.1	26.0	24.8
Luxembourg	26.5	23.5	25.2	26.2
The Netherlands	30.1	32.5	33.7	30.9
Austria	--	26.7	29.0	29.5
Portugal	12.9	15.5	21.0	21.6
Finland	--	25.5	35.4	32.1
Sweden	--	32.9	38.6	34.8
United Kingdom	20.5	23.1	28.8	27.7
European Union (15)	--	25.4	29.0	28.7

The question which remains is which direction will spontaneous convergence take and what will be the results in terms of the quality of social protection for individual citizens. In the final analysis, European economic integration is part of the on-going internationalisation of the economy, which has led to a marked toughening of economic competition throughout the world. In Europe, economic integration embodied in the EMU reflects and emphasises this development. This internationalisation process reduces the relevance and effectiveness of national economic policies. National macro-economic policies will be curtailed as more and more decisions are being taken by central agencies in Brussels and Frankfurt. Even with the undivided European market still in the coming, the EMU already cast its

---

[3] G.A. Ritter, *Der Sozialstaat. Entstehung und Entwicklung im internationalen Vergleich* [The Welfare State. Its rise and development in international perspective] (München: Oldenbourg, 1991, 2nd ed.), p. 198-199.

[4] Source: Eurostat, 1999.

shadow. The Maastricht Treaty of 1991 and the 1996 Stability Pact have compelled European governments to control their public deficits. Apart from some creative budgetary measures, the resulting financial strain may eventually have repercussions on social security schemes. In this way, the systems of social security in the European Union member states may display a degree of convergence. Moreover, countries in Northern and Southern Europe have demonstrated a rapprochement in their social expenditure as a percentage of their GDP (see Table 2, and Figure 1 which has been derived from it). It will be interesting to see if this trend has continued after 1996: in some countries, such as the Netherlands, considerable financial shifts have taken place.

Figure 1: Social protection expenditure in the European Union as a percentage of GDP, in 1980 and 1996, with linear regression lines.[5]

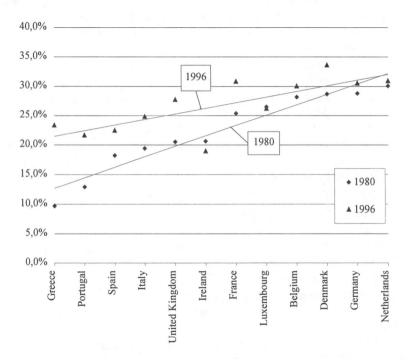

As competition within the internal European market becomes tougher, a harmful extension of economic competition to competition between national systems of social security may ensue: the 'social dumping' phenomenon which was mentioned in the introductory chapter to this book. It goes without saying that not all member states have reached the same level of social and economic development. Nor have they reached the same level of social security: "(...) there are disparities

---

[5] Source: Eurostat, 1999.

in development between Member States as regards social protection".[6] Economic competition between the countries of Europe will put pressure on the social policies of those countries which have the most developed and hence, most expensive social systems. For this reason, it was often suggested that the European Union would fall into serious discord unless the countries involved achieved a much higher degree of convergence in social security *before* its monetary union was introduced. A pessimistic view since, as we pointed out, there was, and still is, little chance of any substantial systematic convergence being achieved. The worst case scenario is that the social security systems of the countries of Europe will eventually be carried along in a 'race to the bottom' until minimal provisions will have become the European norm. Of course, European governments are well aware of this danger, but can it be avoided?

As a result of global developments and European economic integration, the various governments within the EMU will enjoy much less leeway for national economic policy than before. They can no longer respond to crises and problems by unilateral monetary manipulation. After the introduction of the Euro, they can only resort to manipulating wage and price levels in order to compete or to respond to external shocks. Governments can manipulate wages and prices through taxation and by adapting the social security system which, after all, lies at the root of a significant component of wage costs. Countries, which have managed to keep wages and social costs low, will achieve an important advantage in a system in which other countries cannot compensate by altering the value of their currency. Countries with higher wages and higher social costs will be forced to adjust by making wage reductions and cuts in social contributions and taxes. For this reason, pressures towards social dumping are likely to become stronger.

For the sake of social peace, the European Union may try to avoid social dumping by a strong co-ordination of social policy at the European level to compensate for the reduced leeway for autonomous national policies. In the Treaty of Maastricht monetary and budgetary criteria for entering EMU were laid down in the hope that these would foster sensible and disciplined behaviour which, in turn, would result in a *de facto* harmonisation of national policies without policy costs at the European Union level.[7] So far, little headway seems to have been made in this area. According to the Dutch economist L.A. Geelhoed, the countries of the European Union are on the road to competition rather than social co-ordination. He points out that, in essence, the EMU is a strong framework within which countries with different policy packages can compete freely and not a cartel aimed at avoiding competition altogether. The fire of competition will be fanned even more because,

---

[6] Council recommendation of 24 June 1992 on common criteria concerning sufficient resources and social assistance in social protection systems (92.441/EEC), in: *Official Journal of the European Communities*, L 245, August 26th, 1992, p. 46-48, esp. preamble no. 11.
[7] L.A. Geelhoed, '1997: Een delta in Europa [1997: A delta in Europe]', in: *Economisch Statistische Berichten* [Economic and Statistical Communications], (1997), January 1st, p. 4-8.

under EMU, companies will be able to make decisions on investments and reloca-tions as if they were operating in one undivided economy. They will be able to base their decisions on cool comparisons of wages and social costs in the various countries. When calculated in a single European currency, these comparisons will be completely transparent.[8] This will have a considerable impact on collective wage bargaining. Companies and governments will find it easier to put pressure on trade unions to accept lower levels of wages and benefits for the sake of a comparative advantage. In this view, neither insistence on national sovereignty nor the resistance of trade unions will be able to slow down the resulting 'race to the bottom' in social policies and services. Social dumping will be inevitable, and will result in a general downgrading of social security provisions, notably at the bottom of the labour market. The combination of these effects may result in pov-erty in those segments of the population who, for some reason or other, are not able to benefit from the economic boost which, hopefully, will spring from Euro-pean integration. On balance, the impact of the EMU in its present form will be a reduction in the quantity and the quality of social security throughout Europe.

Is this all inevitable? It depends.

First of all, wage costs are not the only issue in international competition. After all, even today companies are able to freely choose the location of their invest-ments. In the bid for their favours, countries with well-developed social security systems are not doing so badly compared to their simpler neighbours. Therefore, it appears that in a company' decision-making such factors as a well-organised na-tional infrastructure, high levels of education, a supportive banking system, State services and, finally, industrial peace are also taken into consideration.

Secondly, the champions of European economic integration never tire of explain-ing that the economic boost created by the creation of a united market will benefit social security, as well. They argue that, in the final analysis, every social security system depends on a country's economic performance. The coming of the EMU may create friction and problems, certainly, but the advantages of a united market will eventually strengthen, not weaken, the foundations of European social secu-rity.

Thirdly, today's social security systems are the outcome of decades of social and political debate and strife. Even during the past decades, almost every inroad on acquired rights has met with serious resistance from political parties, unions, and citizens who were opposed to any downgrading of the existing provisions. An illustration of this is the Thatcher Cabinet in the United Kingdom, which, for all its aversion of 'idlers', did not succeed in lowering the expenditure on social secu-rity. In none of the European countries will the adjustment of the national social

---

[8] G. Miller, *The future of social security in Europe in the context of Economic and Monetary Union. The role of the social partners and EC institutions*, Brussels 1993.

security system to a lower European standard be achieved without a struggle being fought first.

Fourthly, as Balandi en Renga point out in their text on Italy, much will depend on the priorities that will be chosen at the central European level of Brussels and Frankfurt. Will the European Union give priority to socio-political considerations or to monetary policies? If socio-political considerations win the day, European social security will be subject to normal political debate and democratic decision-making. The forces which try to improve and expand social security arrangements will remain in a rough equilibrium with the forces that try to economise on social expenditure and to cut back on too generous provisions. However, if monetary policies get the upper hand, the development of social security will largely with-draw from normal politics and find a momentum of its own. In that case grave dangers to the social security systems of all European countries may loom ahead.

So far, neither the European governments nor their citizenry show any signs of panic concerning the approaching united market and its possible effects on social security. Of course, by now many Europeans have come to consider European integration as something inevitable. But, although the differences between the various countries of Europe are substantial, each has a reason for optimism and for pessimism. For countries such as Greece, Spain, Portugal and, to some extent, Italy, any European influence on social security holds both a danger and an op-portunity. The danger lies in the financial strains caused by the EMU; the oppor-tunities lie in the European incentive towards modernisation, greater efficiency and financial soundness, and the much-needed implementation of minimum re-quirements on basic benefits, equal pay, health, and work safety. For Greece in particular, entrance into the EMU is expected to have far-reaching effects. Greece has met the EMU requirements with great difficulty and, according to Stergiou, the financial basis of its social security system is inadequate. On the other hand, countries such as Denmark, Belgium and the Netherlands seem confident that their economic and financial strength will prevent their social policies from being unduly affected by European integration. In the Netherlands, in particular, there is confidence that the painful reforms of social security since the 1980s will prove enough to weather the storm. For Ireland there is optimism too, but for a different reason. Its social security system is one of the few that can be said to be still in the process of construction and expansion. Because of its current relatively low con-tribution and expenditure levels, its social policies will probably be stimulated rather then downgraded by European integration. France feels the pressure of EMU's financial demands but it is unlikely that, in the short run, European inte-gration will do more than put a slight restraint on its social expenditure.

4.3 Towards the Anglo-Saxon economic model?

In the long run, European integration may even have more fundamental consequences for Europe's economies. According to M. Albert, within the amalgam of
Western free market capitalist economies a meaningful distinction can be made
between two different and competing varieties: the Rhineland model and the Anglo-Saxon model.[9] Within Europe, Germany and the Netherlands perhaps represent most convincingly the variety of the Rhineland model or social market economy. This model is characterised by State involvement and by tripartism (between
government, employers and employees) as a co-ordinating device, by bargaining
and consensus instead of confrontation and conflict, and by an emphasis on securing long-term investments instead of making short-term profits. The United
States and, in Europe, the United Kingdom may be considered to be varieties of
the Anglo-Saxon model which is characterised by little government involvement,
by price stability as a top priority, by co-ordination through market forces, and by
an emphasis on achieving short-term results. Both models have produced their
own social security systems which reflect the values underlying their differences.
In the highly competitive environment of a full-fledged EMU, the more cumber-
some and expensive Rhineland model of social market economy may well yield to
the Anglo-Saxon model which is more suited to fierce economic competition.

5 Persistent problems

5.1 Persistent financial problems

Regardless of their differences, European social security systems have a number
of serious problems in common. Perhaps the most pressing problem regards
funding. Some social security provisions are paid from taxation and burden the
State budget; others are paid from contributions and send wage costs up to the
detriment of national competitiveness and, eventually, the State budget, as well.
Moreover, the financing of social security suffers from the succession of economic recessions and upswings. In times of recession, social security has to ab-
sorb rising unemployment figures. As a consequence, the costs of social security
increase while the overall financial situation is more \ than is usually the case. On
the other hand, economic upswings tend to foster financial optimism among politicians and to increase demands and expectations among workers, unions, and
political parties. This often results in the expansion of social security provisions
and in rising expenditure. Any problems countries may have with the financing of

---

[9] M. Albert, *Capitalisme contre capitalisme*, Paris 1991.

social security are compounded by the steadily rising costs of health care and by the prospect of an ageing population which, according to Ritter, will prevent any major reduction of social expenditure in the decades to come.[10]

In most European countries, the age distribution of the population is changing steadily as a result of the decline in the birth rate since the 1960s. Some countries, *e.g.* Germany, have already wrestled with this problem for many years while others, *e.g.* Ireland, may not experience these effects for many years to come. Nevertheless, the trend is clear and comprehensive. At the moment, the share of citizens in the active age bracket of 20 to 60 is at its peak but the number of pensioners is already rising and will increase dramatically once the baby-boom generation reaches the pensionable age. In countries where old age benefits are financed on a 'pay as you go'-system, the younger generation is in effect paying for the elderly. This system works fine as long as there is a balance between the generations. However, the tacit 'contract between the generations' will be broken once the proportion between active citizens and pensioners has shifted against the former – as it will.[11] In countries where pension funding is largely based on a capitalisation system, the effects will not be so dramatic but even there the ageing of the population will cause rising social expenditure because of rising State pensions and health care costs. In some countries governments are considering a switchover to a capitalisation system.

The rising costs of health care are also a continuing concern of Western governments. This development is partly caused by endemic factors within health care, such as the expansion of bureaucracy, higher medical standards, the rising cost of medication and higher salaries for medical personnel. It is also partly caused by the ageing of the population: the elderly are by far the largest consumers of health care. In some countries, health care is considered to be an integral part of social security; in others, it has organisational and financial structures of its own, independent of the social security systems but hardly without similar problems.

5.2 Persistent unemployment

Perhaps the most pressing problem within European social security concerns the (re)integration into the labour market of those who were made redundant or never

---

[10] Ritter, *Der Sozialstaat*, p. 213.
[11] Winfried Schmähl *et al.*, *Generationenvertrag und Generationengerechtigkeit* [Generational pact and generational equity], Frankfurt a.M.: Bund-Verlag, 1999. Series: *WSI Mitteilungen*, 52 (1999), no. 1 (*Schwerpunktheft*); *Internationales Kolloquium über 'Solidarität zwischen den Generationen'*, Lissabon, September 1990 [International Conference on 'Solidarity between generations', Lisbon, September 1990], Graz: EURAG, 1991; Axel Schütz, 'Pensionsfonds statt Generationenvertrag? [Pension funds instead of generational pact?]', in: *Zeitschrift für das gesamte Kreditwesen* [Journal for General Financing], 50 (1997), no. 4, p. 170.

even held a job. Since the 1970s, European countries have been confronted with a structurally high unemployment level. To some extent, this is a result of the vagaries of the world economy but structural factors are involved too. Moreover, technology has brought about a social shift against unskilled labour. Increasingly, unskilled labour has become too expensive and, even worse, unwanted. Thus, a large and persistent reservoir of the long-term unemployed has been created. Ironically, social security itself has also been blamed for the persistence of unemployment. It is said that, for all its social merits, it has acerbated the unemployment problem. Its very existence has prevented the wage level from adjusting to the consequences of technological change. Moreover, according to many, social security provisions have killed the incentive for citizens to take responsibility for their own lives, to adapt to training standard, and to search actively for jobs. Many cuts in benefits, tightening of eligibility requirements and shifts in the responsibility for social security schemes may be placed in this perspective, along with efforts to make benefits (especially for young adults) dependent on personal commitments to accept jobs which are offered by the social security organisation, to join additional training programmes or to continue searching for a job.

In the 1990s, the countries of Western Europe have felt great financial and economic pressures to combat unemployment, to increase labour participation rates and to improve their employment/population ratio. Governments have set their hopes on economic growth, believing that growth alone will more or less automatically increase the number of people gainfully employed. So far, governments have tried to promote growth by deregulating the labour market, by forcing wage adjustments and by making reforms in social security. Thus many restrictive social security measures are linked to the objective of reducing the number of beneficiaries and subsequently reducing expenditure. Of course, a return to the exceptional growth rates of the fifties and sixties would solve many problems, but it seems too unrealistic to hope for. But even if high growth rates could be attained some problems would still remain. It is clear that in a booming economy unemployment will evidently decline. This was demonstrated, in some European countries, by the favourable closing years of the 1990s which saw a marked decline in unemployment levels. At the same time, the limitations of the effect of economic growth have become obvious, too. Economic growth in a deregulated market, especially in so far as it is brought about by technological innovation, increases productivity and work-pressure, produces and reinforces inequalities between strong and disadvantaged groups in the labour market, and between countries and regions. Predictably, it is the unskilled, the elderly, the disabled and the ethnic minorities who are left behind. Unemployment may decline, but the remaining unemployment is even more persistent and even more hopeless. Finally, one must consider that, historically, economic growth is a precarious phenomenon. Dropping growth rates will affect the weaker first.

Governments have also tried to make the labour market more flexible, thus enabling it to accommodate more citizens than before. Several instruments have been deployed, such as introducing training programmes, restricting employment protection, promoting temporary work through agencies, *etc.* One means of achieving flexibilisation is speeding up the flow rate of jobs by promoting the gradual withdrawal from the labour market by employees over 60 years of age.[12] Although the advantages of this policy are obvious, current trends within European countries are contradictory. In some countries, actual or expected labour shortage – the result of the economic boom and the ageing of the population – has led to pleas for actually *raising* the pensionable age. In others, the necessity of *lowering* the pensionable age is advocated in order to make room for younger people on the labour market. In countries with adequate pension schemes there is a tendency among employees to choose some form of early retirement – often because the increasing work-pressure is becoming too much for them. Disability benefit schemes sometimes provide a convenient, if unintended, transition from full-time employment to full retirement.

Governments have tried their hand at many employment creation schemes, which are particularly aimed at the young and unemployed (which are considered the largest social risk). Schemes of this kind may be beneficial to individuals, but they can cover only a small part of all beneficiaries and claimants. They often provide low paid work only, which is intended to be additional to the regular labour market. Moreover, for elderly, disabled and untrained beneficiaries, prospects remain bleak. Employers tend to recruit only healthy, young and well-qualified applicants. Although recruitment policy is influenced by the situation in the labour market, this observation will, in general, remain valid for the coming years. This means that an important part of long-term beneficiaries who can – in theory – work, will have to seek work, although their opportunities to actually find work have been and will continue to be few. Meanwhile, their benefit conditions are often affected by the government policy to enforce work incentives. The right to a 'real', *i.e.* regular and more or less permanent job, in so far as it used to exist, is no longer an objective of the welfare state.

Although the sum of all government measures (in happy co-operation with an expanding economy) may have reduced unemployment levels among employable men, no substantial headway was made in reintegrating other categories of citizens: the (partially) disabled, members of ethnic minorities and unemployed

---

[12] C. Euzéby, 'De Europese sociale-zekerheidsregelingen in de strijd tegen de sociale uitsluiting [European social security provisions in the fight against social exclusion]', in: *Belgisch Tijdschrift voor Sociale Zekerheid* [Belgian Social Security Review], 38 (1996), no. 3, p. 677-698, p. 694; C. Euzéby, 'Social security for the twenty-first century', in: *International Social Security Review*, 51 (1998), no. 2, p. 3-16, esp. p. 15; O. Giarini and P. Liedtke, 'The employment dilemma and the future of work. Working in the new service economy. Summary by J. Arkell', in: *Progress Newsletter*, annex to issue no. 27 (July 1998), esp. p. 10; L. Delsen and S. Reday-Mulvey, *Gradual retirement in the OECD countries. Macro and micro issues and policies*, Dartmouth, Aldershot 1996.

women and single mothers. It goes without saying that mass unemployment seriously compounds the problems and tensions surrounding ethnic minorities in Europe. Although the proportion of women in paid employment has risen over the years, a substantial number of unemployed women and single mothers remain outside the labour market. Lack of training, opportunities and incentives have plunged them into the relative poverty of minimum benefits and, eventually, this has taken away their hope of ever getting out of the mire. Many of the citizens who have been unemployed for a longer period of time, have become victims of the 'poverty trap'. When they find or accept work their benefits and various additional subsidies are withdrawn. As a result, they are not better off, or even worse off, than they were before. What is more, the resulting 'culture of poverty' tends to extend over generations, causing an ever sharper and enduring divide between those who profit from an affluent society and those who do not. An underclass of dependent poor has emerged – an undesirable development both in regard to social equity and to societal stability.

The problem of marginalisation particularly affects two categories of recipients of benefits: those with few chances on the labour market and those with substantial social responsibilities outside the labour market. It is very doubtful whether policies aimed at creating incentives and obligations are productive *vis-à-vis* these categories. There are obviously big differences between the two.

The *first* category consists of people who have had few opportunities on the labour market. They pose the greatest problem. To make them exempt from the usual obligation of having to find work would mean that their chances of finding work on the labour market will diminish even further. Besides, only on the labour market can people in this category expect an improvement of their income position and receive a higher esteem for their activities. When asking to which extent reintegration into work is really a viable proposition in the context of social security, we should keep in mind that for substantial categories of beneficiaries reintegration into work may not be the best course of action. At least, it should be carefully investigated as to how we can define the categories concerned, what can be expected from them, and whether there can be, for instance, employment creation schemes which are more useful to them than those which are presently operating.

The *second* category consists mainly of single parents, predominantly women. An exemption from the obligation to find work might not be very problematic here, and would be beneficiary for the purpose of raising children. One problem might be that a substantial gap in their work careers will be felt in later years, but an investigation into a better combination of work and childcare, and into better childcare facilities, might create alternatives. One obstacle for many people – especially women with children – from re-entering the labour market is an inability to arrange childcare. Facilities for contracting domestic care to be done by paid caretakers would enable many of them to seek new employment. To this end, of course, crèches and day-care facilities at school are needed, but the social security system can also make a substantial contribution by allowing or even urging certain categories of unemployed (especially women with children) to work on socially useful jobs while retaining unemployment benefits. One obvious way to promote the level of care within society is to extend the full social protection of workers' insurance schemes to workers who are on paid or unpaid leave in order to take care of young children or ill or dying relatives. The effect of this extension could even be increased by stipulating that any vacancies as a result of care leave must be filled either by a person drawing a benefit or by a returner. In some countries, measures have already been introduced to fulfil this need; in other countries, no headway has been made so far. Obviously, much depends on a country's culture in regard to the division of tasks between men and women, *e.g.* on a woman's willingness to accept paid work, and on a man's willingness to perform certain domestic chores.

Government policies which have been implemented in order to combat long-term unemployment raise the question of whether these policies are not *too* focused on the labour market. Its feasibility in the face of labour market realities is a case in point. One might wonder whether labour market reintegration policies interfere too much with alternative methods of social participation for those with little or no likelihood of finding work on the labour market and for those who do unpaid, but important volunteer work and care? From a normative perspective, one could even criticise this development as the 'economising of social relations': money becoming the dominant and only medium of exchange in personal relations, even in the former areas of voluntary work and care. The predominance of paid work could mean a degradation of our norms in regard to social relations. It may reflect a one-sided perspective on social participation, which does not correspond to the experiences of millions of (jobless) people, and which marks them as second-rate citizens.

5.3 Atypical employment patterns

Instead of hopelessly aspiring to a restoration of full employment, governments are well advised to adopt policies which take into account the changed structure of the labour market and the altered lifestyle of European citizens.

In Western countries, social security arrangements, health care, education and old age pensions are lagging behind social change. They are largely based on the concept of the employee who has a full-time and long-term attachment to one company and who is the sole breadwinner of his family. In this capacity, he has enjoyed a whole series of statutory guarantees and benefits. For several decades after World War II, this concept was realistic and beneficial. Since the 1970s, however, it no longer tallies with social realities. A much greater diversity in employment patterns has emerged, typically because of a decline in full-time employment in manufacturing and the rise of part-time employment in the services sector. Many forms of atypical employment, however, exclude their holders from the blessing of job security, social security and pension schemes. This results in the marginalisation of many jobs and in the segmentation of the labour market in regular, well-paid steady jobs and irregular, underpaid and volatile jobs. Even if full employment in its old post-war shape was still a viable goal, it would remain to be seen if full-time regular jobs are what people in European countries really want. For many people, especially women re-entering the labour market or persons approaching their pensionable age, part-time employment is a conscious choice. Therefore, increasing the supply of part-time jobs would be a positive development because it would encourage the labour market participation of women and solve many problems which are associated with the employment of older or partially disabled workers.

One urgently needed reform regards the social protection of workers in 'atypical' employment: part-time, temporary, or stand-by jobs. In the European Union atypical employment contracts are often excluded both from employment protection legislation and from social security coverage.[13] As a result, many workers lack adequate protection due to their inability (or unwillingness) to obtain and keep full-time steady employment. A reform is even more imperative as in most national economies there is a trend, both on the side of employees and that of employers, to prefer less binding forms of employment with a view to, respectively, personal freedom and managerial flexibility. Improvement of the social protection surrounding these forms of employment would increase their attractiveness and, therefore, accommodate both employees and employers. A segmentation of the labour market in attractive and less attractive forms of employment could then also be avoided.

6 Policy recommendations: two scenarios

In this paragraph, two scenarios are presented, one representing a short-term cautious strategy for alleviating some of the problems besetting social security and the other, a long-term, visionary strategy aimed at a wholesale restructuring of the labour market and the social security system. Both scenarios have their pros and cons, which will be further discussed at length. Although these two scenarios suggest different means and measures, their eventual goal is the same: a system of employment and social security which does not foster the marginalisation of certain categories of citizens and which offers sufficient security to those who are in paid (regular or temporary, full-time or part-time) employment or who are self-employed.

---

[13] See L. Delsen, 'Changing work relations in the European Union', in: I.U. Zeytinoglu (Ed.), *Changing work relationships in industrialized economies,* Amsterdam 1999.

6.1 Scenario I: short-term and practical

The first scenario is the more cautious of the two. It aims at the short term rather than the long term. Therefore, it suggests three practical measures which can be introduced without resorting to radical reform:

- The introduction of adequate social protection for workers in atypical employment (i.e. part-time jobs, short-term temporary jobs, irregular jobs, stand-by jobs);
- The expansion and improvement of facilities for workers to contract out all sorts of domestic care to professional paid caretakers;
- The introduction of a 'workfare' system, aimed at eliminating the 'poverty trap' embodied in many social security schemes.
- Measures regarding care leave may be made part of more generic statutory regulations concerning sabbatical leave and career breaks, thus reinforcing the trend toward flexibility in employment. In this way employees can be enabled to combine work and care in a way which is beneficial to their own well-being and that of their families.

Ultimately, these measures aim at a more equitable distribution of paid work. Even without a structural revolution in social security many improvements could possibly be achieved which not only enhance the level of social protection, but also the flexibility of the labour market.

The deployment of social security arrangements to create more part-time paid care jobs might well be a way of killing two birds with one stone. To the unemployed it offers a way out of the social security system; to those who are employed or want to enter the labour market, it offers more leeway for delegating several of their domestic duties.

One pitfall is to be avoided. The creation of better conditions for solidarity of *care* – particularly by creating part-time care jobs – may not result in the exclusion of many people from the regular labour market. As far as the unemployed are concerned, the system should result in their (re)introduction into the labour market.[14] In order to achieve real solidarity of *work*, the creation of part-time jobs should be more than a mere addition to the existing and constant volume of full-time employment. Instead, it should be an integral part of an effort made toward the redistribution of work and an internal flexibilisation of the labour market.

---

[14] See P. Buijs, 'Combineren van arbeid en zorgtaken. Mannen weten niet wat ze missen [Combining work and care. Men do not know what they are missing]', in: *Zeggenschap. Tijdschrift voor vakbewegingsvraagstukken* [Representation. Journal for Trade Union Issues], 7 (1996), no. 1, p. 49. Buijs also stresses the emotional advantages for men which will result from a more equitable distribution of work involving care, especially where the care of children is involved.

One way to offer people 'openings' out of the social security system may be 'workfare'. In its biennial reports over 1994 and 1996, the Dutch *Sociaal en Cultureel Planbureau* (Social and Cultural Planning Bureau) discussed three alternative suggestions for a workfare system. Whatever their differences, they all aim at eliminating the poverty trap which awaits people who have remained in the social security system too long. For them, re-entering the labour market becomes increasingly difficult, for psychological and other reasons, *e.g.* lack of training, advanced age and the stigma of having been on relief for such a long time. Any measure, within reason, which might help them to break out of this predicament and to regain the ability to support themselves is worth serious consideration.

The first alternative is to lower benefits after one year of unemployment. In exchange for this deduction, the unemployed can apply for an extra 'activity allowance' on the condition that he or she accepts a part-time paid job or – as an optional addition to the notion of workfare – performs some socially useful activity. This exchange of money for work may be repeated periodically until, *e.g.* after three years, the unemployment benefits are largely replaced by workfare. The workfare system aims at stimulating the unemployed to accept a job (or, in the optional version, to search for an equivalent alternative). In principle, the unemployed can refuse to co-operate but he or she has to do then without the extra activity allowance. Exceptions should be made for categories which cannot in due fairness be asked to accept work, *e.g.* single parents or the partially disabled. To achieve the desired effect, workfare should be linked to a guarantee of paid part-time work on a minimum wage level, either in the private sector or in the public sector.[15] The workfare system can be supplemented by measures intended to stimulate employers to offer paid part-time jobs.[16]

The second alternative is to stimulate the acceptance of paid work while retaining a secure benefit. This can be achieved by gradually extending the exemption for extra earnings, thus increasing the financial incentive to leave the social security system.

The third and most far-reaching alternative is the introduction of a general work obligation for every citizen under 65 years of age. An unemployed or a partially disabled person who fails to find work, will be offered a job at minimum wages.[17]

For several reasons, the cautious and gradual approach of the first scenario may well be the only viable way of tackling the problems of European social security. On principle, because politicians and other policy-makers should not overestimate

---

[15] Sociaal en Cultureel Planbureau (SCP, Social and Cultural Planning Bureau), *Sociaal en Cultureel Rapport 1996* [Social and Cultural Report 1996] (Rijswijk 1996), p. 183.

[16] Sociaal en Cultureel Planbureau (SCP, Social and Cultural Planning Bureau), *Sociaal en Cultureel Rapport 1994* [Social and Cultural Report 1994] (Rijswijk 1994), p. 236.

[17] SCP, *Sociaal en Cultureel Rapport 1996*, p. 220, note 48.

their capacity to implement wholesale and yet, effective reforms in such a vast terrain as the social security system. The more so because any miscalculation could badly affect those who are dependent on the system. In practice, because the current political climate is much more favourable to gradual improvement and modernisation than radical reform is. For most countries included in the European Union, the 1990s were a period of economic prosperity. Although the prospects of regaining the post-war full employment situation are still dim, it seems that, in some countries at least, large-scale non-specific unemployment is giving way to hard-core unemployment among citizens with specific handicaps: lack of training, lack of work experience, advanced age, partial disability, personal problems – exactly the categories which do *not* benefit from an economic boom. In order to tackle this phenomenon specific, well-aimed measures seem to be more adequate than wholesale generic reforms are.

This true in practice as well, because the gradual approach is feasible for all European countries in spite of their differences in social security policies, politics, and financial possibilities. At best, it may promote European convergence on social security; at worst, it will not hinder it. In practice, finally, because the four objectives – adequate social protection for workers in atypical employment, improvement of care facilities, the introduction of a workfare system, and the elimination of the 'poverty trap' – could be achieved step by step, by the successive introduction of measures which entail calculable costs and predictable gains.

The approach set out above fits the future objective of social security in the countries of the European Union. In 1997, the official Dutch *Wetenschappelijke Raad voor het Regeringsbeleid* (Scientific Board for Government Policy) described the future social security system as 'lubricant [...] for a much more differentiated pattern of labour and mobility'. According to the Board, a 'contemporary system must cushion the risk inherent to any change in one's personal situation, not just from one full-time job to another, but also, for example, from a full-time job to a part-time job, from a steady job to a temporary job, from employment to self-employment, from work to further training'.[18] Social security must give people the confidence to accept the risk-taking necessary for a flexible supply of labour.

Social solidarity in regard to income might not seem to be a priority in this scenario, but the existing solidarity can be maintained and for some categories, particularly people in atypical employment, considerable improvements could be made.

---

[18] Wetenschappelijke Raad voor het Regeringsbeleid (WRR, Scientific Board for Government Policy), *Van verdelen naar verdienen. Afwegingen voor de sociale zekerheid in de 21e eeuw* [From distributing to earning. Reflections on social security in the 21st century] (The Hague 1997. Rapporten aan de regering [Reports to the Government], no. 51/1997), p. 60-61.

One of the scenario's strongpoints is the balance the workfare system strikes between rights and obligations. It eliminates the current public discontent over social security arrangements which are 'too soft' on those reluctant to work. Yet, it does much more than merely tightening rules and regulates. It does not impose obligations without offering rewards in the shape of a job guarantee and the prospect of re-entering the labour market.

Facilitating care leave, as advocated above, may be very useful in promoting further flexibilisation of the labour market, but ultimately the trend is not toward extended care leave but toward delegating care work to professional caretakers. In most countries belonging to the European Union, people set great store by paid work as a way of building their personal future. In recent years, European governments have promoted this attitude in many ways, especially in respect to women. As a result, shifting people's priorities back from paid work to unpaid care work seems hardly feasible. On the other hand, many of them might be willing to spend a substantial part of their income on professional caretakers, thus enabling themselves to pursue their careers. To anticipate this growing demand for professional care, part of the existing volume of unpaid care work could be converted into paid care work.[19] A workfare system would be an excellent way to achieve this, especially because it creates new (and socially secure) employment in the private sector without competing with existing employment.

Workfare is primarily a way of promoting solidarity of work (while retaining solidarity of income). It securely links paid work and social security rights and thus bridges the gap between those *outside* and those *inside* the social security system. It fits in with the current work ethic in which paid work is valued as a social obligation, and as a way of realising one's personal development. Because of its 'tough' aspects, the workfare system could, therefore, hope to earn broad public acclaim (unlike measures which appear to 'pamper' too much). The concept of workfare also suits the preoccupation of European governments and politicians with the flexibilisation of their labour markets.[20]

Workfare contributes to the social activation of people who have been in the social security system for some time. Its helps them to get out of their rut and to develop work experience.[21]

As we have seen, the workfare system may optionally incorporate the possibility of performing unpaid socially useful work while retaining one's full benefit. Some of the main advantages of workfare – social activation, breaking isolation, stimu-

---

[19] See the conclusions of the Dutch *Commissie toekomstscenario's herverdeling onbetaalde arbeid* (Committee on Scenarios of the Future Redistribution of Unpaid Work), quoted in SCP, *Sociaal en Cultureel Rapport 1996*, p. 140-141.

[20] SCP, *Sociaal en Cultureel Rapport 1994*, p. 236.

[21] SCP, *Sociaal en Cultureel Rapport 1996*, p. 179.

lating work experience – are then preserved without the necessity of large public investments. This scenario contributes to a more equitable relation between paid and unpaid work, not only because it promotes the amount of community work available, but also because it imports a statutory recognition of the intrinsic worth of unpaid socially useful work.

The main drawback of the cautious first scenario is that it leaves several problems of European social security unsolved. First of all, it does nothing to amend the costly complexity of various national social security systems, a complexity which often bewilders politicians and civil servants, let alone the people who are thrown back on social security benefits.

Secondly, the scenario might very well be successful in circumstances where relatively low unemployment levels are concerned, but it will fail miserably once economic hard times return – as they inevitably will – and high levels of unemployment will put the national social security systems to the test once more. It is doubtful whether the scenario can improve the financial conditions of social security or not. The workfare concept, which is at the core of the scenario, is based on the expectation that the private sector can create many part-time paid jobs in all kinds of care work. Whether this expectation is realistic or not will depend on the marketability of paid care services. If the results are disappointing, the public sector will have to step in, because the State is bound to honour the work guarantee of the workfare system. This will result in a costly expansion of the public sector. In that case, positive (financial) effects will only appear in the long run when (and *if*) a flow of workers from the public to the private sector is accomplished.[22]

Using the workfare concept to promote unpaid care work may be a positive goal in itself, but it will not help to lower the costs of social security as a whole. In some circumstances it may even have adverse effects, *e.g.* because it keeps people comfortably within the system who would otherwise have moved to private sector employment.

On balance, workfare will at least be an additional useful instrument to fight long-term unemployment even if it does not offer a wholesale remedy against mass unemployment, let alone against the many woes of current social security systems.

6.2 Scenario II: long-term and visionary

The scenario is based on the assumption that in the European economies a recovery of the post-war full employment cannot be achieved.

---

[22] *Ibid.*, p. 183.

According to this scenario, all citizens will be awarded a guaranteed basic income in the form of a *tax credit* and also the right to *at least* part-time paid work in order to supplement this tax credit up to the level of *a basic income* (or above).[23] Acceptance of part-time work is obligatory. Several authors believe that, in the long run, such an arrangement may bring about real solidarity, both in regard to income and work.[24] Some suggest that it will also promote economic efficiency. "A new full employment concept, based on the complementarity of equality and efficiency, is needed. We need a concept which fits the desire to improve the labour utilisation rates and which contributes to and does not hamper the flexibility of the labour market. This concept could very well be part-time employment [...] for all people in the workforce. [...] The public sector would act as an employer of last resort. [...] The basis employment right could then be combined with a basic income, made available to all by the state."[25] To this must be added that the basic income must be made dependent upon the individual's acceptance of the part-time employment offered to him or her by the State. Unjustified unwillingness to work will be punished by a withdrawal of the tax credit.

The level of the basic income (tax credit *plus* income from part-time employment) must be pegged with delicacy: high enough to provide a decent living and real social security for those who have to depend upon it, but not so high as to deaden all ambition to earn *more*. Whether the scenario will indeed result in a flexibilisation of the labour market, largely depends on the level of the basic income. If it is pegged too low, no positive effects will be achieved and social problems will increase. On the other hand, if it is pegged too high it will result in a stiffening of the labour market because for many people the incentive to work will prove too weak. Even if the basic income is fixed with discernment, it may still act as a break on labour mobility. Particularly low income earners (for whom the basic income represents a large percentage of their total income) may feel little incentive to search for new jobs which will only improve their income marginally.

This scenario may, potentially, solve many of the problems besetting current national social security systems. To begin with the most serious of these problems:

---

[23] L. Delsen, 'A new concept of full employment', in: *Economic and industrial democracy*, 18 (1997), p. 119-135, esp. 121, 128-132; Euzéby, 'De Europese sociale-zekerheidsregelingen in de strijd tegen de sociale uitsluiting', p. 691-693; Giarini and Liedtke, 'The employment dilemma', p. 1-2, 11-13.

[24] Delsen, 'A new concept of full employment'; Giarini and Liedtke, 'The employment dilemma'; Euzéby, 'De Europese sociale-zekerheidsregelingen in de strijd tegen de sociale uitsluiting'; Euzéby, 'Social security for the twenty-first century'; Centraal Plan Bureau (Central Planning Bureau), *Challenging neighbours. Rethinking German and Dutch economic institutions* (Berlin 1997), p. 175-221; L. Delsen, 'Employment opportunities for the disabled', in: G. Schmid, J. O'Reilly, and K. Schömann (Eds.), *International handbook of labour market policy and evaluation* (Cheltenham 1996), p. 528-529, 533-534.

[25] Delsen, 'A new concept of full employment', p. 128, 130.

on the whole, social security has proven rather effective in preventing people from being reduced to poverty, but it has been less effective in rehabilitating them in terms of work, social participation and regular income. For millions of European citizens social assistance has become a relentless, if well-intentioned trap. In some countries equally well-intentioned disability pensions schemes have become a hidden receptacle for people who, because of age or unemployability, are squeezed out of the labour market. The social marginalisation of so many citizens causes many personal and social problems, from ill-health, depression and alcoholism – to name but a few – to social unrest and crime. Apart from these implications, it also threatens the financial viability and social acceptability of social security schemes. Moreover, it has serious economic consequences. In conjunction with demographic developments, social security systems have contributed to the deteriorating ratio between citizens who enjoy steady jobs and steady incomes and those who do not. From a macro-economic point of view a huge amount of human capital remains unused while the financial burden and the work-pressure of the active part of the population has increased (and will increase even further in the near future).

Secondly, the national contributions show that almost all European social security systems are beset by serious financial difficulties. These difficulties are caused by persistently high levels of unemployment (although these levels vary considerably between various countries), by adverse demographic developments (in most European countries the average age of the population is rising rapidly) and by a growing discrepancy between the number of people who are gainfully employed and the number of people who, for some reason or other, are not.

Thirdly, there are serious organisational problems. European social security has developed piece-meal over the course of many decades. For example, as we have seen in the national contributions, some national systems consist of a tangle of Bismarckian and Beveridgean elements. All systems have been subject to equally haphazard and *ad hoc* adaptations, improvements and cutbacks. As a result their legal structure, organisation and administration have become impossibly complex, inefficient and consequently expensive.

The scenario has many merits. First of all, from an organisational point of view, it has the merit of representing an alternative which goes far beyond the usual tinkering at just details. It offers a framework for co-ordinated and coherent measures for confronting the problems described above. One of its main attractions is that it would make social assistance arrangements largely superfluous. A statutory basic income (composed of tax credit and earnings) would largely replace such arrangements as a financial safety net for all citizens. A whole mass of eligibility requirements (and their inspection and administration) could be done away with. In short, various systems of social security could be partly abolished, partly simplified – thus solving many of the current organisational complexities. However, the scenario will not make all existing social security arrangements redundant. A number of benefits will still be necessary, particularly benefits in regard to old age and temporary or permanent disability.

From a social point of view, the scenario will tackle the problem of social marginalisation by greatly enlarging the supply of part-time and other atypical forms of labour. Apart from the economic benefits, this is good news for young people, for women with young children, for the partially disabled, and for older people who would like to ease their work load in preparation for their retirement. They will be able to work at secure part-time jobs and receive a proper income without having to resort to moonlighting and without fear of losing any social protection against temporary unemployment, illness, or a destitute old age. The benefits of the scenario may be further enhanced by the explicit equalisation of regular paid work with unpaid socially useful activities. Rearing young children, taking care of elderly or ill relatives, or performing voluntary community services could be considered as real jobs which provide an income above the tax credit. In this way a sound basis can be created for solidarity of *care,* for the extension and improvement of primary social care which so far has always depended on moral obligations and unpaid charity. The scenario thus offers a real perspective on realising solidarity in regard to income, work and care – which is more than the current system does. The most important effect is that social exclusion and marginalisation will be largely eliminated in spite of the fact that full employment in the traditional sense cannot be attained. For elderly, partially disabled or unskilled citizens the State will provide work. True: many jobs will be part-time and moderately paid but, in conjunction with the tax credit, they will provide enough income to live on, to participate in normal social life, and to maintain one's personal dignity. In this way, one of the most pressing social problems in European society will be tackled more effectively than by first cutting wages and benefits in the hope that economic growth will redress the initial social consequences.

From an economic point of view, the success or failure of the scenario depends on the quality of the system by which it is put into practice, and on the reaction of the labour market to its introduction.[26] There is no guarantee for success but even from a purely economic point of view, the scenario is not merely *viable.* It has much to offer. First of all, it will increase the flexibility of the labour market by freeing a mass of human potential and by encouraging people to change jobs more freely. Being able to choose one's job more freely will create more work satisfaction and less absenteeism. On the other hand, the greater social security of their employees will provide employers with more leeway in adapting wages and other conditions of employment to changing economic circumstances – which is a positive development for national economies as a whole. Moreover, the abolition of social security contributions to be paid by the employers and the shift from taxes

---

[26] See R. van der Veen *et al., De toekomst van de sociale zekerheid* [The future of social security] (Amsterdam 1996), p. 97-99.

on labour to taxes on value added will make hiring cheaper, thus promoting a growth of available jobs.[27] A positive side-effect will be that most of the existing 'grey' and 'black' labour markets will disappear.

Finally, from the point of view of European integration, the scenario will not in itself prevent social dumping practices between European countries but it will establish a floor under the national security provisions beneath which they will not, and cannot, drop. It may not prevent a general lowering of social security standards, but it will prevent a race to the bottom.

No plan is immune to criticism. This scenario is no exception.

The scenario does not entail a 'basic income scheme' in the traditional sense since one's income results from a tax credit and earned income in roughly equal parts. However, the objections against the cost of a basic income scheme could be raised again. The system might be too expensive. However, the outlay will be largely compensated by the reduction of government subsidies, the abolition of the full social security system, and the increased tax revenues out of labour. Initial simulations by the Dutch *Central Planning Bureau* (CPB) have indicated that the scenario is financially viable. A substantial increase in production and a substantial reduction of the unemployment rate, notably at the lower end of the labour market, are the result. Nevertheless, even if the scenario would not live up to these expectations, it does offer a more solid alternative, because the level of expenditure is less dependent upon the vagaries of the national economies and therefore more predictable. Ultimately, the State guarantees employment for everyone. As long as the private sector creates the bulk of the necessary jobs, this should not pose a problem. Critics fear a considerable expansion of the public sector in times of economic adversity, because the State may well have to create a large number of jobs without the certainty of a compensating increase in public income.[28]

Another objection raised against any plan involving a kind of basic income concerns the adverse effect on one's motivation to work. In this scenario, however, basic income is dependent on the willingness to work. The security provided by a secure basic income is not going to make people lazy, but it will instead encourage them to take new initiatives: to change jobs or to start businesses of their own without the fear of a dramatic loss of income if things do not go as planned. This freedom will provide employees with a greater autonomy and a stronger position *vis-à-vis* their employer.

---

[27] Delsen, 'A new concept of full employment', p. 121, 128-132; Euzéby, 'De Europese sociale-zeker-heidsregelingen in de strijd tegen de sociale uitsluiting', p. 691-693; Giarini en Liedtke, 'The employment dilemma', p. 1-2, 11-13.

[28] Delsen, 'A new concept of full employment', p. 128, 130-132; Euzéby, 'De Europese sociale-zeker-heidsregelingen in de strijd tegen de sociale uitsluiting', p. 692; Giarini en Liedtke, 'The employment dilemma', p. 13 (item 6.6).

6.3 Conclusion

In the European Council's Recommendation of 24 June 1992 social exclusion is described as the main problem facing European social security: "(...) social exclusion processes and risks of poverty have become more prevalent and more diversified over the last 10 years, owing primarily to a combination of developments in the labour market with, in particular, the growth in long-term unemployment, and in family structures with, in particular, an increase in social isolation".[29] Consequentially, the re-integration of those concerned is considered to be the primary aim of European social policy. The recommendation quotes the European Parliament which declared itself in favour of establishing a guaranteed minimum income in all the Member States to help ensure that the poorest citizens are integrated into society. It is precisely on these two points that the second, long-term scenario focuses.

Nevertheless, it can be argued that at first sight the short-term scenario will appear more attractive to governments and policy-makers than the long-term scenario. As long as the economic prospects are promising and radical reform is affordable, they will prefer to be cautious because the problems have become less urgent, and perhaps forget that only a few years ago the social security system groaned under both financial and organisational pressures. Once the economic boom grinds to a standstill, and the need for reform has become more urgent than before, they will still be reluctant because it is doubtful whether they can afford the costs and uncertainties involved in a policy of reform. However, as we have pointed out, the first scenario does have its merits. Most noteworthy is the fact that its effects are more predictable and more calculable.

The two scenarios are not mutually exclusive. Advocates of the long-term scenario might well think that the short-term scenario is a first step towards their own preference. On the other hand, advocates of the short-term scenario might find that their cautious approach has quite acceptable consequences which will lead towards the long-term scenario. In this sense, the two scenarios both link current practicalities with more ambitious aspirations. What unites them, however, is their appeal to reform European security for the benefit of those who are still dependent upon its services, while at the same time taking into account the economic realities of Europe in the twenty-first century.

---

[29] Council recommendation of 24 June 1992 on common criteria concerning sufficient resources and social assistance in social protection systems (92.441/EEC), in: *Official Journal of the European Communities*, L 245, August 26th, 1992, p. 46-48, esp. preamble no. 3.

XIII Solidarity: An indispensable concept in social security[1]

Kees Tinga and Egon Verbraak

1 General remarks on the concept of solidarity

In the previous chapters much has been said about the performance of social security systems. In this contribution, we will present a normative approach to this performance. Social security should be considered a mechanism for society to care for those who are in need. In this sense, social security is not only a matter of structures, interests and calculations but it also is an ethical issue, reflecting both the self-interest of the well-to-do and the ethical obligation of the young, the healthy, the employed, and the well-to-do *vis-à-vis* the old, the sick, the unemployed, and the poor. We will reflect on this ethical dimension by using the concept of solidarity. In this paragraph, we will make some general remarks on solidarity. In paragraph 2, we will focus on the relationship between solidarity and social security. Next, we will focus on a few of the consequences which the development of social security systems in Europe seems to have on solidarity (paragraph 3). After an excursion into the social teaching of the churches (paragraph 4), we will draw some conclusions (paragraph 5).

Etymologically, the term solidarity goes back to the Latin adjective *solidus* (solid, firm) and the Neo-Latin substantive *solidaritas,* which was mainly used in the context of Roman Law. The word derives its juridical meaning of 'mutual liability' from this background, particularly for a collective debt. In the nineteenth century, solidarity gained a more social meaning. It referred to the interdependency of humans, which is the basis of social life, and to a moral obligation, which is to build a just society. In this sense, solidarity became a keyword for the labour movement, for left-wing political parties and for Christian social movements.

The concept of solidarity is often used in a highly normative sense. Its normative power appears especially in connection with social movements against injustice, *e.g.* the labour movement, movements against oppression in Latin-America, the Polish trade union *Solidarnosz.* Morally, solidarity implies sharing the pursuit of social improvement or, more generally, a just society. It also implies the shared

---

[1] The authors wish to thank Dr. Jan Peet for his contributions to this chapter.

belief that this can only be achieved by working as a group. Solidarity often reflects a particular view on how a just society can be realised. The struggle for a just society reveals conflicting interests. Different social groups have different interests and therefore they can take an opposing stand. This may result in a division of society into two opposite groups (or classes): the oppressed versus the oppressors, the exploited versus the exploiters, the underprivileged versus the privileged, the poor versus the rich. In these circumstances, solidarity is a reflection of the political consciousness and identity of the oppressed, but also of the moral consciousness of those who share the ambitions of the oppressed without being oppressed themselves, thus taking a position against their own social group or class.[2]

However, solidarity may also be used with a more neutral meaning. It then refers to the interdependency of people as a basis of social cohesion. Interdependency implies a responsibility of the members of a group to provide mutual support and assistance.[3] Interdependency exists at different levels. At the philosophical level, solidarity is an expression of the equality of mankind, which is embodied in the *Universal Declaration of Human Rights*. Anthropologically, solidarity exists at the level of kinship and ethnicity. It then reflects equality on the basis of a shared membership of a family or a people. Strongly connected to (and sometimes in conflict with) the ethnic level is the national level: the equality on the basis of citizenship. On an occupational level, solidarity refers to equality on the basis of a shared profession or – in a broader sense – of the shared experienced of being a worker. Finally, solidarity is used with reference to the mutual bonding of two people.[4]

On all levels the concept of solidarity refers to a balance of rights and obligations between individuals and between the collective and the individual. This balance is the backbone of social cohesion. It gives the concept of solidarity a normative sting even in its more neutral meaning. This normative sting is sharpest at the philosophical level. The philosophical notion of the fundamental equality of all humans makes it possible to transcend national and ethnic borders into global, world-wide solidarity. It sustains the aspiration to fight all efforts to legitimise

---

[2] *Cf. Brockhaus Enzyklopaedie in vierundzwanzig Bänden*, F.A. Brockhaus, Mannheim 1993, 19th edition, keyword *Solidarität*.

[3] The website of the French *Ministère de l'emploi et de la solidarité* (Ministry of Employment and Solidarity) describes solidarity as one of the fundamental principles of French society and defines it as follows: *"Interdépendance impliquant une responsabilité mutuelle d'assistance et d'entraide réciproques entre les membres d'un groupe, fondée sur le contrat et/ou la communauté d'intérêts* [Interdependency implying mutual responsibility with regard to mutual assistance and aid between the members of a group, founded on a contract and/or on common interests]*"* (*www.social.gouv.fr/htm/modedemploi/lesmots.htm*).

[4] *Cf.* the French *pacte civil de solidarité* [Civil solidarity pact], in: *Loi no. 99-944 du 15 novembre 1999 relative au pacte civil de solidarité.*

inequality. In this context, solidarity represents a shared ambition to realise equal opportunities and equal rights, not only within certain societies, but also on a global level.

Solidarity also exists on a historical level. It connects past, present and future. Philosophers such as Benjamin, Horkheimer and Habermas stress the critical potential of solidarity with the past and, especially, with past generations. This solidarity is based on *memory*. Remembering the experience of past generations and acting on that experience is an expression of this solidarity. Solidarity with the future, and with future generations, is based on *foresight*. Concern for future prosperity is an expression of solidarity for future generations. Concern for the environment, as initiated by the Club of Rome in the 1970s, is also an expression of solidarity for the generations to come. This form of solidarity focuses attention on sustainability, which implies a reconsideration of economic goals and organisation, particularly concerning the polluting effects of industrial activities and the use of raw materials.

2 Solidarity and social security

Solidarity is linked to social security in different ways. First of all, there is a historical link: many social security arrangements were the result of labour movement campaigns. As indicated earlier, solidarity is one of the keywords of this movement. Today, solidarity (together with universality) is considered to be one of the basic principles of the classic welfare state.[5] Furthermore, important sections of social security are organised on the basis of solidarity amongst workers. The German word *Solidargemeinschaft* (community of solidarity) refers to an organisation in which its members share risks (*i.e.* occupational hazards) by mutual contributions.[6] The close link between solidarity and social security is illustrated by the fact that in France social security comes under the *Ministère de l'émploi et de la solidarité*, the Ministry of Employment and Solidarity.

In this chapter we use solidarity in the sense of interdependency. This is in keeping with the two *Recommendations of the Council of the European Communities* to the member states (see Preface), which have provided a point of departure for the project of this book. In these recommendations, solidarity is considered as a fundamental obligation towards the poor. Thus, it implies that every citizen has a

---

[5] *Cf.* R.H. Cox, 'The consequences of welfare reform. How conceptions of social rights are changing', in: *Journal of Social Policy*, 27 (1998), no. 1, p. 1-16, esp. p. 1. Cox states that solidarity can no longer be considered the main principle to evaluate welfare states. The question still remains relevant, however, how developments in social security influence the understanding and the shape of solidarity.
[6] In Belgium and France health insurance is performed by *mutualités* (mutualities).

right to income protection and that every citizen has a duty to contribute to the financing of the system according to his or her private means. Solidarity is also presented as the antithesis of social exclusion.

Council Recommendation no. 92/441/EEC 'on common criteria concerning sufficient resources and social assistance in social protection systems' (of 24 June 1992) states that encouraging solidarity with the least privileged and the most vulnerable, reinforces social cohesion. Moreover, solidarity inspires the fight against social exclusion. Social policy should therefore aim at the economic and social integration of people who have to rely on social assistance. Social assistance should be developed in the context of 'a comprehensive and consistent drive to combat social exclusion'.

Income protection is an important instrument against social exclusion. Council Recommendation no. 92/442/EEC 'on the convergence of social protection objectives and policies' (of 27 July 1992) recommends that all employed persons be provided with a level of social security, sufficient to maintain their standard of living in a reasonable manner at the end of their working lives, or in the event that they have 'to interrupt their careers owing to sickness, accident, maternity, invalidity or unemployment'. Council Recommendation no. 92/441/EEC recommends a general minimum level of social assistance and protection, 'considered sufficient to cover essential needs with regard to respect for human dignity'. This level of assistance and protection should be set on the basis of appropriate statistical indicators. Although the level of assistance and protection should be defined *vis-à-vis* individuals, the needs of different types and sizes of households should be taken into account.

In line with these recommendations, two primary social rights play a role: the right to earn an income and the right to work. Covenants of international law generally support the view that in any society, ideally, every member of that society who is considered fit for work, should be able – and should be enabled – to earn his or her own living by a paid job or by any other work he or she chooses. In addition, these covenants state that every member of society who, owing to circumstances beyond his or her control, lacks the necessary means of existence should receive sufficient financial support from other members of society. These principles are reflected by the following provisions of the *International Covenant on Economic, Social and Cultural Rights* (ICESCR, 1966):[7]

---

[7] The *International Covenant on Economic, Social and Cultural Rights* is quoted from 'Internationaal Verdrag inzake Economische, Sociale en Culturele Rechten [International Covenant on Economic, Social and Cultural Rights]', published in: E.A. Alkema and H.E. Timmerman (Eds.), *Europees Sociaal Handvest. Turijn 18 oktober 1961. Internationaal Verdrag inzake Economische, Sociale en Culturele Rechten. New York 16 december 1966. Internationale Arbeidsconventies. Diverse internationale verdragen en verklaringen* [European Social Charter. Turin, October 18th, 1961. International Covenant on Economic, Social and Cultural Rights. New York, December 16th, 1966. International

'The States Parties to the present Covenant recognise the right to work, which includes the right of everyone to the opportunity to gain his living by work which he freely chooses or accepts [...].' (Article 6, paragraph 1)

'The States Parties to the present Covenant recognise the right of everyone to social security, including social insurance.' (Article 9)

'The States Parties to the present Covenant recognise the right of everyone to an adequate standard of living for himself and his family, including adequate food, clothing and housing, and to the continuous improvement of living conditions. [...]' (Article 11, paragraph 1).

These principles imply that any system of social security, which is set up in a spirit of solidarity, ought to do more than merely provide an adequate financial support to any citizen in need. It should also, within reason, contribute to the implementation of the right to work of every member of society.[8]

3 Solidarity and social security in Europe

We will now discuss to what extent changes in European social security systems have affected solidarity. We will pay attention to these changes with regard to the level of solidarity which is realised by social security. Next, we will reflect on the way in which the right to income and the right to work is implemented.

3.1 The level of solidarity

In the field of social security solidarity is an issue at two different levels: the national and the occupational level. This reflects the historical development of social security. Some systems were originally set up at the occupational level, and have been organised on the basis of the solidarity amongst workers in certain professions. Others were set up to provide social protection on the basis of citizenship. In general, these two types of solidarity have merged in the course of the development of social security. As a result, most individuals are protected by provisions on which they can lay a claim as citizens and by arrangements on an occupational basis. In recent years, however, the trend seems to be towards provisions based on citizenship.[9] The national contributions in this book reveal that in some European

Labour Conventions. Various international covenants and declarations], vol. II (Zwolle 1984), p. 415-497.

[8] The right to work has two faces. The right to work of a beneficiary of social security may come into conflict with the right of a working person to work. *Cf.* D. Mieth, 'Solidarity and the right to work', in: *Concilium. Theology in the age of renewal,* (1982), p. 58-65.

[9] *Cf.* Euzéby, 'Social security for the twenty-first century', p. 12. See also the contribution on France, where it is stated that "[since] the right to work cannot be guaranteed for all, the right to an income and

countries a third type of basic interdependency has emerged: the interdependency of those who have taken out private insurance against social risks.

From the point of view of social security, people are therefore increasingly addressed at several levels simultaneously. These levels converge in the individual's responsibility for his or her own future and that of his or her dependants (children, partner, family). To appreciate the impact of this development on the perception of solidarity, a distinction must be made between a 'horizontal' and a 'vertical' organisation of solidarity. In a horizontal organisation, members bear social risks by mutual support. This is the case with any occupational insurance type of social security. A vertical organisation, on the other hand, does not focus on the mutual responsibility of its members, but on the responsibility of the organisation (*e.g.* the State) to observe the rights of its members (*e.g.* the citizens). From the point of view of solidarity, the difference between the two is not in the groups concerned, but in the level of commitment: in the horizontal type members are more involved and particularly more committed than in the vertical type.

In recent years, there has been a tendency to change the balance between rights and obligations within the social security of the vertical type. Citizens are, to a larger extent than before, confronted with obligations when they claim their rights.[10] These obligations aim at activating and (re)integrating claimants into the labour market, and thus they tend to stress individual responsibility. This could have major consequences on the solidarity within the system of social security because the summons to take responsibility for one's own life will not find a response with those individuals who are, for some reason or other, unable to take that responsibility. Their position will become even more vulnerable, even though they are the precise group at which solidarity should be aimed. Eventually, this could mean that in the field of social security the principle of solidarity by all citizens has to give way to the principle of self-interest by each citizen.[11]

3.2 The right to income

Individuals who depend on benefits for their livelihood, are increasingly referred to benefits at the level of the social minimum.[12] Each member country of the European Union, with the exception of Greece, has some sort of minimum benefit. Greece does not as yet have a general mechanism to guarantee a social minimum income, but it does have various provisions in its system which provide roughly the same. In some countries short-term benefits are granted at a level which de-

---

to fundamental goods (health, housing) will have to be based upon citizenship, rather than on participation in the labour market."

[10] Cox, 'The consequences of welfare reform', p. 13.

[11] Cox (*ibidem*, p. 14) claims that social rights have become discursive.

[12] Cox (*ibidem*, p. 6) observes a shift from the social optimum towards the social minimum.

pends on previously earned income, working history and/or paid contributions. This is often the case with unemployment or disability benefits. In the long term, however, the right to these type of benefits expires.[13] Social protection is then taken over by benefits at a minimum level. Since most short-term unemployment and disability benefits are based on the social insurance principle; the individual's claim to a benefit largely depends on the amount he or she has contributed to the insurance fund. People who have not contributed much or who do not meet certain eligibility requirements are instantly referred to a social minimum benefit. The same goes for people who previously earned a low income, since earnings-related benefits grant a percentage of the previously earned income.

With regard to the level of the social minimum, Council Recommendation no. 92/441/EEC advises that it should be determined on the basis of appropriate statistical indicators and that it should be sufficient to cover essential needs with regard to respect for human dignity. From the contributions from the European correspondents it is not always clear how the level of the social minimum is set, nor to what extent it is 'appropriate', *e.g.* given a country's price level.

In most countries, the social minimum is not fixed according to any objective indicators but to political and budgetary considerations. Even in countries which do use objective indicators, these objective indicators are sometimes set aside if the circumstances dictate accordingly. In Belgium, no official poverty line exists. In Italy the level of benefits is set 'with no specific reference to any poverty line indicator whatsoever' while in Greece the indicators which are used, are arbitrary. The French and German correspondents explicitly point at the trade-off that must be made in setting the level of social minimum benefits. On the one hand, the minimum benefit must cover the needs of beneficiaries and guarantee humane conditions. Living on a minimum benefit for a longer time erodes a person's standard of living, even in countries where the social minimum is set comparatively high. On the other hand, beneficiaries should be encouraged to participate in the labour market: the level of social minimum must not be so high as to be a disincentive for finding a paid job. The dilemma posed by the twofold goal of the minimum benefit, meeting 'subsistence needs of individuals and households' (UK) and activating beneficiaries to (re)enter the labour market, is reflected in all contributions. The difference between the social minimum and the minimum wage should be large enough to make work profitable. From the point of view of solidarity, however, the gap should not be too wide, because this could create an inappropriate division between those who have work and those who do not.

In this context it should be reminded that a just level of social minimum is particularly a matter of solidarity towards people who have little or no opportunity to improve their financial position by finding a paid job: the disabled and the aged.

---

[13] Belgium is a rare exception: in this country the right to unemployment benefit is not restricted in time.

In regard to disability benefits, European countries have a wide variety of provisions, which seem to have no tendencies in common. Some countries have different benefits for disability caused by illness as opposed to disability caused by work accidents. In most countries, the level of the benefits varies according to the remaining earning-capacity of the potential beneficiary.

The developments in the field of old age pensions show an overall trend towards three-layered systems: a guaranteed social minimum pension provided by the State (first layer), which is then supplemented by benefits from social insurance (second layer) and from private savings (third layer). The individual is responsible for the second and third layer, by working and thus contributing to insurance funds, and by saving for his or her old age. This three-layered model (sometimes called the *cappuccino* model) has proven to be an effective instrument from the point of view of intergenerational solidarity. By adjusting the levels of the different layers the model can respond to demographic changes (ageing) and still provide acceptable old age pensions.[14] In the French contribution, the question emerges as to whether the level of old age pension should be left to the responsibility and, more particularly, the opportunity of people to save income. The principle of solidarity seems to require that even the minimum pension is set at a fair level which enables people to live according to human dignity even if they have not been in a position to build up supplementary provisions. In its discussions, the Committee of the Catholic Study Centre assumed that a level of at least 10% above the current poverty line – a level which would allow a level of spending of at least 50% of the median spending level for households – would be an appropriate bottom-line. But even when a just level has been established, there may still be a widening gap between those who were able to provide for a supplemental income for their old age and those who were not.

3.3 The right to work

For most individuals in receipt of some kind of benefit the right to work comes down to the aspect of reintegration into the labour market. The *Renta Mínima de Inserción* (Spain), the *Revenu Minimum d'Insertion* (France), *Minimex* (Belgium), the *Income Support and Jobseeker's Allowance* (United Kingdom) and the *Bijstand* (the Netherlands) are types of social minimum provisions in which eligibility is linked to the obligation to search for a paid job or, at least, to be available for jobs offered. In other systems, there is no strict obligation linked to the grant of a minimum benefit, but job hunting is nevertheless encouraged by applying incentives on the 'carrot-and-stick' principle. The general trend is summarised by the Danish correspondent: "The trend [...] seems to be [...] towards a system in which

---

[14] *Cf.* L. Delsen, *Exit poldermodel? Sociaal-economische ontwikkelingen in Nederland.* [Exit the Dutch consensus model? Socio-economic developments in the Netherlands], Assen 2000.

the continuation of various short-term benefits is made conditional on accepting offers to work, training or further education".

Is this present-day focus on reintegration – as the first remedy against hard-core unemployment – a positive contribution towards the realisation of the right to work, in spite of the fact that reintegration efforts invariably include a moment of obligation or conditionality? It is clear that job-seeking is the most obvious instrument for helping people to leave the social security system. The answer to the question is therefore affirmative. However, some considerations must be added.

Firstly, the question presents itself whether reintegration means that people leave the social security system permanently and totally. Successful reintegration presupposes the availability or creation of a sufficient number of jobs.[15] However, in many European countries the increase in jobs which was realised in the last decade of the twentieth century consisted to a large extent of part-time jobs.[16] Between 1994 and 1997, 50% of the new jobs in the European Union were of a temporary and flexible nature. Many people who work in these jobs still have to rely on supplementary or temporary benefits because their jobs do not pay enough to live on. Moreover, in many cases finding a paid job does not mean an improvement in real income because there are extra costs (*e.g.* commuting or childcare) while certain subsidies (*e.g.* housing benefits) are withheld. Research in the Netherlands has shown that it takes at least four years of steady employment to escape from this so-called poverty trap![17] Finally, it should be mentioned that people who work in temporary and part-time jobs are not always able to build up supplementary old age provisions. As a result, they will have to manage on a social minimum pension in their old age.

Secondly, as has been stated in one of the previous chapters, *too much* focus on reintegration could have a negative effect on solidarity. Efforts to activate beneficiaries into active job-seeking may be valuable, especially if they coincide with active labour market policies to create suitable jobs and to raise the opportunities of job-seekers. But they could also, eventually, lead to a conception of social life in which social participation has been reduced to paid work and in which social relations are largely economised. In such a cultural environment, people who have remained jobless will be marked as second-rate citizens. This will particularly affect those who have, for reasons beyond their control, little opportunity on the

---

[15] O. Giarini and P. Liedtke, 'The employment dilemma and the future of work. Working in the new service economy. Summary by J. Arkell', in: *Progress Newsletter*, annex to issue no. 27 (July 1998), p. 1-13, esp. p. 6.

[16] P. van Schilfgaarde, *Werk voor iedereen* [Work for everyone], Assen 1994. The feasibility of full-time full employment for everyone is discussed in a previous chapter.

[17] Sociaal en Cultureel Planbureau (Social and Cultural Planning Office) and Centraal Bureau voor de Statistiek (Central Office for Statistics), *Armoedemonitor 1999* [Poverty Monitor 1999], The Hague 1999. Cahier 163.

labour market and for those who have social responsibilities outside the labour market, such as the care of children or other dependants.

Thirdly, it should be noted that work represents more than merely a way of earning an income. It has also consequences for the environment. Various groups (*e.g.* the Club of Rome, some churches, the ecology movement) insist on a discussion on sustainability as a principle in the organisation of labour and production. In the field of social security this aspect seldom attracts attention. Where the necessity and desirability of growing employment is concerned, there seem to be no alternatives and no freedom of choice. Nevertheless, the principle of solidarity should urge for a revaluation of the status of paid labour within society. The results should be applied to the system of social security.[18] The question whether reintegration does indeed contribute to the right to work can be answered affirmatively, but only if this background is taken into consideration. Offering beneficiaries the opportunity to (re)integrate into the labour market is just one option. A system of social security should contribute to or at least not interfere with a future reorganisation and redistribution of paid labour.

Council Recommendation no. 92/442/EEC points to alternatives. The Recommendation suggests that the drive for greater equality of opportunities includes not only opportunities for paid work but also opportunities for unpaid socially valuable activities – as an alternative for, or in combination with paid work. The Recommendation states that, for purposes of calculating pension rights, the penalty for workers who give up work temporarily to bring up children or other dependants, should be abandoned or reduced, in particular by opening up the possibility of voluntary contributions. It also recommends that social security systems contribute to the integration of those who, having brought up children, wish to re-enter the labour market, and that these systems facilitate parental occupational activity by enabling them to reconcile both family and professional responsibilities. However, judging by the present trend in European social security systems, alternative visions on paid and unpaid work are as yet hardly a major topic.

4 Excursion: a note on the social teaching of the churches

With regard to the fundamental right to work and to a sufficient income, the social teaching of the churches and their declarations on social affairs merit special attention because they put these rights in a broader context, thus providing a frame-

---

[18] *Cf.* Giarini and Liedtke, 'The employment dilemma', p. 9-13. See also the *long-term scenario* as described in the previous chapter.

work for a revaluation of paid work. Moreover, in their declaration they attempt to voice the experience of the unemployed and the poor.

The social teaching of the Roman Catholic Church, as elaborated in encyclicals such as *Rerum Novarum* (1891), *Quadrigesimo Anno* (1931) and *Centesimus Annus* (1991), has always supported the right of every member of society to work, the right of every worker to fair wages that enable him to support himself and his family (if he has one), and, inherent to the right to fair wages, the right to social insurance.[19] In January 1997, the joint Christian churches of the member states of the European Union reported the result of a consultation in which they supported the right to a sufficient standard of living, and the right to a sufficient level of social security. The churches also, implicitly, supported the right to work.[20]

In general, Christian churches proclaim, as a point of departure for their social teaching, the fundamental and inalienable dignity of every human person.[21] Starting from the tenet of human dignity, the churches have developed two other basic principles of social ethics. Firstly, the churches confess to a special involvement with those whose human dignity may be said to have been violated the most, that is: with the poor and the least privileged in society. Secondly, the churches have developed the theme of the anthropological value of work as a means by which man can develop and fulfil himself as an individual and as a social being.

The Christian churches' notion on the value of work (and of paid work in particular) is relevant to the discussion on the 'right to work'. According to their declaration of January 1997, the churches support the fundamental right to work and consider unemployment a social evil. Social conditions which exclude people from work are incompatible with the principle of human dignity. Therefore, the churches plead for a more equal distribution of paid work. The churches link this argument, however, to a broader argument for a redistribution of, on the one hand,

---

[19] *Cf.* Jean Paul II, *'Lettre Encyclique Centesimus Annus 'à l'occasion du centenaire de l'encyclique Rerum Novarum'* [Encyclical letter Centesimus Annus 'on the occasion of the centennial of the encyclical Rerum Novarum']', in: *De 'Rerum Novarum' à 'Centesimus Annus'. Textes intégraux des deux encycliques avec deux études de Roger Aubert et Michel Schooyans* [From 'Rerum Novarum' to 'Centesimus Annus'. The complete and unabridged texts of two encyclicals with two essays by Roger Aubert and Michel Schooyans] (Vatican City 1991), p. 115-189 (paragraphs 8, 34, 48).
[20] *Consultations among the churches and their organizations in the European Union on issues of poverty and social exclusion. Third draft* (Version 09.01.97). *Final Report*, p. 4-5, 8-9.
[21] *Cf.* J. Verstraeten, *De sociale leer van de Katholieke Kerk en de 'Derde Weg'* [The social teachings of the Catholic Church and the 'Third Way']', in: L. Bouckaert and G. Bouckaert (Ed.), *Metafysiek en engagement. Een personalistische visie op gemeenschap en economie* [Metaphysics and commitment. A personalistic view on community and economy], Leuven, Amersfoort 1992, 51-63, 60-61. See also: *Europese commissies Justitia et Pax, verklaring over armoede in Europa. Europese conferentie Justitia et Pax, Kerkrade, 12 oktober 1996.* [The European Committees of 'Justitia et Pax': Declaration on poverty in Europe. European Conference 'Justitia et Pax', Kerkrade, October 12th, 1996]', in: *121 Kerkelijke Documentatie* [121 Ecclesiastical Documentation], 25 (1997), p.115-117.

paid work and, on the other hand, time to be spent in other pursuits, such as education, training, cultural activities and leisure. In this context, the churches specifically require that special attention be given to family life, to the education of children, and to a general renewal of the 'style of life' in present-day European society. Moreover, from an economic point of view, a redistribution of paid work *and* other pursuits of social and cultural importance could, according to the churches, generate new paid jobs. However, the main thrust of their argument appears to be that work, and the redistribution of work, is not a matter of economics alone, but also (and perhaps even primarily) a matter of a more general cultural and social relevance.

The churches intend to place paid work within a broader perspective.[22] Their main objective is not a redistribution of (paid) work as such, but the development of a new way of life, in which a paid job may be of major importance to human self-fulfilment but not of sole importance and ultimately, perhaps, not of foremost importance. From a point of view of social cohesion, human dignity and solidarity, the importance of voluntary social and cultural work is stressed – for the benefit of a humane social environment.

This trend in Christian social thought seems to imply that a sound system of social security should not only provide sufficient financial support and opportunities for reintegration into the labour market. Social security, from a present-day Christian perspective, should also be an instrument of socio-cultural improvement and economic reform. In these decades of economic and social development, all over Europe more or less substantial reductions in welfare state provisions coincide with mass unemployment and the availability of a vast human potential for voluntary work. In these circumstances, the advancement of voluntary social and cultural work by means of social security regulations and provisions has been proposed as a reasonable course of action. Furthermore, social security provisions and regulations could facilitate (or at least not interfere with) the fulfilment of basic tasks in human life, such as the creation of a healthy primary social environment, the education of children and the care of the sick, the disabled and the elderly.

Generally, a strong trend in present-day Christian social thought implies that social security could well be an instrument for bringing about a redistribution of work. It could also contribute to a shift in our attitude towards work: from a predominant perspective of economic growth to a perspective of social and cultural improvement, and of ecologically sustainable development.

---

[22] The joint European churches point to the danger of an economic and social polarisation in European societies, and demand a more equitable distribution of wealth in Europe. *Centesimus Annus* indicates a cultural polarisation in modern societies, which prevents substantial parts of the population from keeping up with the rapid development of knowledge and information, and – therefore – from operating successfully in the modern labour markets.

5 Conclusions

Present-day changes and developments in the field of European social security can be considered a threat to solidarity and, at the same time, they can be seen as a challenge for building a new and adjusted sense of solidarity which may lead to new formulas and forms.

5.1 Threats

Most of the contributions in this book show a trend in which the costs of social security are to be cut back. This trend has started in the 1980s and was caused by the fact that economic recession, demographic trends (ageing of the population) and cultural shifts (individualisation) led to rising social expenditure. Part of the financial problem was caused by the principle of solidarity itself. To avoid the faults of pre-war paternalistic charity, modern state-organised social security took on anonymous forms. Eventually, this strength turned into a weakness: under the pressure of economic crisis, social security became an easy and overcharged refuge for many – even for those who were not exactly entitled to its provisions. Cutbacks have been achieved by decreasing (or not increasing) the level of benefits, by tightening eligibility criteria and by promoting the reintegration of claimants into the labour market. Cutting back costs does not automatically imply an erosion of solidarity. Austerity may be instrumental in saving the system amidst economic setbacks and adverse demographic trends. Thus, solidarity between the employed and the unemployed and between generations may be maintained as well. However, the contributions in this book show that the burden of this operation is not equally distributed. Certain categories of citizens run a greater risk of falling into poverty than others, in particular the elderly, the long-term unemployed, and single parents with children. The resulting inequality detracts from the level of solidarity.

In recent years, Europe has displayed a trend towards social polarisation, both in its economy as a whole and within its social security systems. Polarisation takes place between people with regular jobs and people without jobs (insiders *vs.* outsiders), between people with opportunities to make a career for themselves and people who lack any perspective, between those who benefit from the booming economy and those who do not. Polarisation is also on the rise between the young and the old: countries such as Germany and the Netherlands are experiencing an erosion of the solidarity between the younger and the older generation in regard to the financing of old-age pensions. But there is also polarisation among the elderly, as well. While State-financed old-age pensions are being reduced, supplementary private old-age savings are being encouraged. As a result, two (or more) categories of old people have been created: those who have been able to build up an adequate pension, and those who have not had this opportunity. In the past, in times of economic growth, a 'right to continuous improvement of living conditions' was often assumed for all European citizens. That right has long since lost all its practical meaning for a considerable part of the European population.

As a result of these developments, solidarity is being put under pressure, both in its vertical and its horizontal dimension. Solidarity presupposes a balance between mutuality and private capitalisation, between freedom of choice and coercive solidarity, and between the responsibilities of all parties involved in social security. Restoring that balance is of vital importance, not only in regard to the financing of the system, but also in regard to its political legitimacy. The notion of solidarity can only be reinforced if as many people as possible are committed to the implementation of social security both as contributors and as potential beneficiaries.

5.2 Opportunities and challenges

Recent developments in social security should not be considered solely as a threat to solidarity. They also present new opportunities and challenges. New opportunities to realise solidarity are provided by new types of employment, characterised by the keyword flexibility, changes in the rhythms and patterns of education, labour and careers. 'Diversity' seems to be one of the keywords in the coming years.[23] Combined arrangements of part-time labour and social security as suggested in the long term scenario of the previous chapter may be a promising elaboration. In the next few decades, the major challenge of social security, besides the fight against poverty, may well be to facilitate the care of dependants, to promote sustainable developments and to support new ways of structuring one's life in regard to the time spent on work, care, and leisure. In Denmark, Belgium and the Netherlands first attempts to legislate these challenges have already been made.

After so many accounts of bureaucratic chaos, improvements in administration appear to offer another way of updating and strengthening solidarity. Although the State can hardly be expected to give up its final responsibility – and as a representative of all citizens it must not give up that responsibility – a fairer distribution of responsibilities among all parties involved in social security is in order. Lazar and Stoyko rightly predict that 'the term welfare 'State' may become a misnomer as social provision becomes the responsibility of a broader network of organisations.'[24] Such a development will test the true social responsibility of governments, employers and employees. Employees have to be willing to develop and to keep developing their 'employability' in order to provide the quality which is required of employees in modern economies. Employers should be stimulated to create opportunities which provide a-typical types of labour (temporary, part-time,

---

[23] H. Lazar and P. Stoyko, 'The future of the welfare State', in: *International Social Security Review*, 51 (1998), no. 3, p. 3-36, esp. p. 31.

[24] *Ibidem*, p. 33.

flexible), which create facilities for training and education, and which offer work for retarded or disabled people. These are fair challenges indeed for today's market economy, which is more famous for its financial incentives than for its social responsibility and solidarity!

5.3 A new social contract?

Solidarity is often seen as a 'Sunday's notion': good for moral motivation but unclear and weak in practical applications. Historically, however, it has been a concept good enough to play a major role in the development of present-day welfare arrangements. The Great Depression of the 1930s, with its day-to-day experience of unemployment and poverty, provided the inspiration of the post-war 'solidaristic' period in the same way as awareness of poverty and starvation in the so-called Third World awakened feelings of solidarity and led to numerous aid and development programmes. Although in the past two decades, the notion of solidarity has lost much of its 'romantic' appeal, it continues to inspire people. It has motivated various new forms of social action and engagement. In spite of their pragmatic culture, Western societies still possess a great mass of social capital. Solidarity, the willingness to mutual or one-sided support in resisting forms of injustice, will remain one of the primary means of making this capital work. As long as there are injustices in the field of labour and social security, we can be confident that solidarity will time and time again surface as a moral attitude and as a legal principle.

In the near future, one radical question will crop up again and again. In most countries solidarity, in whatever organisational form, is still linked to the traditional labour order. Although the welfare state has met with many problems, most countries have succeeded in finding a new balance in their social policies without resorting to radical reform. The economic growth of the last decade of the twentieth century has helped them substantially to do this. Still, it remains to be seen whether the future of social security and solidarity can be built on regular paid employment. With many poorer countries and regions having joined the common market, a continuation of the traditional link between employment and social security does not seem advisable, neither on a European level nor on a global one. The traditional link also deserves reconsideration in the light of environmental concerns.

Ideally, social security in the European Union should incorporate a just distribution of various types of paid employment and social participation. It should be strong enough to provide protection and cost-effective enough to offer a sustainable perspective for future generations. In a globalising economy, existing social security systems will, sooner or later, be forced to change radically and fundamentally. This should inspire designs for a new balance, between labour and leisure, work and care, economic growth and ecological conservation, between rights and obligations, between rich and poor on many levels, both globally and locally. A new social contract is called for, but not without solidarity.

Appendices

Appendix A

Council recommendation of 24 June 1992 on common criteria concerning sufficient resources and social assistance in social protection systems (92.441/EEC)[1]

THE COUNCIL OF THE EUROPEAN COMMUNITIES,

Having regard to the Treaty establishing the European Economic Community, and in particular article 235 thereof,

Having regard to the proposal from the Commission,[2]

Having regard to the opinion of the European Parliament,[3]

Having regard to the opinion of the Economic and Social Committee,[4]

(1) Whereas reinforcing social cohesion within the Community requires the encouragement of solidarity with regard to the least privileged and most vulnerable people;

(2) Whereas respect for human dignity is one of the fundamental rights underlying Community law, as recognised in the preamble to the Single European Act;

(3) Whereas social exclusion processes and risks of poverty have become more prevalent and more diversified over the last 10 years, owing primarily to a combination of developments in the labour market with, in particular, growth in long-term unemployment, and in family structures with, in particular, an increase in social isolation;

(4) Whereas there is a need for general development policies capable of contributing towards halting the perceived structural trends to be accompanied by specific, systemic and coherent integration policies;

(5) Whereas, consequently, social policy efforts need to be continued, there achievements reinforced and these policies adapted to the multi-dimen-

---

[1] In: *Official Journal of the European Communities*, L 245, August 26th, 1992, p. 46-48.
[2] *Official Journal of the European Communities*, C163, June 22nd, 1991, p. 3.
[3] *Official Journal of the European Communities*, C150, June 15th, 1992.
[4] *Official Journal of the European Communities*, C14, January 20th, 1992, p. 1.

sional nature of social exclusion, which involves linking the various forms of immediate assistance needed to measures aiming expressly at the economic and social integration of the people concerned;

(6) Whereas people with insufficient, irregular and uncertain resources are unable to play an adequate part in the economic and social life of the society in which they live and to become successfully integrated economically and socially; whereas the right of the least privileged to sufficient, stable and reliable resources should therefore be recognised as part of a consistent, overall policy for supporting there integration;

(7) Whereas on 29 September 1989 the Council and the Ministers for Social Affairs meeting within the Council adopted a resolution on combating social exclusion[5] which stressed that combating social exclusion may be regarded as an important part of the social dimension of the internal market;

(8) Whereas the Community Charter of the Fundamental Social Rights of Workers, adopted at the European Council in Strasbourg on 9 December 1989 by the Heads of State or Government of 11 Member States, states, *inter alia*, in its eighth recital and in points 10 and 25:

'Whereas, [...] in a spirit of solidarity, it is important to combat social exclusion';

'According to the arrangements applying in each country:

10. Every worker of the European Community shall have a right to adequate social protection and shall, whatever his status and whatever the size of the undertaking in which he is employed, enjoy an adequate level of social security benefits.

Person(s) who have been unable either to enter or re-enter the labour market and have no means of subsistence must be able to receive sufficient resources and social assistance in keeping with their particular situation.'

'25. Any person who has reached retirement age but who is not entitled to a pension or who does not have other means of subsistence, must be entitled to sufficient resources and to medical and social assistance specifically suited to his needs.';

(9) Whereas the Commission has included this fundamental aspect of the fight against social exclusion in its action programme relating to the implementation of the Community Charter of the Fundamental Social Rights of Workers, while noting in particular the value of a Community

---

[5] *Official Journal of the European Communities*, C277, October 31st, 1989, p. 1.

initiative, in a spirit of solidarity, to assist the least privileged citizens of the Community, including the elderly, whose situation all too often resembles that of persons excluded form the labour market;

(10) Whereas the implementation of a guarantee of resources and social assistance comes within the sphere of social protection; whereas it is for Member States to define, in this connection, the legal nature of the provisions intended to ensure this guarantee, which in Most Member states do not come within the sphere of social security;

(11) Whereas it is important to take account during the progressive implementation of this recommendation of the availability of financial resources, of national priorities and of balances within national social protection systems; whereas there are disparities in development between Member States as regards social protection;

(12) Whereas, in its resolution on combating poverty in the European Community,[6] the European Parliament declared itself in favour of establishing in all the Member States a guaranteed minimum income to help ensure that the poorest citizens are integrated into society;

(13) Whereas, in its opinion on poverty of 12 July 1989,[7] the Economic and Social Committee also recommended the introduction of a minimum social income, both to act as a safety net for the poor and to boost their reintegration into society;

(14) Whereas this recommendation does not affect national and Community provisions on right of residence;

(15) Whereas the Treaty does not, in respect of the attainment of these objectives, provide for any means of action other than those laid down in article 235,

I   HEREBY RECOMMENDS MEMBER STATES:

A   to recognise the basic right of a person to sufficient resources and social assistance to live in a manner compatible with human dignity as part of a comprehensive and consistent drive to combat social exclusion, and to adapt their social protection systems, as necessary, according to the principles and guidelines set out below;

B   to recognise this right according to the following general principles:

1. it is to be a right based on respect for human dignity;

---

[6] *Official Journal of the European Communities*, C262, October 10th, 1989, p. 194.
[7] *Official Journal of the European Communities*, C221, August 28th, 1989, p. 10.

2. the scope of that right is to be defined *vis-à-vis* individuals, having regard to legal residence and nationality, in accordance with the relevant provisions on residence, with the aim of progressively covering all exclusion situations in that connection as broadly as possible, in accordance with detailed arrangements laid down by the Member States;

3. every person who does not have access individually or within the household in which he or she lives to sufficient resources is to have access to such right:

– subject to active availability for work or for vocational training with a view to obtaining work in the case of those persons whose, age, health and family situation permit such active availability, or, where appropriate, subject to economic and social integration measures in the case of other persons, and

– without prejudice to the Member States' option of not extending this right to persons in full-time employment or to students;

4. access is not to be subject to time limits, assuming compliance with the eligibility conditions and on the understanding that, in practice, the right may be granted for limited but renewable periods;

5. the right is auxiliary in relation to other social rights. An effort should be made in parallel to reintegrate the poorest people into the systems of general rights;

6. it is to be accompanied by those policies deemed necessary, at a national level, for the economic and social integration of those concerned, as laid down in the resolution of the Council and of the Ministers for Social Affairs, meeting within the Council, of 29 September 1989 on combating social exclusion;

C to organise the implementation of this right according to the following practical guidelines:

1. (a) fixing the amount of resources considered sufficient to cover essential needs with regard to respect for human dignity, taking account of living standards and price levels in the Member State concerned, for different types and sizes of household;

(b) adjusting or supplementing amounts to meet specific needs;

(c) in order to fix the amounts, referring to appropriate indicators, such as, for example, statistical data on the average disposable income in the Member State, statistical data on household consumption, the legal minimum wage if this exists or the level of prices;

(d) safeguarding an incentive to seek employment for persons whose age and condition render them fit for work;

(e) establishing arrangements for periodic review of these amounts, based on these indicators, in order that needs continue to be covered;

2. granting, to people whose resources taken at the level of the individual or the household are lower than the amounts thus fixed, adjusted or supplemented, differential financial aid to bring them up to these amounts;

3. taking the necessary measures to ensure that, with regard to the extent of the financial support thus granted, the implementation of the regulations in force in the areas of taxation, civil obligations and social security takes account of the desirable level of sufficient resources and social assistance to live in a manner compatible with human dignity;

4. taking every measure to enable those concerned to receive appropriate social support, comprising measures and services such as, in particular, advice and counselling, information and assistance in obtaining their rights;

5. adopting arrangements in respect of persons whose age and condition render them fit for work, which will assure they receive effective help to enter or re-enter working life, including training where appropriate;

6. taking the necessary measures to ensure that the least privileged are informed of this right;

7. simplifying as far as possible the administrative procedures and arrangements for examining means and situations involved in claiming this right;

8. organising, in so far as possible and in accordance with national provisions, the machinery for appeals to independent third parties, such as tribunals, to which the persons concerned should have easy access;

D   to guarantee these resources and benefits within the framework of social protection arrangements;

to determine detailed arrangements, finance costs and organise their administration and implementation in accordance with national legislation and/or practice;

E   to implement the measures laid down in this recommendation progressively as from now in such a way that a report can be drawn up after five years,

– taking into account economic and budgetary resources as well as the priorities set by national authorities and balances within social protection systems, and

– where appropriate, varying their scope according to age group or family situation;

F   to take appropriate measures:

– to collect information systematically on the actual arrangements for access to these measures for the people concerned, and

– to carry out a methodical evaluation of their implementation and impact;

II AND THEREFORE ASKS THE COMMISSION:

1. to encourage and organise, in liaison with the Member States, the systematic exchange of information and experiences and the continuous evaluation of the national provisions adopted;

2. to submit to the European Parliament, the Council and the Economic and Social Committee, on a regular basis, reports based on information supplied by the Member States describing the progress achieved and obstacles encountered in implementing this recommendation.

Done at Luxembourg, 24 June 1992.

For the Council

The President

José da Silva Peneda

Appendix B

Council recommendation of 27 July 1992 on the convergence of social protection objectives and policies (92.442/EEC)[8]

THE COUNCIL OF THE EUROPEAN COMMUNITIES,

Having regard to the Treaty establishing the European Economic Community, and in particular article 235 thereof,

Having regard to the proposal from the Commission,[9]

Having regard to the opinion of the European Parliament,[10]

Having heard to the opinion of the Economic and Social Committee,[11]

Whereas, under the terms of article 118 of the Treaty, the Commission has as its task the promotion of close co-operation between Member States in the social field;

Whereas the Community Charter of the Fundamental Social Rights of Workers, adopted at he Strasbourg European Council on 9 December 1989 by the Heads of State or Government of 11 Member States, states in the 7th, 13th and 16th recitals and in points 10, 24 and 25:

'Whereas the completion of the internal market must offer improvements in the social field for workers of the European Community, especially in terms of [...] social protection [...];'

'Whereas (the) aim (of this Charter) is [...] to declare solemnly that the implementation of the Single European Act must take full account of the social dimension of the Community and that it is necessary in this context to ensure at appropriate levels the development of the social rights of workers of the European Community, especially employed workers and self-employed persons;'

'Whereas the solemn proclamation of fundamental social rights at European Community level may not, when implemented, provide grounds for

[8] *Official Journal of the European Communities*, L 245, August 26th, 1992, p. 49-52.
[9] *Official Journal of the European Communities*, C194, July 25th, 1991, p. 13.
[10] *Official Journal of the European Communities*, C67, March 16th, 1992, p. 206.
[11] *Official Journal of the European Communities*, C40, February 17th, 1992, p. 91

any retrogression compared with the situation currently existing in each Member State;'

'According to the arrangements applying in each country:

10. Every worker of the European Community shall have a right to adequate social protection and shall, whatever his status and whatever the size of the undertaking in which he is employed, enjoy an adequate level of social security benefits.

Persons who have been unable either to enter or re-enter the labour market and have no means of subsistence must be able to receive sufficient resources and social assistance in keeping with their particular situation.'

'According to the arrangements applying in each country:

24. Every worker of the European Community must, at the time of retirement, be able to enjoy resources affording him or her a decent standard of living.

25. Every person who has reached retirement age but who is not entitled to a pension or who does not have other means of subsistence must be entitled to sufficient resources and to medical and social assistance specifically suited to his needs.';

Whereas social protection is an essential instrument of solidarity among the inhabitants of each Member State, in the context of the general right of all to social protection;

Whereas the Commission in its action programme relating to the implementation of the Community Charter of the Fundamental Social Rights of Workers noted that differences in social security cover might act as a serious break on the free movement of workers and exacerbate regional imbalances, particularly between the north and the south of the Community; whereas, based on this, it has been proposed that a strategy be promoted for the convergence of Member States' policies in this field, underpinned by objectives established in common, making it possible to overcome such disadvantages;

Whereas, having noted that comparable trends in most of the Member States may lead to common problems (in particular the ageing of the population, changing family situations, a persistently high level of unemployment and the spread of poverty and forms of poverty), the Council proposed, at its meeting on 29 September 1989, that this *de facto* convergence should be further promoted by establishing common objectives as a guide for national policies;

Whereas the aim of this convergence strategy is to fix common objectives able to guide Member States' policies in order to permit the co-existence of different national systems and to enable them to progress in harmony with one another towards the fundamental objectives of the Community;

Whereas the specific common objectives must act as pointers to the way in which these systems are modified to take account of protection needs, particularly those resulting from changes in the labour market, family structures and demographic trends;

Whereas this convergence seeks also to guarantee the continuation and stimulate the development of social protection within the context of the completion of the internal market; whereas this will facilitate the mobility of workers and their families within the Community and whereas steps should be taken to ensure that this mobility is not impeded by too great a disparity in levels of social protection;

Whereas, because of the diversity of the schemes and their roots in national cultures, it is for Member States to determine how their social protection schemes should be framed and the arrangements for financing and organising them;

Whereas this recommendation does not affect national and Community provisions on right of residence;

Whereas the social protection objectives laid down in this recommendation are without prejudice to each Member State's option to establish the principles and organisation of its health system;

Whereas this action appears necessary in order to achieve, as part of the operation of the common market, one of the aims of the Community,

I   HEREBY RECOMMENDS THAT MEMBER STATES SHOULD:

A   allow their general policy in the area of social protection, without prejudice to the powers of the Member States to establish the principles and organisations of their own systems in the sectors concerned, to be guided by the following principles:

1. Taking account of the availability of funds, of priorities and balances within social protection systems and according to those systems' own organisational and funding procedures, social protection should attempt to fulfil the following tasks:

(a) in conformity with the principles enunciated in the Council Recommendation of 24 June 1992 on common criteria concerning sufficient resources and social assistance in social protection systems, to guarantee a level of resources in keeping with human dignity;

(b) under conditions determined by each Member State, to give any person residing legally, within its territory, regardless of his or her resources, the chance to benefit from the system for the protection of human health existing in the Member State;

(c) to help to further the social integration of all persons legally resident within the territory of the Member State and the integration into the labour market of those who are in a position to exercise a gainful activity;

(d) to provide employed workers who cease work at the end of their working lives or are forced to interrupt their careers owing to sickness, accident, maternity, invalidity or unemployment, with a replacement income, fixed in the form of flat-rate benefits, or benefits calculated in relation to their earnings in their previous occupation, which will maintain their standard of living in a reasonable manner in accordance with their participation in appropriate social security schemes;

(e) to examine the possibility of introducing and/or developing appropriate social protection for self-employed persons.

2. Social benefits should be granted in accordance with the following principles:

(a) equal treatment in such away as to avoid any discrimination based on nationality, race, sex, religion, customs or political opinion, providing that applicants fulfil the provisions regarding length of membership and/or residence required to be eligible for benefits;

(b) fairness, so that beneficiaries of social benefits will receive their share from improvements in the standard of living of the population as a whole, while taking account of priorities set at national level.

3. Social protection systems must endeavour to ad(a)pt to the development of behaviour and of family structures where this gives rise to the emergence of new social protection needs, related in particular to changes on the labour market and demographic changes.

4. Finally, social protection systems must be administered with maximum efficiency having regard to the rights, needs and situations of those concerned, and with maximum effectiveness in terms of organisation and functioning;

B adapt and, where necessary, develop their social protection systems, without prejudice to the powers of the Member States to establish the principles and organisation of their own systems in the sectors concerned in order progressively to attain the following aims and to take the necessary measures to this end:

1   Sickness

Organise the role of social protection in preventing illness and in treating and rehabilitating the persons concerned so as to meet the following objectives:

(a) under conditions determined by each Member State, to ensure for all persons legally resident within the territory of the Member State access to necessary health care as well as to facilities seeking to prevent illness;

(b) to maintain and, where necessary, develop a high-quality healthcare system geared to the evolving needs of the population, and especially those arising from dependence of the elderly, to the development of pathologies and therapies and the need to step up prevention;

(c) to organise where necessary the rehabilitation of convalescents, particularly following serious illness or an accident, and their subsequent return to work;

(d) to provide employed persons forced to interrupt their work owing to sickness with either flat-rate benefits or benefits calculated in relation to their earnings in their previous occupation, which will maintain their standard of living in a reasonable manner in accordance with their participation in appropriate social security schemes.

2   Maternity

(a) to organise for all women legally resident within the territory of the Member State coverage of the costs of treatment necessary due to pregnancy, childbirth and their consequences, subject to participation by the women concerned in appropriate social security schemes and/or subject to cover by social assistance;

(b) to ensure that employed women who interrupt their work due to maternity enjoy appropriate social protection.

3   Unemployment

(a) in accordance with the provisions of the recommendation of 24 June 1992 and subject to their active availability for work, to guarantee minimum means of subsistence for unemployed persons legally resident in the territory of the Member State;

(b) to make available to the unemployed, particularly to young people arriving on the job market and to the long-term unemployed, a range of measures against exclusion designed to foster their integration into the labour market, subject to their active availability for work or for vocational training with a view to obtaining employment;

(c) to provide employed workers who have lost their job with either flat-rate benefits, or benefits calculated in relation to their earnings in their previous occupation, which will maintain their standard of living in a reasonable manner in accordance with their participation in appropriate social security schemes subject to their active availability for work or for vocational training with a view to obtaining employment.

4   Incapacity for work

(a) in accordance with the provisions of the recommendation of 24 June 1992 to guarantee minimum means of subsistence to disabled persons legally resident within the territory of the Member State;

(b) to foster the social and economic integration of persons suffering from a chronic illness or from a disability;

(c) to provide employed workers forced to reduce or interrupt work due to invalidity with either flat-rate benefits, or benefits calculated in relation to their earnings in their previous occupation, adjusted where appropriate according to the degree of their incapacity, which will maintain their standard of living in a reasonable manner in accordance with their participation in appropriate social security schemes.

5   The elderly

(a) in accordance with the provisions of the recommendation of 24 June 1992, to guarantee minimum means of subsistence to elderly persons legally resident within the territory of the Member State;

(b) to take appropriate social security measures, having regard to the specific needs of the elderly where they are dependent on care and services from outside;

(c) to take steps to combat the social exclusion of the elderly;

(d) having regard to specific national circumstances as regards unemployment and demographic conditions, to seek to remove obstacles to work for persons who have reached the minimum age at which entitlement to retirement pension begins;

(e) to put in place mechanisms to enable former employed workers who have retired with no gap in their working lives to benefit from a reasonable replacement income throughout their retirement, taking into account, wherever appropriate, statutory and supplementary schemes, while maintaining a balance between the interests of the working population and those who have retired;

(f) for purposes of calculating pension rights, to reduce, in particular by opening up the possibility of voluntary contributions, the penalty for those workers who have gaps in their careers as a result of periods of illness, invalidity or long-term unemployment, and for those who gave up work temporarily to bring up their children or, where appropriate, in accordance with national legislation, other dependants;

(g) to adapt pension schemes to the trend of behaviour and family structures;

(h) to promote, where necessary, changes to the conditions governing the acquisition of retirement and, especially, supplementary pension rights with a view to eliminating obstacles to the mobility of employed workers;

(i) in due course, to adapt pension schemes to demographic changes, while maintaining the basic role of statutory pension schemes.

6 Family

(a) to develop benefits paid to:

– families with the greatest child-related costs, for example because of the number of children,

and/or

– the most disadvantaged families;

(b) to contribute to fostering the integration of persons who, having brought up children, wish to enter the labour market;

(c) to help remove obstacles to occupational activity by parents through measures to reconcile family and professional responsibilities.

II AND, TO THIS END, REQUESTS THE COMMISSION TO:

1. submit regular reports to the Council on progress achieved in relation to the objectives set out above and to determine and develop, in co-operation with the Member States, the use of appropriate criteria for that purpose;

2. organise regular consultation with the Member States on the development of social protection policy.

Done at Brussels, 27 July 1992.

For the Council

The President

N. LAMONT

Contributors

Prof. Irene Asscher-Vonk studied law at the University of Amsterdam, the Netherlands, where she successfully defended her Ph.D. thesis in 1989. She has been a teacher of and researcher in social law since 1967. Since 1990 she has been Professor of Social Law at the Catholic University of Nijmegen, the Netherlands. She is a member of the Social and Economic Council. From 1981 to 1985 she was also a member of the national Emancipation Council. She has held honorary functions as a judge and has published widely on social law, especially on matters of equal treatment and non-discrimination.

Prof. Gian Guido Balandi (1948) is Professor of Labour Law at the University of Ferrara, Italy. Having held various posts at the Universities of Pisa and Ferrara, he is also a member of several groups and committees for the study of social security reform. He has lectured extensively at several universities in Europe and Latin America. Among his publications are *Tutela del reddito e mercato del lavoro nell' ordinamento italiano* (Income protection and the labour market in the Italian system, 1984) and, recently, 'La direttiva comunitaria sul distacco dei lavoratori: un passo in avanti verso il diritto comunitario del lavoro' (The UE directive on the workers' detachment: a step forward towards a European labour law, in: *Scritti in onore di Giuseppe Federico Mancini*, 1998).

Dr. Mel Cousins (1959) is a researcher and lecturer in social policy in Dublin, Ireland. He qualified as a barrister-at-law at the Kings Inns, Dublin. He has written extensively on social policy issues and, in particular, the Irish welfare system. Publications include a book entitled *The Irish Welfare System: Law and Social Policy* (1995).

Dr. Simon Deakin (1961) gained his Ph.D. at the University of Cambridge, UK, in 1990. He is currently Reader in Economic Law at the University of Cambridge and Fellow of Peterhouse. His main teaching interests are labour and social security law, tort law, and the economics of law. He is the director of the corporate governance research programme of the ESRC Centre for Business Research at Cambridge. His books include: *Tort Law* (4th ed. 1998, with Markesinis), *Labour Law* (2nd ed. 1999, with Morris), *Contracts, Cooperation and Competition* (1997, ed., with Michie), and *Tortious Liability of Statutory Bodies: An Economic and Comparative Analysis* (1999, with Markesinis, Auby, and Coester-Waltjen).

Dr. Lei Delsen (1952) studied economics at the University of Groningen (the Netherlands) and received his Ph.D. in economics from the University of Maastricht (the Netherlands). He was a research fellow at the European Centre for Work and Society in Maastricht and, since 1987, has been Assistant Professor at the Department of Applied Economics of the University of Nijmegen, the Netherlands. His current research deals with a number of topical European labour market problems and issues, including new forms of work, retirement from work, employment policy and economic performance and institutions. He has published several books and articles in journals. His publications include *Gradual Retirement in the OECD Countries. Macro And Micro Issues and Policies* (with G. Reday-Mulvey, 1996); 'A New Concept of Full Employment' (in: *Economic and Industrial Democracy,* 1997), and *The German and Dutch economies: Who follows whom?* (with E. de Jong, 1998).

Dr. Nicolette van Gestel (1957) studied social geography at the Catholic University of Nijmegen (the Netherlands), specialising in political geography. In 1985, she graduated cum laude on a study of employment policies and regional politics. Since 1986 she has been affiliated with the department of Public Administration and Management Science at the University of Nijmegen as a part-time researcher and lecturer; since 1991 as a senior lecturer. In 1994 she received her Ph.D. for her dissertation entitled *The Invisible Government. Towards new ways of steering; the Employment Service Act case.* Since 1999 she has been a senior lecturer at the Nijmegen School of Business. She is presently engaged in research on new forms of governance in the socio-economic sector, in particular in the area of social security and in labour market policy.

Dominique Greiner (1963) is M.A. in economics and moral theology. He is currently senior-fellow in economics and ethics at the Catholic University of Lille (France) and in theology at the Catholic University of Paris. His interests lie in the field of social policy and labour market, business ethics, normative economics, and economic philosophy. He is preparing a Ph.D. thesis on theories of justice and compensation of disadvantage in health status (with reference to the disabled, the elderly and people awaiting transplants because of renal fealure).

Prof. Bent Greve (1953) is M.A. in economics, Ph.D. in public administration. Currently Jean Monnet Professor and Head of the Social Sciences Department at Roskilde University, Denmark, he has visited most European countries on lecturing tours. Recent publications include: (ed.) *Comparative Welfare Systems* (1996), (ed.) *What constitutes a good society* (1999), and *Historical Dictionary of the Welfare State* (1998). In Danish: *Væksten i de offentlige udgifter* (Growth in public sector expenditure, 1992), *Skatteudgifter i teorisk og empirisk belysning* (Tax-expenditures: theoretical and empirical taxes, 1994). He has written extensively on social and labour market policies in welfare state and European perspective.

Pilar Nuñez-Cortés studied law. She works as a lecturer in labour law and social security at the Faculty of Business Administration of the *Universidad Pontificia Comillas de Madrid.* Among her publications are: *El Estatuto de los Trabajadores. Antecedentes, Proyectos y Reformas* (The Worker's Statute. Antecedents, projects, and reforms) (*et al.,* 1987), and 'La interpretación de las cláusulas de blindaje en los contratos de alta dirección (Interpretation of cushioned contracts for top executives)' (in: *Revista ICADE,* 1999). She is currently working on a Ph.D. thesis entitled *Maternity leave for the working woman under Spanish Law.*

Dr. Jan Peet (1952) obtained his degree in the history of Eastern Europe at Utrecht University (the Netherlands). Since 1979 he has worked for the Catholic Documentation Centre and the Catholic Study Centre of the Catholic University of Nijmegen (the Netherlands). He completed his Ph.D. thesis on the Young Christian Workers (YCW) in the Netherlands in 1987. Since 1998 he has worked at the Netherlands Economical-Historical Archive and at the International Institute of Social History, both in Amsterdam. He publishes mainly on the history of trade unionism and social security in the Netherlands.

Frans Pennings (1957) studied law at the University of Utrecht (the Netherlands), where he gained his Ph.D. on a thesis entitled *Benefits of Doubt. A comparative study of the legal aspects of employment and unemployment schemes in Great Britain, Germany, France and the Netherlands* (1990). Since 1990 he has been Associate Professor of Social Law at the University of Tilburg. He has published extensively on social law issues and is an expert in social security law of the European Communities.

Prof. Dr. Eugenio M. Recio (1926) is Professor in the Fundamentals of Management Sciences at the *Escuela Superior de Administración y Dirección de Empresas* (Higher School of Business Administration and Management) of the *Universidad Ramon Llull,* Barcelona. He has taken his Ph.D. at the University of Cologne (Germany) and the *Universidad Central de Barcelona,* and has held numerous positions in the field of business administration, economics and human resources planning. Among his publications are *El Estado des Bienestar* (The Welfare State, 1996), *El Estado des Bienestar y el Mercado de Trabajo* (Welfare State and Labour Market, 1997), and *El Sistema Educativo y el Estado del Bienestar* (The Educational System and the Welfare State, in press).

Dr. Hannah Reed is a Junior Research Fellow at the ESRC Centre for Business Research and an Affiliated Lecturer in Law at the University of Cambridge. Her principal research interests include labour law and welfare reform, job insecurity and labour market flexibility.

Dr. Simonetta Renga studied law at the University of Perugia (Italy), at Brunel University, London, and the University of Bristol. In 1989, she gained her Ph.D. at Bristol University. Her main findings were published as 'Unemployment, social security system, new working patterns' (in: *Anglo-American Law Review,* 1991). She has participated in numerous seminars and research projects in Italy and abroad. In 1992, she qualified as barrister-at-law at Perugia. At present, she works as a lecturer and researcher at the universities of Ferrara and Perugia. Among her publications are *Mercato del lavoro e diritto* (The labour market and the law, 1996) and *La tutela contro la disoccupazione* (Social protection for the unemployed, 1997).

Prof. Dr. Josef Schmid (1956) is Professor of Political Science at the University of Tübingen (Germany). He gained his Ph.D. at the University of Constance (Germany) and his academic teaching qualification (*Habilitation*) at the Ruhr-University of Bochum (Germany). He teaches and researches in the fields of comparative public policy, political economy, labour market and the welfare state. Among his publications are *Wohlfahrtsverbände in modernen Wohlfahrtsstaaten* (Voluntary associations in modern welfare states, 1996), *Wohlfahrtsstaaten im Vergleich. Soziale Sicherung in Europa* (Welfare states in comparison. Social security in Europe, 1996), *Vom Wohlfahrtsstaat zum Wettbewerbsstaat? Arbeitsmarkt- und Sozialpolitik in den 90ern* (From welfare to competition? Labour market and social policy in the 1990s, 1999).

Cees Sparrius (1960) studied law at the University of Leiden (the Netherlands) and is preparing a Ph.D. thesis on the division of responsibilities for the income protection of sick employees. He teaches labour law and social security law at the Catholic University of Nijmegen (the Netherlands). Since 1999, he has also served as secretary to the *Adviescommissie Duaal Ontslagstelsel* (Advisory Committee on the Dual Dismissal System), a committee which advises the government on the future of dismissal law in the Netherlands. He publishes mainly on social security law issues. His most recent publications are: 'REA's reïntegratie-instrumentarium en verantwoordelijkheidsverdeling: een verbetering? (REA's reintegration instruments and the distribution of responsibility: an improvement?) (in: *Sociaal Maandblad Arbeid*, 1999) and two chapters on income protection and secondary labour conditions of sick employees in: Asscher-Vonk *et al.*, *De zieke werknemer* (*The sick employee*) (1999).

Prof. Dr. Angelos Stergiou (1957) studied law at the University of Thessaloniki (Greece) and social law at the Université Paris I, Panthéon, Sorbonne (France), where he gained his Ph.D. *cum laude* on a thesis entitled *L'organisation interne des syndicats en droit grec* (1985). Since 1982 he has been working as barrister-at-law in Thessaloniki, and since 1990 has been Assistant Professor of Social Law at the University of Thessaloniki. He published extensively on social law issues, most recently: *Le juge communautaire et la coordination des systèmes de sécurité sociale* (1997) and *Invalidité* (1999).

Kees R. Tinga (1947) studied theology at the Free University of Amsterdam, the Netherlands. He was active in industrial pastoral work. Since 1992 he has been a staff member for matters of Church and society in the national office of the Dutch Reformed Churches. He took part in the preparation and publishing of several Protestant and ecumenical reports and papers on labour, poverty and social security. Among others: *Deelnemen en meedelen. Sociale zekerheid van uitsluiting naar participatie. Een aanzet tot discussie* (Participating en sharing. Social security from exclusion to participation. Elements for discussion) (1995).

Dr. Egon Verbraak (1957) studied theology at the University for Theology and Pastoral Care in Heerlen, the Netherlands, where he gained his Ph.D. in 1990 on a thesis entitled *Arbeidsongeschikten in beweging. Een toetssteen voor de theologie van de arbeid van M.-D. Chenu en de nieuwe politieke theologie van J.B. Metz* (Disabled in movement. A touchstone for the theology of labour of M.-D. Chenu and the new political theology of J.B. Metz). In this study the movement of the disabled is taken as a touchstone for theological concepts. He works as a theologist in service of religious orders for the benefit of the movement against poverty. He publishes on matters concerning theology and economy.

Maureen Verhue (1969) studied economics and graduated as Master of Science in Economics in 1998. She currently works at the Ministry of Flanders, Department of Economics, Employment, Internal Affairs and Agriculture. She is also finishing her Ph.D. thesis. Her field of interest comprises income distribution, social security, and public opinion with respect to social security. One of her publications is: 'De kloof tussen laag- en hooggeschoolden en de politieke houdbaarheid van de Belgische werkloosheidsverzekering: een empirische analyse (The gap between unskilled and highly-skilled employees and the political sustainability of the Belgian unemployment insurance system: an empirical analysis)' (with E. Schokkaert and E. Omey, in: *Economisch en Sociaal Tijdschrift,* March 1999).

Dr. Joos van Vugt (1953) studied contemporary history at the Catholic University of Nijmegen. In 1994, he gained his Ph.D. in 1994 on a thesis on the history of congregations of religious brothers, entitled *Broeders in the katholieke beweging* (Brothers in the Catholic movement). At present, he works at the Catholic Study Centre of Nijmegen University as a researcher and as secretary to several academic discussion groups. He specialises in the history of convent life and national education. He published in this field and on various social issues.

Contributions to Economics

Bruno Jeitziner
Political Economy of the
Swiss National Bank
1999. ISBN 3-7908-1209-9

Irene Ring et al. (Eds.)
Regional Sustainability
1999. ISBN 3-7908-1233-1

Katharina Müller/Andreas Ryll/
Hans-Jürgen Wagener (Eds.)
Transformation of Social Security:
Pensions in Central-Eastern Europe
1999. ISBN 3-7908-1210-2

Stefan Traub
Framing Effects in Taxation
1999. ISBN 3-7908-1240-4

Pablo Coto-Millán
Utility and Production
1999. ISBN 3-7908-1153-X

Frank Riedel
Imperfect Information
and Investor Heterogeneity
in the Bond Market
2000. ISBN 3-7908-1247-1

Kirsten Ralf
Business Cycles
2000. ISBN 3-7908-1245-5

Michele Bagella/Leonardo Becchetti (Eds.)
The Competitive Advantage
of Industrial Districts
2000. ISBN 3-7908-1254-4

Frank Bohn
Monetary Union and Fiscal Stability
2000. ISBN 3-7908-1266-8

Michael Malakellis
Integrated Macro-Micro-Modelling
Under Rational Expectations
2000. ISBN 3-7908-1266-8

Stefan Baumgärtner
Ambivalent Joint Production and
the Natural Environment
2000. ISBN 3-7908-1290-0

Henri Capron, Wim Meeusen (Eds.)
The National Innovation System
of Belgium
2000. ISBN 3-7908-1308-7

Tobias Miarka
Financial Intermediation and Deregulation
2000. ISBN 3-7908-1307-9

Chisato Yoshida
Illegal Immigration and Economic Welfare
2000. ISBN 3-7908-1315-X

Nikolaus Thumm
Intellectual Property Rights
2000. ISBN 3-7908-1329-X

Max Keilbach
Spatial Knowledge Spillovers
and the Dynamics of Agglomeration
and Regional Growth
2000. ISBN 3-7908-1321-4

Alexander Karmann (Ed.)
Financial Structure and Stability
2001. ISBN 3-7908-1332-X

Druck: Strauss Offsetdruck, Mörlenbach
Verarbeitung: Schäffer, Grünstadt